Kids Having Kids

Economic Costs and Social Consequences of Teen Pregnancy

REBECCA A. MAYNARD
Editor

THE URBAN INSTITUTE PRESS
Washington, D.C.

Library of Congress Cataloging in Publication Data

Kids Having Kids: Economic Costs and Social Consequences of Teen Pregnancy/
Rebecca A. Maynard, editor.

1. Teenage parents. 2. Teenage pregnancy—Economic aspects. 3. Teenage pregnancy—Social aspects. I. Maynard, Rebecca A.

HQ759.64.K53	1996	96-33522
305.23′5—dc20		CIP

ISBN 0-87766-654-7 (cloth, alk. paper)

Printed in the United States of America

Distributed in North America by
National Book Network
4720 Boston Way
Lanham, MD 20706

THE URBAN INSTITUTE is a nonprofit policy research and educational organization established in Washington, D.C., in 1968. Its staff investigates the social and economic problems confronting the nation and public and private means to alleviate them. The Institute disseminates significant findings of its research through the publications program of its Press. The goals of the Institute are to sharpen thinking about societal problems and efforts to solve them, improve government decisions and performance, and increase citizen awareness of important policy choices.

Through work that ranges from broad conceptual studies to administrative and technical assistance, Institute researchers contribute to the stock of knowledge available to guide decision making in the public interest.

Conclusions or opinions expressed in Institute publications are those of the authors and do not necessarily reflect the views of staff members, officers or trustees of the Institute, advisory groups, or any organizations that provide financial support to the Institute.

ACKNOWLEDGMENTS

The substantive content of the book is largely the product of work by the analysts who authored chapters 2 through 9. They had been working on their research for nearly two years when I was enlisted to conduct the cost analysis and prepare a nontechnical overview of the findings. This team not only conducted their independent research projects, but also worked patiently with me. I am especially grateful to Seth Sanders for his assistance in conducting the complementary analyses of maternal outcomes needed for the cost analysis and in helping me work through several key technical details.

The *Kids Having Kids Research Project* benefited greatly from the input of an outstanding project advisory group: Elijah Anderson, University of Pennsylvania; Wendy Baldwin, National Institutes of Health; Douglas Besharov, American Enterprise Institute; Claire Brindis, University of California, San Francisco; Sara Brown, National Institute of Medicine; Michael A. Carrera, Children's Aid Society of New York; Mary Elizabeth Corcoran, University of Michigan; Sheldon H. Danziger, University of Michigan; Joy Dryfoos, Consultant; David Ellwood, Harvard University; Jacqueline D. Forrest, The Alan Guttmacher Institute; Frank Furstenberg, University of Pennsylvania; Irving B. Harris, The Harris Foundation; Karen Hein, United States Senate; Evelyn Kappeler, U.S. Department of Health and Human Services; Marianna Kastrinakis, U.S. Department of Health and Human Services; Arleen Leibowitz, RAND Corporation; Sara S. McLanahan, Princeton University; Robert A. Moffitt, Johns Hopkins University; David Myers, Mathematica Policy Research; Susan Newcomer, National Institute of Child Health and Human Development; Susan O. Philliber, Philliber Research Associates; Carol Roddy, U.S. Department of Health and Human Services; Robert F. St. Peter, Mathematica Policy Research; Robert Valdez, U.S. Department of Health and Human Services; and Terry Watkins, U.S. Department of Health and Human Services.

The *Kids Having Kids Research Project* was the vision of Paul Tudor Jones, founder of the Robin Hood Foundation and Chair of its Board of Directors, and David Saltzman, executive director of the Robin Hood Foundation. They enlisted the assistance of the Catalyst Institute to commission comprehensive, scientific research on the consequences of teen childbearing and provided significant financial support for the individual studies.

I am grateful to the Urban Institute Press for the benefits of its review and editorial process and for undertaking the publication of the book under extreme time pressure. Finally, I am grateful for the expert research assistance and production support provided by Louise Alexander, Meredith Kelsey, and Dan McGrath of the University of Pennsylvania.

The authors, the advisors, the sponsors, and the research assistance and production team together made this one of the most rewarding, if challenging, projects of my career. I hope the labors of the entire team will pay off in shaping the future course of social policies directed at teenage pregnancy and parenthood.

Rebecca A. Maynard

CONTENTS

Much of the discussion of teen pregnancy might lead one to believe that it is a new and rapidly escalating social problem. In fact, the U.S. teen pregnancy rate, though much higher than in other developed countries, is below its all-time high reached in the 1950s and is currently falling slightly. The issue is of policy concern, however, because teen mothers are more likely to encounter a variety of economic and social ills than women who delay childbearing. They are less well educated, less successful in the job market, more likely to be and remain unmarried, and more likely to depend on public assistance for extended periods of time.

The analytic and policy challenge, however, is that early parenting is strongly correlated with other factors that lead to bad outcomes. Policy intervention aimed at preventing or reducing teen pregnancy and motherhood is only justified if there is evidence that it would also reduce the undesirable outcomes associated with it. To find such evidence requires disentangling the influence of early parenting from the wide array of social forces that influence the overall life course of the mothers, including the behaviors and choices leading to their adolescent parenting.

Kids Having Kids: Economic Costs and Social Consequences of Teen Pregnancy is the first comprehensive effort to identify the extent to which the undesirable outcomes of teen pregnancy are attributable to adolescent pregnancy itself rather than to the wider environment in which most of these pregnancies and the subsequent child rearing take place. It is also the first study to look at the consequences of adolescent pregnancy for the fathers of the children and, even more important, for the children themselves.

The basic message of the book is that early parenting itself has little effect on the mothers' education or earnings. The mothers' background and individual characteristics are considerably more important factors. Even after background and individual characteristics are taken into account, however, adolescent mothers are less likely to marry than similar women who delay childbearing. And their children, on average, are less healthy, more likely to suffer from child abuse and be placed in foster care, more likely to engage in criminal activity as adolescents and young adults, and less likely to be economically and socially successful as adults.

These findings indicate that adolescent parenting results in a loss of human potential and other economic and social costs that our society can ill afford. It is my hope that the book will help inform the wider public debate about teen pregnancy and contribute to the formulation of policies and programs that have a realistic chance of being successful in reducing these costs.

William Gorham
President

Chapter One

THE STUDY, THE CONTEXT, AND
THE FINDINGS IN BRIEF

Rebecca A. Maynard

Each year, about 1 million teenagers in the United States—approximately 10 percent of all 15- to 19-year-old women—become pregnant. Of these pregnancies only 13 percent are intended. The U.S. teen pregnancy rate is more than twice as high as that in any other advanced country and almost 10 times as high as the rate in Japan or the Netherlands. About a third of these teens abort their pregnancies, 14 percent miscarry, and 52 percent (or more than half a million teens) bear children, 72 percent of them out of wedlock. Of the half a million teens who give birth each year, roughly three-quarters are giving birth for the first time. Over 175,000 of these new mothers are age 17 or younger.

Teen pregnancy has come very much into the public debate in recent years, at least partly as a result of three social forces. First, child poverty rates are high and rising. Second, the number of welfare recipients and the concomitant costs of public assistance have risen dramatically. And third, among those on welfare we see a much higher proportion of never-married women, younger women, and women who average long periods of dependency. No work to date, however, has made a comprehensive effort to identify the extent to which these trends are attributable to teen pregnancy *per se*, rather than to the wider environment in which most of these pregnancies and the subsequent child rearing take place, or to look at the consequences of teen pregnancy for the fathers of the children and for the children themselves. *Kids Having Kids* begins to fill this gap.

GUIDANCE FROM PRIOR RESEARCH

The *Kids Having Kids* research was undertaken in the context of literature describing trends in adolescent childbearing and factors that lead to or exacerbate these trends and their consequences. Aspects of the literature have helped shape this research. So, too, the results of the *Kids Having Kids* research underscore the emerging consensus that the poor outcomes observed for teenage parents and their children are the product of myriad factors, among which early childbearing is only one.

FACTORS RELATED TO THE TRENDS IN TEEN BIRTH RATES

The likelihood that teenagers engage in unprotected sex, become pregnant, and give birth is highly correlated with multiple risk factors. These factors include growing up in a single-parent family, living in poverty and/or in a high-poverty neighborhood, having low attachment to and performance in school, and having parents with low educational attainment (Moore, Miller et al. 1995). For example, teenagers living in single-parent households are one and a half to two times more likely to become teenage parents than those in two-parent families (Zill and Nord 1994). Probabilities increase for those with low aspirations and low aptitude test scores. More important, each of these factors increases not only the risk of teen parenthood but also many other negative outcomes, such as poor school performance, weak social skills, and low earnings potential.

CONSEQUENCES FOR ADOLESCENT CHILDBEARING

Earlier studies have found that adolescent mothers have high probabilities of raising their children in poverty and relying on welfare for support. More than 40 percent of teenage moms report living in poverty at age 27 (Moore et al. 1993). The rates are especially high among black and Hispanic adolescent mothers, more than half of whom end up in poverty and two-thirds of whom find themselves on welfare. Indeed, a recent study found that more than 80 percent of young teen mothers received welfare during the 10 years following the birth of their first child, 44 percent of them for more than 5 years (Jacobson and Maynard 1995).

This results from a combination of factors, including their greater-than-average income needs to support themselves and their children, lower earning potentials, and more limited means of support from other sources, including male partners. Adolescent mothers have an average of six-tenths more children than do older childbearers, and they have their children over a shorter time span. This fertility pattern both increases their income needs over the long haul and adversely affects the likelihood that they will complete high school and have decent earnings prospects (Nord et al. 1992; Rangarajan, Kisker, and

Maynard 1992; Grogger and Bronars 1993; Geronimous and Korenman 1993; Hoffman, Foster, and Furstenberg 1993; Ahn 1994).

Although past literature is consistent in pointing out these poor outcomes for adolescent parents and their children, it is less clear how much of the poor outcomes observed for adolescent parents and their children is directly attributable to early childbearing as opposed to other background and contextual factors common among young mothers. The accumulating evidence suggests that at least half and plausibly considerably more of the poor outcomes can be attributed to factors other than the early childbearing—factors that in many cases may have contributed to the teen becoming a parent (Wolpin and Rosenzweig 1992; Bronars and Grogger 1994; Geronimus, Korenman, and Hillemeier 1994; Haveman and Wolfe 1994; Hoffman, Foster, and Furstenberg 1993). Four such factors are particularly noteworthy.

Single Parenthood. Over time, adolescent mothers have become increasingly likely to be single parents and the sole providers for themselves and their children. Most teen parents are unmarried five years after giving birth. Moreover, fewer than half of the teens who give birth out of wedlock marry within the next 10 years (Jacobson and Maynard 1995). Not surprisingly, therefore, marital status at the time of the first birth is a powerful predictor of subsequent poverty status and welfare dependence, regardless of the age of the woman when she has her first child. More than two-thirds of all out-of-wedlock childbearers end up on welfare, as do 84 percent of young teen mothers who are unmarried when their first child is born. Especially notable about the adolescent mothers is that so many of them give birth out of wedlock and that, when they go onto welfare, they tend to do so for long periods of time—more than 5 of the 10 years following the birth of their first child.

Young mothers, in particular, have limited support either from the fathers of their children or from other adults. Among all unwed teen parents, only about 30 percent of single teen parents live with adult relatives, and less than one-third receive any financial support, including informal support, from the nonresident fathers of their children (Congressional Budget Office 1990).

School Completion. Young teen mothers have exceptionally low probabilities of completing their schooling and thus show weak employment prospects. Just over half of teenage mothers complete high school during adolescence and early adulthood; many who complete high school do so with only an alternative credential—the General Educational Development (GED) certificate (Cameron and Heckman 1993;

Murnane, Willett, and Boudett 1994; Cao, Stromsdorfer, and Weeks 1995). Many of those who do complete regular high school have very low basic skills (Strain and Kisker 1989; Nord et al. 1992). The combination of low education credentials, low basic skills, and parenting responsibilities means that teenage parents have limited employment opportunities, primarily restricted to the low-wage market (Moore et al. 1993; Hoffman et al. 1993; Rangarajan et al. 1992).

Social and Economic Circumstances. The logical consequence of these outcomes is high poverty rates, even for those who are employed. Among adolescent mothers, almost two-thirds of blacks, half of Hispanics, and just over one-quarter of whites are still in poverty by the time they reach their late 20s (Moore et al. 1993). The poverty rates for the more than 60 percent of adolescent mothers who live on their own and for those who are not employed are particularly high. Poverty rates exceed the national average even among teen mothers who are employed (24 percent) and those living with a spouse (28 percent) or relative (34 percent) (Congressional Budget Office 1990).

The high poverty rates are accompanied by numerous other life-complicating factors, some caused by the poverty and some contributing to its perpetuation. Teenage parents are disproportionately concentrated in poor, often racially segregated communities characterized by inferior housing, high crime, poor schools, and limited health services. Many of the teens have been victims of physical and/or sexual abuse. For example, recent studies of Washington State welfare recipients estimate that half of those women who give birth before age 18 have been sexually abused and another 10 percent or more have been physically abused (Roper and Weeks 1993; Boyer and Fine 1992). Data from the National Survey of Children indicate that 20 percent of sexually active teenagers have had involuntary sex and over half of those who are sexually active before age 15 have experienced involuntary sex (Alan Guttmacher Institute 1994).

These statistics have been corroborated by recent experiences of paraprofessional home visitors working with a representative sample of teenage parent welfare recipients in three cities (Johnson, Kelsey, and Maynard, forthcoming). In one of these sites, home visitors reported that roughly two-thirds of these teenagers are victims of physical and/or sexual abuse and as many as 20 percent are currently abused or at risk of being abused.

Roles of the Fathers. The male partners of teenage mothers tend not to be teens themselves. Even so, they generally are not a consistent source of support for the teenage mothers or their children. Only 20 to 30 percent marry the mother of their child, and only about 20 percent of the nonresident fathers are ordered by the court to pay child support. Those with orders pay only a small fraction of the award amount (Congressional Budget Office 1990).

Among those fathers whose children end up on welfare, only about one-third have regular contact with the mother by the time of the birth. Another third have intermittent contact, and the remaining fathers have no involvement whatsoever (Maynard, Nicholson, and Rangarajan 1993). Moreover, the father's rate of contact and support declines substantially over time.

STUDY DESIGN

Unlike most previous research, which compared teenage (under age 20) mothers with those who delay childbearing until age 20 or later, *Kids Having Kids* focuses on the more than 175,000 adolescent women annually who give birth before age 18 and places primary importance on assessing the likely consequences of delaying their childbearing for an average of about four years, or until they reach age 20 to 21. The particular focus on young teens reflects the strong public concern about the high rate of childbearing among young teens, the vast majority of which results from unplanned pregnancies. Still school age, unlikely to be married, even less likely to be prepared for parenthood, these very young mothers highlight the dimensions of teen pregnancy and parenthood in this country. The delay until age 20 or 21 was chosen as a goal that could plausibly be achieved by policy intervention.

One of the primary purposes of the study was to begin untangling the pathway of early parenting from the intricate web of social forces that influence the life course of the mothers, including the behaviors and choices leading to their adolescent parenting. Disentangling the various types of factors associated with teen childbearing in this way is extremely important for any policy discussion about the benefits to be expected from preventing teen pregnancy.

Policy intervention is only justified if there is evidence to suggest that preventing or reducing teen pregnancy and motherhood would indeed improve the lot of the mothers, fathers, and/or children. The analytical strategy for estimating the impacts of different policy alternatives comes down to three types of comparison. Figure 1.1 shows

Figure 1.1 HYPOTHETICAL IMPACT ON CHILD'S LIFETIME EARNINGS OF
THREE LEVELS OF "POLICY" CHANGE

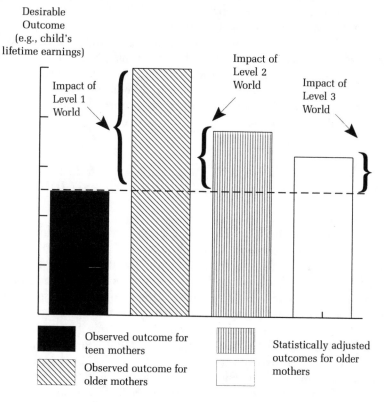

Level 1: A world where teen mothers were equal to older mothers in age of first birth
and *all* other characteristics and circumstances.

Level 2: A world where teen mothers were equal to older mothers in age of first birth
and characteristics that are changeable by policy (e.g., education, job
opportunities, motivation).

Level 3: A world where all births were delayed until age 20 to 21 but nothing else
changed.

how these comparisons allow us to measure the potential impacts of
different "policy" scenarios.

The most radical of these scenarios would create a world in which
all adolescent moms would *both* delay their first birth until their early
20s *and* look like their older childbearing counterparts in all other
respects. For example, they would have parents with similar levels of
education; they would attend schools of similar quality; they would

live in neighborhoods with similar economic opportunities and crime rates; and they would have similar cultural backgrounds. Total fantasy, of course, but useful to illustrate the extreme case. This comparison is readily measured and, indeed, the one that tends to shape public opinion. Under this scenario, the benefits of instituting the policy change are equal to the full difference in observed outcomes between early and later childbearers—as reflected in the research reviewed briefly above and measured by the Level 1 world in the figure.

Next, imagine a world in which we had a policy that would delay the first birth and at the same time compensate for or eliminate those differences between adolescent mothers and later childbearers that are susceptible to short-term policy change. Such a change might be a successful pregnancy prevention program that addressed the full spectrum of closely linked factors—such as motivation, economic opportunities, and school quality issues—that contribute to the poor outcomes of early childbearers and that also may have contributed to the early childbearing. The hypothetical benefits of the policy are indicated by the Level 2 world in the figure. The contributing authors estimate the benefits of such a policy by comparing outcomes for adolescent moms with those for later childbearers, controlling statistically for factors not influenceable by the policy package (such as education of parents, race, cultural background, crime in the neighborhood).

Now, imagine that we had a highly effective, widely accepted, long-acting contraceptive that all sexually active teens used automatically, with no side effects, until they were 20 to 21. In this scenario, nothing else would change for the mother or her children except those things caused directly by the early childbearing. This comparison measures the consequence of adolescent childbearing itself. The benefits of such a policy are depicted for the Level 3 world in the figure.

The last comparison can be approximated by adding more statistical controls to the analysis, but it can only be made definitively if a comparison group is found that is like the young teen mothers in all respects, on average, except for the childbearing itself. The chapter assessing consequences for the mothers does this by using the subsequent experiences of teens who miscarry as a measure of what would have happened to the young teen moms if they had postponed childbearing. Miscarriages are generally considered to be close to random events that force a delay in the timing of the first birth but have no other major consequences. Without the miscarriage these women would have been young teen mothers. As a result of the miscarriage, all will experience a near random delay in childbearing, in many cases until the young women enter their twenties. The chapter on the likelihood of the children being incarcerated uses the fact that a woman who has more than one child is necessarily older when she gives birth to her second child, again allowing the analyst to separate the effect of early childbearing from the effects of other maternal characteristics. The difference between this impact and the larger impacts of the Level 1 and Level 2 worlds is attributable to factors *that will not go away simply by delaying the childbearing.*

FINDINGS IN BRIEF

The *Kids Having Kids* study consists of a background study of trends in teenage and adolescent childbearing and seven coordinated studies, each focusing on a particular dimension of adolescent childbearing. Each study is based on the best available data set to address that particular set of questions (shown in table 1.1). Each study also uses statistical analyses to control for a variety of non-pregnancy-related factors that might affect outcomes (shown in table 1.2).

Teen Pregnancy and Childbirth in the Larger Context of Social and Economic Change (Chapter 2)

Although teen birth rates are much higher in the United States than in other developed countries, contrary to what many assume this does not represent a recent crisis. In fact, the teen birth rate now is lower than 40 years ago. Nor is the difference between the United States and other developed countries the consequence of a more diverse population. Teen pregnancy rates for the white population are substantially higher in the United States than in European countries with comparable white populations.

The major story, rather, is critical changes in the wider environment that make the implications of teen pregnancy and motherhood quite different from what they were a generation ago. Four, in particular, deserve emphasis.

The teenage population has been, and is again, increasing rapidly. Between 1950 and 1980, for example, it doubled (with adolescent females increasing from 5.3 million to 10.4 million and adolescent males increasing from the same base to 10.7 million). The numbers stayed about the same through the 1980s but are again increasing. During the decade of the 1990s, for example, the number of teen women is expected to increase by another million. Even if teen birth

Table 1.1 STUDIES AND DATA SOURCES

Study	Data Source
Trends in Early Childbearing (Susan W. McElroy and Kristen A. Moore)[a]	Vital Statistics; U.S. Bureau of the Census; various published reports
Consequences for the Mothers (V. Joseph Hotz, Susan W. McElroy, and Seth G. Sanders)[a]	National Longitudinal Survey of Youth (females ages 18 to 21 in 1979)
Consequences for the Fathers (Michael J. Brien and Robert J. Willis)[a]	National Longitudinal Survey of Youth (males age 27 in one year of the follow-up survey); 1989 National Maternal and Infant Health Survey (NMIHS), linked with Vital Statistics
Consequences for the Offspring	
Lives as Children and Adolescents (Kristen A. Moore, Donna R. Morrison, and Angela D. Greene)[a]	National Longitudinal Survey of Youth, 1990—Child Supplement (children ages 4 to 14); National Survey of Children, 1981 (children ages 12 to 16) and 1987 (children ages 18 to 22)
Health and Medical Care (Barbara Wolfe and Maria Perozek)[a]	1987 National Medical Care Expenditure Survey (children under age 14 with a mother under age 33)
Child Abuse/Neglect and Foster Care (Robert M. Goerge and Bong Joo Lee)[a]	Illinois Integrated Database on Children and Family Services; Illinois birth certificate data
Incarceration (Jeff Grogger)[a]	National Longitudinal Survey of Youth (males ages 27 through 34 in 1991)
Success as Adults (Robert Haveman, Barbara Wolfe, and Elaine Peterson)[a]	Panel Study of Income Dynamics (persons 0 to 6 years old in 1968 and surveyed each year through 1988)

[a] Study authors.

rates remain the same or fall, the number of children born to teen mothers will almost inevitably increase.

Changes in marriage rates and family structure have also affected the nature and consequences of teen pregnancy and childbirth. As the age of first marriage has risen, a greater proportion of teens remains unmarried. This carries the inevitable implication that births among teens are considerably more likely to occur outside marriage than in the past.

Table 1.2 CONTROL VARIABLES USED IN THE ANALYSES

	Consequences for the Mothers	Consequences for the Fathers	Consequences for the Offspring				
			Lives as Children and Adolescents	Health and Medical Care	Abuse/Neglect and Foster Care Placement	Incarceration	Success as Adults
Demographic Characteristics							
Marital status	✓	✓a		✓			
Race/ethnicity	✓	✓a	✓a	✓	✓	✓	✓
AFQT	✓	✓					
Child's age			✓a	✓a			
Birth order				✓		✓	✓
Mother's age at birth	✓a	✓a	✓a	✓a	✓a	✓b	✓
Family Background							
Living arrangement as teen	✓	✓	✓				✓
Mother's education	✓	✓	✓				✓
Father's education	✓	✓					✓
Mother's achievement test score							
Family income	✓						
Years lived in poverty							✓
Mother on welfare/family in poverty	✓						✓
Religion		✓					
Number of children		✓					
Home resources		✓		✓		✓	
Other							
Region of residence		✓					
Child's health				✓	✓	✓	
Birth year			✓		✓	✓	
State per capita spending on family planning							
Neighborhood unemployment rate							✓
State maximum welfare benefits							✓

a. Variable was used as a subgroup identifier.
b. Variable was used only in models that included correction for selection bias.

Women with young children are also increasingly likely to work outside the home, in part because of rising wages relative to men and in part because of increasing educational levels among women. Single women are more likely to be in the labor force than married women, continuing a long-term trend. But among women with young children, participation rates are higher for married than for unmarried women—a difference that is widening over time.

Finally, because of structural changes in the economy, the employment and earnings potential of people with the least education have worsened.

The combination of these trends has led to two major consequences. The rising rate of out-of-wedlock childbearing and age of marriage has made it much more likely that teen mothers will have only their own earnings to support themselves and their children. And the stronger link between dropping out of school and unemployment, low wages, and poverty has put teen mothers at much greater risk of becoming dependent on welfare.

Consequences for the Mothers (Chapter 3)

If young women who are "at risk" of becoming teen mothers are somehow convinced to delay their childbearing, how substantially would their life prospects be changed and how much would this affect what the government spends on cash welfare and food stamps for these women? The authors address this question using an innovative evaluation design in which teen women who miscarried become a comparison group for teen women who gave birth. This allows the effect of the birth itself to be separated from all other factors.

The descriptive statistics that begin the discussion confirm the evidence from previous research reviewed earlier that teen mothers do worse along many dimensions than mothers who delay childbearing. But analysis of the miscarriage data contradicts the conventional wisdom that these women would themselves be better off if they delayed their childbearing to a later age and nothing else changed.

Failure to delay childbearing significantly reduces the likelihood that a woman will ever obtain a high school diploma, according to the authors. But teen mothers are more likely to obtain a GED diploma. With respect to earnings, early childbearers, according to this study, start their labor market careers later, but tend to work more hours and earn more overall than comparable women who postponed childbearing as a result of a miscarriage. These results on earnings are paralleled by findings on welfare receipt. Although teen childbearers have a different pattern of cash welfare and food stamp receipt over time, they depend on welfare no more overall than do women who delay childbearing. The combined effects of teen childbearing on tax revenues from mothers' earnings, and on AFDC and food stamp benefits add up to a small net gain to the government.

The authors do identify some effects of early childbearing that are likely to have adverse consequences for teen mothers and their children. Most notably, because of their early childbearing teen mothers will spend a larger fraction of their life as a single mother than if they had delayed their childbearing. As the authors themselves note, "given that teen mothers have less formal education, work more hours, and are more likely to be and remain single parents than if they had delayed their childbearing, it is natural to ask if the failure of these women to postpone parenthood may pose threats to the development and well-being of their children." The rest of *Kids Having Kids* examines the likely consequences of teen childbearing for the fathers and the children, including any public costs incurred as a result.

Consequences for the Fathers (Chapter 4)

This chapter distinguishes two perspectives when assessing the consequences of teen parenting for fathers. The first is the fathers' perspective: What are the consequences for men who father children when they are themselves teenagers? The second is the mothers' perspective: What resources are potentially available from their partners and how do these resources vary with the age at which the women become mothers?

Although men who have children as young teens begin their careers by having higher incomes and working more hours than those who delay, men who wait to have a child have higher levels of education, earn more, and work more hours by the time they reach their late 20s. The important question for policy is how much this difference has to do with differences in the characteristics of those who become young fathers and those who do not, and how much with the fact of the birth and whether the man takes responsibility for the child by marrying the mother.

The authors pursue answers to these questions with a series of statistical analyses designed to isolate the various influences at work. When differences in the characteristics of the fathers are taken into account, the authors find evidence of only modest effects of fathering a child in and of itself on the educational level and earnings trajectories of the fathers in later life. There does, however, seem to be a substantial "marriage penalty" for those who choose to take responsibility for their children by marrying the mother. Irrespective of their other characteristics, these men earn more by working substantially more hours than their counterparts with the same characteristics who do not accept responsibility for the child, suggesting that they work more in order to provide for the children they have chosen to support.

In examining the child support implications of early childbearing, the authors focus on the men who father the children of teen mothers, and how delayed childbearing would affect their earnings patterns during the first 18 years of those children's lives. This information is then used to estimate differences in the amount they would pay in child support (assuming full enforcement of Wisconsin's relatively generous child support system).

These fathers have little to provide in their early years, but their incomes, and therefore the potential amount of the child support payments, uniformly increase with the age of the woman at the child's birth. If a 17-year-old mother delayed childbearing until she reached the age of 20 to 21, for example, simulations suggest that she would receive almost $200 a year more over the 18-year period following the child's birth. This assumes full enforcement of Wisconsin's child support obligations under both scenarios. If the comparison is between young teen childbearing and current enforcement versus delayed childbearing and full enforcement, of course, the additional child support would be substantially greater.

Consequences for the Lives of the Children (Chapter 5)

To assess the effects of early childbearing on the children themselves, the authors of this chapter look at four types of outcomes: the quality of the home environment provided to the child; the child's cognitive development and educational attainment; physical and psychological well-being; and behavior problems and substance abuse. They consider these potential impacts for the children when young as well as when adolescents. And they examine whether firstborns fare differently from their siblings.

Their major finding are in the areas of home environment and cognitive and educational development. When the mother's background characteristics are controlled, the quality of the home environment (including both emotional support and cognitive stimulation) is over 4 points lower (on a normal scale where the mean is set at 100) for the offspring of young teen mothers than for children whose mothers were 20 to 21 at their birth. The children of young teen mothers also score lower in mathematics and reading recognition (4 points) and in reading comprehension (3 points) in the period up to age 14. These differences carry over into adolescence in the form of greater likelihood of repeating a grade and being rated unfavorably by teachers in high school. Birth order is not important. These deficits are found for subsequent children as well as the firstborn children of young teen mothers.

Children's Health and Medical Outcomes and Costs (Chapter 6)

This chapter compares the health of the children of teen mothers from birth to age 14 with the health of children of the same age born to nonteen mothers. Health measures include whether or not the children are in excellent health, whether or not they are in fair to poor health, whether they have an acute condition, and whether they have a chronic condition.

The overall proportion of children reported to be in excellent health is substantially greater for the offspring of nonteen mothers than for the offspring of young teen mothers. The children of nonteen mothers are also somewhat less likely to be reported as in fair or poor health. The children of nonteen mothers are more likely, however, to have a reported acute or chronic condition than the children of young teen mothers.

A wide range of measures of medical care utilization also are explored in this chapter, including visits to doctors, clinics, and emergency rooms, and hospital stays. Except for emergency room visits, of which there is greater use by the infants of teen mothers than by other groups, all indicators of utilization show that the children of nonteen mothers have higher utilization rates. (The earlier finding that the children of nonteen mothers have more acute and more chronic conditions than the children of young teen mothers may be reflecting these utilization differences at least in part.)

How do these utilization differences translate into sources of payment and costs of care? Children of nonteen mothers have more of their care paid for directly by their families (47 percent versus 38 percent) and by private insurance (32 percent versus 16 percent). In sharp contrast, much more of the care of young teen parents was paid for by public sources (49 percent versus 20 percent). Consistent with these findings, the costs of medical care were greater for the children of nonteen mothers than for young teen mothers, but the amount paid by other members of society was greater for children born to young teen mothers than for children born to nonteen mothers.

To better isolate the impact of having a mother who first gave birth as a teen, the analysts also provide estimates that control for a variety of factors that can be expected to have independent effects on medical care use and costs. The multivariate findings confirm that the children of young teen mothers are much less likely to have excellent health than the children of nonteen mothers, a finding that extends beyond the firstborns to later children in the family.

If a mother who was younger than 18 at her fist birth were to postpone childbearing until after age 21, according to simulations by the authors based on their multivariate results, she would use more medical care on behalf of her children and the costs of her children's care would increase. But the expenses paid by others for the care of her children would decrease by almost 50 percent—a large enough reduction to imply an absolute reduction in the amount others would have to pay for her children's medical care. These simulations, it should be noted, are based on the assumption that current teen mothers would "act" like older mothers, not only in their fertility behavior but also in the education attainment, earnings, and insurance.

Abuse and Neglect of the Children (Chapter 7)

This chapter uses Illinois state records to assess the impact of teen childbearing on child abuse and neglect cases and foster care placement. This is one of the few data bases that provides detailed family information. In addition, the overall demographic characteristics of the Illinois child population are very comparable with those of the population in the nation.

The authors' descriptive statistics indicate that children born to young teen mothers are much more likely to be indicated victims of abuse and neglect than those born to nonteen mothers. And new families in which the mother's age was under 18 at the time of first birth are also much more likely to become an indicated case of child abuse and neglect than other families. The unadjusted data also show that once a child is in foster care, the duration of the foster care placement is higher for children of young teen mothers than for other children.

When birth order is controlled, it becomes apparent that subsequent children of mothers who bore their first child as a young teen are considerably more likely to be victims of abuse and neglect than the firstborns of those mothers. When other demographic factors are also controlled, the size of the differences between the children of young teen mothers and the children of nonteen mothers is reduced, but the children of young teens are still considerably more likely than the children of nonteens to be victims of abuse and neglect and to be placed in foster care. The duration of time in foster care is no longer significantly different for the two groups, however.

As can be expected given these results, simulations of the costs of abuse/neglect and foster care placement indicate that society would reap substantial savings if childbearing could be delayed. If women now bearing children at age 17 or younger delayed childbearing until at least ages 20 to 21, the annual savings in foster care nationwide could reach about $1 billion. A similar delay could reduce the costs of abuse/neglect investigations by almost $100 million a year. The causal chain leading to incidents of reported abuse and neglect and to foster care placement is as yet unclear, however. These simulations assume that a policy that leads to childbirth delays will also ameliorate whatever it is that leads to child abuse/neglect and foster care placement.

The Children's Risk of Incarceration (Chapter 8)

This chapter begins by presenting descriptive statistics showing that the children of young teen mothers are almost three times as likely to be behind bars at some point in their adolescence or early 20s as are the children of mothers who delayed childbearing. When the analysis controls for a number of important background factors the link between young teen childbearing and incarceration remains, although the extent of the difference is greatly reduced.

In a further effort to tease out the effect of teen childbearing per se, the author takes a novel approach to controlling for unobservable characteristics of the mother that may be correlated with her early age at first birth. He uses a comparison group consisting of the subsequent children of mothers who first gave birth as a young teen. The mothers are the same. They are simply older. The link between young teen childbearing and higher incarceration rates among the offspring remains, although its magnitude is further reduced.

On the basis of this last comparison, the author performs a series of simulations to assess the expected savings from the reduced risk of incarceration implied by postponing the age of first childbirth. The savings are considerable. If young teens delayed their first childbirth until ages 20 or 21, their child's risk of incarceration would fall by an estimated 12 percent and the correction costs incurred by more than $900 million. These savings almost certainly understate the full crime-related costs of early childbearing. They also represent only a fraction of the correctional costs currently incurred by the sons of young teen mothers. This is because the age of the mother has less of an effect on delinquency than other differences in the circumstances facing the children of young teen versus nonteen mothers.

The Life Chances of the Children (Chapter 9)

Does having a young teen mother affect the chances of her children having a successful adulthood? This is the question to which the authors of this chapter seek an answer. They measure success along four dimensions for which data were gathered when the children were in their mid-20s: graduating from high school, not giving birth as a teen, not giving birth as an unmarried teen, and being economically active (specified as certain combinations of educational activity, or working outside the home, and/or parenting a preschooler).

The authors approach this task in three stages. First, they estimate the gross differences between the success of the two groups of children as young adults. Then, they add controls to adjust for the influence of background and personal characteristics of the mother. Finally, they add controls to adjust for aspects of the state/local policy environment that might influence children's choices in adolescence.

The gross differences indicate that being a child of a young teen mother substantially reduces the chances of success as a young adult educationally, economically, and in terms of family formation. When mothers' characteristics are controlled, the children of teen mothers are still less likely to succeed along all four dimensions, although the differences between the children of young teens and nonteens are smaller. Introducing the policy variables again shrinks but still does not remove the difference in the chances of success between the two groups of children.

These multivariate findings suggest that, even given the differences in the mothers' characteristics and the policy environment in which the children were raised, delaying childbearing from ages 16 to 17 until ages 20 to 21 would increase the probability that the children would graduate from high school by about 9 percent. The probability of the daughters giving birth as a teen would drop by about 22 percent. The probability that the daughters would give birth out of wedlock as a teen would fall by about 10 percent. And the probability of being economically inactive as young adults would decrease by about 19 percent.

Adding Up the Costs (Chapter 10)

The purpose of the final chapter in the book is to develop, from the separate components of the picture provided by the contributing authors, an overall sense of the range of savings that could be achieved if public policy interventions were able to prevent young teens from having children until they were age 20 or 21. Previous attempts to estimate the costs of early childbearing have focused rather narrowly on public welfare costs. The range of outcomes examined in the *Kids Having Kids* studies allows a much broader perspective.

Deriving a more comprehensive set of cost estimates is an extremely complex enterprise, however. Because of data limitations and methodology differences among the component studies, as well as a whole variety of assumptions that always have to be made in order to build a comprehensive cost picture, there is no "best" answer to the cost question. Therefore, this chapter first provides "baseline" cost estimates that combine the impacts as estimated by the contributing authors with only a minimum set of assumptions necessary to fit them into a cost-accounting framework. It then provides an additional range of estimates that illustrate how the findings change as assumptions underlying the separate analyses are altered.

For the baseline estimates as well as for the sensitivity analysis, two policy scenarios are costed out. The first, which yields lower bound savings estimates, is that policy intervention succeeds in delaying childbearing until the mother is age 20 to 21 but makes no other changes to the wider environment. The second, which yields higher estimated savings, assumes that the policy that is successful in postponing the age of the first childbirth also addresses the maximum set of policy-influenceable factors that lead to poor outcomes (such as motivation, educational opportunities, and various social and economic support needs).

Baseline Estimates. The lower bound estimates indicate that early childbearing alone costs U.S. taxpayers nearly $7 billion annually for social services and forgone tax revenues. The upper bound estimates indicate that taxpayers potentially could save as much as $15 billion annually if they were successful in both preventing young teen childbearing and addressing many of the other problems that contribute to the poor outcomes observed for teen parents. The record of interventions to date, however, suggests that even strong policies may leave us closer to the lower bound estimates than to this higher figure.

The costs of society are about twice the costs to taxpayers—an estimated $15 billion a year due to early childbearing itself, and up to $30 billion a year if all the risk factors amenable to policy influence were successfully eliminated.

This study indicates that the economic welfare of the teens would not be greatly affected by policies that prompted them to delay childbearing. Policies that delayed their childbearing but changed nothing else would in fact leave the teens with about $850 a year less income. If they simultaneously addressed the maximum set of related disadvantages that conceivably could be affected by policy, the young women could find themselves with roughly $1,000 more income annually during their early parenting years.

Sensitivity Analysis. The sensitivity analysis experimented with six different assumptions. The first reflects experts' disagreements about the estimated effect of early parenting on the mothers' earnings and welfare receipt and assumes the mothers lose more than in the baseline estimates. The second assumes that early parenting makes no difference to the income available to the mothers from a resident spouse. The third cuts in half the measured effect on fathers' earnings from delayed parenting by the mothers. The fourth adds an estimate of criminal justice costs over and above those associated with incarceration. The fifth adds an estimate for child welfare costs in addition to those for foster care. The sixth ignores the estimated long-term gains to the children being born to older mothers.

Combining the assumptions included in the sensitivity analysis in various ways, not surprisingly, produces a wider range of estimated savings. The lower bound costs borne by taxpayers range from 12 percent below to 32 percent above the $7 billion a year baseline estimate. The lower bound costs to society range from 24 percent below to 15 percent above the $15 billion a year baseline estimate.

The Basic Message. The cost chapter provides a good summary of the book's basic message. The economic costs for the mothers of early childbearing are small to nonexistent. Rather, the consequences for them are nonmonetary and often not observable for several years following their first birth. Young teen mothers are much less likely to complete high school, spend more of their early years of parenthood single, and have their children over a somewhat shorter period of time. During their children's elementary and middle school years, early child bearers also spend slightly more time out of the home and in the labor force than if they had delayed childbearing. So too, they create less supportive home environments for their children.

What is unambiguously clear—from both the cost analysis and from the companion studies reported earlier in the book—is that young teen childbearing has significant adverse consequences for the children and that these consequences are costing taxpayers and society enough to merit close policy attention.

References

Ahn, G. 1994. "Teenage Childbearing and High School Completion: Accounting for Individual Heterogeneity." *Family Planning Perspectives* 26(1): 17–21.

Alan Guttmacher Institute. 1994. *Sex and America's Teenagers.* New York: Alan Guttmacher Institute.

Boyer, D., and D. Fine. 1992. "Sexual Abuse as a Factor in Early Pregnancy and Maltreatment." *Family Planning Perspectives* 24(1): 4–19.

Bronars, Stephen G., and Jeff Grogger. 1994. "The Economic Consequences of Unwed Motherhood: Using Twin Births as a Natural Experiment." *American Economic Review* 84 (December): 1141–1156.

Cameron, S. V., and J. J. Heckman. 1993. "The Nonequivalence of High School Equivalents." *Journal of Labor Economics* 11(1): 1–47.

Cao, J., E. Stromsdorfer, and Gregory Weeks. Forthcoming. "The Human Capital Effect of the GED on Low Income Women." Olympia, WA: Washington State Institute for Public Policy, Evergreen State College. Forthcoming in *Journal of Human Resources*.

Congressional Budget Office. 1990. *Sources of Support for Teenage Parents.* Washington, DC: U.S. Government Printing Office.

Geronimus, A., and S. Korenman. 1993. "The Socioeconomic Consequences of Teen Childbearing Reconsidered." *Quarterly Journal of Economics* 107(4): 1187–214.

Geronimus, A., S. Korenman, and S. Hillemeier. 1994. "Does Young Maternal Age Adversely Affect Child Development? Evidence from Cousin Comparisons in the United States." *Development Review* 20: 585–609.

Grogger, J., and S. Bronars. 1993. "The Socioeconomic Consequences of Teenage Childbearing: Findings from a Natural Experiment." *Family Planning Perspectives* 25(4): 156–61.

Haveman, R., and B. Wolfe. 1994. *Succeeding Generations: On the Effects of Investments in Children.* New York: Russell Sage Foundation.

Hoffman, S. E., M. Foster, and F. Furstenberg Jr. 1993. "Reevaluating the Costs of Teenage Childbearing." *Demography* 30(1, February): 1–13.

Jacobson, J., and R. Maynard. 1995. "Unwed Mothers and Long-Term Welfare Dependency," in *Addressing Illegitimacy: Welfare Reform Options for*

Congress. Washington, DC: American Enterprise Institute, September 11.

Johnson, A., M. Kelsey, and R. Maynard. Forthcoming. "What are the Real Barriers to Self-Sufficiency for Teenage Parents?" Paper prepared for the Henry J. Kaiser Family Foundation. Philadelphia: University of Pennsylvania.

Moore, K. A., B. C. Miller, D. Glei, and D. R. Morrison. 1995. *Early Sex, Contraception, and Childbearing: A Review of Recent Research.* Washington, DC: Child Trends.

Moore, K. A., D. Myers, D. R. Morrison, C. Nord, B. Brown, and B. Edmonston. 1993. "Age at First Childbirth and Later Poverty." *Journal of Research on Adolescence* 3(4): 393–422.

Murnane, R., J. B. Willett, and K. P. Boudett. 1994. "Do High School Dropouts Benefit from Obtaining a GED?" Working Paper. Harvard Labor Economics Seminar, August 11.

Nord, C., K. Moore, D. Morrison, B. Brown, and D. Myers. 1992. "Consequences of Teen-Age Parenting." *Journal of School Health* 62(7, September): 310–18.

Philliber, S. 1994. *Carrera/Dempsey Replication Programs: 1993–94 Summary of Client Characteristics and Outcomes.* Accord, NY: Philliber Research Associates.

Rangarajan, A., E. E. Kisker, and R. Maynard. 1992. *Selecting Basic Skills Tests for Program and Evaluation Purposes.* Princeton, NJ: Mathematica Policy Research.

Roper, P., and G. Weeks. 1993. *Child Abuse, Teenage Pregnancy, and Welfare Dependency: Is There a Link?* Olympia, WA: Washington State Institute for Public Policy, Evergreen State College, October.

Strain, M., and E. E. Kisker. 1989. *Literacy and the Disadvantages: Analysis of Data from the National Assessment of Educational Progress.* Princeton, NJ: Mathematica Policy Research.

Wolpin, K., and M. Rosenzweig. 1992. "Sisters, Siblings, and Mothers: The Effects of Teenage Childbearing on Birth Outcomes." Paper presented at the NICHD conference, "Outcomes of Early Childbearing: An Appraisal of Recent Evidence," Bethesda, MD, May 18–19.

Zill, N., and C. W. Nord. 1994. *Running in Place: How American Families Are Faring in a Changing Economy and an Individualistic Society.* Washington, DC: Child Trends.

Chapter Two

TRENDS OVER TIME IN TEENAGE PREGNANCY AND CHILDBEARING: THE CRITICAL CHANGES

Susan Williams McElroy and Kristin Anderson Moore

Before the consequences of teen pregnancy in the United States are examined in detail, we set the stage with a brief overview of recent trends in U.S. teen pregnancy and childbearing and their place in the larger context of social and economic change over recent decades. We first compare teen pregnancy and childbirth in this country with that in other countries. Then, we describe the changing social and economic context within which recent trends in teen pregnancy and childbirth have taken place in the United States. Following this discussion is a statistical picture of teenage sexual and contraceptive behavior, teen pregnancy outcomes, birth rates of teen women from 1960 to 1993, the increasing incidence of childbearing outside of marriage, and the link between teen childbirth in one generation and family formation in the next.

THE INTERNATIONAL CONTEXT

The international context highlights two important facts about U.S. teen childbearing (figure 2.1). First, the United States has the highest teenage birth rate of all Western developed countries.[1] The United States, with its 1992 teenage birth rate of 61 births per 1,000 females ages 15 to 19, has a teen birth rate nearly twice that of the United Kingdom, whose 1992 teen birth rate is the second highest, at 32 per 1,000. It is sometimes presumed that the high incidence of teenage pregnancy and childbearing in the United States results from the

The research assistance of Dana Glei, Angela Romano, and Gregory Kienzl, the production assistance provided by Fanette M. Jones and the editorial assistance provided by Charlotte Koelling are greatly appreciated. We would like to thank Robert Willis and V. Joseph Hotz for their comments.

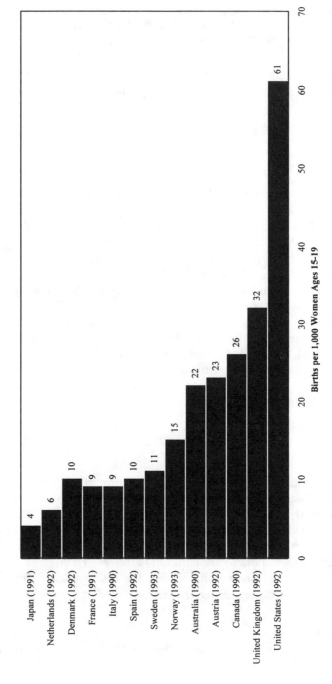

Figure 2.1 BIRTH RATES OF TEENS AGES 15 TO 19, FOR SELECTED COUNTRIES

Sources: United Nations (1994, 1995); U.S. Department of Health and Human Services (1994).

greater racial and ethnic diversity of the population compared to the populations of other industrialized nations, Western Europe in particular. This is not the major explanation, however, because the birth rate among non-Hispanic U.S. white females ages 15 to 19 is 40 per 1,000, noticeably higher than the birth rate for comparable populations in Western industrialized countries.

The United States also registered the largest percentage and absolute increase in the birth rate of 15- to 19-year-olds among the major industrialized countries between 1977 and 1990 (figure 2.2). Of the eight countries shown in figure 2.2, only the United States and the United Kingdom registered sizable increases in the teen birth rate during this period: from 53 to 60 per 1,000 in the United States and from 30 to 33 per 1,000 in the United Kingdom. Japan's teen birth rate barely increased, from 3 per 1,000 in 1977 to 4 per 1,000 in 1990. By contrast, the teen birth rate declined in the Netherlands, Sweden, France, Australia, and Canada.

In the United States the overwhelming majority of births to women age 19 and younger occurs outside marriage. In this respect the United States is similar to a number of other Western industrialized countries (figure 2.3). In 1981, 50 percent of all births to women age 19 and younger in the United States occurred outside marriage. By 1991, this figure had climbed to 69 percent (and to 76 percent by 1994). The same pattern emerges for each of the six other countries shown. In Canada, England and Wales, and France, even larger percentages of teen births occur outside marriage than in the United States.

THE CHANGING SOCIAL AND ECONOMIC CONTEXT OF TEEN PREGNANCY AND CHILDBEARING

In recent decades, the social and economic context of teenage pregnancy and childbearing has changed in major ways. We highlight four major changes:

- Growth of the teenage population
- Changes in marriage and family structure patterns
- Women's rising rates of labor force participation
- Changing educational demands of the U.S. labor market

These are not the *only* ways in which the social and economic context of teenage pregnancy and childbearing in the United States has changed over time. However, they are particularly important.

Figure 2.2 BIRTH RATES OF WOMEN (MARRIED AND UNMARRIED) AGES 15 TO 19, 1977 TO 1990

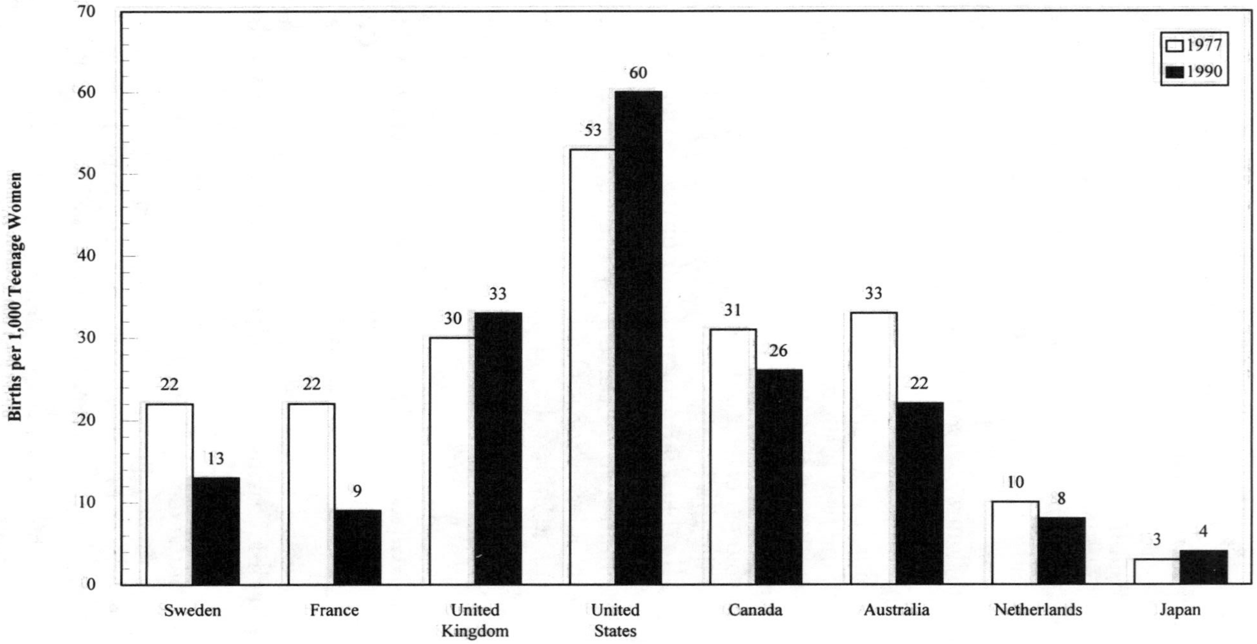

Source: United Nations (various years).

Table 2.1 TOTAL U.S. POPULATION BY AGE GROUP AND GENDER, 1950–2000
(IN THOUSANDS)

	Males			Females		
	10–14	15–19	20–24	10–14	15–19	20–24
1950	5,660	5,311	5,606	5,459	5,305	5,876
1960	8,524	6,634	5,272	8,249	6,586	5,528
1965	9,636	8,656	6,884	9,323	8,395	6,794
1970	10,622	9,714	8,034	10,230	9,517	8,544
1975	10,534	10,757	9,640	10,112	10,465	9,677
1980	9,316	10,726	10,697	8,925	10,376	10,678
1985	8,590	9,398	10,820	8,207	9,019	10,481
1990	8,586	8,670	9,443	8,207	8,299	9,137
1995	9,706	9,131	9,385	9,233	8,659	9,088
2000	9,986	9,681	8,723	9,532	9,262	8,422

Sources: U.S. Bureau of the Census 1975, 1983, and 1988.

Growth of the Teenage Population

Between 1950 and 1980, the number of females ages 15 to 19 almost doubled, increasing from 5.3 million to 10.4 million (table 2.1). The population of teenage males (ages 15 to 19) literally doubled, increasing from 5.3 million to 10.7 million in 1980. Although their number declined in the 1980s, the population of adolescents has recently begun again to increase. Between 1990 and 2000, the number of females ages 15 to 19 will increase by a million. Unless significant reductions are achieved in the teen birth rate, this trend can be expected to increase substantially the number of births to teen mothers.

Changes in Patterns of Marriage and Family Structure

Significant changes in marital and family structure patterns have also affected the nature and meaning of teenage pregnancy and childbearing in the United States. In past decades, for example, women typically married soon after high school, whereas men waited until they were able to support a family. In this regard, marital patterns in the United States followed Western European patterns. In 1950, for example, the median age at first marriage for women was 20.3 and for men was 22.8 (U.S. Bureau of the Census 1975). By 1988, the median age at first marriage had risen to age 23.7 for women and to 25.5 for men (U.S. Bureau of the Census 1993). Black women tend to marry later than white women do. In 1988, the median age at first marriage for black women was 26, compared with age 23 for white women (DaVanzo and Rahman 1993). Now many women remain single long

Figure 2.3 PERCENTAGE OF ALL BIRTHS TO TEENS (AGE 19 AND UNDER) THAT OCCUR OUTSIDE MARRIAGE

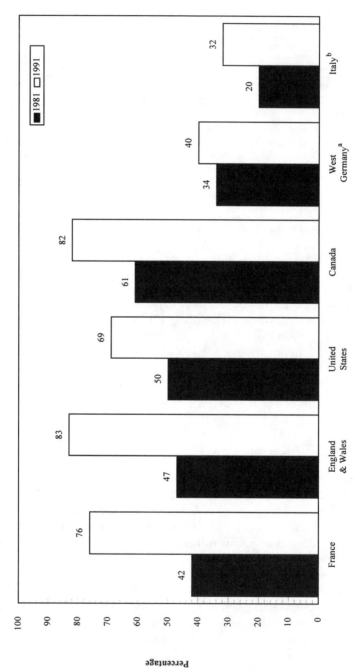

Source: Compiled by the office of Senator Daniel Patrick Moynihan using data from the National Center for Health Statistics and various countries.

a. 1984 and 1990 data.
b. 1981 and 1990 data.

after they have completed high school, with young black women less likely to have ever been married than young white and Hispanic women. For example, in 1992, among women ages 25 to 29, 62.2 percent of black women had never been married, compared with 30.6 percent of white women and 29.1 percent of Hispanic women (U.S. Bureau of the Census 1992).

What difference do such changes make in the social and economic context of teenage pregnancy and childbearing? In the first place, virtually all adolescents are now unmarried. In 1960, 83.9 percent of all females ages 15 to 19 had never been married. The corresponding figure for males was 96.3 percent (table 2.2). By 1993, those proportions had risen respectively to 95.2 percent and 98.8 percent. Only about 1 in 100 adolescents ages 15 to 17 were married in 1993. Thus, conceptions among teens are considerably more likely to occur outside marriage than in previous decades. In addition, teens who become pregnant outside of marriage are less likely to marry before the birth

Table 2.2 PERCENTAGE OF MALES AND FEMALES, NEVER MARRIED, BY AGE AND RACE, 1960–1993

	Males			Females		
	15–17	18–19	15–19	15–17	18–19	15–19
1960						
Total	99.1%	91.1%	96.3%	93.2%	67.8%	83.9%
White	99.1	91.0	96.2	93.3	67.6	83.9
Nonwhite	99.2	91.9	96.6	92.3	69.3	83.8
1980						
Total	99.4	94.2	97.3	97.0	82.8	91.1
White	99.4	93.6	97.0	96.7	81.5	90.4
Black	99.4	97.7	98.8	98.3	90.9	95.4
Hispanic	98.5	92.2	95.8	94.6	79.2	88.2
1990						
Total	99.8	96.8	98.5	98.5	90.3	95.0
White	99.7	96.5	98.4	98.2	89.1	94.3
Black	100.0	98.9	99.6	100.0	95.5	98.1
Hispanic	99.8	93.8	97.1	96.3	80.2	89.3
1993						
Total	99.9	96.9	98.8	98.7	89.9	95.2
White	99.9	96.7	98.7	98.6	88.3	94.5
Black	100.0	97.7	99.2	98.8	96.9	98.0
Hispanic	99.6	92.9	96.8	96.9	84.0	91.5

Note: Hispanic persons may be of any race, and black and white totals may include Hispanics.
Source: U.S. Bureau of the Census, *Current Population Reports*, various years.

of the child than in previous decades (U.S. Bureau of the Census 1991). One result of these changes is that young women are more likely to raise children on their own.

Women's propensity to marry at all differs by race, with black women less likely to ever marry than white women (U.S. Bureau of the Census 1994). A corollary of this fact is that black women are less likely to be married throughout their childbearing years (Bennett, Bloom, and Craig 1989). However, during the teen years, the vast majority of young women are unmarried, irrespective of race or ethnicity. The primary implication of later age at first marriage is that teenagers who become pregnant are much less likely to be married than in previous decades.

Women's Rising Rates of Labor Force Participation

Women's labor force participation rates have risen dramatically, and women with young children are considerably more likely to participate in the paid labor force than in previous decades. Rising rates of female labor force participation during the postwar period constitute one of the most profound and far-reaching social changes of this century (Bergmann 1986; Goldin 1990; Kessler-Harris 1982). That increase cannot be separated from a number of other social and economic changes, including rising wages paid to women and women's higher levels of educational attainment.

The increase in women's wages in the post World War II period explains, in part, rising rates of labor force participation. That is, as women's actual and potential wages increased, not participating in the paid labor market became considerably more costly for women; the rising value of their time meant that the opportunity cost of working only in the home (that is, the income lost because of the decision not to enter the paid labor market) became significantly higher.

> Women have always had to sell their time cheaper than men. But the price employers have paid for women's time has risen along with the price paid for men's. The key to women's economic emergence is that women's time has risen in price until it has become, in the eyes of family members, too valuable to be spent entirely in the home. (Bergmann 1986, p. 15)

Women's levels of educational attainment also rose, enabling them to command higher wages. And the narrowing gender gap in earnings made even more costly the traditional gender division of labor that forms the basis of the economic theory of the family: that is, men working outside the home—in the paid labor market—and women doing unpaid work inside the home (Becker 1973, 1985, 1991).

Black women traditionally have had higher rates of labor force participation than white women have. In recent years, however, participation rates of young black women have leveled off, whereas those of their white counterparts have continued to rise, narrowing the labor force participation gap between the two (McElroy 1996).

Single women have traditionally had higher rates of labor force participation than have married women, and they still do. During recent decades, participation rates of both single and married women have risen markedly. Perhaps the most notable change in women's labor force participation is the rise in participation rates of women with young children and infants (Hayghe 1986). Among women with children under age six, the participation rates of married women are higher than those of single women. Whereas the labor force participation rate of married women with children under age six rose from 45.1 in 1980 to 59.9 in 1992, the rate for single women with children rose only slightly, from 44.1 in 1980 to 45.8 in 1992 (U.S. Bureau of the Census 1993). These differences in labor force participation by marital status suggest two alternative possibilities. Either something about being married, or about policies that vary by marital status, make married women more likely to participate in the paid labor force. An alternative explanation is that differences in education, experience, or on-the-job training, or unobservable characteristics between single and married women, affect their labor force participation.

Changing Educational Demands of the U.S. Labor Market

The educational demands of the U.S. labor market have increased dramatically, and the employment and earnings prospects of high school dropouts and others at the lower end of the educational spectrum have worsened (Murphy and Welch 1993). For young women, being a high school dropout also has additional and *different* implications than in earlier periods, in part because young women, who used to marry soon after high school, now are much less likely to do so and therefore are more likely to be supporting their child or children alone once they become mothers.

It is also true that, in relative terms, high school completion is no longer as high an educational attainment level for women as it was in the 1950s. In 1960, 42.5 percent of all women age 25 and over had completed high school or more. By 1990, 77.5 percent of women in this age group had completed high school or more. College completion rates also serve as an indicator of women's rising levels of educational attainment: in 1960, 5.8 percent of women age 25 and over had completed college; by 1993, the proportion had risen to 19.2 percent.

Taken together, the sweeping social and economic changes outlined above suggest that the social and economic implications of teenage childbearing have indeed changed in fundamental ways. The link between dropping out of high school, on the one hand, and unemployment, low earnings, welfare participation, and poverty, on the other hand, has grown increasingly strong during recent decades, most notably in the 1980s and 1990s. At the same time, teenagers have become less likely to marry, increasing the likelihood that a young mother will have only her own earnings with which to support herself and her child.

SEXUAL ACTIVITY AND USE OF CONTRACEPTION AMONG TEENAGERS

Not surprisingly, the percentage of teens who report ever having had sex increases with age. It also differs by race and ethnicity, with the percentage reporting that they have had sex higher for black than for white or Hispanic teenagers. This pattern holds at all ages and for both men and women (figure 2.4).

For example, 56 percent of non-Hispanic black female 17-year-olds report having had sex, compared to 52 percent of comparable non-Hispanic white females and 52 percent of Hispanic females. Similarly, 78 percent of non-Hispanic black 17-year-old males report having had sex, as compared to 46 percent of non-Hispanic white males and 50 percent of Hispanic males. These proportions are uniformly lower for 15-year-olds and uniformly higher for 19-year-olds.

Although some teenage sexual activity takes place within marriage, most is premarital sex. And the proportion of women ages 15 to 19 who reported having had premarital sex has increased steadily. Between 1970 and 1988, for example, the proportion grew from less than one-third to over one-half (figure 2.5).

Nonvoluntary Sexual Intercourse

Another dimension of teenage sexual activity is the distinction between voluntary and nonvoluntary sexual activity (table 2.3). Table

Figure 2.4 PERCENTAGE OF TEENS AGES 15, 17, AND 19 WHO REPORT HAVING HAD INTERCOURSE IN THE PREVIOUS THREE MONTHS, BY GENDER AND RACE/ETHNICITY, 1992

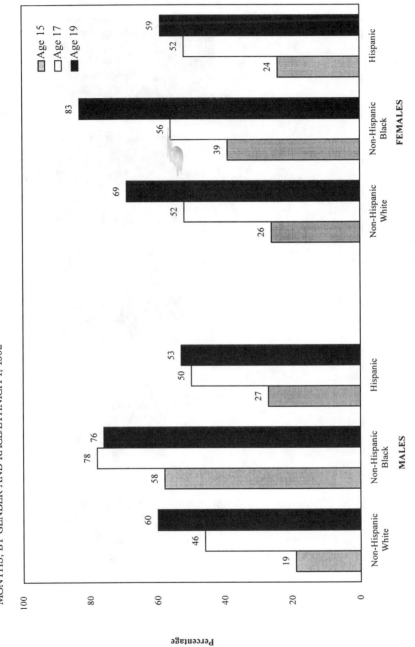

Source: National Health Interview Survey—Youth Risk Behavior Supplement (1992), tabulations by Child Trends, Inc., weighted analyses.

Figure 2.5   PERCENTAGE OF FEMALES (AGES 15 TO 19) WHO HAVE HAD PREMARITAL SEX, 1970 TO 1988, VARIOUS YEARS

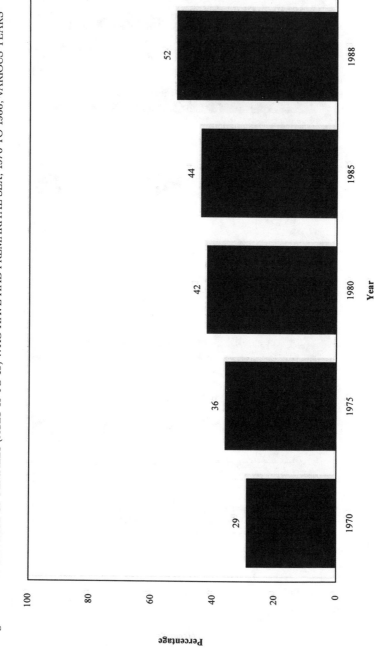

Source: Trussell and Vaughan (1991).

Table 2.3 PERCENTAGE OF 18- TO 22-YEAR-OLDS REPORTING NONVOLUNTARY INTERCOURSE, BY AGE, GENDER, AND RACE

White Females			
Age	Nonvoluntary	Voluntary	Any Intercourse
<14	5.8	2.3	6.9
15	6.3	4.2	8.5
16	7.5	10.6	15.3
17	9.1	28.0	31.7
18	10.8	48.6	51.7
19	11.9	64.5	65.6
20	12.7	76.2	76.9

White Males			
Age	Nonvoluntary	Voluntary	Any Intercourse
<14	0.3	4.1	4.1
15	0.4	11.8	11.8
16	0.4	20.6	20.6
17	0.4	41.6	41.6
18	0.4	59.2	50.2
19	1.9	74.7	74.7
20	1.9	82.1	82.1

Black Females			
Age	Nonvoluntary	Voluntary	Any Intercourse
<14	2.9	6.2	9.0
15	3.2	13.8	16.7
16	3.5	20.7	23.5
17	5.1	36.2	38.4
18	5.6	52.7	54.2
19	6.0	74.0	75.6
20	8.0	82.6	82.3

Black Males			
Age	Nonvoluntary	Voluntary	Any Intercourse
<14	0.0	13.9	13.9
15	1.4	20.8	22.1
16	4.8	36.0	37.4
17	5.6	61.1	61.1
18	6.1	72.4	72.4
19	6.1	77.8	77.8
20	6.1	88.1	88.1

Sources: Moore, Nord, and Peterson (1989); data from the 1987 National Survey of Children.

2.3 shows the percentage of 14- to 20-year-olds who reported having experienced sexual intercourse, according to whether the intercourse was nonvoluntary or voluntary (Moore, Nord, and Peterson 1989). For both blacks and whites, teenage women are considerably more likely to have experienced nonvoluntary intercourse than are their male counterparts. Second, at every age, black teenage females are less likely to report having experienced nonvoluntary intercourse than are white teenage females but more likely to have experienced voluntary intercourse. Third, black teenage males are more likely to have experienced both nonvoluntary and voluntary intercourse than are white teenage males.

Teen Pregnancy Rates by Sexual Experience

Reflecting increased levels of sexual activity, pregnancy rates for all teen women ages 15 to 19 have risen during the past two decades. However, the pregnancy rate for sexually experienced teen women has declined (figure 2.6). In 1972, for example, the pregnancy rate for teenage women was 95 per 1,000 women; by 1990, the rate had climbed to 117 per 1,000. However, the pregnancy rate for female teens ages 15 to 19 who had ever had sexual intercourse declined from 254 to 207 per 1,000 over the same period. That pregnancy rates have been climbing for all teens while declining among sexually experienced teen females suggests that changes in sexual activity constitute a major driving force underlying changes in the overall teen pregnancy rate.

Contraceptive Use

During the 1980s, condom use among teenagers increased dramatically. The proportion of sexually experienced females ages 15 to 19 who used a method of contraception at first sexual intercourse increased from 39 percent in 1976, to 48 percent in 1982, to 65 percent in 1988 (Forrest and Singh 1990; Zelnik and Kantner 1978). The most popular methods of contraception among teenagers ages 15 to 19 who used contraception in 1988 were the birth control pill (59 percent) and the condom (33 percent). Of the more than one million women ages 15 to 19 who became pregnant in 1987, almost three-quarters (71 percent) were not using contraception and only 13 percent of these pregnancies ended in an intended birth (figure 2.7).

Although most teens who became pregnant were not using contraception when they conceived, those who were practicing birth control

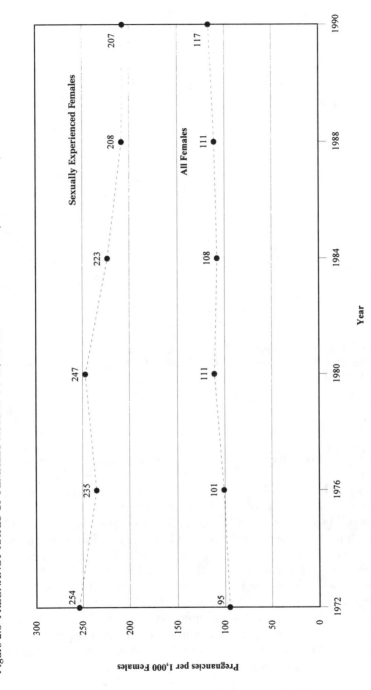

Figure 2.6 PREGNANCY RATES OF FEMALES AGES 15 TO 19, BY SEXUAL EXPERIENCE (1972 TO 1990)

Note: Sexually experienced is defined as females who have ever had sexual intercourse.
Source: Alan Guttmacher Institute (1994).

Figure 2.7 CONTRACEPTIVE USE AT CONCEPTION, BY PREGNANCY OUTCOME
FOR FEMALES AGES 15 TO 19 (1987)

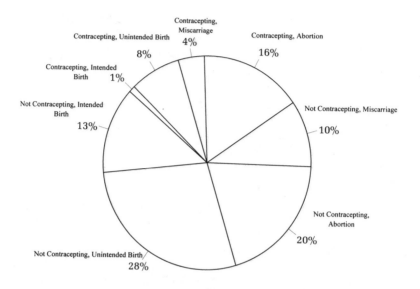

Source: Tabulations provided to Child Trends, Inc., by the Alan Guttmacher Institute,
from the 1988 National Survey of Family Growth (U.S. Department of Health and
Human Services).

were much more likely to obtain an abortion—55 percent versus 28
percent of those practicing unprotected sex. Thus, contraceptive use
not only reduces the risk of pregnancy, it serves as an indicator of the
depth of a teen's motivation to prevent pregnancy.

The pill has the lowest failure rates for teens, as is the case for older
populations, and the condom the next lowest. Periodic abstinence and
foam have the highest failure rates (figure 2.8). Low-income teen
women have higher failure rates than other teen women whatever the
method used.[2] For example, for condom use the failure rate for low-
income women is 27.3 percent, as opposed to 13.2 percent for their
higher income counterparts. Possible explanations for the difference
include lower reading levels, lower motivation, less cooperation from
partners, and lower levels of parent education and knowledge to support teen contraceptive use.

Figure 2.8 PERCENTAGE OF CONTRACEPTIVE FAILURE RATES AMONG NEVER-MARRIED WOMEN UNDER 20, BY POVERTY STATUS (1988 NSFG)

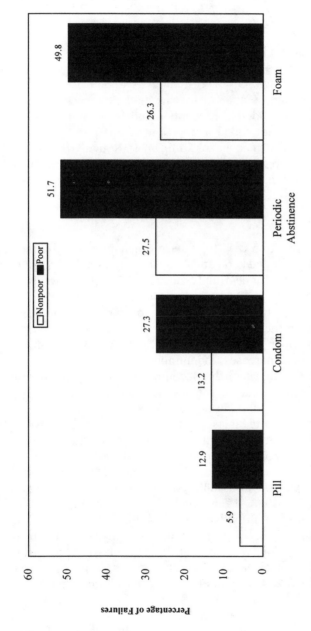

Notes: Failures are defined as conceptions that occurred when the respondent reported using a method of contraception. All rates are first-year failure rates, corrected for the underreporting of abortions. Poverty status is defined as having a family income that falls below 200 percent of the poverty line.
Source: Jones and Forrest (1992).

TEENAGE PREGNANCY RESOLUTIONS: BIRTHS, ABORTIONS, AND MISCARRIAGES

Not all pregnancies end in live births. Specifically, three outcomes, or resolutions, to a pregnancy are possible: (1) live birth, (2) abortion, and (3) miscarriage. Of an estimated 1,040,000 pregnancies among young women age 19 and younger in 1990, 51 percent ended in birth (37 percent unintended at conception and 14 percent intended at conception), 35 percent ended in abortion, and 14 percent ended in miscarriage (Alan Guttmacher Institute 1994). Roughly the same proportion of teenage pregnancies, about one-third, end in unintended births as end in abortions.

Births

Despite the attention paid to teenage pregnancy and childbearing by researchers, policymakers, and educators, the total number of births to teens has actually declined since the 1960s. The number of births to females ages 15 to 19 rose in the 1960s, peaked in 1970 at 664,708 births, fell below a half million during the mid-1980s, and then began to rise again in the late 1980s, reaching 521,826 births in 1990. Since 1990, the number has declined slightly, to 505,488 in 1994. As the teen population increases, the number may rise again.

For blacks, teenage births account for a larger percentage of all births (23 percent) than is the case for whites (11 percent) (U.S. Department of Health and Human Services, 1996a). It is also true, however, that births to teens as a percentage of all births have been declining steadily for both blacks and whites since the mid-1970s.

Since the early 1970s the percentage of teen pregnancies ending in a birth has also declined, from 76 percent in 1972 to 60 percent in 1990. Between 1972 and 1980, the percentage declined rapidly. Between 1980 and 1988, it remained almost constant. Then, from 1988 to 1991, it began to climb back upward (figure 2.9).

Teen mothers give birth to a higher percentage of low-birth-weight babies than do older women, and the percentage of low-birth-weight babies among black teens is nearly twice as high as among white teens.[3] In 1994, 13.1 percent of all the babies born to black teens were low birth weight compared to 7.9 percent for white teens (U.S. Dept. of Health and Human Services, 1996a).

What do we know about the biological fathers of children born to teen mothers? At present, we know much too little. We do know that

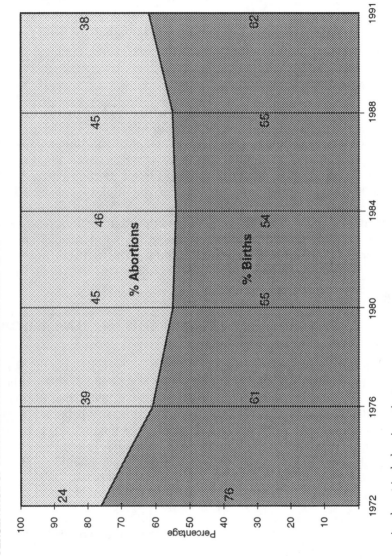

Figure 2.9 PERCENTAGE OF PREGNANCIES AMONG WOMEN AGES 15 TO 19 ENDING IN BIRTH AND ABORTION, 1972 TO 1991

Note: Pregnancies do not include miscarriages.
Source: Alan Guttmacher Institute (1994).

men who are fathering children born to teen mothers are somewhat older than the mothers. In 1988, for example, half of the biological fathers of children born to adolescent mothers age 17 or younger were themselves age 20 or older (Landry and Forrest, 1995). The fathers are nearly always older and two-thirds of the fathers of babies born to females ages 15 to 19 are not themselves teenagers.

Abortions

The proportion of teen pregnancies ending in abortion has increased since the 1970s (figure 2.9). In 1972, for example, 24 percent of pregnancies among women ages 15 to 19 ended in abortion, compared to 38 percent in 1991. In 1991, 314,000 women between the ages of 15 and 19 had abortions, which translates to an abortion rate of 37.6 per 1,000 women in that population. Teens from high-income families are more likely to abort an unplanned pregnancy than are teens from low-income or poor families. According to the Alan Guttmacher Institute (1994), 70 percent of unplanned pregnancies to women from high-income families end in abortion, compared with 39 percent for women from poor families.

FERTILITY RATES OF TEENAGE WOMEN

The birth rate for teens ages 15 to 19 has declined over the past 40 years from 90 per 1,000 in 1955 to 59 per 1,000 in 1994. Although this rate was considerably higher in the early 1990s than in the mid-1980s, it remains lower than during the post-war baby boom years. Teen birth rates differ by race, however (see figure 2.10), with white teen women having the lowest rate (40 per 1,000) and black and Hispanic teen women having the same rate (108 per 1,000) in 1994 (U.S. Department of Health and Human Services, 1996a).

BIRTHS OUTSIDE MARRIAGE

While the number of births to teens each year has declined slightly compared with the 1950s, as has the birth rate for teenagers, the trends for births outside marriage have been strikingly different (figure 2.11). The percentage of all teen births that occur outside marriage has risen

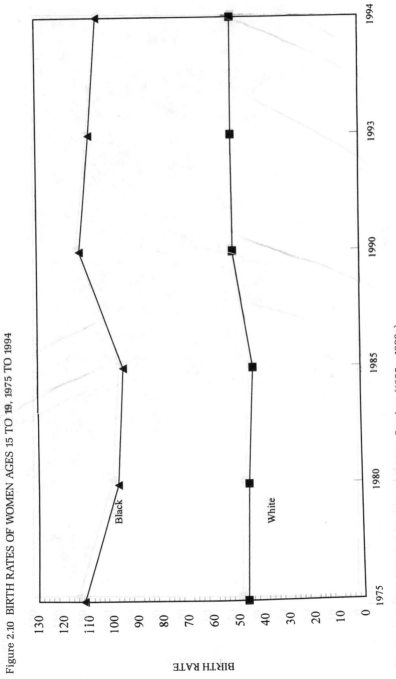

Figure 2.10 BIRTH RATES OF WOMEN AGES 15 TO 19, 1975 TO 1994

Source: U.S. Department of Health and Human Services (1995a, 1996a).

Figure 2.11 PERCENTAGE OF TEEN BIRTHS THAT OCCURRED OUTSIDE MARRIAGE, 1955 TO 1994

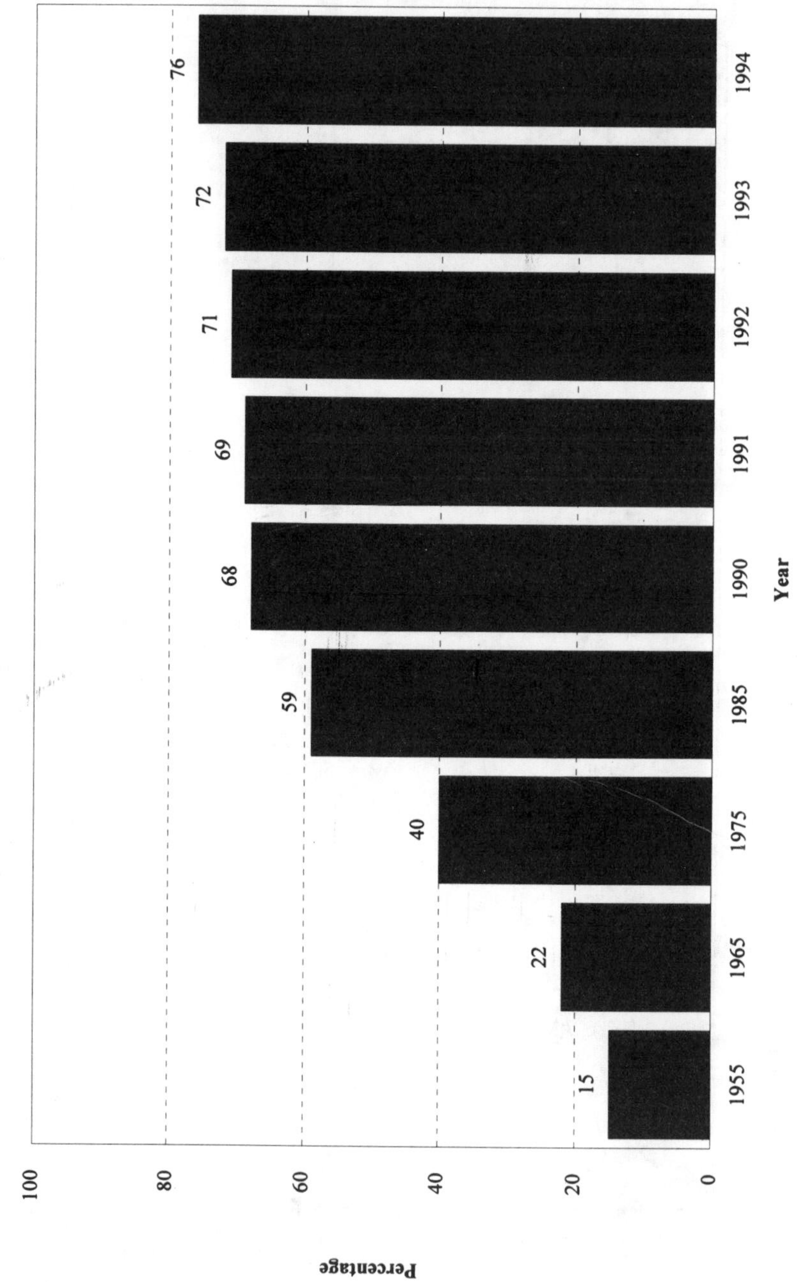

Source: U.S. Department of Health and Human Services (various years).

more than fourfold in the span of four decades. Between 1955 and 1994, for example, the percentage of teen births that occurred outside of marriage increased from 15 percent in 1955 to 76 percent in 1994. By definition, then, the percentage of teen births that were marital births declined during the same period. The older the teen, the more likely she is to be married when she gives birth; 66 percent of births occur outside of marriage among 18- to 19-year-olds compared with 80 percent among 15- to 17-year-olds.

The percentage of teen births that occur outside marriage has consistently been higher among blacks than among whites (figure 2.12). This percentage has also been increasing at a faster rate among whites than among blacks. In 1970, 17 percent of births to white teens were to unmarried women, compared with 65 percent of births to black teenage women. Twenty-four years later, in 1994, 68 percent of births to white teens were outside of marriage, as compared to 95 percent of births to black teens. For both black and white teens, the proportion who are married when they give birth increases with age.

It should be noted that teenagers are not the only age group for whom the percentage of all births that occurred outside marriage has risen rapidly. In fact, the percentage of births which occurred outside of marriage has risen for women of all childbearing age groups. Two decades ago (1973), for instance, among women 20 to 24, 11 percent of all births occurred outside marriage in comparison to 35 percent in 1994. Nor do teens account for the majority of births to unmarried women. Births to teens accounted for only 31 percent of all births outside of marriage in 1994 (figure 2.13). During the same year, nonmarital births to women ages 20 to 24 accounted for 35 percent of all births. The corresponding figures for women ages 25 to 29 and those 30 and older were 18 percent and 16 percent, respectively. The United States is not unique in this regard. In a number of other industrialized countries an increasing percentage of all births have occurred outside marriage during recent decades (Ermisch 1991).

TEENAGE CHILDBIRTH AND FAMILY FORMATION

Two indicators of the link between teenage childbirth and family formation are (1) the percentage of births to teens that are first births and (2) the percentage of mothers who have had a grandchild by a specified age (which is a proxy for generation length).

Figure 2.12   PERCENTAGE OF ALL BIRTHS TO WOMEN AGES 15 TO 19 THAT OCCUR OUTSIDE OF MARRIAGE BY RACE (1970 TO 1994)

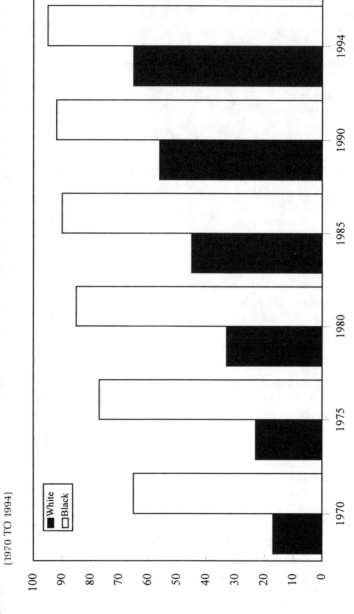

Source: U.S. Department of Health and Human Services, various years.

Figure 2.13 BIRTHS TO UNMARRIED WOMEN, BY AGE GROUP (1994)

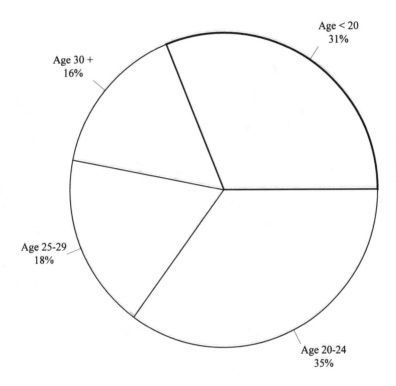

Source: U.S. Department of Health and Human Services (1994).

Of the 518,389 births in 1994 to women age 19 and younger, 78 percent (402,444) were first births, an indicator that varies somewhat by race and ethnicity. Among white teens in 1994, 82.4 percent of all births were first births; the corresponding percentages for black and Hispanic women were 70.2 percent and 75.0 percent, respectively. For all three groups, the proportion of teen births that are second or higher-order births has risen over the past decade.

A pattern of early childbearing is linked with social disadvantages. Thus, mothers who live in high-poverty areas become grandmothers at much younger ages, on average, than do women who live in lower-poverty areas (figure 2.14).[4] Women who live in zip codes with a higher incidence of poverty tend to become grandmothers at much

Figure 2.14 PERCENTAGE OF MOTHERS WHO HAVE HAD A GRANDCHILD, BY AGE AND LEVEL OF POVERTY IN ZIP CODE AREA, LIFE TABLES, NSC (WEIGHTED)

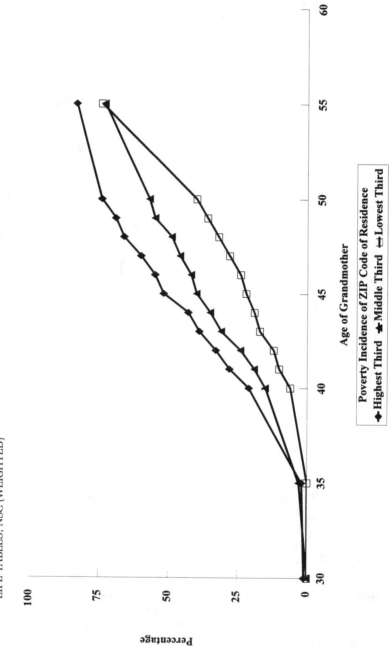

earlier ages than do women who reside in zip codes with lower con-
centrations of poverty. In the highest poverty areas, a quarter of mothers become grandmothers in their early forties, compared with approximately 5 percent in the lowest third of areas by poverty
incidence.

CONCLUSION

Our central conclusion is that teenage pregnancy and childbearing in
the United States are quite different phenomena in the 1980s and the
1990s than in previous decades. The most profound changes have
taken place in the *circumstances* of teenage pregnancies and births.
Contrary to the conventional wisdom and media reports suggesting
that the actual numbers of births to teenagers have skyrocketed in
recent decades, neither the numbers of births nor birth rates have
changed dramatically. In fact, the teen birth rate in 1995 was actually
lower than in 1955. On the other hand, teen pregnancy rates were
higher in the early 1990s than in the early 1970s. Thus, although the
teenage birth rate in the United States is the highest of all developed
countries, there is scant evidence of a sudden "epidemic" (Vinovskis
1988). Rather, changes in what we call "the social and economic
context of teenage pregnancy and childbearing" constitute the real
story.

Four major changes in the context of teen pregnancy and childbearing deserve emphasis. First, although during the 1980s the size
of the teenage population declined, the population of adolescents recently has begun to increase. Second, young men and women have
begun to marry at later ages, and a larger percentage of young people
remain single throughout their teen years. Third, women's rates of
participation in the paid labor force have risen dramatically across all
racial and ethnic groups, particularly among younger women and
women with children. Finally, during recent decades, the labor market
prospects of persons with low educational attainment and low skills
have become increasingly bleak. In addition, the average educational
attainment level of young women has risen markedly, such that high
school completion is no longer considered a high attainment level for
women. These social and economic changes, in conjunction with one
another, have provided a rapidly changing context for teenage sexual
activity, fertility, and marriage.

Striking changes in the premarital sexual behavior of teenagers have also transpired during recent decades. For example, the percentage of teens who report ever having experienced sexual intercourse has risen over time. As would be expected, the older the teens, the more likely they are to report that they have experienced sex. Improved contraceptive use has also occurred. In particular, during the 1980s, condom use among teens rose. The birth control pill and the condom are the two most popular forms of contraception among those teens who practice contraception.

Since we know that not all teen sexual activity results in a pregnancy and not all pregnancies end in a live birth, it is useful to review the three possible outcomes of a pregnancy: live birth, 51 percent of teen pregnancies; abortion, 35 percent; and miscarriages, 14 percent (statistics are for 1990). Throughout most of the 1980s, the fraction of all teen pregnancies ending in a live birth changed little, but in the late 1980s and early 1990s there was an increase in the percentage of pregnancies ending in a live birth, and a corresponding decline in the proportion ending in abortion.

There is no doubt that one of the most salient transformations in teen pregnancy and childbearing is in the marital status of teenage mothers, that is, the increasing percentage of teen births that occur outside marriage. In 1993, nearly three-quarters of all teen births were to unmarried teens. Nevertheless, teen births do not constitute the majority of all nonmarital births. At the same time, less than one-third of all births to unmarried women were to women younger than age 20.

Finally, we note that the great majority of births to teens are unintended by the teen at the time of conception. This fact suggests that, despite high levels of teen pregnancy, most teens would prefer to delay parenthood. In this regard, teens would appear to agree with their parents and with taxpayers. The success of other industrialized nations in achieving low levels of teen childbearing suggests that lower rates are also possible in the United States.

Notes

1. Recently released data indicate that by 1995 the U.S. teen birth rate had declined to 56.9 births per 1,000 females ages 15 to 19 (U.S. Department of Health and Human Services, 1996b).

2. Low income here is defined as family income below 200 percent of poverty.
3. Low birth weight is defined as less than 2,500 grams.
4. Statistics are weighted to reflect the composition of the U.S. population.

References

Alan Guttmacher Institute. 1994. *Sex and America's Teenagers*. New York: Alan Guttmacher Institute.

Becker, G. S. 1973. "A Theory of Marriage: Part I." *Journal of Political Economy* 81(4): 813–46.

———. 1985. "Human Capital, Effort, and the Sexual Division of Labor." *Journal of Labor Economics* 3(1, pt. 2): S33–S58.

———. 1991. *A Treatise on the Family*. Cambridge, Mass.; London: Harvard University Press.

Bennett, N. G., D. E. Bloom, and P. H. Craig. 1989. "The Divergence of Black and White Marriage Patterns." *American Journal of Sociology* 95(November): 692–722.

Bergmann, B. 1986. *The Economic Emergence of Women*. New York: Basic Books.

DaVanzo, J., and M. O. Rahman. 1993. "American Families: Trends and Correlates." *Population Index* 59(3): 350–86.

Ermisch, J. F. 1991. *Lone Parenthood: An Economic Analysis*. Cambridge: Cambridge University Press.

Forrest, J. D., and S. Singh. 1990. "The Sexual and Reproductive Behavior of American Women, 1982–1988." *Family Planning Perspectives* 22: 206–214.

Goldin, C. 1990. *Understanding the Gender Gap: An Economic History of American Women*. New York: Oxford University Press.

Hayghe, H. 1986. "Rise in Mother's Labor Force Activity Includes Those with Infants." *Monthly Labor Review* 109(2, February): 43–45.

Jones, E. F., and J. D. Forrest. 1992. "Contraceptive Failure Rates Based on the 1988 National Survey of Family Growth." *Family Planning Perspectives* 24: 12–19.

Kessler-Harris, A. 1982. *Out to Work: A History of Wage-Earning Women in the United States*. New York: Oxford University Press.

Landry, D.J., and J.D. Forrest. 1995. "How Old Are U.S. Fathers?" *Family Planning Perspectives* 27(4): 159–165.

Matthaei, J. A. 1982. *An Economic History of Women in America: Women's Work, the Sexual Division of Labor, and the Development of Capitalism*. New York: Schocken Books.

McElroy, S. W. 1996. "The Effect of Teenage Childbearing on Young Black and White Women's Educational Attainment, Labor Force Participation, and Earnings." Ph.D. diss., Stanford University.

Moore, K. A., C. W. Nord, and J. L. Peterson. 1989. "Nonvoluntary Sexual Activity among Adolescents." *Family Planning Perspectives* 21(3): 110–14.

Moore, K. A., N. Snyder, and J. L. Peterson. 1993. *Teen Fertility: National File. A data file on teen fertility.* Publication #DD-01. Washington, D.C.: Child Trends.

Murphy, K. M., and F. Welch. 1993. "The Structure of Wages." *Quarterly Journal of Economics* 107(February): 35–78.

Trussell, J., and B. Vaughan. 1991. "Selected Results Concerning Sexual Behavior and Contraceptive Use." From the 1988 National Survey of Family Growth and the 1988 National Survey of Adolescent Males, Office of Population Research Working Paper No. 91-12, Princeton University.

United Nations, Department of Economic and Social Development. 1994, 1995. *Demographic Yearbook.* New York: United Nations.

U.S. Bureau of the Census. 1975. *Historical Statistics of the United States: Colonial Times to 1970.* Washington, D.C.: U.S. Government Printing Office.

————. 1983. *1980 Census of Population. Vol. I: Characteristics of the Population*, Chapter B: General Population Characteristics, Part 1: United States Summary. Washington, D.C.: U.S. Government Printing Office.

————. 1988. *Projections of the Population of the United States by Age, Sex, and Race: 1988 to 2080*, by G. Spencer. *Current Population Reports.* Series P-25, no. 1018. Washington, D.C.: U.S. Government Printing Office.

————. 1991. *Fertility of American Women 1990*, by A. Bachu. *Current Population Reports.* Series P-20-454. Washington, D.C.: Government Printing Office.

————. 1992. *Marital Status and Living Arrangements: March 1992*, by A. Saluter. *Current Population Reports.* Series P-20-468. Washington, D.C.: U.S. Government Printing Office.

————. 1993. *Money Income of Households, Families, and Persons in the United States: 1992. Current Population Reports.* Series P-60, no. 184. Washington D.C.: U.S. Government Printing Office.

————. 1993. *Statistical Abstract of the United States 1993.* Washington, D.C.: U.S. Government Printing Office.

————. 1994. *Statistical Abstract of the United States 1994.* Washington, D.C.: U.S. Government Printing Office.

————. Various years. *Marital Status and Living Arrangements. Current Population Reports.* Washington, D.C.: U.S. Government Printing Office.

U.S. Department of Health and Human Services; Public Health Service; Centers for Disease Control and Prevention; National Center for Health Statistics. 1993. "Advance Report of Final Natality Statistics, 1990." *Monthly Vital Statistics Report* 41(9), supplement.

_____. 1995a. "Advance Report of Final Natality Statistics, 1993." *Monthly Vital Statistics Report* 44(3, September), supplement.

_____. 1995b. "Trends in Pregnancies and Pregnancy Rates: Estimates for the United States, 1980–92." *Monthly Vital Statistics Report* 43(11, May), supplement.

_____. 1996a. "Advance Report of Final Natality Statistics, 1994." *Monthly Vital Statistics Report* 44 (11, June), supplement.

_____. 1996b. "Births and Deaths: United States, 1995." *Monthly Vital Statistics Report* 45 (3, October), supplement.

_____. Various years. *Vital Statistics of the United States.*

_____. 1994. "Advance Report of Final Natality Statistics, 1992." *Monthly Vital Statistics Report* 43(5), supplement.

Vinovskis, M. A. 1988. *An "Epidemic" of Adolescent Pregnancy: Some Historical and Policy Considerations.* New York: Oxford University Press.

Zelnik, M., and J. Kantner. 1978. "Contraceptive Patterns and Premarital Pregnancy Among Women Aged 15–19 in 1976." *Family Planning Perspectives* 10(3): 135–142.

Chapter Three

THE IMPACTS OF TEENAGE CHILDBEARING ON THE MOTHERS AND THE CONSEQUENCES OF THOSE IMPACTS FOR GOVERNMENT

V. Joseph Hotz, Susan Williams McElroy, and Seth G. Sanders

There is growing concern in the United States about the number of children born to teen mothers and the proportion of these births that occur out of wedlock. A decade ago, the National Research Council concluded that "adolescent pregnancy and childbearing are matters of substantial national concern" (Hayes 1987, p. ii) and President Bill Clinton, in his 1995 State of the Union Message, asserted that teenage pregnancy is "our most serious social problem." Part of the concern centers around the plight of teen mothers. The everyday hardships of teen motherhood come into public consciousness through media attention to and the prevalence of teen childbearing throughout the United States. Furthermore, there is a strong statistical association between the age at which a woman has her first child and her subsequent socioeconomic well-being. For example, one finds that women who have a baby in their teens are subsequently less likely to complete school, less likely to marry (and thus have a parenting partner), less likely to participate in the labor force, likely to earn less in their jobs, and more likely to rely on various forms of public assistance than are women who do not give birth in adolescence.

This association has helped fuel the view that teen childbearing is the *cause* of the poor socioeconomic outcomes endured by teen mothers, and there appears to be a compelling logic behind this perception. Adolescence is an important period for one's educational attainment, especially with regard to the completion of high school and preparation for one's vocation, and this attainment has become even more crucial as the earnings prospects for unskilled workers has declined (Juhn, Murphy and Pierce 1993). Furthermore, adolescence is an important period of a person's psychosocial development. A young mother—particularly a single mother—will have less time and energy than her counterpart without a child to socialize, develop as an individual, and learn how to develop healthy interpersonal relationships (and, hence, a support network). All of these are presumably important for her socioeconomic well-being in later life. Thus, it is no wonder that childbearing during adolescence is perceived as a trap door that propels the young mother on a downward spiral in socioeconomic terms.

The apparent adverse consequences of teen motherhood have also become an important issue in the current debate over reforming the U.S. welfare system. An increasing fraction of the Aid to Families with Dependent Children (AFDC) caseload consists of women who first gave birth as teenagers. In 1992, for example, 52 percent of the mothers on AFDC had their first birth as teens, costing U.S. taxpayers an estimated $12.8 billion (Moore 1995). Such trends and costs to government have fueled calls, from liberals and conservatives alike, for enactment of provisions to limit the access of teen mothers to welfare benefits.

It is hard to dispute the evidence that teen mothers have tough lives and limited options. As we show in the next section, recent data show a grim picture of teen motherhood when one compares the socioeconomic attainment of teen mothers with those of women who delay their childbearing. What is at issue is the appropriateness of such standard comparisons and the validity of the conclusions about the *causal* link between teenage childbearing, the well-being of young mothers, and the costs this behavior imposes on government and taxpayers. In this chapter, we address the following question: *What would be the adolescent mother's (behavioral) outcomes if she were to delay her childbearing until she was older but nothing else changed in the wider socioecononomic context?* This question is, we argue, the relevant one for assessing both the extent to which teenage childbearing, per se, is the reason young mothers appear to fare so poorly over their subsequent lives and the source of the substantial costs government currently bears.

Obtaining reliable answers to this question is difficult. This is because the adverse outcomes attributed to teenage childbearing may simply reflect pre-existing differences in family background such as poverty and other factors which make teen mothers different from those women who delay their childbearing. As such, the apparent consequences noted above, and illustrated below, may have little to do with the timing of motherhood. Random assignment to "treatment" and "control" groups is the standard evaluation method for dealing with the confounding influences of such pre-existing factors when estimating causal effects. Therein, "treatments" are randomly assigned to some members of a sample and not to others. Then, estimates of the average causal effect of the treatment are obtained from the mean difference in subsequent outcomes for the treatment and "control" groups.

Unfortunately, use of such experimental designs is simply not feasible in the context of teen childbearing. Rather, social scientists must resort to nonexperimental (or quasi-experimental) statistical methods in their attempt to sort out these causal links. The latter methods attempt to adjust for the influence of these pre-existing differences between comparison groups by using such statistical techniques as regression analysis to eliminate their influence and, thus, isolate the causal relationship between teenage childbearing and the socioeconomic attainment of such mothers. Such techniques may not completely adjust for all the background differences between teen mothers and women who did not bear a child in their teens and, as such, produce biased estimates. This is because many factors not measured in available data sets—or factors that cannot be measured, or even identified, directly or reliably—are likely to affect the age at which a woman has her first child. In addition, the various factors that affect when a woman has a child may well exert other independent effects on the woman's subsequent socioeconomic attainments.

To avoid obtaining biased estimates of the causal effects of the consequences and costs of early childbearing, we exploit a "natural experiment" associated with human reproduction. Drawing on our previous work (Hotz, McElroy, and Sanders 1996), we compare the behavior of teen mothers with that of women who became pregnant as teens but who experienced a miscarriage. To the extent that miscarriages are purely random events *and* the only way in which pregnancies do not result in births, women who experience them constitute the ideal control group that a randomized experiment would provide. While these conditions are not met in practice, use of this comparison group appears to provide a valid approximation to the ideal conditions that would be achieved with a randomized experimental design (Hotz, Mullin, and Sanders 1995).

Before proceeding, it is important to stress the limits of our analysis. We address but one facet of the teen childbearing issue, namely, the effects on the teen mothers themselves and whether these particular effects are the reason that this group of women requires government subsidies. Our analysis does not consider the consequences and costs of teenage childbearing to at least two other groups of individuals: the fathers of children born to teen mothers and, more importantly, the children themselves. While we find little evidence that

teenage childbearing, per se, harms mothers or that taxpayers or society would realize any cost savings if all early childbearing were
eliminated, our results do not preclude the possibility that early
childbearing does adversely affect these other two groups and imposes
social costs for that reason. These costs and consequences are the
subject of other chapters in this book.

THE APPARENT CONSEQUENCES OF
TEENAGE CHILDBEARING

The Data

We use the National Longitudinal Survey of Youth (NLSY) to present
a statistical portrait of the prevalence of teenage childbearing in the
United States and its apparent consequences for teen mothers. The
NLSY is a nationally representative sample of young men and women
who were 14 to 21 years old in 1979. Thus, the teenage years of women
in our study (ages 13 to 19) occurred between 1970 and 1985. Respondents have been interviewed each year since 1979; we make use of
data through the 1992 interview in our analysis. The female respondents were asked a range of questions about their pregnancy and
childbearing, marital arrangements, and educational and labor force
activities. We make use of two samples from the NLSY. To describe
the general characteristics of young women growing up during the
1980s, we focus on the sample of women that includes a subsample
of women who were drawn to be representative of the U.S. population
of women in the 14 to 21 age range as of 1979 (3,108 non-Hispanic
white women are in this subsample) as well as women in two supplemental subsamples of young black (1,067) and Hispanic women (751),[1]
for a total sample of 4,926 women.[2] We refer to this sample as our *All
Women's Sample*. We focus much of our regression analysis described
below on the subset of women in this sample who reported that they
experienced their first *pregnancy* as a teenager; we refer to it as our
Teen Pregnancy Sample. We provide a more detailed description of
this second sample later in the chapter.

Estimates of Teenage Childbearing and Its Apparent Consequences

The rate of teenage childbearing among young women growing up
during the last two decades was substantial. In the All Women's Sam-

ple, 14.7 percent of white women, 36.9 percent of black women, and 30.0 percent of Hispanic women reported having their first birth prior to reaching the age of 18. (As elsewhere in the book, we define teenage childbearing as births which women have at ages less than 18. Where appropriate, we comment on the childbearing patterns of women who are slightly older, 18 or 19, when they had their first birth.) In terms of the U.S. population as a whole, 18.9 percent of women who were teenagers during the 1970s and early 1980s had their first birth as teens. Using our data from the NLSY, we briefly compare the attainment of teen mothers with women who did not experience a birth prior to age 18.

The differences in the childbearing and marital experiences as of age 30 between teen mothers and those women who postponed their childbearing indicate that teen mothers bear one and a half more children on average than do women who delay (figure 3.1). They also spend more than twice as much of their time between ages 14 and 30 as single mothers compared to women who delay.

One also finds substantial disparities in the educational attainment of teen mothers compared to young women who delay (figure 3.2). Only 35 percent of teen mothers have graduated from high school, that is, have received a regular high school diploma, by age 30 compared with over 85 percent of women who delay motherhood. This figure is not surprising; the presence of a young child makes it very difficult for teen mothers to continue their education. Many of these mothers do ultimately attain a high school degree by obtaining a General Educational Development (GED) certificate. Some 26 percent of teen mothers complete high school via this route. As we discuss below, there is a good deal of controversy about whether the GED is "equivalent" to a regular high school diploma, especially with respect to an individual's ability to compete for jobs and wages in the labor market. However, regardless of the method of completing high school, only 61 percent of teen mothers attain a high school diploma or GED certificate by the time they reach age 30. In contrast, over 90 percent of women who do not give birth as teens end up obtaining a high school diploma or GED by the same age.

Given their lower educational attainment, it is not surprising that teen mothers are less successful in the labor market compared to women who do not become mothers at such a young age (figure 3.3). Not only do teen mothers earn less, on average, at almost every age, but the gap between them and women who delayed grows with age. By age 30, for example, the annual earnings of teen mothers is only 58 percent of the earnings of those who delayed childbearing ($18,544

Figure 3.1 CHILDBEARING AND SINGLE MOTHERHOOD EXPERIENCES BY AGE
30 FOR TEEN MOTHERS AND WOMEN WHO DELAYED THEIR
CHILDBEARING

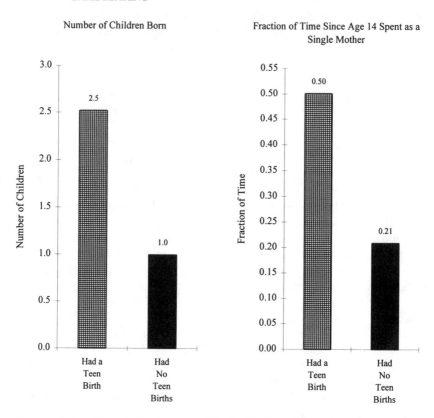

Source: National Longitudinal Survey of Youth, *All Women's Sample.*

versus $32,935 in 1993 dollars). Part of this gap can be accounted for
by the greater number of hours women who delay work compared
with teen mothers (1,280 versus 966 per year, not shown) as well as
the substantially lower wage rates of teen mothers.

Finally, consistent with other estimates, we find that teen mothers
receive substantially higher levels of public assistance than do those
women who delay their childbearing (figure 3.4). By age 30, teen
mothers receive over four times more in public assistance benefits
than do women who delay ($1,984 versus $467).

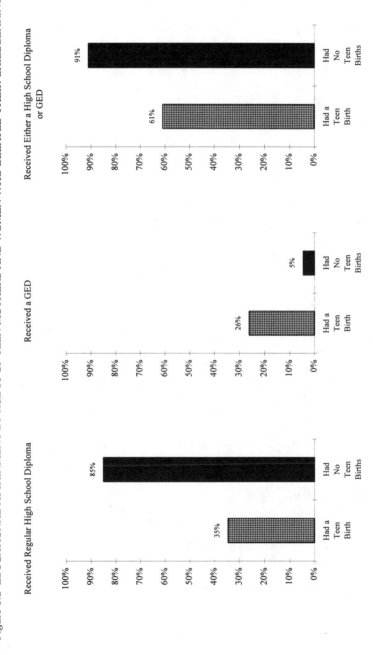

Figure 3.2 EDUCATIONAL ATTAINMENT BY AGE 30 OF TEEN MOTHERS AND WOMEN WHO DELAYED THEIR CHILDBEARING

Source: National Longitudinal Survey of Youth, *All Women's Sample.*

Figure 3.3 ANNUAL LABOR MARKET EARNINGS OF TEEN MOTHERS AND WOMEN WHO DELAYED THEIR CHILDBEARING

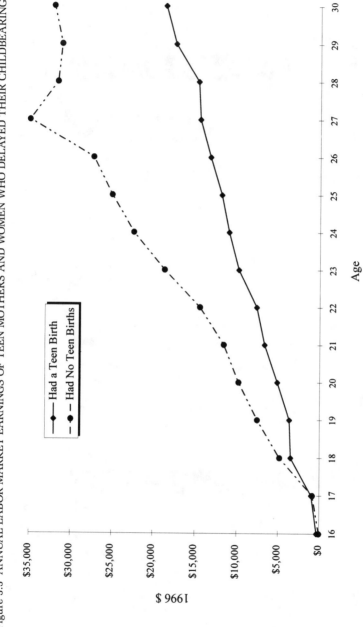

Source: National Longitudinal Survey of Youth, *All Women's Sample.*

Figure 3.4 ANNUAL AFDC AND FOOD STAMP BENEFITS RECEIVED BY TEEN MOTHERS AND WOMEN WHO DELAYED THEIR CHILDBEARING

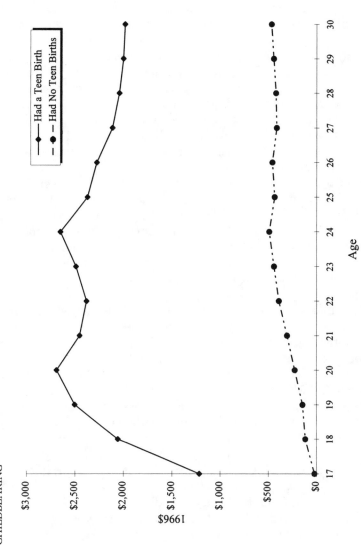

Source: National Longitudinal Survey of Youth, All Women's Sample.

**Teen Mothers and Those Observed to Delay Childbearing:
An Inappropriate Comparison?**

As the evidence just cited makes clear, the *gross*, or *unadjusted*, disparities in socioeconomic attainment of teen mothers and those who
delay are substantial, making a strong *prima facie* case that teen mothers impose substantial costs on U.S. taxpayers. It is tempting to conclude from these findings that if we could only convince teen mothers
to delay motherhood until they were older, they would substantially
improve their material well-being and, as a result, reduce their burden
on society. But does such a conclusion follow? Can we conclude that
failure to delay childbearing causes these disparities?

The assertion that teenage childbearing is the *cause* of the poor
socioeconomic outcomes presented above implies that a teenage
mother was on the same upwardly mobile life course as her counterpart who did not have a child as a teenager but, *by having her first
birth as a teenager*, altered the remainder of her life in very detrimental ways. For these two groups of women to be *comparable*, teen
mothers and the women with whom they are being compared would
have to have virtually identical socioeconomic and background characteristics prior to the age at which teen mothers had their first child.
In fact, this is not the case.

Teen mothers come from much more disadvantaged backgrounds
than do women who delay childbearing (table 3.1). For example, teenage mothers grew up in homes that were poorer (the average annual
income of the households in which women who had had teen births
resided in 1978 was $13,676 versus $22,816 for their counterparts),
had parents who were less educated (the fathers of women who later
became teenage mothers completed an average of only 10 years of
school versus 12 years of schooling for the fathers of other women),
were more likely to grow up in single-parent families (21 percent
versus 11 percent), and were more likely to have been in a family on
welfare when growing up (19 percent versus 11 percent) than women
who did not have a child as a teen.

One can, in principle, "adjust" for these differences in background
characteristics by using statistical techniques, such as regression analysis. One then uses comparisons of the adjusted estimates of socioeconomic attainment to estimate the causal effects of early childbearing. At issue is the adequacy of these adjustments for dealing with
selection bias, namely the possibility that selective differences remain
between women who have children as teenagers and those who do

Table 3.1 BACKGROUND CHARACTERISTICS OF TEENAGE MOTHERS AND
WOMEN WHO DELAYED CHILDBEARING UNTIL AFTER AGE 18

Characteristic	Teenage Mothers		Not Teenage Mothers	
	Mean	Standard Deviation	Mean	Standard Deviation
White	0.51	0.50	0.81	0.39
Black	0.39	0.49	0.13	0.33
Hispanic	0.11	0.31	0.06	0.25
Family on welfare in 1978	0.19	0.39	0.11	0.31
Family income in 1978[a]	$13,676	$10,122	$22,816	$13,995
In female-head household at age 14	0.21	0.41	0.11	0.32
In intact household at age 14	0.68	0.47	0.85	0.36
Mother's education	9.88	2.91	11.73	2.72
Father's education	9.98	3.35	11.97	3.56
AFQT score[b]	25.73	21.13	49.99	27.42

Source: National Longitudinal Survey of Youth, *All Women's Sample.*
[a] Denominated in 1978 dollars
[b] Armed Forces Qualifying Test Score

not. The potential for such bias clouds the internal and external validity of many nonexperimental methods for estimating the causal effect of early childbearing.

One concern often raised when estimating the socioeconomic attainment of young women is the importance of heterogeneity in their cognitive abilities and in market-related skills that are not captured by educational attainment. While most data sources do not have measures of such attainment for respondents, one is available in the NLSY—the Armed Forces Qualifying Test (AFQT). This aptitude test, which was administered in 1981 to all respondents of the NLSY, has been found to be a good predictor not only of the likelihood that enlistees will be successful in the military but also of initial success in the civilian labor force. The AFQT score of teenage mothers, 25.7, is almost one standard deviation below the mean score of women who were not teenage mothers (50.0), providing further evidence that the two groups were not comparable at the outset (see also table 3.1).

While the AFQT scores enable us to control for achievement, there are likely to be a host of other dimensions along which teen mothers may differ from women who delay their childbearing and which are likely to have independent effects on their socioeconomic attainment, most of which are not measured in data sets like the NLSY.[3] Thus, one must find alternative strategies for isolating the causal effects of early childbearing on the socioeconomic attainment of teen mothers.

EXPLOITING A NATURAL EXPERIMENT

The most common strategy used in scientific evaluations of causal effects is experiments in which treatments, including a treatment which represents the status quo, are randomly assigned to a sample of subjects and their subsequent behavior monitored. When properly conducted, such experiments ensure that, on average, the group receiving the treatment of interest and the group representing the status quo are the same in all ways except for their treatment status and that the differences in average outcomes for these two groups provide a direct measure of the average effect of the treatment under consideration.

While the postponment of births cannot be investigated with controlled randomized experiments, nature does provide the opportunity to conduct a very similar investigation. Many pregnancies end in spontaneous abortions, or miscarriages, which evidence from epidemiological studies of miscarriages indicates are mostly random events.[4] If so, women who miscarry as teenagers constitute an almost random sample of women who become pregnant as teenagers but are precluded from having a child at that age. While women who experience random miscarriages may be an appropriate comparison group for women who are *at risk* to have a birth, they do not constitute, per se, the appropriate comparison group for women who actually have births. This is because pregnant women can elect to have an induced abortion rather than have a birth. Furthermore, there are strong, *ex ante*, reasons to suspect that women who have abortions are *not* a random sample of pregnant women.[5]

Under certain conditions, however, one can use an adjusted difference in mean outcomes of *pregnant women who do not experience a miscarriage* and *those who do*—where the adjustment consists of weighting this difference by the proportion of nonmiscarrying women who have births—to obtain unbiased estimates of the effect of the failure of a teen mother to delay motherhood.[6] The conditions required for the validity of this method are that (a) all miscarriages are random events; (b) all women truthfully report whether they experienced a pregnancy and the way it was resolved; and (c) there is no additional "effect" of having an induced abortion beyond not experiencing a birth. Each of these conditions is potentially violated in practice. Some miscarriages appear to be induced by the excessive use of alcohol or tobacco by pregnant women. There is clear evidence that abortions—especially among young women—are underreported and that abortions are, in and of themselves, traumatic events. However, relaxing each of these assumptions (by forming conservative upper and lower bounds on the effects of teenage childbearing for a number of the socioeconomic outcomes of mothers considered here) does not change the central conclusions drawn about the effects of teenage childbearing based on the adjusted differences in means outcomes for teen women who experience miscarriages and those who do not (Hotz, Mullin and Sanders 1995).

Thus, under the above conditions, the natural experiment of using data on teenagers who experience miscarriages allows us to address the following causal question concerning teenage childbearing: "If, in the socioeconomic environment currently facing them, women who gave birth as a teen had delayed their childbearing, how would their subsequent outcomes have been different?" Obtaining reliable answers to this question is central to the social and policy debates over teenage childbearing in the U.S. For example, one of the important issues, and a central focus of this volume, is the costs to government associated with teenage childbearing. Previous analyses of this question (Burt and Haffner, 1986, and Burt 1992) have estimated how much government spends in the form of AFDC, food stamps and other forms of public assistance on women who began motherhood as teenagers. While an important baseline, such costs do not necessarily represent the costs to government that are directly attributable to early childbearing (or the failure of these women to delay motherhood). By obtaining reliable estimates of the question of causality posed above for outcomes such as receipt of public assistance benefits, we can draw conclusions about what government might save if teen mothers were all to delay their childbearing until they were older.[7]

Estimation Methods and Sample Used

The estimates of the effects of teen childbearing presented below are produced with a modified version of the design involving data on women whose first births end in a miscarriage. In particular, we use a variant of regression analysis, called the *method of instrumental variables*,[8] which further adjusts the differences in outcomes for women who do and do not experience a miscarriage as a teen for differences in number of personal and background characteristics of these women. Means and standard deviations of these characteristics are presented in table 3.2 for the Teen Pregnancy sample. We distinguish between two subsamples of women: those whose first pregnancy occurred prior to age 18 and those for whom it occurred at ages 18 or 19. Our focus in this chapter is on the effects of births for those

Table 3.2 BACKGROUND CHARACTERISTICS OF TEENAGE WOMEN BY THE AGE
AT FIRST PREGNANCY

Characteristic	First Pregnancy Occurred before Age 18		First Pregnancy Occurred at Ages 18 or 19	
	Mean	Standard Deviation	Mean	Standard Deviation
White	0.61	0.49	0.73	0.44
Black	0.30	0.46	0.18	0.38
Hispanic	0.10	0.29	0.09	0.28
Family on welfare in 1978	0.15	0.36	0.12	0.32
Family income in 1978[a]	$16,768	$9,616	$17,445	$9,115
Missing family income	0.52	0.50	0.48	0.50
In female-head household at age 14	0.18	0.38	0.15	0.36
In intact household at age 14	0.73	0.44	0.77	0.42
Mother's education	10.44	2.66	10.76	2.69
Missing mother's education	0.08	0.27	0.05	0.22
Father's education	10.41	2.94	10.54	3.22
Missing father's education	0.19	0.40	0.14	0.35
AFQT score[b]	31.81	23.40	39.19	25.18
Distribution of Timing of First Pregnancy:				
at Age < 16				
at Ages 16 or 17				
at Ages 18 or 19				
Distribution of How First Pregnancy Ended:				
in a Miscarriage	0.07		0.11	
in a Birth	0.69		0.66	
in an Abortion	0.25		0.23	
No. of Women	980		764	

Source: National Longitudinal Survey of Youth, *All Women's Sample.*
[a] Denominated in 1978 dollars
[b] Armed Forces Qualifying Test Score

women who have their first pregnancies prior to age 18; nonetheless,
we include both subsamples in all of our regression analyses, estimating separate effects of births for the two age groupings. First pregnancies (and the risk of a first birth) at these older ages are generally
viewed with less concern in much of the literature about teenage
childbearing in the U.S. In most states, women at these ages are
considered adults and have legal responsibility for such actions as
whether they continue to attend school. Women who delay their first
pregnancy until 18 or 19 tend to come from less disadvantaged backgrounds and have higher scores on the AFQT than do women who
first become pregnant prior to age 18 (table 3.2).[9]

In the instrumental variable regression analysis, we estimated the effects for each year of the woman's life from age 15 to age 40 to determine the timing and duration of the effects, as well as the net "lifetime" effect.[10]

Before reporting our findings, we call attention to how women in our Teen Pregnancy sample resolved their first pregnancies (see also table 3.2). While the majority of these pregnancies resulted in a live birth, almost 35 percent of these pregnancies did not. Induced abortion, the most prevalent way in which childbearing is avoided, accounted for between 23 and 25 percent of these pregnancies. Between 7 and 11 percent of teen pregnancies are reported to have ended in miscarriages. Our data (not shown) indicate that the median age at first birth among women whose first teen pregnancy results in a live birth is about age 17 while the median age at first birth among women whose first teen pregnancy ended in a miscarriage is about age 20. Looking at the mean (rather than the median) age at first birth, we find that women who would have had a teen birth had they not miscarried actually had their first birth some time after their twenty-first birthday. On average, for these women a miscarriage delayed a first birth a minimum of three to four years.[11] Therefore, our estimates of the effects of teenage childbearing can be reliably used to infer what the levels of socioeconomic attainment would be for teen mothers if they were to delay their childbearing for at least three to four years, a length of time which is consistent with a realistic goal for policy interventions that might cause at-risk teenage women to postpone entry into motherhood. This length of delay is similar to that used for estimates elsewhere in this book.

It is important to note that the statistics on pregnancy resolutions and the incidence of pregnancies in the NLSY data are based on self-reports. It is likely that there is significant underreporting of abortions, miscarriages, and pregnancies in this data. Abortions among young women, in particular, appear to be substantially underreported (Jones and Forrest 1990). Furthermore, epidemiological clinical-based studies of spontaneous abortions (miscarriages) find that between 11 to 14 percent of pregnancies end in miscarriages (Klein, Stein, and Susser 1989). We explicitly investigated the implications of such underreporting for our estimates of the effects of early childbearing on the socioeconomic attainment of teen mothers, making use of more reliable data sources on the incidence of abortions and births to supplement our analysis of the NLSY data (Hotz, Mullin, and Sanders 1995). Our findings and inferences about these causal effects do not change when we account for this source of bias in the data used in our instrumental variable regression analysis.

ESTIMATED EFFECTS OF DELAYING CHILDBEARING ON ADULT OUTCOMES AMONG TEEN MOTHERS

In this section, we discuss our estimates of the effects of early childbearing, or, put differently, the likely effects of delaying childbearing for over 3 to 4 years on a range of socioeconomic outcomes for teenage mothers.[12] Coefficient estimates and standard errors from our instrumental variable regressions are displayed in table 3A.1 of the appendix. We used these coefficient estimates to produce more readily interpretable estimates of what the average outcomes of teen mothers would be at various ages *if these mothers had delayed their childbearing at least three to four years.*

At the outset, several general comments are in order. Our findings indicate that it is important to distinguish between two types of effects of early childbearing on a teenage mother's subsequent socioeconomic status: permanent effects and those that represent temporary substitution of behaviors over the life course. In some respects, early childbearing has permanent effects on the mothers. For example, we find that early childbearing permanently increases the total number of children she will bear and the proportion of her lifetime she will spend as a single mother. In contrast, some of the effects of early childbearing appear to alter only the *timing* of events and activities over the mother's lifetime. For example, we find that although teenage mothers have lower labor-market earnings in their late teens and early 20s compared to what they would have earned had they postponed their childbearing, they actually earn more money in their late 20s and in their 30s than if they had delayed childbearing. In such cases, the ultimate effect and costs of early childbearing for the mother, or for the government, may be negligible when tallied over a mother's entire lifetime.

We also caution the reader about the interpretation of our estimated effects on outcomes measured at older ages. For most of the outcomes, we simply do not have much data for the older ages. Because we have no observations after age 34, we cannot be confident in the estimates derived for outcomes measured after ages 30 to 34. One important exception to this is the results for birthrate patterns. We can reasonably assume that a negligible percentage of the women will bear children beyond the age of 34.[13] Thus, we believe that our estimates accurately reflect the consequences of early childbearing on the subsequent number of children a teen mother will eventually bear.

Childbearing, Marriage and Financial Resources from Spouses

Consider first the effects of teen childbearing on the number of children teen mothers bear by age 20. While gross differences shown earlier in fertility between teen mothers and women who did not bear children as teens indicate that the former group of women had 1.5 more children than the latter, most of this disparity cannot be attributed to early childbearing per se. In fact, we estimate that only 20 percent of this difference can be attributed to the failure of teen mothers to delay childbearing. Once one accounts for the selective differences in the background and personal characteristics of teen mothers, one finds that by age 30 teen mothers would be expected to have one-third of a child less, on average, than if they delayed their childbearing for at least 3 to 4 years (figure 3.5A). This difference implies that teen mothers have 12 percent more children by age 30 that they will have to support, an addition that is statistically significant.[14]

Failure to delay childbearing, though much smaller than suggested by the earlier comparisons, has a negative and lasting effect on a teen mother's marriage prospects. We estimate that teen mothers would spend 20 percent less of their early years of motherhood (ages 14 through 30) as a single mother if they had delayed childbearing (43 versus 53 percent), a result that is also statistically significant (figure 3.5B). This result is particularly disturbing given the growing concerns about the consequences of single parenthood, and the absence of fathers, on the well-being and development of young children (Furstenberg and Harris 1993).

In contrast to the effects of teen childbearing on the likelihood of a teen mother being married, early childbearing does not significantly reduce the amount of income available from husbands.[15] In fact, we find that at least until their mid-30s, teen mothers are likely to have significantly *higher* levels of income from husbands than if they had delayed childbearing (figure 3.6).[16] At age 30, the typical woman who was a teen mother can expect $23,359 per year in income provided by her spouse; if this same woman had delayed her childbearing, income from her spouse would amount to $14,874. Thus, while the level of income that the typical teen mother can expect from her spouse is low at almost any stage of her early adulthood, her prospects

Figure 3.5 CHILDBEARING AND SINGLE MOTHERHOOD EXPERIENCES BY AGE
30 FOR TEEN MOTHERS VERSUS WHAT WOULD HAPPEN IF THEIR
CHILDBEARING WERE DELAYED

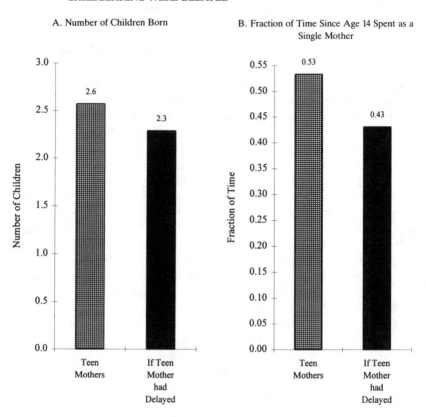

Source: National Longitudinal Survey of Youth, *Teen Pregnancy Sample.*

for having this source of financial support for her and her children do
not improve if she delays her childbearing by several years.

High School Completion

Although the unadjusted difference between teen mothers and women
who did not have births as teens overstates the consequences of early
childbearing on high school completion, as on marriage rates, the
failure of teen mothers to delay their childbearing does adversely

Figure 3.6 ANNUAL SPOUSAL INCOME RECEIVED BY TEEN MOTHERS VERSUS WHAT WOULD HAPPEN IF THEIR CHILDBEARING WERE DELAYED

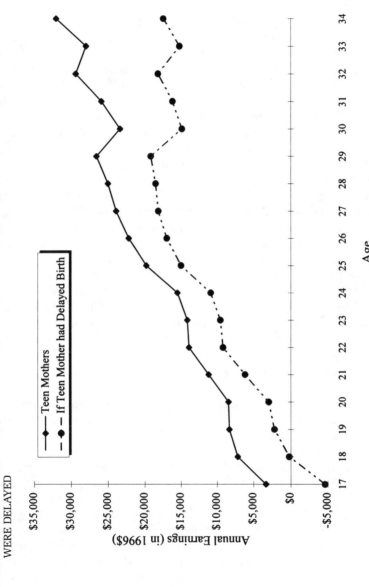

Source: National Longitudinal Survey of Youth, *Teen Pregnancy Sample*.

affect their rates of high school graduation. On average, teenage child-bearing reduces the likelihood of obtaining a standard high school degree by 20 percentage points (41 versus 61 percent, figure 3.7A).[17] With respect to the likelihood of receiving a GED, however, the gross difference does not overstate the causal impact of teen childbearing. Teen mothers are more likely to receive a GED (by 21 percentage points, figure 3.7B) than women who delay childbearing, regardless of how one forms the comparison group. Finally, there is no significant causal effect of early childbearing on the probability that teen mothers obtain a high school–level education (figure 7C), if high school diplomas and GEDs are taken as equivalent.

At issue are differences in the returns to these two alternative forms of high school completion for this group of women. For men, the value of the GED in the labor market is minimal, with its recipients earning no more than high school dropouts (Cameron and Heckman 1993). However, the labor market returns to the GED are no different from those of a high school diploma for the typical *woman* (Cao, Stromsdorfer, and Weeks 1996). What remains undetermined is whether this equivalence in the labor market returns holds for women who become teen mothers as well as for all women. We do not address this issue directly. But our findings for the effects of early childbearing on the labor market outcomes of teen mothers, to which we now turn, are not inconsistent with the equivalence of GED and high school graduation effects found in recent analysis for women generally.

Hours Worked and Earnings

Our natural experiment provides little evidence that early childbearing has the sort of persistent adverse effect on the labor market activity of teen mothers suggested by the unadjusted comparison, although the timing of this activity varies substantially. At early ages, teen mothers supply significantly fewer hours to the labor market (between 370 and 90 hours per year), while, by their mid-20s and early 30s, these mothers work more (130 to 500 hours) than if they had delayed their childbearing (figure 3.8).[18] These effects are not trivial. On average, teenage mothers work 820 hours per year during their 20s; over the same age range, we estimate that these mothers would work 20 percent *fewer* hours per year if they delayed their childbearing by over 3 to 4 years. The effects of early childbearing on the probability of a teen mother working for pay follow the same age pattern (Hotz, McElroy, and Sanders 1996).

Figure 3.7 EDUCATIONAL ATTAINMENT BY AGE 30 FOR TEEN MOTHERS VERSUS WHAT WOULD HAPPEN IF THEIR CHILDBEARING WERE DELAYED

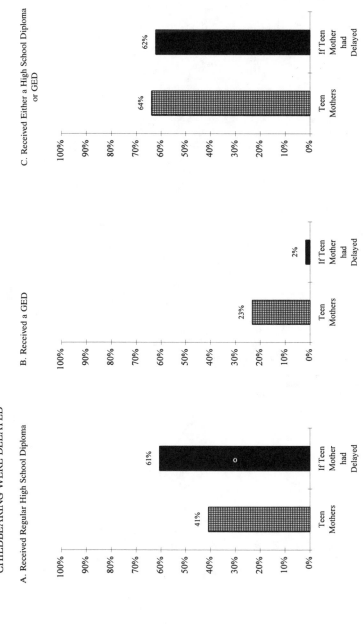

A. Received Regular High School Diploma

B. Received a GED

C. Received Either a High School Diploma or GED

Source: National Longitudinal Survey of Youth, *Teen Pregnancy Sample.*

Figure 3.8 ANNUAL HOURS OF WORK FOR TEEN MOTHERS VERSUS WHAT WOULD HAPPEN IF THEIR CHILDBEARING WERE DELAYED

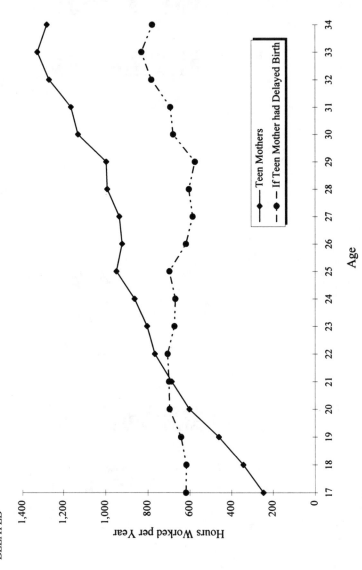

Source: National Longitudinal Survey of Youth, *Teen Pregnancy Sample.*

Studies of women's labor supply patterns typically show that women work less when their children are very young and more when the children get older. Consequently, the effects of early childbearing on hours worked (and labor force participation) estimated from our natural experiment reflect, in part, differences in the timing of the childbearing between teen mothers and the comparison group of women who had miscarriages. It is an open question as to whether these greater levels of work for teen mothers will persist over the remainder of their adult lives. But it is clear from figure 3.8 that the estimated effect appears to be growing through age 34, the last age for which we have data on these women.

Finally, our natural experiment indicates that the earnings of teen mothers is *higher* at *every* age through 34 than would be the case if these women delayed their childbearing, differences that are statistically significant at the 0.01 level for ages 26 through 30 (figure 3.9). Through age 34, teen mothers earn, on average, $12,745 per year in 1996 dollars; their earnings would be 35 percent lower, or $8,237 per year, if they had delayed their childbearing.[19]

Two comments are in order about our findings with respect to the labor market consequences of teen motherhood. First, they are extremely robust. Even if we violate each of the conditions required for our natural experiment to be valid—that miscarriages are random, that all women report truthfully, and that there is no additional "effect" of having an induced abortion other than lack of a birth—we still cannot reject that teen mothers work and earn more than if they had delayed their births from the mid-20s through mid-30s (Hotz, Mullin, and Sanders 1995). Furthermore, our method is sufficiently powerful, in a statistical sense, to *reject* that these effects are *negative* at these same ages.

Second, while a definitive explanation of why teen mothers appear to benefit from not delaying their childbearing when it comes to the labor market awaits further research, we offer the following speculation. Our evidence, and that of others, documents that women who begin motherhood as teens come from less advantaged backgrounds, are less likely to be successful in school, and, as such, are less likely to end up in occupations which require higher education than are women who postpone motherhood. Further, our evidence suggests that these women are more likely to acquire the skills on the job (rather than in school) and work in jobs where educational credentials are less important than continuity and job-specific experience. For such women, concentrating their childbearing at early ages may prove more compatible with their likely labor market career options than

Figure 3.9 ANNUAL LABOR MARKET EARNINGS FOR TEEN MOTHERS VERSUS WHAT WOULD HAPPEN IF THEIR CHILDBEARING WERE DELAYED

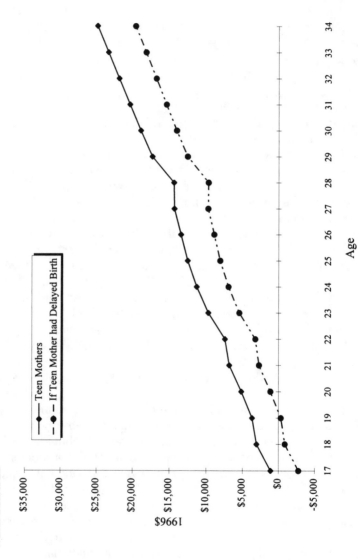

Source: National Longitudinal Survey of Youth, *Teen Pregnancy Sample*.

would postponing motherhood and/or spacing births over their child-bearing years. If this characterization is accurate, forcing teen mothers to postpone their childbearing, as miscarriages do, may "explain" why they both appear to acquire no more formal education and actually end up doing less well in the labor market than if they had been able to follow their preferred life cycle plan.

Receipt of Public Assistance

As for labor market outcomes, we find little evidence that early child-bearing, per se, accounts for the heavy dependence of teen mothers on various forms of public assistance. Early childbearers and women who delay follow the same general pattern—increasing receipt of AFDC and food stamps through their teens, leveling off in their early 20s and finally reducing benefit receipt as they continue to age (figure 3.10). But within the general trajectory, differences in the age pattern of receipt are again striking. Delaying childbirth appears to reduce benefit receipt during the teen years. But it seems to make no difference during the early 20s and actually increase the amount of benefits received at older ages.[20] The same age pattern holds for AFDC and food stamp benefits when evaluated separately and for the rates of participation in these two programs as well as the likelihood of receiving some form of housing assistance such as public housing or rent subsidies. Through age 34, the average effect of delaying child-bearing on the amount of welfare received is essentially zero; the welfare benefits received by teen mothers would be lowered by only 4 percent ($88 per year) if they delayed motherhood by over 3 to 4 years.[21]

Are We Right? Evidence from other Recent Studies

No single piece of scientific evidence should be taken as proof of any proposition, whether or not the evidence is contrary to conventional wisdom. Although we are alone in approximating a controlled experiment to reduce the intrusion of selection bias, many researchers have recognized the importance of the selection bias issue in estimating the consequences of teenage childbearing[22] and have used a variety of approaches to limit it.

We cite three recent studies. Geronimus and Korenman (1992, 1993) based their studies on pairs of sisters who were raised in the same family (and therefore assumed to be of very similar background) but who differed in timing of childbearing, one sister of each pair having

Figure 3.10 ANNUAL AFDC AND FOOD STAMP BENEFITS RECEIVED BY TEEN MOTHERS VERSUS WHAT WOULD HAPPEN IF THEIR CHILDBEARING WERE DELAYED

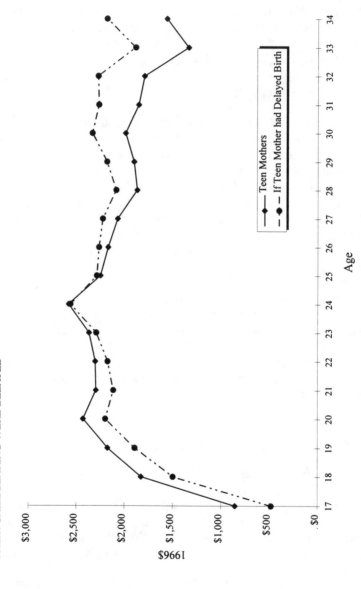

Source: National Longitudinal Survey of Youth, *Teen Pregnancy Sample.*

given birth as a teenager and the other having had her first child in adulthood.[23] The average difference in the outcomes of sisters was interpreted as the effect of teenage childbearing. Grogger and Bronars (1993) and Bronars and Grogger (1995) compared the outcomes of women who gave birth to twins as teen and unwed mothers with those who bore a single child. Because the occurrence of twins is thought to be random, the differences in the adult outcomes of the two groups of teen mothers are measures of the effects of teenage childbearing (under the presumption that the effect of an extra child is the same as the effect of a first child). Ribar (1995) used a set of statistical assumptions to reduce the mean outcomes of women who did not give birth as teenagers to what they would likely have been if these women had the same backgrounds as teen mothers. If his statistical assumptions are correct, the difference between the adult outcomes of teen mothers and his adjusted group of mothers who did not have a first birth as a teenager measures the effect of teenage childbearing.

All three studies come to the same conclusion: the failure to account for selection bias vastly *overstates* the negative consequences of teenage childbearing and certainly provides no support for the view that there are large, negative consequences of teenage childbearing per se for the socioeconomic attainment of teen mothers. What remains uncertain is whether the effects of teen childbearing on such outcomes as labor market attachment and earnings are slightly negative as in Bronars and Grogger (1995), negligible as in Ribar (1995), or positive as in Geronimus and Korenman (1992, 1993) and in Hotz, Mullin and Sanders (1995).

THE COSTS TO GOVERNMENT OF TEENAGE MOTHERS AND EARLY CHILDBEARING

One of the concerns that has been expressed about the teenage childbearing "problem" in the United States is the public assistance costs it imposes on society. We have argued that previous studies of the costs to government of teenage childbearing have confused what we spend on teen mothers with the portion of these expenditures which can be *attributed* to the failure of these women to delay their childbearing. To make this distinction clear, we use our estimates of causal effects to estimate what government spends each year on public assistance for women who became mothers as teens and what they would save if all these women delayed. We estimate both the direct costs that government incurs for teen mothers on public assistance programs as well as those costs *net* of the taxes that women who were teen mothers will pay at various stages of their lifetimes. Obviously, the taxes paid by teen mothers must finance more than just what they incur in expenditures on public assistance. But given our finding that the effect of early childbearing is to raise the labor market earnings of teen mothers at older ages, it is worthwhile to determine the extent to which the taxes these women pay "cover" what they cost government in public assistance over their lifetimes.

We calculated as comprehensive an estimate of the public assistance costs incurred by teen mothers as possible. The NLSY yields data on annual benefits received from AFDC and food stamps, as well as the benefits from other social programs, including Supplemental Security Income (SSI) and General Assistance (GA). Another important form of public assistance for teen mothers is the medical care they and their children often receive under the Medicaid program. While information is not available in the NLSY, we estimated the dollar value of the public assistance teen mothers receive in the form of medical care through this program from other sources.[24] We added these derived estimates for Medicaid received to those for the other benefits teen mothers received at various ages and used this measure to estimate the causal effects of early childbearing for this measure of public assistance, using the instrumental variables regression methods described earlier.[25]

We used the following strategy to estimate what teen mothers pay in federal, state, and local sales and income taxes at each age of their early adulthood. We assumed that the average teenage mother faces a federal marginal tax rate of 15 percent and pays an additional 8 percent of her income in state and local income and sales taxes. Using the resulting tax rate of 23 percent, we multiplied the annual earnings of teen mothers, as well as our estimates of the causal effects of early childbearing on annual earnings, to produce annual estimates of taxes paid by teen mothers and the additional taxes they would pay if they had delayed their childbearing.

To obtain estimates of the total annual costs and savings to government associated with teen motherhood, we also must estimate the total number of women in the U.S. population in 1996 who first became mothers as teens, that is, had their first birth prior to age 18. We assumed that the number of early childbearers at each age, from 17 through 34, was equal to the number of women who became teen mothers for the first time in 1993. The U.S. Vital Statistics yields an estimate of 175,259 new teen mothers in 1993.

We use these estimates to simulate the total amount all levels of government will spend in 1996 on public assistance for women who became mothers as teen mothers, what these costs will be net of the taxes government collects from these women, and what the gross and net *savings* would be in these costs if all these women had delayed their childbearing (figure 3.11). Our results indicate that each year government spends $11.3 billion (in 1996 dollars) on AFDC, food stamps, Medicaid and other forms of public assistance for women, ages 17 through 34, who began motherhood as teens. This expenditure represents 6 percent of total expenditures on AFDC, food stamps, and Medicaid in the United States in 1993 and amounts to an annual expenditure of $3,596 per woman.[26] While these costs to government are substantial, they are offset, in part, by the taxes that women who bore their first child as a teenager can be expected to pay. In fact, the total annual public assistance costs of early childbearers, net of the taxes they pay, amounts only to a net annual cost, per woman, of $665. Nonetheless, this is a substantial net governmental outlay to women who chose not to delay their childbearing.

Most of this governmental outlay is not attributable to the failure of teen mothers to delay their childbearing, however. In fact, the total annual expenditures on public assistance would increase slightly, rising by $0.8 billion, if all of these women had delayed their first births by over 3 to 4 years. Moreover, the *net* (of taxes) annual outlays by government for cash-assistance and in-kind transfers to these women would actually *increase* by 35 percent, or $4.0 billion. This increase in net expenditures associated with delaying childbearing would amount to over $1,200 per teen mother. That getting teen mothers to delay their childbearing would result in additional costs to taxpayers, rather than savings, is a direct consequence of our finding that teen mothers would earn less over their lifetimes if they were forced to delay their first births. This loss in earnings translates to a reduction in taxes paid by these women and an increase, rather than decrease, in the net costs to government associated with the postponement of motherhood.

To assess the robustness of our findings we recalculated all our cost estimates, varying both the ranges of ages of teen mothers used to calculate these costs (estimates also were derived using women, ages 17 through 40 and ages 17 through 30) and the tax rate used to derive tax revenue estimates (we also used a rate of 15 percent). While the magnitudes of the four cost entries displayed in figure 3.11 change under these alternative assumptions, the general pattern does not: government spending on public assistance will not decline and net

Figure 3.11 TOTAL ANNUAL GOVERNMENT EXPENDITURES ON TEEN MOTHERS FOR AFDC, FOOD STAMPS, AND MEDICAID AND SAVINGS TO U.S. TAXPAYERS IF TEEN MOTHERS DELAYED THEIR CHILDBEARING

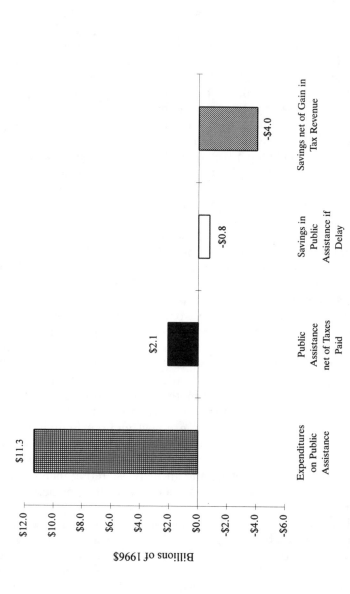

Source: National Longitudinal Survey of Youth and U.S. Vital Statistics.
Note: See text for explanation of how estimates of public assistance expenditures and savings were obtained. "Net of Taxes Paid" refers to estimated tax revenues derived from teen mothers over their lifetimes.

spending will increase even if society were able to get these women to postpone their childbearing by substantially more than 3 to 4 years.[27]

These rather startling findings call into question the view that teenage childbearing is one of the nation's most serious social problems, at least when one measures its severity in terms of costs to taxpayers. More generally, our analysis of the costs and consequences of teenage childbearing highlights the potential for drawing very misleading conclusions if one fails to use adequate evaluation designs when making causal inferences about the effects of such selective phenomena as teen childbearing. At the same time, we caution the reader to not overgeneralize from what we have found. As we noted at the beginning, we have considered only a limited range of the potential consequences and costs of teenage childbearing. Furthermore, standards of scientific inquiry dictate that further replications and scrutiny of our findings are required before one can confidently draw strong conclusions about the causal influence of teenage childbearing.

Notes

Our research has been funded by a grant from the National Institute of Child Health and Human Development. Preparation of this chapter, which summarizes parts of our larger research project, was paid for by the Robin Hood Foundation. We wish to thank Sarah Gordon, Stuart Hagen, Terra McKinnish, Charles Mullin, Carl Schneider, and Daniel Waldram for able and conscientious research assistance on this project. We wish to thank Robert Moffitt, Frank Furstenberg, Arlene Leibowitz, John Strauss, Susan Newcomer, Arline Geronimus, and participants in the Workshop on Low Income Populations at the Institute for Research on Poverty at the University of Wisconsin-Madison for helpful comments on an earlier draft and Charlotte Koelling, Frances Margolin, Deborah Sanders, Simon Hotz, and Gregory Kienzl for their editorial assistance in preparing this chapter. We especially wish to thank Robert Willis for numerous helpful discussions during the course of this study. All remaining errors are the responsibility of the authors.

1. The NLSY drew random oversamples of these two minority groups to ensure adequate sample sizes for conducting separate analyses by race.

2. Where appropriate, we use sampling weights provided with the NLSY to account for the use of the minority oversamples.

3. For example, the psychological literature on teenage childbearing suggests that low self-esteem (Patten 1981; Vernor, Green, and Frothingham 1983), religiosity (Michael and Tuma 1985), and low educational aspirations and expectations (Abrahamse et al. 1988) all increase the chances that a teenager will become a mother. One suspects that these factors affect a woman's educational attainment and her rates of labor force and welfare participation. None of these factors is well measured in the NLSY or most other data sources. That existing data sets are unlikely to allow one to convincingly adjust

out background differences via ordinary regression analysis between teen mothers and women who delayed is substantiated in recent work (Hotz, Mullin, and Sanders 1995), establishing that one can reliably reject the validity of standard regression-adjustment methods when analyzing the socioeconomic outcomes of teen mothers.

4. Epidemiological studies find that while smoking and drinking during pregnancy and the use of an intrauterine device (IUD) at conception increase the likelihood that a woman miscarries, other factors, such as a woman's socioeconomic status, her nutrition, or drug use, do not increase miscarriage rates, although the latter factors do affect birth weight. See Klein, Stein and Susser (1989) for a summary of this evidence.

5. In Hotz, McElroy and Sanders (1996), we show that the background characteristics of women who have induced abortions as teenagers are significantly different from those of the women who had miscarriages (spontaneous abortions) as teens.

6. This adjustment was first noted by Bloom (1984) in the context of manpower training evaluations. Also see Angrist and Imbens (1991), Heckman, Smith, and Taber (1994), Hotz and Sanders (1994a, 1994b), and Heckman (1995) for further descriptions of this method.

7. There is an important qualification to our results. We are estimating the effects of teenage births on the socioeconomic attainments of those women in the population who would likely be observed to have their first births as a teenager unless they were to experience a random denial of that birth by miscarrying. Because pregnancies are not random events, we do not make inferences about the causal effects of early child-bearing for an individual randomly chosen from the population of all teenage women in the United States; such inferences would be meaningless for policymaking. Instead, we are focusing on what the data *can* identify. In general, such data, even when considered through the "natural experiment" framework of random miscarriages, will tell us very little about the likely consequences for a typical woman of having her first birth as a teen relative to delaying her childbearing. But that is not the point of this analysis. We are more interested in what portions of the mothers' apparently lowered life prospects can be considered the consequences of early childbearing. This focus is adequate for making inferences about factors like the costs to government imposed by the teenagers having babies in the United States today.

8. See Greene (1993) for a discussion of the instrumental variables method. See Hotz, McElroy, and Sanders (1996) for a detailed description of the implementation of this instrumental variables method to estimate the effects of teenage childbearing.

9. Details of these results, as well as separate estimates of effects by the mother's age at first birth, can be found in Hotz, McElroy, and Sanders (1996).

10. While we also have investigated how the effects of teen births differed by race and ethnicity, herein we focus on results for all racial and ethnic groups taken together. Again, see Hotz, McElroy, and Sanders (1996) for more detailed descriptions of these analyses by race-ethnicity group.

11. We estimate that 12 percent of women who would have given birth as a teenager had they not miscarried (latent-birth women) had not had any children by the 1992 survey, when they were ages 27 to 34. Because we do not know the age at which these women first gave birth, it is not possible to calculate exactly the mean age at first birth among all latent-birth women. If we assume that all of the latent-birth women who had not given birth by the 1992 survey had a first child in 1993, then on average latent-birth women first gave birth when they were age 21. This implies that miscarriages delay the age at first birth for latent-birth women from sometime between the woman's seventeenth and eighteenth birthdays to sometime between the woman's twenty-first and twenty-second birthdays, or for three to four years. Of course not all latent-birth women who had not had a child by 1992 had a child in 1993. Therefore, a 3- to 4-year delay is the lower bound on the average delay from a miscarriage for this group of women.

12. In Hotz, McElroy, and Sanders (1996), we present results for a slightly broader and more detailed list of outcomes than considered in this chapter.

13. According to the Current Population Survey (CPS), for example, the birth rates (numbers of births per 1,000 women) in 1992 were 76 for women of ages 30–34, 38 for women of ages 35–39, and 9 for women of ages 40–44 (U.S. Bureau of the Census 1993).

14. One rejects that this delay effect is significantly different from zero at the 0.01 level.

15. We counted the spousal-earnings variable as the annual labor-market earnings of a woman's husband if she is married and as zero if she is single.

16. The estimates of spousal earnings associated with delaying childbearing are significantly lower (at the 0.01 level) than those for teen mothers at ages from 25 through 30.

17. This estimated difference in completion rates is statistically significant at the 0.01 level. We note that the completion rates in the first two panels of figure 3.7 for teen mothers are different from those in the corresponding panels of figure 3.2. This is due to differences in the samples used to derive the estimates in these figures. In figure 3.7, the estimates are obtained from the Teen Pregnancy sample and are based on women whose *first pregnancy* that occurred *prior* to their eighteenth birthday ended in a birth, regardless of when that birth occurred. In figure 3.2, the estimates are calculated with the All Women's sample, i.e., for women who experienced a *birth prior* to age 18, regardless of how many pregnancies she had experienced (and terminated) at earlier ages. Since most regular high school graduations occur around age 18, there is great scope for differences in the estimates of receipt of a high school diploma or a GED across the two samples.

18. These differences in hours are statistically significant by conventional levels of significance from ages 17 through 20 and from ages 23 through 34.

19. In her independent assessment of the costs of teenage childbearing, Maynard (1996) calculates the likely impact of delayed childbearing among teen mothers by comparing the earnings that teen mothers receive over their first 13 years of motherhood with estimates of what women who delayed childbearing until age 21 would be expected to earn over their first 13 years of motherhood. (She uses this same approach in calculations for annual hours of work and welfare benefits received.) This approach differs from ours only in how the outcomes associated with delay are calculated. Moreover, we find that using this approach does not change our basic finding that delaying teen motherhood will lower on average, rather than increase, the labor market earnings of women who become teen mothers.

20. The estimated effects of delaying childbearing among teen mothers on total AFDC and food stamp benefits are statistically significant at ages 18 and 19 and for ages 29 through 34.

21. Using the method of comparison proposed by Maynard (1996), which is described in footnote 19, does not change the conclusion that average annual level of welfare benefits received by teen mothers would not be expected to decline if these women delayed their childbearing.

22. As noted in a summary of a recent National Institute of Child Health and Human Development (NICHD) conference assessing evidence on the effects of early childbearing, "the size and importance of this effect [of early childbearing on a young mother's educational and economic outcomes], and the extent to which a causal interpretation can be made, remain in dispute. Recent studies have given new emphasis to earlier concerns that traditional multivariate approaches have not adequately controlled for selectivity into early childbearing" (Bachrach and Carver 1992, pp. 20–21).

23. Rosenzweig and Wolpin (1995) use a much more elaborate variant of differencing across family members (sisters and cousins) in modeling the effects of early childbearing on the mother's outcomes and the well-being of her children.

24. Using state aggregate data on the maximum monthly AFDC and food stamp benefits for a family of four (consisting of one adult and three children) and average monthly Medicaid expenditures for a family of this size in the years between 1984 and 1989, we

regressed the Medicaid benefits against the sum of food stamp and AFDC benefits, controlling for a linear time trend to account for the rising level of expenditures on Medicaid relative to those for the other programs over this period. The results produce an estimate that in each month a typical family on public assistance receives $250 plus 0.193 times the benefits received (in 1993 dollars) from the AFDC and food stamp programs combined. Based on this formula, the average monthly Medicaid expenditure on a family of four receiving the maximum allowable AFDC and food stamp benefits would be $404. In 1993, the median state's maximum monthly AFDC benefit for a family of four was $435, and the maximum monthly food stamp allotment for such a family was $375 (U.S. House of Representatives 1994). Since the average monthly expenditure in 1993 for a family of four receiving assistance under the Medicaid program was $386 (U.S. House of Representatives 1994), the above estimation procedure appears to yield reasonable estimates. While the NLSY contains information on whether its respondents receive rental subsidies or subsidized housing, it does not contain information on the dollar value of these forms of assistance. Because we were unable to obtain reliable data with which to estimate the costs of housing subsidies, they are not included in our cost calculations.

25. The estimates for this regression are presented in table 3A.1 in the appendix.

26. In 1993, the total expenditures, in terms of 1996 dollars, for AFDC, food stamps, and Medicaid were $27.3 billion, $28.4 billion, and $197.1 billion, respectively (U.S. House of Representatives 1994).

27. Under these alternative assumptions, our estimates of total annual governmental expenditures on public assistance to teen mothers vary from $12.5 to $9.3 billion. These same costs, net of taxes paid by teen mothers, range from $5.6 to −$4.1 billion. Estimates of the total expected savings in public assistance from postponement of teen births vary from $0.002 to −$2.5 billion. And the net savings to government of such a postponement range from −$1.6 to −$7.2 billion a year.

References

Abrahamse, A., et al. 1988. *Beyond Stereotypes: Who Becomes a Single Teenage Mother.* Santa Monica, Calif.: RAND Corporation.

Angrist, J., and G. Imbens. 1991. "Sources of Identifying Information in Evaluation Models." Unpublished manuscript, Harvard University, August 1991.

Bachrach, C., and K. Carver. 1992. "Outcomes of Early Childbearing: An Appraisal of Recent Evidence." Summary of a conference. National Institute of Child Health and Human Development, May 1992.

Bloom, H. 1984. "Accounting for No-Shows in Experimental Evaluation Designs." *Evaluation Review* 8(2): 225–246.

Bronars, S., and J. Grogger. 1995. "The Economic Consequences of Unwed Motherhood: Using Twin Births as a Natural Experiment." *American Economic Review* 84(5): 1141–1156.

Burt, M. 1992. "Teenage Childbearing: How Much Does It Cost?" Washington, DC: Center for Population Options.

Burt, M., and D. Haffner. 1986. "Estimates of Public Costs for Teenage Childbearing: A Review of Recent Studies and Estimates of 1985 Public Costs." Washington, DC: Center for Population Options.

Cameron, S., and, J. Heckman. 1993. "The Nonequivalence of High School Equivalents." *Journal of Labor Economics* 11, Part 1 (January): 1–47.

Cao, J., E. Stromsdorfer, and G. Weeks. 1996. "The Human Capital Effect of the GED on Low Income Women." *Journal of Human Resources* 31(1): 206–228.

Furstenberg, F., and K. M. Harris. 1993. "When and Why Fathers Matter: Impacts of Father Involvement on the Children of Adolescent Mothers." In R. Lerman and T. Ooms, eds., *Unwed Fathers: Changing Roles and Emerging Policies*. Philadelphia: Temple University Press.

Geronimus, A., and S. Korenman. 1992. "The Socioeconomic Consequences of Teen Childbearing Reconsidered." *Quarterly Journal of Economics* 107: 1187–1214.

Geronimus, A., and S. Korenman. 1993. "The Costs of Teenage Childbearing: Evidence and Interpretation." *Demography* 30: 281–290.

Greene, W. 1993. *Econometric Analysis*. Second Edition. New York: Macmillan.

Grogger, J., and S. Bronars. 1993. "The Socioeconomic Consequences of Teenage Childbearing: Results from a Natural Experiment." Unpublished manuscript, University of California-Santa Barbara, February 1993.

Hayes, C. 1987. *Risking the Future: Adolescent Sexuality, Pregnancy, and Childbearing*. Vol. I. Washington, DC: National Academy Press.

Heckman, J. 1995. "Randomization as an Instrumental Variable." NBER Technical Working Paper No. 184, September 1995.

Heckman, J., J. Smith, and C. Taber. 1994. "Accounting for Dropouts in Evaluations of Social Experiments." Unpublished manuscript, University of Chicago, September 1994.

Hotz, V. J., S. McElroy, and S. Sanders. 1996. "Assessing the Effects of Teenage Childbearing on Maternal Outcomes in the United States: Exploiting a Very Natural Experiment." Unpublished manuscript. University of Chicago.

Hotz, V. J., C. Mullin, and S. Sanders. 1995. "Bounding Causal Effects Using Contaminated Instrumental Variables: Analyzing the Effects of Teenage Childbearing Using a Natural Experiment." Unpublished manuscript. University of Chicago.

Hotz, V. J., and S. Sanders. 1994a. "Bounding Treatment Effects in Experimental Evaluations Subject to Post-Randomization Treatment Choice." *Bulletin of the International Statistical Institute.*

Hotz, V. J., and S. Sanders. 1994b. "Bounding Treatment Effects in Controlled and Natural Experiments Subject to Post-Randomization Treatment Choice." Unpublished manuscript, March 1994.

Jones, E., and J. Forrest. 1990. "Underreporting of Abortions in Surveys of U.S. Women: 1976–1988." *Demography* 29: 113–126.

Juhn, C., K. M. Murphy, and B. Pierce. 1993. "Inequality and the Rise in Returns to Skill." *Journal of Political Economy* 101(3): 410–442.

Klein, J., Z. Stein, and M. Susser. 1989. *Conception to Birth: Epidemiology of Prenatal Development.* New York: Oxford University Press.

Maynard, R. 1996. *Kids Having Kids: A Robin Hood Foundation Special Report on the Costs of Adolescent Childbearing.* New York: Robin Hood Foundation.

Michael, R., and N. Tuma. 1985. "Entry Into Marriage and Parenthood by Young Men and Women: The Influence of Family Background." *Demography* 22 (November): 515–44.

Moore, K. 1995. "Background Data on Teenage Fertility." Washington, DC: Child Trends, Inc.

Patten, M. 1981. "Self Concept and Self Esteem: Factors in Adolescent Pregnancy." *Adolescence* 64 (Winter): 765–78.

Ribar, D. 1995. "The Socioeconomic Consequences of Young Women's Childbearing: Reconciling Disparate Evidence." Unpublished manuscript. Penn State University.

Rosenzweig, M., and K. Wolpin. 1995. "Sisters, Siblings, and Mothers: The Effect of Teen-age Childbearing on Birth Outcomes in a Dynamic Family Context," *Econometrica* 63(2): 303–326.

U.S. Bureau of the Census. 1993. "Fertility of American Women 1992." *Current Population Reports.* Series P-20-470. Washington, DC: U.S. Government Printing Office.

U.S. House of Representatives, Committee on Ways and Means. 1994. *Green Book: Background Material and Data on Programs within the Jurisdiction of the Committee on Ways and Means.* Washington, DC: U.S. Government Printing Office.

Vernon, M., J. Green, and T. Frothingham. 1983. "Teenage Pregnancy: A Prospective Study of Self-esteem and Other Sociodemographic Factors." *Pediatrics* 72: 632–35.

APPENDIX 3A

Table 3A.1 COEFFICIENT ESTIMATES FOR THE INSTRUMENTAL VARIABLE (IV) REGRESSIONS FOR THE EFFECT OF EARLY CHILDBEARING ON SOCIOECONOMIC OUTCOMES OF TEEN MOTHERS

Independent Variables	Dependent Variables				
	Number of Children Born by Age t	Fraction of Time Spent as Single Mom Since Age 14 at Age t	Annual Earnings from Spouse at Age t (= 0 if spouse not present)	Obtained a High School Diploma by Age t	Obtained a GED by Age t
First pregnancy prior to age 18 ending in a birth	0.8315	−0.3320	51471.6094	0.3358	−1.4046
	(1.0845)	(0.9353)	(46902.4102)	(2.1110)	(1.6046)
First pregnancy at age 18 or 19 ending in a birth	0.4239***	0.0367***	1463.0170	−0.1390***	0.0623***
	(0.0366)	(0.0077)	(1509.1650)	(0.0173)	(0.0131)
Teenage Birth*Current Age	0.0083	0.0458	−4033.2329	−0.0632	0.1558
	(0.0965)	(0.1221)	(3961.1831)	(0.2750)	(0.2091)
Teenage Birth*Current Age^2	−0.0009	−0.0012	86.6786	0.0029	−0.0052
	(0.0021)	(0.0052)	(81.6950)	(0.0116)	(0.0088)
Teenage Birth*Current Age^3		4.91e-6		−4.70e-5	5.88e-5
		(7.10e-5)		(1.59e-4)	(1.21e-4)
Current Age	0.4522***	0.1589***	4267.4712**	0.7889***	0.0188
	(0.0481)	(0.0578)	(1849.3640)	(0.1296)	(0.0985)
Current Age^2	−0.0065***	−0.0056**	−46.0938	−0.0306***	−0.0002
	(0.0010)	(0.0024)	(37.4506)	(0.0053)	(0.0041)
Current Age^3		0.670e-4**		0.391e-3***	−2.06e-6
		(3.23e-5)		(7.20e-5)	(5.48e-5)
Black	0.1084***	0.2094***	−13609.7695***	0.2503***	−0.0764***
	(0.0161)	(0.0034)	(670.3544)	(0.0076)	(0.0058)
Hispanic	0.0783***	0.0216***	−3885.3540***	0.0131	−0.0135*
	(0.0216)	(0.0046)	(915.2986)	(0.0103)	(0.0078)
Family on Welfare in 1978	0.0946***	0.0643***	−2325.5110***	−0.0336***	−0.0245***
	(0.0193)	(0.0041)	(788.4078)	(0.0091)	(0.0069)
Family Income in 1978	−0.525e-5***	4.42e-8	0.0510*	0.271e-5***	−0.136e-5***
	(7.11e-7)	(1.49e-7)	(0.0287)	(3.36e-7)	(2.56e-7)

continued

Table 3A.1 COEFFICIENT ESTIMATES FOR THE INSTRUMENTAL VARIABLE (IV) REGRESSIONS FOR THE EFFECT OF EARLY CHILDBEARING ON SOCIOECONOMIC OUTCOMES OF TEEN MOTHERS (continued)

Independent Variables	Number of Children Born by Age t	Fraction of Time Spent as Single Mom Since Age 14 at Age t	Annual Earnings from Spouse at Age t (=0 if spouse not present)	Obtained a High School Diploma by Age t	Obtained a GED by Age t
			Dependent Variables		
Missing Family Income (0–1)	0.1760***	−0.0403***	491.7833	−0.0648***	−0.0102**
	(0.0131)	(0.0028)	(546.6868)	(0.0062)	(0.0047)
in Female-Headed Hsehold. at Age 14	−0.0875***	0.0343***	432.0361	0.0429***	−0.0425***
	(0.0242)	(0.0051)	(1013.6130)	(0.0115)	(0.0088)
in Intact Hsehold. at Age 14	0.0005	−0.0086*	3199.6101***	0.1348***	−0.0784***
	(0.0212)	(0.0045)	(891.6422)	(0.0101)	(0.0077)
Mother's Educ.	−0.0214***	−0.0021***	−0.5981	0.0132***	0.0107***
	(0.0026)	(0.0005)	(108.6487)	(0.0012)	(0.0009)
Missing Mother's Educ. (0–1)	0.0849***	0.0227***	−1920.1150*	−0.0563***	−0.0598***
	(0.0241)	(0.0051)	(1019.7230)	(0.0115)	(0.0087)
Father's Educ.	−0.0202***	0.0018***	314.5903***	0.0022**	−0.0045***
	(0.0022)	(0.0005)	(91.4316)	(0.0010)	(0.0008)
Missing Father's Educ. (0–1)	−0.0081	0.0005	−595.8063	−0.0224***	0.0014
	(0.0167)	(0.0035)	(697.8730)	(0.0080)	(0.0061)
AFQT	−0.0039***	−0.421e-3***	96.3101***	0.0054***	0.0007***
	(0.0003)	(6.16e-5)	(12.0697)	(0.0001)	(0.0001)
First pregnancy occurred before age 16	0.4904***	0.0939***	−7568.1128***	−0.2967***	0.0636***
	(0.0393)	(0.0058)	(1606.3850)	(0.0188)	(0.0143)
First pregnancy occurred at ages 16 or 17	0.1236***	0.0058	−4996.5361***	−0.1552***	−0.0022
	(0.0405)	(0.0086)	(1660.9500)	(0.0193)	(0.0147)
Constant	−5.4360***	−1.4711***	−60671.8789***	−6.4439***	−0.2260
	(0.5675)	(0.4572)	(22566.2500)	(1.0273)	(0.7809)
No. of Person-Years	22,102	24,572	20,458	25,432	25,432

* Denotes significance at 0.10 level; ** denotes significance at 0.05 level; *** denotes significance at .0025 level.

Table 3A.1 COEFFICIENT ESTIMATES FOR THE INSTRUMENTAL VARIABLE (IV) REGRESSIONS FOR THE EFFECT OF EARLY CHILDBEARING ON SOCIOECONOMIC OUTCOMES OF TEEN MOTHERS (continued)

Independent Variables	Dependent Variables				
	Obtained a High School Diploma or GED by Age t	Annual Number of Hours Woman Worked for Pay at Age t	Woman's Annual Labor Market Earnings at Age t	Annual Monetary Value of AFDC and Food Stamp Benefits Received at Age t	Annual Monetary Value of AFDC, Food Stamps, and Medicaid Benefits Received at Age t[a]
First pregnancy prior to age 18 ending in a birth	-1.1401*** (0.4214)	-2940.5171** (1325.5510)	3238.9951 (13640.7598)	930.3288 (2366.4680)	3047.8779 (3567.6470)
First pregnancy at age 18 or 19 ending in a birth	-0.0783*** (0.0160)	-153.9541*** (38.4753)	831.3946 (960.8264)	434.2270** (170.3709)	700.8003*** (256.8482)
Teenage Birth*Current Age	0.0913** (0.0361)	200.9372* (109.4288)	11.5281 (1102.1410)	-19.6750 (192.5919)	-136.6693 (290.3483)
Teenage Birth*Current Age^2	-0.0018** (0.0008)	-2.9311 (2.2098)	1.4393 (21.7880)	-.7622 (3.8187)	.2897 (5.7571)
Teenage Birth*Current Age^3					
Current Age	0.1135*** (0.0178)	90.0399* (52.3367)	2037.2090*** (636.0340)	3773.5449*** (510.4857)	6926.1289*** (769.5995)
Current Age^2	-0.0020*** (0.0004)	-1.3549 (1.0414)	-11.2287 (12.5659)	-140.0084*** (20.3360)	-257.9422*** (30.6581)
Current Age^3				1.7130*** (.2683)	3.1657*** (.4045)
Black	0.1724*** (0.0070)	25.8367 (17.3872)	1929.1010*** (434.4171)	1100.4590*** (76.2963)	2146.8840*** (115.0229)
Hispanic	-3.89e-5 (9.48e-3)	24.0697 (23.3255)	3069.3201*** (584.5808)	484.4153*** (102.6161)	977.9039*** (154.7023)
Family on Welfare in 1978	-0.0559*** (0.0084)	-190.4840*** (20.6845)	-2000.9530*** (512.2833)	788.7813*** (90.2428)	1391.1360*** (136.0485)
Family Income in 1978	0.131e-5*** (3.10e-7)	0.0023*** (0.0008)	0.1105*** (0.0186)	-.0049 (.0033)	-.0059 (.0050)

continued

Table 3A.1 COEFFICIENT ESTIMATES FOR THE INSTRUMENTAL VARIABLE (IV) REGRESSIONS FOR THE EFFECT OF EARLY CHILDBEARING ON SOCIOECONOMIC OUTCOMES OF TEEN MOTHERS (continued)

	Dependent Variables				
Independent Variables	Obtained a High School Diploma or GED by Age t	Annual Number of Hours Woman Worked for Pay at Age t	Woman's Annual Labor Market Earnings at Age t	Annual Monetary Value of AFDC and Food Stamp Benefits Received at Age t	Annual Monetary Value of AFDC, Food Stamps, and Medicaid Benefits Received at Age t[a]
Missing Family Income (0–1)	-0.0699***	-135.3658***	-3113.9839***	-64.4300	56.7415
	(0.0057)	(14.2131)	(352.1359)	(61.9188)	(93.3477)
in Female-Headed Hsehold. at Age 14	-0.0021	-24.2717	147.5678	-234.8956**	-400.3635**
	(0.0106)	(26.2608)	(657.5315)	(115.1432)	(173.5879)
in Intact Hsehold. at Age 14	0.0572***	-23.4033	-680.6509	-481.5816***	-810.8190***
	(0.0093)	(23.0307)	(577.5261)	(101.0498)	(152.3409)
Mother's Educ.	0.0236***	13.6385***	503.6415***	-9.1344	-22.0243
	(0.0011)	(2.7845)	(69.4840)	(12.1895)	(18.3767)
Missing Mother's Educ. (0–1)	-0.1160***	-2.6849	-1075.4659	-18.6754	47.0347
	(0.0106)	(26.3669)	(654.5994)	(114.7723)	(173.0288)
Father's Educ.	-0.0019**	6.4641***	166.6109***	-52.9031***	-68.6893***
	(0.0009)	2.3399	(58.7920)	(10.3047)	(15.5352)
Missing Father's Educ. (0–1)	-0.0196***	-62.1035***	-592.1396	-50.1624	75.6484
	(0.0073)	(18.1160)	(452.7890)	(79.3874)	(119.6831)
AFQT	0.0061***	6.2850***	170.2729***	-15.4928***	-30.0301***
	(0.0001)	(0.3141)	(7.8034)	(1.3775)	(2.0767)
First pregnancy occurred before age 16	-0.2571***	-209.5872***	-1210.0260	1158.5720***	1984.4020***
	(0.0171)	(41.7343)	(1035.8979)	(182.8159)	(275.6101)
First pregnancy occurred at ages 16 or 17	-0.1644***	-243.1763***	-1769.3760*	648.5098***	1098.7520***
	(0.0177)	(43.0508)	(1068.8660)	(188.2354)	(283.7804)
Constant	-1.2486***	-659.9171	-43529.4492***	-31240.5996***	-57437.5703***
	(0.2180)	(649.4204)	(8011.5352)	(4244.0781)	(6398.2988)
No. of Person-Years	25,432	21,772	20,621	21,964	21,964

* Denotes significance at 0.10 level; ** denotes significance at 0.05 level; *** denotes significance at .0025 level.
[a] Estimates from this instrumental variable regression were used for estimates of public assistance costs displayed in figure 3.11.
Source: NLSY, *Teen Pregnancy Sample.*

Chapter Four

COSTS AND CONSEQUENCES
FOR THE FATHERS

Michael J. Brien and Robert J. Willis

What are the consequences of young men entering fatherhood as teenagers or when their partners are teenagers?[1] This chapter addresses both parts of this question. Similar to the extensive literature on teen childbearing for young mothers, our first goal is to measure the impact of teen fatherhood on the father himself. In particular, we will examine the role of teen childbearing on the education and skills he brings to the labor market and his subsequent earnings. Our second goal is to consider associated costs for the child and for the larger society.[2] Specifically, we measure the resources that could be provided by the fathers of children born to young mothers, constructing a profile of the potential support available to a child over the first 18 years of the child's life. These two goals are interrelated since to quantify the resources available from a father, we must understand how men and their earnings, for example, are affected by the birth of a child. Our overall aim is to determine the consequences of teenage childbearing in both the short and the long term and to consider how these consequences interact with decisions about marriage and contributions of resources by both parents and by the state in behalf of the child. The first part of this chapter examines the consequences for men of having a child when they are teenagers. The second part is more from the mother's perspective and considers the resources potentially available from her partner and how these resources vary with the age a woman becomes a mother.

CONSEQUENCES FOR FATHERS

The substantive and measurement issues surrounding the implications of early fatherhood for the young man himself are analogous to those presented by Ellwood in "Teenage Unemployment: Permanent Scars or Temporary Blemishes?" (1982). In particular, he addresses a question of great importance to policymakers concerning which of two possible effects of early unemployment on the long-run economic capacities of young men is correct. The notion of permanent scars emphasizes the possibility that periods of unemployment during the critical early years in which youths accumulate large amounts of human capital may cause permanent damage to their lifetime career paths. The alternative notion of a blemish emphasizes that unemployment, however painful at the time, usually fades away and leaves no lasting effects. Consistent with the scar hypothesis, data in this area typically display a strong correlation between the current employment and earnings of men in their late 20s and their prior experience of unemployment during their teen years. However, as Ellwood correctly notes:

> The fundamental problem in capturing the long term effects of unemployment is separating differences in employment and wages which are causally related to early unemployment, from the differences due to unobserved personal characteristics correlated with early unemployment. (1982, p. 349)

In contrast to earlier studies, Ellwood found that some scar effects do exist but, when unobserved individual differences are controlled for, are much smaller than uncontrolled estimates would indicate.

The issues raised by Ellwood for the case of teen unemployment can be applied to teenage fatherhood, although with some new and interesting aspects. As in the case of teen unemployment, teen childbearing might impose either a short-term blemish or a long-term scar. Furthermore, it is important to distinguish causal links from simple correlations between (observed and unobserved) personal characteristics and the likelihood of the event. But, unlike unemployment, which is typically a temporary episode, the birth of a child typically has long-term, irreversible consequences for the custodial parent or parents.

"What If" Questions

To give more precision to the concept of the private costs of teenage fatherhood, it is useful to begin with carefully posed counterfactual questions. The first question we address is what are the consequences if a man delays the transition into fatherhood by one year. The effect of delaying fatherhood from, say, age 16 to age 21 can then be calculated as the cumulative effect of five one-year delays.

The basic idea behind this approach is illustrated in figure 4.1. The vertical axis measures the expected present discounted value of the lifetime earnings of three youths: A, B, and C, who differ in "economic potential." The horizontal axis measures the age at which a young man fathers his first child, marries the mother, and assumes the status of family breadwinner. Consider first the curve BB, corresponding to a youth with average potential. The inverse-U shape of the curve reflects the net outcome of two countervailing forces, one associated with optimal human capital investment in education and postschool training and the other with the benefits of marriage for male earnings—the "marriage premium" found in a number of recent studies (Korenman and Neumark 1991; Daniel 1993).

Initially, the lifetime earnings of youth B will increase by delaying marriage and fatherhood. Presumably this is because as a single person, responsible only for himself, he will be able to complete the optimal amount of schooling, participate in postschool training or apprenticeship programs, and find a job that is a good match given his skills, training, and interests. At some point, when he has completed his schooling and has found a "career job," additional delay of

Figure 4.1 FATHERHOOD AND HUMAN CAPITAL

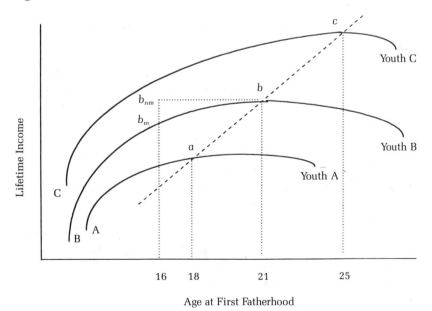

Age at First Fatherhood

family responsibilities offers no further benefits to his economic prospects. Indeed, as noted above, family responsibilities are likely to provide a married man with greater incentives for economic success; additionally, his earnings potential may benefit from the household division of labor afforded by marriage. Thus, for youth B, delay of marriage and fatherhood past age 21 would be detrimental to the value of his lifetime earnings as seen by the declining portion of the BB curve. The curves AA and CC represent the similarly shaped corresponding curves for youths with low and high economic potential, whose lifetime earnings are maximized when family responsibilities are delayed until age 18 and age 25, respectively.

For simplicity, assume that the optimal age of marriage and first fatherhood for a young man of a particular economic potential is given by the age at which the corresponding present value curve reaches a maximum.[3] Thus, a youth who chooses to have a child and assume family responsibilities (or has a "shotgun wedding") at an age earlier than this optimal age forgoes additional lifetime earnings, an effect analogous to Ellwood's scar effect. The magnitude of the cost of becoming a teenage father at, say, age 16 is given by the difference between the height of the lifetime earnings curve at age 16, denoted by b_m, and the height of the curve at the optimal age, denoted by b_{nm}. In addition, the marginal value of delaying fatherhood by one year is given by the difference between the height of the curve at ages 16 and 17.

The curves for youths A, B, and C are drawn under the assumption that higher long-run economic potential is correlated with higher marginal returns to delaying fatherhood. This assumption implies that if young men time marriage and fatherhood optimally, youths with higher potential will delay fatherhood longer, and that the cost of early fatherhood is higher the greater the economic potential of the youth. The empirical relationship between age of fatherhood and lifetime income in this model is given by the dashed line abc in figure 4.1, which connects the points corresponding to the optimal choices made by A, B, and C, respectively. This dashed line greatly overstates the scarring effect of early fatherhood because it fails to control for the economic potential of the youth.[4]

The theory suggests two things for our empirical work. First, controlling for differences in the economic potential of men is extremely important in isolating the impact that entering fatherhood at a nonoptimal age has on the realization of their potential. Second, factors must exist that would cause young men with a given level of economic potential to make different choices so that, after controlling for potential, the observed variations in age at first fatherhood and long-run outcomes (e.g., education, occupation, midcareer earnings) trace out a given curve such as BB. A number of sources of "chance variation" in age of first fatherhood that are found among the many nonmonetary elements of the "mating game" may lead a man to become a father at an age different from the age that would maximize his net lifetime income. Examples include romantic love, sexual desire, difficulties in finding and attracting a girlfriend, and "accidental" pregnancies.

We assume that the variations in age at first fatherhood remaining after controlling for variables associated with a young man's economic potential reflect the chance outcomes of nonmonetary factors uncorrelated with his economic potential. Given this assumption, estimates of the effect that variation in age at first fatherhood has on long-run outcome variables, controlling for economic potential, do identify the scarring effects of early fatherhood. However, the underlying theory itself implies that this assumption is unlikely to be completely correct. For example, the cost to a 16-year-old male of impregnating his girlfriend is much greater for a young man with high potential (e.g., youth C) than it is for a person with lower potential (e.g., youth A). Even though both A and C have an incentive to avoid conception, the higher cost of an "accident" to C suggests that he would be more apt to reduce the likelihood of an accident. Thus, even if all unwed conceptions were unintended, the observed relationship between age of fatherhood and outcome variables may be biased because men with higher economic potential would be less likely to have accidents. Our hope is that the observable variables we use to control for a young man's economic potential are strong enough (i.e., account for a sufficiently large portion of the true variance in the economic benefits of delaying fatherhood) to eliminate most of this bias.[5]

To this point, we have focused on the counterfactual question, "What is the consequence for a male of delaying his transition into fatherhood from age X to age X + 1?" In asking this question, we have implicitly assumed that fatherhood and marriage are inextricably linked. We now wish to relax this assumption and consider how the answer to the question may depend on marriage and child support decisions.

The theoretical framework represented in figure 4.1 can be extended to deal with marital and child support decisions associated with fatherhood. We consider two alternatives to the fatherhood/marriage case considered above. First, youth B fathers a child at age 16, but instead of marrying the mother and becoming a breadwinner, he "walks away" and provides no support for the child; indeed, his paternity is never legally established.[6] In this case, assuming that he makes no further "mistakes," he may continue on his optimal path and delay marriage and fathering additional children until the optimal age. His level of lifetime earnings is depicted by point b_{nm} if he walks away. Compared with a decision to marry, the youth benefits from higher lifetime earnings, and society benefits from the additional income taxes he will pay based on his higher earnings. However, the mother and child are deprived of the resources that he would have contributed to the family. If the mother's resources (including any resources made available by the mother's family) are insufficient, society will bear the costs of providing support for the child through Aid to Families with Dependent Children (AFDC). In this scenario, an implicit transfer takes place from the rest of the society to the teen father—who bears no cost for his actions, not even a temporary blemish.

As a second case, a father whose paternity is established chooses not to marry the mother of the child. The costs to him as well as to others depend on the level of support he provides to the child. He may, for example, choose to provide an amount equivalent to the married father, although there are theoretical reasons (Weiss and Willis 1985) and much empirical evidence (e.g., Weiss and Willis 1993) to expect a nonresident father to provide considerably less. If the father pays significant child support, he may have to forgo continued schooling or training opportunities similar to those depicted for married fathers in figure 4.1.

The underlying reason for such scar effects is an imperfection in the credit market, whereby a young man who has an immediate need for cash to help support a family is prevented from borrowing against his future earnings and continuing to follow an optimal pattern of investment in schooling and training that would carry him to the peak of his present value curve in figure 4.1. Of course, if the youth comes from a prosperous background, his family may provide the needed resources so that the boy "does right" by the mother and child without handicapping his own career. Additionally, if the boy's parents know they will get stuck with the bill, they have a strong incentive to exercise paternal power to reduce their chance of becoming premature grandparents. Conversely, the options of cushioning the effects of teen fatherhood and of his family's incentives to prevent it happening are both greatly reduced for youths from poor backgrounds. Of course, to the extent they care about their sons' futures, rich and poor parents alike are motivated to try to keep their teenage sons from becoming fathers if that would disrupt their careers.

The Data

The primary data set for this analysis is the National Longitudinal Survey of Youth (NLSY). The NLSY is a nationally representative sample of 12,686 young men and women of all races who were ages 14–21 in 1979.[7] Individuals were surveyed each year from 1979 until the latest wave in 1992. Overall, these data provide detailed information for a large number of respondents on a variety of topics. Relevant to the issues examined in this chapter, the NLSY allows us to construct childbearing and marriage histories for a large number of male respondents. Educational achievement, employment status, measures of labor supply and income, and a large number of background variables are available in addition. Also important, the NLSY includes the respondent's score on a standardized aptitude test, the Armed Forces Qualifying Test (AFQT).

Although the NLSY is one of the best available data sets for studying the impact of teenage fatherhood, it has weaknesses. Perhaps the most important drawback of any survey data on fatherhood is the strong likelihood that men will fail to report some of the children they father.[8] This problem can be severe for males who become fathers when they are young and unwed and are less likely to have contact with the child. A strength of the NLSY is, however, that starting from relatively young ages men are asked about their childbearing behavior. This feature of the data implies that we need not rely solely on retrospective fertility histories and the reporting of births that might be influenced by whether or not the father has remained in contact with the child.

Efforts have been made to examine the validity of the male fertility reports in the NLSY. Mott (1985) compared the fertility behavior of the male respondents of the NLSY to a comparable cohort of males in the U.S. Vital Statistics.[9] His results suggest that males of all races, ages 20–24 in the NLSY, underreport births by 15 percent. For black males, the underreporting grows to 23 percent. This drawback is clearly a problem in any attempt to assess the impact on the father from having a child. The men who do not report the birth are most likely those who completely walk away from the parenting responsibility and who therefore suffer little consequence of their parental status. This bias should be kept in mind in any interpretation of the results presented in this chapter. For our analysis, we use the fertility and marriage histories constructed by the Center for Human Resource Research. Technical reports (see, for example, Mott 1983) suggest that the cleanup procedures used in the construction of these variables greatly reduced the number of discrepancies in these histories.

In addition to marriage and fertility histories, a number of outcome and control variables are constructed (table 4.1). To capture the notion of long-run outcomes, we want to measure the outcomes as far into the future as possible. To construct a consistent measure for all NLSY respondents, the status of the individual at age 27 (the latest available age for all cohorts in the NLSY) is chosen for examination.[10] The associated value of human capital, labor supply, and earnings measures are considered at this age. The total number of years of education is used as a measure of the level of human capital; the total number of hours worked in the calendar year was constructed as a measure of labor supply.

Individual income, the closest indicator of the potential resources the father could provide to the child, is considered in two ways. The first and most basic is the actual income at age 27. This measure, however, has a drawback. Even though we are choosing to evaluate all individuals at one age, they may actually be at different points in their life cycles. Individuals who choose high levels of schooling or career paths that require considerable training may not have yet achieved the income benefits associated with their chosen occupations. For example, a plumber with a high school education may have been working in his profession for 5 to 10 years by age 27, whereas a newly

Table 4.1 OUTCOME AND CONTROL VARIABLES

Age 27 outcomes
    Years of education
    Census occupational income
    Actual annual income
    Hours worked in calendar year
Control variables
    Marital status
    Living arrangement status at age 14 (father/mother, mother only)
    Mother's education
    Father's education
    Magazines in home at age 14
    Newspapers in home at age 14
    Library card in home at age 14
    Lived in urban area at age 14
    Race (Hispanic, black)
    Armed Forces Qualifying Test Score
    Religion in which respondent was raised (none, Protestant, Catholic, Jewish)

Source: National Longitudinal Survey of Youth.

graduated lawyer might be just starting his first job at age 27. Although their actual earnings at this age may not be different, their long-run earnings prospects are probably very different. To get around these problems, we also consider the occupations chosen at age 27. To measure a long-run or permanent income, we attach to this occupation the mean income recorded, by race and education, in the 1990 U.S. Census for a cohort of men slightly older than those found in the NLSY. We refer to this measure as census income.

The control variables used in the analysis are also shown in table 4.1. Our choices are dictated by a desire to include variables that can be considered independent of the behaviors being examined. These variables are the race of the respondent, the education of the respondent's parents, the living arrangements at age 14 (residing with mother only, urban residence, and the learning environment in the home), and the religion in which the respondent was raised. Finally, as a measure of ability, we include the respondent's normalized AFQT score.[11]

To construct a sample for our analysis we need to make certain restrictions on the data. The largest restriction is exclusion of the military sample and the supplemental sample of economically disadvantaged, nonblack, non-Hispanics (824 and 742 respondents, respectively). Our primary motivation for exclusion is our focus on long-run outcomes: both samples were dropped from the survey prior to the most recent wave of data and therefore provided insufficient long-run information.[12] In a similar way, we exclude respondents who dropped out of the sample prior to age 27 or did not provide information in the surveys around their 27th year. We also exclude the few individuals who did not provide the appropriate data for the construction of marriage and fertility histories. Finally, the respondents who did not take the AFQT are also dropped (221 respondents after the other restrictions were imposed). The final analysis includes 4,231 male respondents.[13]

Basic statistics on marriage and childbearing (table 4.2) show that 64 percent of the men report having a first marriage prior to the 1992 survey. The average age at first marriage is 24 years. Clearly evident in this table are the racial differences in marriage behavior that have been found in other data. A smaller proportion of blacks report having a first marriage, and their average age at first marriage is higher. Approximately 60 percent of the respondents have at least one birth. Suggesting a close relationship, the average age at first birth is virtually identical to the average age at first marriage. The racial pattern,

Table 4.2 SUMMARY STATISTICS ON MARRIAGE AND FERTILITY BY RACE

	White	Black	Hispanic	Total
Living arrangements				
Percentage reporting first marriage	72.5	48.0	68.4	64.3
Average age at first marriage (years)	23.9	24.4	23.2	23.9
Fertility				
Percentage reporting first birth	54.4	65.2	66.0	59.8
Average age at first birth (years)	25.0	22.7	23.5	24.0
Sample size	2,149	1,285	797	4,231

Source: National Longitudinal Survey of Youth.

Table 4.3 MARITAL STATUS AT TIME OF FIRST BIRTH AND AT
FIRST PREGNANCY BY RACE

	White	Black	Hispanic	Total
First pregnancy				
Never married	33.9%	81.0%	52.9%	53.4%
Married +	66.1	19.0	47.1	46.6
First birth				
Never married	13.4	71.5	30.2	36.1
Married +	86.6	28.5	69.8	63.9
Sample size	1,168	838	526	2,532

Source: National Longitudinal Survey of Youth.
Note: "Married +" denotes that the event occurred after the date of the first marriage.

while still apparent in the fertility behavior, reverses. A higher percentage of blacks report having a birth, and the difference between blacks and whites in the age at first birth is over two years.

Statistics on the relationship between marital status and fertility show that the majority of first births occur to men who are married (table 4.3).[14] The majority of first pregnancies are caused by men prior to their first marriages, however. Examining these numbers within race reveals large differences between blacks and the other two groups. Blacks are much more likely to have their first birth prior to the first marriage. Although nonmarital childbearing is less common for white and Hispanic men, it still composes, respectively, 13.4 percent and 30.2 percent of first births. Comparing the status at the time of each event, we see for all groups a movement to marriage when the man's partner becomes pregnant. For example, the percentage of white respondents who were never married moved from 33.9 to 13.4 in the time between conception and birth.

As an alternative way of examining the dynamic nature of these decisions, we consider the waiting time to marriage and the waiting time to the first birth, both before and after marriage. [15] Approximately 50 percent of the white and Hispanic samples had a first marriage by age 26 (figure 4.2). At all ages, a substantially lower proportion of blacks have had a first marriage. Figure 4.3 shows the percentage of respondents at each age that have experienced a birth either before marriage, after marriage, or regardless of marital status. Each racial group is presented in a separate panel. By age 30, for example, slightly greater than 50 percent of the white males have experienced a first birth, the vast majority of which occurred within marriage. Also clearly evident are the racial differences in nonmarital childbearing, with a much higher percentage of births to blacks occurring outside marriage.

Effect of Fatherhood on a Male's Economic Well-Being

This section examines a major focus of this chapter: how the economic well-being of young men is affected by the birth of a child. We want to determine the extent to which the age of entry into fatherhood and marital status at that time is associated with a young man's economic well-being.[16] We argued above that entry into fatherhood may have a scarring effect on a male if it causes him to assume responsibility for a family before he can complete his schooling and

Figure 4.2 PROPORTION OF MEN MARRIED BY AGE AND RACE

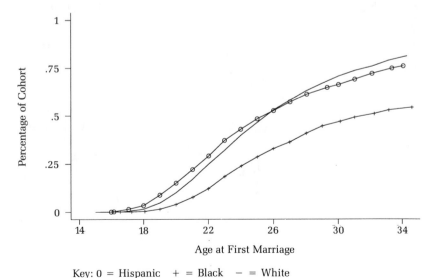

Key: 0 = Hispanic   + = Black   — = White

Figure 4.3 PROPORTION OF MEN WHO HAVE BECOME FATHERS, BY AGE AT BIRTH OF FIRST CHILD AND MARITAL STATUS

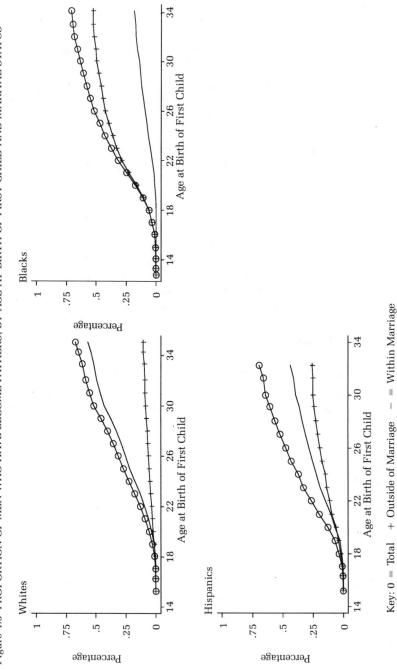

Key: 0 = Total   + = Outside of Marriage   – = Within Marriage

find a stable job. Conversely, if the young man can father a child outside of marriage and escape the burden of marriage or child support payments, fatherhood may have no effect on his educational attainment or postschool investment in human capital. Before we discuss the long-run economic well-being of these young men, we briefly consider the evolution of education, earnings, and hours of work over their life paths.

PATTERNS OVER MEN'S LIFE CYCLES

The left-hand panels of figures 4.4–4.6 show mean outcomes by age for men who had their first child prior to age 20, had it after age 20 but before the end of the NLSY sample period, or were childless by the end of the survey period. The top two panels present the means for nonblack respondents (whites and Hispanics); the bottom panels present the comparable material for blacks.[17] For both racial groups, men who wait to have a child have higher levels of education, higher income, and work more hours by the time they reach their late 20s.[18] With the exception of education, however, this pattern differs across the life cycle. Men who have children at young ages appear briefly to have higher incomes and work more hours than the other fathers. This evidence is consistent with the argument that childbearing has affected these men by forcing them into the labor market earlier than would have been optimal, as seen by their greater earnings and hours worked at younger ages and their lower earnings and hours at later ages. But the age pattern is also consistent with the argument that men who are more attached to the labor market, and perhaps more prepared to have a child, begin childbearing at an earlier age. The regression analysis presented below attempts to disentangle the direction of causation.

The same age patterns for men who have had a child, broken down by whether the man was married at the time of the birth of the child, are shown in the two right-hand panels of figures 4.4–4.6. The education findings show the widest range for men who were married at the time of the birth of the child. Married men who were teen fathers have the least schooling of all groups. Married men who delayed fatherhood until after their teen years have the most schooling of all. For men who were unmarried at the birth, the age at which they begin childbearing has a relatively modest impact on their years of schooling. For earnings and hours worked, men who were married at the birth generally did better than fathers of the same age who were not. As with the previous analysis, this evidence is subject to several interpretations.

Figure 4.4 MEAN YEARS OF SCHOOL BY GIVEN AGE

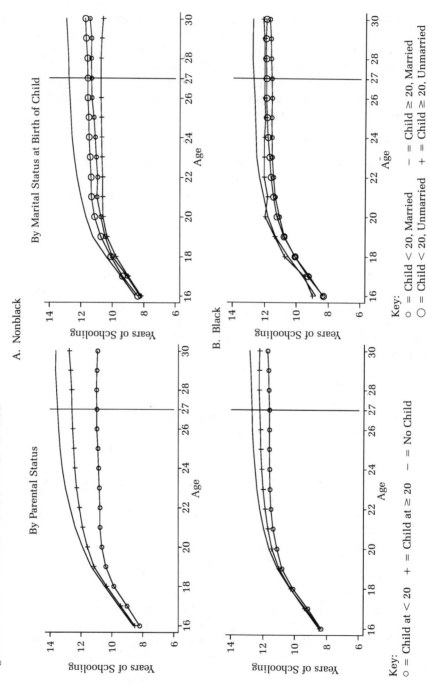

A. Nonblack

By Parental Status

By Marital Status at Birth of Child

B. Black

Key:

o = Child at < 20   + = Child at ≥ 20   − = No Child

Key:

o = Child < 20, Married   − = Child ≥ 20, Married
O = Child < 20, Unmarried   + = Child ≥ 20, Unmarried

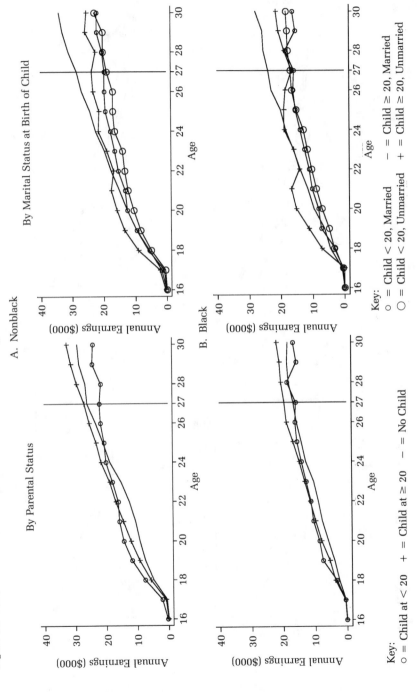

Figure 4.5 MEAN ANNUAL EARNINGS BY GIVEN AGE

A. Nonblack

By Parental Status

By Marital Status at Birth of Child

B. Black

Key:

o = Child at < 20   + = Child at ≥ 20   – = No Child

Key:

o = Child < 20, Married   – = Child ≥ 20, Married
O = Child < 20, Unmarried   + = Child ≥ 20, Unmarried

Figure 4.6 MEAN ANNUAL HOURS OF WORK BY GIVEN AGE

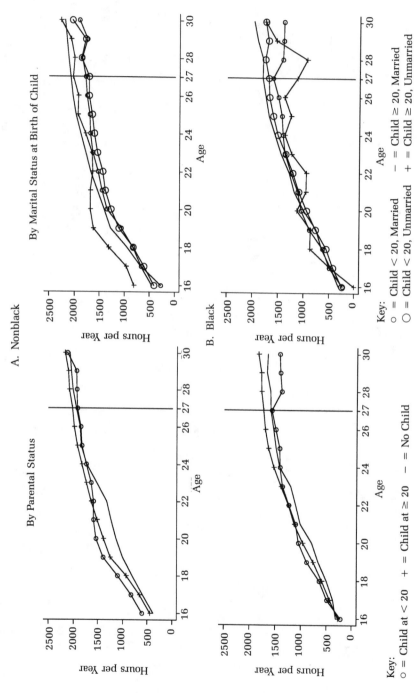

IMPACT OF AGE AT FIRST FATHERHOOD ON AGE 27 OUTCOMES

To address these and other issues more formally, we estimate a series of equations that relate four outcome variables evaluated at age 27 to a set of variables that measure the age at which the individual makes a transition into fatherhood, controlling for a large number of observed characteristics available in the survey. The outcomes of interest are education, census income (which is a measure of the occupational income attained in his chosen career), actual earnings, and hours worked.[19] Special attention is given to disentangling the extent to which teen fatherhood inflicts scars on a young man that hurt his economic prospects from the extent to which men who have poor long-run prospects in any case become teen fathers. The question, in other words, is which way the causation runs. The issue is especially critical in view of our theoretical expectation that the costs of teenage fatherhood will be lower for males with lower potential.[20]

We assume that, in general, most men do not make "mistakes." They choose to marry and to become fathers largely in terms of what is in their best interests. This is of course conditional on their abilities to find a mate in the marriage market, on their returns from investments in education and postschool training, and on the constraints that marriage and fatherhood may impose on their capacity to make human capital investments. On this assumption, the statistical relationship between the age of first fatherhood and the age 27 outcomes can be depicted in a series of figures.[21] Predicted values are plotted in the left-hand panels of figures 4.7–4.10 labeled All Male Respondents. We generally see a positive relationship between the age at first fatherhood and each of the four outcome variables. This pattern reflects the age-specific means for several broad groups of age-at-fatherhood categories.

These figures cannot answer the counterfactual question posed earlier: "What effect would assuming the responsibilities of fatherhood at age x have on a young man's long-run well-being, relative to delaying fatherhood to age x^*, where x^* is the optimal age at first fatherhood?" The reason is that, since these regressions approximate the relationship between economic well-being and x^*, the slope of the relationship may only reflect the correlation between a man's potential returns from human capital and x^*. The positive slopes of the line marked "All Male Respondents" in figure 4.7, for example, may show only that men with high potential have an incentive to delay fatherhood.

Figure 4.7   EDUCATIONAL ATTAINMENT AT AGE 27, BY FIRST FATHERHOOD

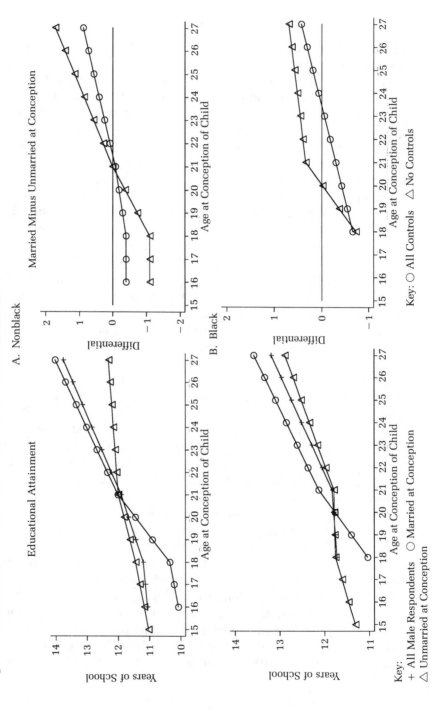

A. Nonblack

Educational Attainment

Married Minus Unmarried at Conception

B. Black

Key: ○ All Controls   △ No Controls

Key:
+ All Male Respondents   ○ Married at Conception
△ Unmarried at Conception

Figure 4.8 OCCUPATIONAL STATUS AS MEASURED BY CENSUS EARNINGS AT AGE 27, BY FIRST FATHERHOOD

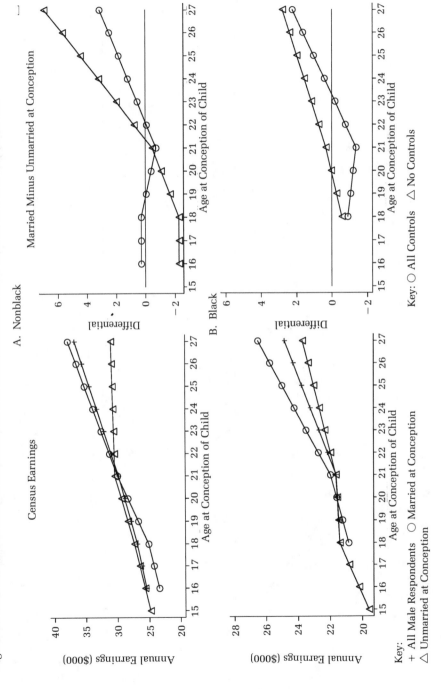

Key:
+ All Male Respondents   ○ Married at Conception
△ Unmarried at Conception

Key: ○ All Controls   △ No Controls

Figure 4.9 ACTUAL EARNINGS AT AGE 27, BY FIRST FATHERHOOD

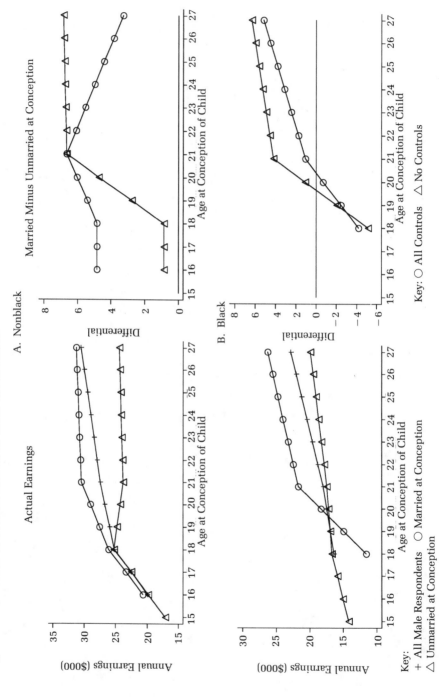

Key:
+ All Male Respondents   ○ Married at Conception
△ Unmarried at Conception

Key: ○ All Controls   △ No Controls

Figure 4.10 ANNUAL HOURS WORKED AT AGE 27, BY FIRST FATHERHOOD

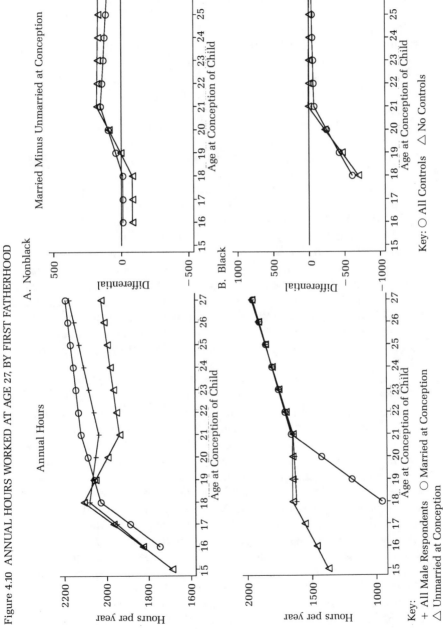

A. Nonblack

Annual Hours

Married Minus Unmarried at Conception

B. Black

Key: ○ All Controls △ No Controls

Key:
+ All Male Respondents ○ Married at Conception
△ Unmarried at Conception

If so, controlling for variables that influence this age (such as ability) should reduce the strength of the relationship between outcomes at age 27 and age at first conception. We examine this possibility by controlling for the person's age-standardized AFQT score and family background measures listed in table 4.1.[22] As expected, the controls flatten the age profiles described above—a result that holds true for each of the outcomes considered and for each racial group. Consider, for example, the regression results for education at age 27. For a typical nonblack male, delaying fatherhood from age 17 to age 21 would, without controls, result in a .8 year increase in years of schooling. With controls this gap is cut in more than half, dropping to about .3 years. For blacks, a comparable delay in fatherhood is estimated to be .2 years without controls and is virtually eliminated when controls are added.

If a young man fathers a child but is able to escape responsibility for support of that child, theory and common sense both suggest that he will be able to carry out his optimal human capital investment program just as he would if he had not become a father. Conversely, if society (or his own conscience) forces the young man to assume responsibility, either by marrying the mother or by providing child support payments to her, his optimal program will be interrupted, and he will incur the cost of lower attainment. We investigate these issues by adding controls for whether the man was married at the time of the conception.[23] The analysis allows for an interaction between the male's age and marital status at conception in order to capture whether the consequences of assuming responsibility are greater at younger ages (e.g., dropping out of school) than at older ages.

The effects of marital status at the time of first conception are illustrated in the left-hand panels of figures 4.7–4.10 and the differences between fathers who were and were not married at the time of conception are given by the line labeled No Controls in the right-hand panels. For education we see that unmarried men who became fathers before age 18 have substantially more education at age 27 than those who are married at the time they became fathers (figure 4.7). At later ages, however, education is not at all sensitive to marital status, as seen by the convergence of the plots for married and unmarried men. This evidence is consistent with the hypothesis that young fathers who conceive a child outside of marriage escape a rather substantial penalty for a forced marriage. Results for the other outcome variables are less clear-cut but basically consistent with this interpretation. On the census earnings measure, the same pattern occurs as for education but it is less pronounced. For actual earnings at age 27, men who were married at the time their first child was conceived always earn more than men who were not married at the same age. In part, this may be due to the greater number of hours worked at age 27 of men who were married before age 18. But few men fall into this category.

One could object to the above interpretation on the grounds that a man's decision to marry is not independent of his own characteristics and depends, rather, on the magnitude of the loss the man would incur if he were forced to bear responsibility for the child. Thus, as discussed above, the optimal age of first fatherhood for the men who choose to marry and father children at an early age may be lower than for those who father children early and fail to marry. If this is true, the results described above may in fact overstate the magnitude of the penalty for a marriage at time of the conception.

We gauge the likely severity of this problem by using the same set of control variables described above (i.e., AFQT and background variables).[24] The difference in predicted attainment by marital status of fathers of a given age, holding these controls constant, is given by the curves marked All Controls in the right-hand panels of figures 4.7–4.10. In general, we see that perhaps half the estimated effect of early fatherhood on education and census earnings remains after these controls are entered. The actual earnings at age 27 of men who were married when their first child was conceived are still substantially larger than earnings of men who were not married. Indeed, the pattern becomes less irregular when the controls are imposed. This is partly explained by higher hours worked by married fathers. A more complete explanation might be the existence of a "marriage premium," although the fact that the effect of marriage is larger on actual hours at age 27 than on census earnings suggests that the higher earnings of married men may simply reflect greater effort.

To assess the effect of being married at the time of the pregnancy and the impact of the controls used, we examine whether the outcomes for the married and the unmarried groups are statistically different at ages 18, 21, and 27.[25] Outcomes reported in table 4.4 can be used to judge whether the predicted plots in figures 4.7–4.10 are significantly different.[26] For nonblacks and without controls, the effect of marital status is occasionally significant for each outcome at some ages. Adding the controls serves to dampen the significance of the effect. For blacks, marital status appears to be generally insignificant.

COSTS TO THE CHILD AND SOCIETY

The most fundamental problem in calculating the cost of teenage childbearing to the youth and to society is finding the fathers of the

Table 4.4 SIGNIFICANCE OF MARITAL STATUS AT VARIOUS AGES OF
FIRST CONCEPTION

	Age 18	Age 21	Age 27
Nonblack			
Education at age 27			
No controls	**	n.s.	***
Controls	n.s.	n.s.	***
Census earnings at age 27			
No controls	n.s.	n.s.	***
Controls	n.s.	n.s.	**
Actual earnings at age 27			
No controls	n.s.	***	**
Controls	n.s.	***	n.s.
Annual hours at age 27			
No controls	n.s.	**	n.s.
Controls	n.s.	n.s.	n.s.
Black			
Education at age 27			
No controls		n.s.	n.s.
Controls		n.s.	n.s.
Census earnings at age 27			
No controls		n.s.	n.s.
Controls		n.s.	n.s.
Actual earnings at age 27			
No controls		n.s.	**
Controls		n.s.	*
Annual hours at age 27			
No controls		n.s.	n.s.
Controls		n.s.	n.s.

Source: National Longitudinal Survey of Youth.
Note: Full regression results available from the authors.
   * denotes significance at the 10% level.
  ** denotes significance at the 5% level.
*** denotes significance at the 1% level.
n.s. = nonsignificant.

children born to teenage mothers. Data bases containing information
on fathers provide little information on the mother if the father and
mother do not live together (or later split up). Similarly, data bases on
teen motherhood with female respondents generally will have no information about the potential resources of the father if the mother and
father do not live together. Using data on the mothers and fathers
available on the National Maternal and Infant Health Survey (NMIHS)
we develop a "statistical matching" procedure. This enables us to
estimate components of the costs of teenage parenthood for highly

policy-relevant cases in which the mother and father never live with one another or split up some time following the birth of their child.

As an example of this procedure, consider a single mother who bears a child and never lives with the father. Although we do not know the father's age, education, or income, we may use information from the NMIHS to calculate a set of probabilities that the father was of a given age and educational attainment.[27] From the NLSY, we predict the expected earnings and number of children for fathers in each age and education class in each year of the child's life. We also estimate the number of children a man may have, since many child support formulas are based on the number of dependents. Multiplying these estimates by the associated probability that the father was in a given class yields an estimate of the expected earnings potential of the child's father. Application of the relevant child support formula to each of these earnings projections yields an estimate of the expected child support payments that would be forthcoming under an ideal system of paternity establishment and child support enforcement.[28]

Policy Considerations

Implementation of the Family Support Act of 1988 has strong and interesting policy implications for the costs of teenage fatherhood and their distribution between the father, the mother and child, and the rest of society. Specifically, the act mandates that each state develop a child support formula to determine the minimum support a father must pay as a function of his own income and, in some states, the income of the custodial mother. These formulas apply to fathers of children born out of wedlock as well as to divorced fathers. In addition, the act emphasizes the importance of establishing paternity for all children, regardless of the marital status of the parents at the time of the child's birth and provides extensive (and potentially expensive) enforcement machinery to ensure that the father pays child support until the child reaches age 18. Beginning in 1994, the enforcement provisions mandate wage withholding for all child support orders.

As a concrete example of the implication of the new laws if perfectly enforced, consider a high school senior living in the state of Wisconsin who becomes an unwed father. If the state establishes his legal paternity and applies the Wisconsin child support formula to him, he will be required to pay 17 percent of his income to the mother as child support. As long as he remains in school and has zero income, the boy owes nothing. During this period, if the mother has no family or personal resources to draw upon, the state will support the child by giving the mother AFDC transfers. Since fatherhood does not require the youth to come up with immediate cash, he will be able to continue on his optimal career path just as if paternity was never established. When he completes his education and begins earning income, however, he must begin paying child support.

We are now in a position to assess both the social and private costs of teenage fatherhood under the Wisconsin law, assuming a 10 percent interest rate. If the youth dropped out of school to earn cash when he became a father and earned $10,000 per year for the rest of his life, he would pay child support of $1,700 per year for the next 18 years. Wisconsin taxpayers, in turn, would pay $1,700 per year less in AFDC than they would if the father did not pay child support. But if the youth remained in school one more year and graduated, he could earn, say, $12,000 a year for the rest of his life—a marginal rate of return to school completion of 20 percent.[29] In this case, upon graduation, Wisconsin law would require him to pay $2,040 per year for the next 17 years. Thus, the state would pay $1,700 more in the first year of the child's life and $340 (= $2,040 − $1,700) less in the next 17 years than if the father had dropped out. The child support formula in combination with the AFDC program implicitly gives the state an "equity position" in the youth's human capital that provides the state with a rate of return approximately equal to the marginal rate of return on investment in the youth's human capital. If this rate of return exceeds the rate of interest faced by the state, the taxpayers will benefit by this policy, as will the youth. The next section describes the data and procedures used to build the statistical match of teen mothers and the fathers of the children involved. Readers interested in the findings more than the procedures used for the analysis may skip the next section without loss of continuity.

Building a Statistical Match

The data used to provide the matching probabilities come from the NMIHS. This survey was administered to a sample of 9,953 women who experienced a birth in 1988 and provides additional information to the data provided in basic vital statistics records. In general, what is needed for the analysis are data on the characteristics of both the mother and father, regardless of their marital status and living arrangement. Basic *Vital Statistics* data are not sufficient for our purpose because they underreport male characteristics. The NMIHS provides a chance to fill in data missing from the original birth certificate.

We first use the NMIHS to examine the age distribution of the partners of mothers. As mentioned above, many of the partners of teen mothers are not teenagers themselves (table 4.5). For example, 3.4 percent of nonblack women who have a child when they are 16 years of age or less have a partner in the same age category. Many of these very young mothers, almost 40 percent, have a partner between the ages of 17 and 19, 31 percent between the ages of 20 and 21, and 26 percent in the age 22 and over group. The data suggest a wider age distribution for nonblack women as evidenced by a larger fraction of partners in the highest age category. Very few women of either racial group have children with younger men.

For the statistical matching procedure, we break down the mother and father characteristics further. For women of a particular race and marital status that give birth at a given age, we calculate the probability that their partner will be in a particular age and education class.[30] These probabilities allow us to know the age, education, race, and marital status of the men with whom women, including teenage women, are having children. To calculate the potential child support payments that these men may be able to provide, we need information on both the income and the additional number of children the men will have over the life of the index child. For this information, we return to the NLSY. The primary advantage of the NLSY is that we are able to use the actual earnings of men who have had a child, and this incorporates any effects that childbearing may have on the income of men.

For the purpose of the child support calculation, we assume that the man is responsible for the first 18 years of the child's life. The

Table 4.5 AGE DISTRIBUTION OF FATHERS BY AGE OF MOTHER

| | Mother's Age | | | |
Father's Age	≤16	17–19	20–21	≥22
Nonblack				
≤16	0.034	0.000	0.000	0.000
17–19	0.392	0.177	0.038	0.000
20–21	0.312	0.248	0.164	0.000
≥22	0.262	0.575	0.797	1.000
Black				
≤16	0.069	0.016	0.000	0.000
17–19	0.503	0.285	0.045	0.003
20–21	0.244	0.281	0.180	0.026
≥22	0.184	0.419	0.775	0.971

Source: National Longitudinal Survey of Youth.

NLSY, however, is only a 14-year panel and cannot cover all years in which support would be necessary. This shortfall is true for both income and the number of children born to the men. We circumvent this problem by estimating a series of predicting equations for both variables for all 18 years of the child's life.[31] The coefficients on which the income and number of children predictions are based are presented in appendix tables 4B.1 and 4B.2, respectively.

Calculated separately by race, the predicted income for each child year is shown in appendix figure 4B.1 for nonblacks and in 4B.2 for blacks. Each figure presents a matrix of graphs by the age at which the man fathered his first child, which varies across columns, and by his educational attainment when he became a father, which varies across rows. These figures show that the earnings of young, poorly educated fathers are extremely low at the time the child is born, but those at the median or above will experience considerable earnings growth during the next 18 years. The predicted earnings of men in the bottom quartile of the earnings distribution hover near zero for all men with less than a high school education, no matter how old they were when they became a father.[32]

In addition to his earnings, a noncustodial father's child support obligation for his first child, as determined by the child support formula in his state of residence, generally depends on the number of other children he has fathered. In figure 4B.3, we present the predicted number of additional children that a man will father as his first child ages. Within each graph, we present separate predictions for nonblack and black males. The most striking feature of these graphs is the strong negative relationship between a man's age at first fatherhood and the predicted number of children he will subsequently father. For example, a young man of either racial group who is 16 or younger when he fathers his first child is, on average, predicted to have more than one additional child by the time his first child reaches age 6 and almost two additional children before his first child reaches age 18. In contrast, a high school dropout in either racial group who delays entry into fatherhood until he is older than 21 is predicted, on average, to have less than 0.5 additional children by the time his first child reaches age 6. By the time the child is age 18, black men will have added about another 0.5 children and nonblacks only about 0.25 children. Although age at first fatherhood has a much stronger effect than educational attainment, the racial differential showing higher fertility for black than white males among the less well educated is reversed among groups with some college or more.

The next step is to calculate how much of the father's income will be devoted to child support. This will clearly vary by both personal preferences and state statutes. As a benchmark, we use the relatively straightforward child support formula mandated in the state of Wisconsin. As described above, this standard requires that a father pay 17 percent of his income as child support for his first child. If the man has an additional child the obligation to the first child drops to 12.5 percent of his income. With three children this obligation is 9.7 percent, and with four children it becomes 7.75 percent.[33] The outcome of this exercise is presented graphically in figure 4B.4 by age of first fatherhood and educational attainment for the median father, based on predicted median earnings and predicted number of children as described above. As shown, the amount a man would be obligated to pay in child support for his first child will grow as the child ages, largely because of growth in the man's earnings capacity. The graphs also show that nonblack fathers will typically owe more support for their first child than do black fathers. For less well educated men, these racial differences in child support obligations largely reflect racial differences in fertility. For better-educated men, the reduction in obligation to their first child caused by the higher fertility of nonblack men is more than offset by the increase in the obligation caused by their higher predicted earnings.

The final component of the calculation is to estimate the amount of child support owed by a man who fathers a child by a woman of a given age. As described above, since we do not know the characteristics of the fathers of the children born out of wedlock, we must use a statistical matching procedure to make our estimates. Thus, we multiply the predicted child support obligations of men of each age, race, education, and marital status by the probability that a man of each type fathered a child by a woman of a given age, and we sum these products across all types of men.

Potential Child Support

The findings from our child support analysis are presented in table 4.6. This table first shows, for women who begin childbearing at different ages, the discounted present value of the income of the predicted partner over the first 18 years of the child's life. All the calculations in this table are repeated for male earnings evaluated at the 25th, 50th, and 75th percentiles and are done separately by marital status and race. For a single nonblack woman who has a child at 16

Table 4.6 ESTIMATED PRESENT VALUE OF FATHER'S TOTAL EARNINGS AND CHILD SUPPORT OVER 18 YEARS, BY AGE OF THE WOMAN

A. Single at Time of Birth	Age of the Woman						
	≤15	16	17	18	19	20–21	≥22
Nonblack							
25th percentile							
Estimated income		$81,624	$86,095	$93,268	$95,876	$100,885	$106,700
Child support		10,773	11,417	12,406	12,798	13,479	14,193
Monthly child support		77	81	88	91	96	101
Median							
Estimated income		195,659	199,990	207,209	209,997	215,308	221,943
Child support		25,942	26,652	27,703	28,190	28,956	29,876
Monthly child support		185	190	197	201	206	213
75th percentile							
Estimated income		294,231	299,807	308,913	312,831	320,375	332,033
Child support		39,301	40,238	41,574	42,261	43,339	44,920
Monthly child support		280	287	296	301	309	320
Black							
25th percentile							
Estimated income	$ 58,148	65,492	69,294	72,287	75,079	83,965	76,058
Child support	7,868	8,952	9,578	10,102	10,603	12,054	10,989
Monthly child support	56	64	68	72	76	86	78
Median							
Estimated income	147,164	156,078	162,099	166,987	171,285	182,721	179,907
Child support	19,887	21,362	22,440	23,358	24,186	26,244	26,075
Monthly child support	142	152	160	167	172	187	186
75th percentile							
Estimated income	247,979	257,001	264,861	271,279	276,405	289,217	288,545
Child support	33,557	35,196	36,680	37,946	39,008	41,513	41,827
Monthly child support	239	251	261	271	278	296	298

Note: All values are in 1994 dollars.

Table 4.6 ESTIMATED PRESENT VALUE OF FATHER'S TOTAL EARNINGS AND CHILD SUPPORT OVER 18 YEARS, BY AGE OF THE WOMAN (continued)

B. Married at Time of Birth	Age of the Woman						
	≤15	16	17	18	19	20–21	≥22
Nonblack							
25th percentile							
Estimated income		$168,033	$178,951	$189,491	$189,222	$191,331	$171,532
Child support		22,618	23,897	25,167	25,153	25,423	23,086
Monthly child support		161	170	179	179	181	165
Median							
Estimated income		265,340	275,587	286,248	286,300	288,840	269,443
Child support		35,816	36,899	38,114	38,160	38,500	36,402
Monthly child support		255	263	272	272	274	260
75th percentile							
Estimated income		358,396	370,788	384,110	384,362	388,039	365,729
Child support		48,547	49,796	51,271	51,359	51,843	49,546
Monthly child support		346	355	366	366	370	353
Black							
25th percentile							
Estimated income	$140,416	128,798	163,131	152,569	167,535	167,038	140,843
Child support	20,044	17,846	23,639	21,951	24,393	24,375	20,786
Monthly child support	143	127	169	156	174	174	148
Median							
Estimated income	229,578	211,420	252,949	242,633	257,770	257,885	239,155
Child support	32,475	28,993	36,483	34,700	37,373	37,471	35,040
Monthly child support	232	207	260	247	266	267	250
75th percentile							
Estimated income	315,180	290,967	336,931	327,819	341,549	341,773	326,713
Child support	44,642	39,998	48,655	46,949	49,584	49,729	47,986
Monthly child support	318	285	347	335	353	355	342

Source: National Longitudinal Survey of Youth.
Note: All values are in 1994 dollars.

years of age, for example, the estimates of the discounted present value of her partner's income over 18 years range from a low of $81,624 for a partner at the 25th percentile to a high of $294,231 for a partner at the 75th percentile. Let us look in detail at the possibilities for a single nonblack woman who has a child at 17 years of age by a man at the median (50th percentile). Her partner's predicted income over 18 years is $199,990. As a result of her delaying the birth one year, her partner's income increases by 2.2 percent. If the woman delays child-bearing until after 22 years of age, that income increases by 13 percent, to $221,943. Consistent with the evidence presented earlier, for each age of the mother, the predicted partner's income is higher for non-black than for black and for married than for single women.

The potential child support payment the partner could provide under the Wisconsin standards for the predicted number of children (see previous section) appears directly below the predicted income in table 4.6. A 16-year-old single nonblack woman, for example, can look forward to $25,942 in child support. In comparison, her black counterpart would be owed $21,362. If the birth is delayed by a year, the predicted discounted present value of support payments increases by approximately 2.7 percent for a nonblack woman and by 5.0 percent for a black woman. In general, the value of the support always increases with the age of the woman and is, again, higher for nonblack than black and for married than single women.[34]

We next consider the impact of early childbearing on society as a whole. Would the predicted child support be enough to offset public expenditures on behalf of the child? Expressing the child support payment as a monthly flow is convenient for this purpose. This is shown immediately below the child support totals.[35] The child support potentially available to the single nonblack women who has a child at age 16 is equivalent to a monthly payment of $185. Similarly, the $21,362 child support obligation for a single, black 16-year-old is equivalent to a monthly payment of $152. The monthly payment, of course, varies with maternal characteristics in the same way as the lump-sum payment. How do these estimates compare with the government transfers received by a comparable woman? As an illustration, consider a woman with one child in the state of Wisconsin. In 1994, the maximum AFDC benefit available in this state to a woman with one child was $440 per month. The predicted child support obligation of the partner of a hypothetical single 16-year-old mother represents 42 percent or 35 percent of the welfare benefit value, respectively, for a nonblack or black woman. By law, additional payments by the father can only increase the mother's income by $50 per month, with the remaining payments going to reduce AFDC payments received by the mother. In this case, if child support laws were perfectly enforced, the taxpayers' burden would decrease from $440 per month to $305 per month, a 30 percent reduction. Wisconsin has relatively generous welfare benefits; in other states, the offset of public versus private expenditure might be even greater.

In reality, of course, perfect enforcement of the child support law is not possible. Enforcement is costly, and the revenue yields will never be as high as the perfect-enforcement results shown here. Consideration of the net effect on taxpayers' obligations is clearly one element in determining the degree to which child support laws should be enforced. However, other factors should also be considered in developing child enforcement policies. One concerns the degree to which society should force fathers to acknowledge paternity and bear economic responsibility for their children. On the negative side, strict enforcement may reduce the development of a young man's economic potential, although (as argued earlier) the combination of AFDC and a child support obligation proportional to the father's income may be less disruptive to his investment in human capital than a forced marriage. On the positive side, strict child support enforcement may change the perceptions of young men and young women concerning the costs of becoming parents and the benefits of doing so within marriage.[36]

CONCLUSIONS

Our research addresses the costs and consequences associated with young men entering fatherhood either when the men are teenagers or when their partners are teenagers. Specifically, we examine the relationship between the age at which a man first becomes a father and his subsequent education, occupational status, earnings, and work effort. In general, we find early entry into fatherhood associated with lower levels of schooling, lower actual and occupational income, and fewer hours worked in the labor market. The impact of early fatherhood is dampened once the analysis includes control variables thought to be associated with these outcomes. One plausible explanation is that the impact of early childbearing is tied to the issue of whether the man takes responsibility for the child. As with Ellwood's (1982) study of early unemployment, we find little evidence of a lasting scar from this behavior.

We also address the issue of whether early childbearing implies lower levels of support for the female partner and the child. In terms of potential support for the child, the evidence indicates that there are gains to delayed childbearing. For a society as a whole, the support provided by men could amount to 40–50 percent of current AFDC benefits. While the partners of the women who become teen mothers may have little to provide in their early years, the evidence does suggest growth in their income and potential child support payments throughout the life of the child. This indicates that more rigorous paternity establishment and child support enforcement could provide gains to the child as well as to society.

NOTES

Support for this research was provided by the Robin Hood Foundation. We wish to acknowledge comments and suggestions by Frank Furstenberg, V. Joseph Hotz, Arlene Leibowitz, Robert Moffitt, Susan Philliber, and Seth Sanders. We also want to thank Charles Mullin and, especially, Honggao Cao for very able research assistance.

1. Evidence from birth certificate data suggests that most births to teenage mothers were with male partners who were already past the teen years. Among nonblacks, for example, 57.4 percent of the births to young teenage women (age 16 or less) in 1988 were fathered by men 20 years of age and over; the corresponding number for blacks is 42.8 percent. Similarly, for older teenage mothers (ages 17–19) the proportion of fathers who were age 20 or more is 82.3 percent for nonblacks and 70.0 percent for blacks (see table 4.5).

2. Though not considered in this chapter, the mothers of the children are also clearly affected by this behavior. In particular, lack of adequate support by an absent father or a lower level of support from a partner who experiences a disrupted career path requires that the woman make choices that are equally disruptive to her life.

3. A more complete analysis would consider the youth's (and mate's) utility functions (e.g., direct preferences for sexual activity, the pleasures of living with the partner, the joys of having a child, the costs of marital search) that would cause the optimal age to be somewhat earlier or later than this point. In particular, even if no marriage premium exists, so that delay of fatherhood and other family responsibilities always increases the man's lifetime earnings (i.e., curves such as BB are always positively sloped), at some point it is reasonable to assume that the marginal monetary benefits of delay become smaller than the marginal nonmonetary disutility of delay, so that the man will wish to begin family life.

4. Ideally, we would like to estimate curves such as AA, BB, and CC, but sorting associated with optimizing behavior by youths induces a positive correlation between economic potential and age at first fatherhood that confounds movements along a given curve with movements across curves.

5. Alternative statistical approaches using instrumental variables do not appear promising because, in our opinion, the data set we use does not contain plausible valid instruments with significant predictive power.

6. Although paternity is not legally established in a large number of out-of-wedlock births to AFDC-eligible mothers (see Nichols-Casebolt and Garfinkel 1991), studies suggest that many fathers voluntarily admit paternity when contacted by child support authorities (Meyer 1992). The issue of the father not knowing of the presence of the child is a topic that must be addressed in assessing the validity of the data used in our study.

7. The survey actually contains three distinct samples that can be used separately or combined. First, there is a cross-sectional sample that is representative of all young men and women in the relevant age category. Second, there is a supplemental sample that includes an oversample of youths identified to be Hispanic, black, or economically disadvantaged non-Hispanic nonblacks. Finally, there is a sample that consists of individuals who, as of September 30, 1978, were serving in the military. As will be discussed below, our study only uses the cross-sectional sample.

8. An alternative approach to this problem is to use information on the sexual and reproductive behavior of males to help understand the degree to which teenage men place themselves at the risk of fatherhood by engaging in sexual activity. This would include the number of partners they have and their own and/or partner's use of contraception. See Ku, Sonenstein, and Pleck (1993) for a study of this type.

9. Even this relatively straightforward comparison can be complicated due to an underreporting of father's characteristics on the *Vital Statistics* data. This is particularly a problem for births to young, unmarried couples.

10. To reduce the amount of nonreporting due to item nonresponse and missed surveys in the construction of the age 27 outcomes, we used an algorithm that also considered outcomes around age 27. We first used the outcomes at age 27. If that was missing, we took values first from age 26 if that was available, then age 28. We did not drift farther than one year in either direction to fill the outcome measures.

11. The AFQT was administered to approximately 93 percent of the male respondents of the NLSY in 1980. The raw AFQT score was constructed using the sum of Armed Services Vocational Aptitude Battery (ASVAB) Sections 2–5. To construct a normalized measure, we used the residual from a weighted regression of the raw score on cohort dummy variables. The purpose of this regression was to control for the different ages at which the test had been administered. We then normalized the residual by the weighted standard deviation for each cohort.

12. The majority of the military sample was dropped after the 1984 wave, and the poor white sample was completely discontinued after the 1990 survey. The respondents used in the analysis, therefore, come solely from the cross-sectional sample. This sample, as noted above, is representative of all young men and women.

13. Due to item nonresponse, additional respondents will be dropped in the analysis presented below. The exact number of observations used in each analysis is given in each model presented below. It should also be noted that the 1979 sample weight was used in the regression analysis presented below.

14. The data for males permit only the analysis of pregnancies that lead to a live birth. This implies that a man may have impregnated a woman prior to this point but it did not result in a live birth. The pregnancy date is calculated as nine months before the birth date.

15. The results in figures 4.2 and 4.3 are based on Kaplan-Meier estimates of waiting time to the event.

16. This issue has also been considered by Lerman (1993) and Pirog-Good (1993).

17. We group nonblacks together because preliminary results (not shown) suggested substantial differences between blacks and nonblacks but not between Hispanics and

whites. Note also that the vertical line at age 27 in figures 4.4–4.6 denotes the point at which the long-run outcomes will be evaluated for use in the regressions below.

18. Census income is not considered in these figures since it is specifically tied to the occupation chosen at age 27. It was felt that earlier occupations are more transitory and would not be as meaningful for this portion of the analysis.

19. As previously defined, census income is the mean income associated with the occupation chosen at age 27 based on the 1990 U.S. Census. It is designed to capture long-run differences in economic status.

20. Willis (1994) also shows that the rate of out of wedlock fatherhood will tend to depend on the overall ratio of females to males in the marriage market and on the capacity of females to rear children without the contributions of the father, either through their own labor or with welfare payments. Willis shows that under conditions in which females outnumber males and are capable of economic independence, a marriage market equilibrium exists in which males and females in the lower part of the income distribution will tend to have children out of wedlock and those in the upper part of the income distribution will tend to marry. The lower the absolute income of males, the higher will be the fraction of men who become out of wedlock fathers.

21. Specifically, we describe this relationship by estimating regression equations of the form $y = a + b_1 age_1 + b_2 age_2 + b_3 age_3$ where the age variables are splines of the male's age at conception of his first child with nodes at ages 18 and 21. For the interested reader, regression results of this specification for each of the four outcome variables being considered are presented in Model 1 of appendix tables 4A.1–4A.4. Each model presented in this section has been estimated separately for black and nonblack respondents and has been weighted using the 1979 sample weights. The means and standard deviations of the variables used in the regressions are available from the authors upon request.

22. Selected results for this regression are presented in Model 3 of appendix tables 4A.1–4A.4. The impact of these controls can be seen by examining across Models 1 and 3 in the appendix tables.

23. We estimated the following regression model:

$$y = a + b_1 age_1 + b_2 age_2 + b_3 age_3 + c_0 m + c_1 age_1 m + c_2 age_2 m + c_3 age_3 m$$

where m is a dummy variable equal to one if the individual was married at the time of the conception of his first child and zero otherwise. The "c" coefficients measure the difference in the level and age profile of men who are married or unmarried. These results can be found in Model 2 of tables 4A.1–4A.4.

24. This specification is labeled as Model 4 in tables 4A.1–4A.4.

25. There were no black respondents married at the time of the pregnancy in the less than 18 years of age category.

26. Specifically, F-tests were conducted on the joint significance of the marriage and age interactions in Models 2 and 4 in tables A.1–A.4.

27. The characteristics on which the match is made are limited by the data available on the NMIHS.

28. For an example of other research in this area, see Garfinkel and Oellerich (1989).

29. For simplicity, assume that the optimal level of education for this youth is high school graduation. Remember that the rate of return to high school graduation varies across individuals, as illustrated by the different curves in figure 4.1.

30. In the construction of matching probabilities for both the mother and father, we use four age categories ($\leq$ 16 years, 17–18 years, 19–21 years, and $\geq$ 22 years), four education categories ($<$ high school, high school graduate, some college, and college graduate

and beyond), two race categories (black and nonblack), and two marital status categories (married and not married).

31. The income equations are based on quantile regressions for the 25th, 50th, and 75th percentiles. The predicted number of children is based on an ordered probit specification.

32. A close examination of figure 4B.2 reveals one cell in which these general results do not necessarily hold. The quantile earnings projections cross for black men who have a college degree and who do not have their first child until age 22 or older. This logically inconsistent crossing is the result of an extrapolation beyond the NLSY sample period and having relatively few men in that cell.

33. We assume that the number of children born to men does not exceed four. Also, these percentage obligations assume that the man fathers all subsequent children with the same mother. Alternatively, if he fathers a second child by a different woman, his obligation to the first child would be 17 percent of his income, net of his obligation to his second child, yielding an obligation of 14.1 percent [.17 × (1 − .17)] rather than 12.5 percent, and so on for additional births by different women. Our data do not permit us to determine whether a given man's children are by the same or different mothers. We choose to make our calculations of potential obligations using the lower percentage obligations listed in the text. In this sense, our estimates of a man's potential child support payments are slightly conservative.

34. The support payment is not directly proportional to the predicted income, due to the potential presence of future children.

35. The flow value, p, is determined with the following formula:

$$p = \frac{[(rV) \div 12]}{[1 - (1 \div (1 + r)^{18})]}$$

where r denotes the interest rate (.05) and V denotes the discounted present value of child support payments.

36. Willis (1994) proposes a theoretical model in which child support enforcement would reduce the incidence of out of wedlock childbearing, but little empirical work has been done on this problem. In one of the few empirical papers dealing with this issue, Sonenstein, Pleck, and Ku (1994) find little evidence of an effect of the strength of child support enforcement on a young male's pregnancy risk behavior (i.e., unprotected sex), but it does appear to affect their perception of the cost of the behavior.

REFERENCES

Daniel, K. E. 1993. "Does Marriage Make Workers More Productive?" Ph.D. dissertation, University of Chicago.

Ellwood, D. T. 1982. "Teenage Unemployment: Permanent Scars or Temporary Blemishes?" In *The Youth Labor Market Problem: Its Nature, Causes, and Consequences*, eds. R. B. Freeman and D. A. Wise. Chicago: University of Chicago Press.

Garfinkel, I., and D. Oellerich. 1989. "Noncustodial Fathers' Ability to Pay Child Support." *Demography* 26(2): 219–33.

Huber, P. J. 1967. "The Behavior of Maximum Likelihood Estimates under Nonstandard Conditions." *Proceedings of the Fifth Berkeley Symposium on Mathematical Statistics and Probability* 1: 221–33.

Korenman, S., and D. Neumark. 1991. "Does Marriage Really Make Men More Productive?" *Journal of Human Resources* 14(4): 579–94.

Ku, L., F. L. Sonenstein, and J. H. Pleck. 1993. "Factors Influencing First Intercourse for Teenage Men." *Public Health Reports* 108(6): 680–694.

Lerman, R. I. 1993. "Employment Patterns of Unwed Fathers and Public Policy." In *Young Unwed Fathers: Changing Roles and Emerging Policies*, eds. R. I. Lerman and T. J. Ooms. Philadelphia: Temple University Press.

Meyer, D. R. 1992. "Paternity and Public Policy." *Focus* 14(2): 1–11.

Mott, F. L. 1983. "Fertility-Related Data in the 1982 National Longitudinal Surveys of Youth: An Evaluation of Data Quality and Some Preliminary Analytical Results." Columbus: Center for Human Resource Research, Ohio State University.

————. 1985. "Evaluation of Fertility Data and Preliminary Analytic Results from the 1983 (5th round) Survey of the National Longitudinal Surveys of Work Experience of Youth." Columbus: Center for Human Resource Research, Ohio State University.

Nichols-Casebolt, A., and I. Garfinkel. 1991. "Trends in Paternity Adjudications and Child Support Awards." *Social Science Quarterly* 72: 83–97.

Pirog-Good, M. A. 1993. "The Education and Labor Market Outcomes of Adolescent Fathers." Wisconsin: Institute for Research on Poverty Discussion Paper 1014-93. August.

Sonenstein, Freya L., Joseph Pleck, and Leighton Ku. 1994. "Child Support Obligations and Young Men's Contraceptive Behavior: What Do Young Men Know? Does It Matter?" Paper presented at the annual meeting of the Population Association of America, Miami, May 7.

Weiss, Y., and R. J. Willis. 1985. "Children as Collective Goods and Divorce Settlements." *Journal of Labor Economics* 3(3): 268–292.

————. 1993. "Transfers among Divorced Couples: Evidence and Interpretation." *Journal of Labor Economics* 11(4): 629–79.

Willis, R. J. 1994. "A Theory of Out-of-Wedlock Childbearing." Unpublished paper.

APPENDIX 4A: AGE 27 OUTCOME REGRESSIONS

Table 4A.1 EDUCATION AT AGE 27: SELECTED REGRESSION RESULTS

A. Nonblack	Model 1	Model 2	Model 3	Model 4
Marital status				
Married at first pregnancy		− 18.595		− 16.930
		(− 2.69)		(− 2.366)
Age at first pregnancy (spline)				
Age < 18	0.065	0.039	− 0.023	− 0.096
	(0.33)	(0.19)	(0.17)	(− 0.67)
18 ≤ age < 21	0.237	0.208	0.095	0.123
	(3.53)	(2.41)	(1.73)	(1.72)
Age ≥ 21	0.307	0.048	0.133	− 0.006
	(8.94)	(0.70)	(5.00)	(− 0.13)
No child by age 27	− 0.233	1.481	0.037	0.920
	(− 1.23)	(3.87)	(0.26)	(3.25)
Marriage and age spline interactions				
Married* (age < 18)		0.990		0.936
		(2.51)		(2.32)
Married* (18 ≤ age < 21)		0.250		− 0.006
		(1.65)		(− 0.05)
Married* (age ≥ 21)		0.292		0.167
		(3.71)		(2.76)

B. Black	Model 1	Model 2	Model 3	Model 4
Marital status				
Married at first pregnancy		− 0.725		− 0.660
		(− 0.89)		(− 1.00)
Age at first pregnancy (spline)				
Age < 18	0.132	0.147	0.065	0.072
	(1.40)	(1.54)	(0.79)	(0.87)
18 ≤ age < 21	0.034	0.011	− 0.034	− 0.014
	(0.44)	(0.13)	(− 0.52)	(− 0.20)
Age ≥ 21	0.227	0.181	0.165	0.125
	(4.47)	(2.99)	(3.79)	(2.40)
No child by age 27	− 0.617	− 0.262	− 0.436	− 0.232
	(− 2.19)	(− 0.76)	(− 1.82)	(− 0.81)
Marriage and age spline interactions				
Married* (18 ≤ age < 21)		0.354		0.119
		(1.17)		(0.47)
Married* (age ≥ 21)		0.059		0.122
		(0.53)		(1.28)

Notes: The dependent variable is years of school at age 27. Models 3 and 4 also include a large number of other control variables. These variables are listed in table 4.1. Full estimates are available from the authors upon request. Regressions are based on 2,946 and 1,285 observations for nonblacks and blacks, respectively. Sample weights were used in the estimation and robust standard errors were obtained using Huber's formula; t-statistics in parentheses. See Huber (1967).

Table 4A.2 CENSUS EARNINGS AT AGE 27: SELECTED REGRESSION RESULTS

A. Nonblack	Model 1	Model 2	Model 3	Model 4
Marital status				
Married at first pregnancy		−21559.650		−24031.380
		(−1.00)		(−1.07)
Age at first pregnancy (spline)				
Age < 18	621.897	587.484	394.948	200.092
	(1.45)	(1.27)	(1.03)	(0.49)
18 ≤ age < 21	821.942	896.825	289.275	521.080
	(3.25)	(2.54)	(1.24)	(1.61)
Age ≥ 21	987.456	83.436	441.580	−0.877
	(5.47)	(0.28)	(2.79)	(0.00)
No child by age 27	−1823.529	3989.238	−1119.857	1529.068
	(−1.85)	(2.49)	(−1.29)	(1.18)
Marriage and age spline interactions				
Married* (age < 18)		1112.936		1374.643
		(0.91)		(1.08)
Married* (18 ≤ age < 21)		368.720		−451.617
		(0.68)		(−0.87)
Married* (age ≥ 21)		1042.181		551.720
		(2.85)		(1.77)

B. Black	Model 1	Model 2	Model 3	Model 4
Marital status				
Married at first pregnancy		−477.476		−768.523
		(−0.17)		(−0.37)
Age at first pregnancy (spline)				
Age < 18	503.172	505.852	252.386	243.989
	(1.95)	(1.96)	(0.98)	(0.93)
18 ≤ age < 21	60.187	65.162	−115.802	−18.059
	(0.27)	(0.27)	(−0.53)	(−0.08)
Age ≥ 21	455.765	292.723	265.526	103.258
	(2.93)	(1.54)	(1.96)	(0.63)
No child by age 27	−995.964	124.238	−671.896	188.254
	(−1.05)	(0.11)	(−0.87)	(0.20)
Marriage and age spline interactions				
Married* (18 ≤ age < 21)		258.593		−127.390
		(0.23)		(−0.15)
Married* (age ≥ 21)		343.438		506.381
		(1.01)		(1.71)

Notes: The dependent variable is census income at age 27. Models 3 and 4 also include a large number of other control variables. These variables are listed in table 4.1. Full estimates are available from the authors upon request. Regressions are based on 2,820 and 1,167 observations for nonblacks and blacks, respectively. Sample weights were used in the estimation and robust standard errors were obtained using Huber's formula; t-statistics in parentheses. See Huber (1967). Income is expressed in 1989 dollars. Coefficients can be converted to 1994 dollars by multiplying by 1.189.

Table 4A.3 ACTUAL INCOME AT AGE 27: SELECTED REGRESSION RESULTS

A. Nonblack	Model 1	Model 2	Model 3	Model 4
Marital status				
Married at first pregnancy		19078.640		−6478.391
		(0.41)		(−0.15)
Age at first pregnancy (spline)				
Age < 18	2204.551	2374.723	2088.098	1872.698
	(1.96)	(1.98)	(1.99)	(1.68)
18 ≤ age < 21	646.660	−412.112	−60.724	−890.097
	(1.07)	(−0.51)	(−0.11)	(−1.18)
Age ≥ 21	427.693	87.333	−15.726	98.643
	(1.51)	(0.17)	(−0.06)	(0.20)
No child by age 27	−2741.079	2697.334	−2026.438	425.548
	(−2.14)	(1.05)	(−1.63)	(0.18)
Marriage and age spline interactions				
Married* (age < 18)		−1037.208		595.275
		(−0.38)		(0.23)
Married* (18 ≤ age < 21)		1736.606		442.644
		(1.22)		(0.32)
Married* (age ≥ 21)		20.299		−465.640
		(0.03)		(−0.79)

B. Black	Model 1	Model 2	Model 3	Model 4
Marital status				
Married at first pregnancy		−4315.030		−3525.620
		(−0.87)		(−0.73)
Age at first pregnancy (spline)				
Age < 18	595.223	697.873	291.673	350.993
	(0.80)	(0.94)	(0.42)	(0.50)
18 ≤ age < 21	443.770	210.342	186.966	146.495
	(0.93)	(0.41)	(0.39)	(0.29)
Age ≥ 21	674.211	346.591	438.007	129.531
	(1.99)	(0.83)	(1.32)	(0.31)
No child by age 27	−5026.925	−2268.286	−4513.675	−2346.787
	(−2.89)	(−1.04)	(−2.67)	(−1.09)
Marriage and age spline interactions				
Married* (18 ≤ age < 21)		2625.642		1472.658
		(1.33)		(0.75)
Married* (age ≥ 21)		296.854		577.849
		(0.40)		(0.77)

Notes: The dependent variable is actual income at age 27. Models 3 and 4 also include a large number of other control variables. These variables are listed in table 4.1. Full estimates are available from the authors upon request. Regressions are based on 2,915 and 1,276 observations for nonblacks and blacks, respectively. Sample weights were used in the estimation and robust standard errors were obtained using Huber's formula; t-statistics in parentheses. See Huber (1967). Income is expressed in 1989 dollars. Coefficients can be converted to 1994 dollars by multiplying by 1.189.

Table 4A.4 ANNUAL HOURS WORKED AT AGE 27: SELECTED REGRESSION
RESULTS

A. Nonblack	Model 1	Model 2	Model 3	Model 4
Constant	−233.628	−1066.456	−192.919	−822.123
	(−0.14)	(−0.59)	(−0.12)	(−0.46)
Marital status				
Married at first pregnancy		7010.816		5854.366
		(1.49)		(1.15)
Age at first pregnancy (spline)				
Age < 18	128.620	177.783	123.873	160.317
	(1.33)	(1.72)	(1.30)	(1.57)
18 ≤ age < 21	−14.903	−66.255	−36.151	−75.426
	(−0.42)	(−1.47)	(−1.01)	(−1.66)
Age ≥ 21	23.438	15.569	16.410	17.113
	(1.71)	(0.59)	(1.20)	(0.62)
No child by age 27	−201.627	−44.609	−184.972	−100.119
	(−3.16)	(−0.31)	(−2.91)	(−0.67)
Marriage and age spline interactions				
Married* (age < 18)		−400.712		−331.365
		(−1.51)		(−1.16)
Married* (18 ≤ age < 21)		132.254		91.172
		(1.73)		(1.17)
Married* (age ≥ 21)		−5.337		−12.228
		(−0.17)		(−0.38)

B. Black	Model 1	Model 2	Model 3	Model 4
Marital status				
Married at first pregnancy		−695.468		−605.687
		(−1.59)		(−1.45)
Age at first pregnancy (spline)				
Age < 18	78.265	90.922	57.271	67.588
	(1.22)	(1.41)	(0.90)	(1.06)
18 ≤ age < 21	7.880	−0.129	4.153	2.310
	(0.19)	(0.00)	(0.10)	(0.05)
Age ≥ 21	53.050	52.078	47.200	45.627
	(2.20)	(1.80)	(1.98)	(1.61)
No child by age 27	−380.080	−378.254	−365.606	−374.121
	(−3.05)	(−2.50)	(−3.00)	(−2.57)
Marriage and age spline interactions				
Married* (18 ≤ age < 21)		234.833		178.173
		(1.39)		(1.07)
Married* (age ≥ 21)		−2.806		7.362
		(−0.05)		(0.14)

Notes: The dependent variable is annual hours worked at age 27. Models 3 and 4 also include a large number of other control variables. These variables are listed in table 4.1. Full estimates are available from the authors upon request. Regressions are based on 2,923 and 1,281 observations for nonblacks and blacks, respectively. Sample weights were used in the estimation and robust standard errors were obtained using Huber's formula; t-statistics in parentheses. See Huber (1967).

APPENDIX 4B: COST CALCULATIONS

Table 4B.1 QUANTILE REGRESSIONS ON ACTUAL INCOME

	Percentile		
A. Nonblack	25th	50th	75th
Constant	−958.528	4230.852	9665.610
	(−0.64)	(2.98)	(5.11)
Age at first birth category (≤ 16 omitted)			
17-18 years	1080.903	−1152.605	−1589.325
	(0.81)	(−0.93)	(−0.96)
19-21 years	1764.431	556.763	880.624
	(1.35)	(0.46)	(0.54)
≥ 22 years	4681.169	4422.385	6206.336
	(3.53)	(3.60)	(3.76)
Age of index child (spline)			
Age < 5	479.264	960.576	988.779
	(2.92)	(6.37)	(4.90)
5 ≤ age < 10	346.057	781.254	1133.057
	(2.27)	(5.57)	(6.08)
Age ≥ 10	9.484	888.994	1176.474
	(0.04)	(4.28)	(4.18)
Marital status			
Married at birth	6272.695	7874.055	8879.320
	(8.65)	(11.86)	(10.26)
Married* age of child	−84.764	−433.597	−638.036
	(−0.80)	(−4.43)	(−4.88)
Education category (≤ high school omitted)			
High school	3137.032	2254.538	1938.799
	(4.94)	(3.79)	(2.40)
Some college	5092.462	5872.028	4321.340
	(5.43)	(7.00)	(3.87)
≥ college graduate	8935.014	14158.730	11996.400
	(8.07)	(13.88)	(8.50)
Education and child age interactions			
(High school)* child age	418.523	512.092	606.623
	(4.30)	(5.65)	(4.99)
(Some college)* child age	501.173	437.196	1030.257
	(2.90)	(2.95)	(5.34)
(≥ college graduate)* child age	1547.378	911.014	2197.360
	(6.55)	(4.22)	(7.20)
Pseudo R^2	0.1105	0.1201	0.1224

Notes: The dependent variable is actual annual income. Regressions are based on 11,643 person/year observations. *t*-statistics are in parentheses.

Table 4B.1 QUANTILE REGRESSIONS ON ACTUAL INCOME (*continued*)

	Percentile		
B. Black	25th	50th	75th
Constant	− 365.435	− 121.420	5697.708
	(− 0.62)	(− 0.14)	(4.96)
Age at first birth category (≤ 16 omitted)			
17-18 years	− 3.396	652.634	− 807.230
	(− 0.01)	(0.99)	(− 0.90)
19-21 years	− 597.373	1043.062	1627.410
	(− 1.36)	(1.58)	(1.82)
≥ 22 years	1143.589	3798.522	4237.352
	(2.39)	(5.37)	(4.49)
Age of index child (spline)			
Age < 5	368.830	1060.652	1316.897
	(3.92)	(7.10)	(6.63)
5 ≤ age < 10	− 64.581	810.727	1131.259
	(− 0.81)	(6.62)	(6.77)
Age ≥ 10	10.037	286.614	460.873
	(0.10)	(1.84)	(2.19)
Marital status			
Married at birth	7057.966	5606.883	6522.895
	(15.18)	(7.82)	(6.48)
Married* age of child	− 340.934	− 240.673	− 545.874
	(− 4.69)	(− 2.10)	(− 3.29)
Education category (≤ high school omitted)			
High school	2756.513	6132.514	4512.678
	(6.60)	(9.34)	(4.89)
Some college	2928.226	4933.793	4446.274
	(4.79)	(5.27)	(3.49)
≥ college graduate	11875.290	19103.870	25010.590
	(12.21)	(11.88)	(11.57)
Education and child age interactions			
(High school)* child age	327.425	− 219.328	− 137.702
	(5.51)	(− 2.37)	(− 1.08)
(Some college)* child age	696.040	262.185	224.595
	(7.53)	(1.84)	(1.18)
(≥ college graduate)* child age	962.018	− 382.814	− 1239.564
	(5.05)	(− 1.19)	(− 3.14)
Pseudo R^2	0.1176	0.1247	0.1132

Notes: The dependent variable is actual annual income. Regressions are based on 11,643 person/year observations. *t*-statistics are in parentheses.

Table 4B.2 ORDERED PROBIT FOR THE ADDITIONAL NUMBER OF
CHILDREN BORN

	Nonblacks	Blacks
Age at first birth category (≤ 16 omitted)		
17-18 years	−0.546	−0.197
	(−6.43)	(−4.15)
19-21 years	−0.747	−0.320
	(−9.14)	(−7.12)
≥ 22 years	−1.361	−0.800
	(−16.70)	(−17.66)
Age of index child (spline)		
Age < 5	0.468	0.380
	(40.48)	(26.09)
5 ≤ age < 10	0.058	0.085
	(8.91)	(11.18)
Age ≥ 10	0.023	0.018
	(4.43)	(3.45)
Marital status		
Married at birth	0.323	0.323
	(6.63)	(6.26)
Married* age of child	−0.016	−0.025
	(−3.90)	(−5.49)
Education category (< high school omitted)		
High school	0.399	−0.001
	(9.72)	(−0.25)
Some college	0.441	−0.002
	(8.29)	(−0.36)
≥ college graduate	0.673	−0.013
	(11.73)	(−1.24)
Education and child age interactions		
(High school)* child age	−0.004	0.070
	(−1.27)	(1.37)
(Some college)* child age	−0.013	0.073
	(−2.76)	(1.01)
(≥ College graduate)* child age	−0.005	−0.050
	(−1.09)	(−0.42)
Ancillary parameters		
Cut point 1	1.588	1.533
	(0.10)	(0.07)
Cut point 2	2.842	2.504
	(0.10)	(0.07)
Cut point 3	3.703	3.258
	(0.10)	(0.08)
Cut point 4	4.347	4.053
	(0.10)	(0.08)
Log likelihood	−29,164.691	−16.237.688

Notes: The dependent variable is number of children born beyond the index child. The
nonblack and black samples contain 30,492 and 15,084 person/year observations, respectively. z-statistics are in parentheses for main parameter estimate; standard errors
are shown for the ancillary parameters.

Figure 4B.1   NONBLACK MEN: PREDICTED EARNINGS AT 25TH, 50TH, AND 75TH PERCENTILE FOR YEARS FOLLOWING BIRTH OF CHILD, BY AGE AND EDUCATION

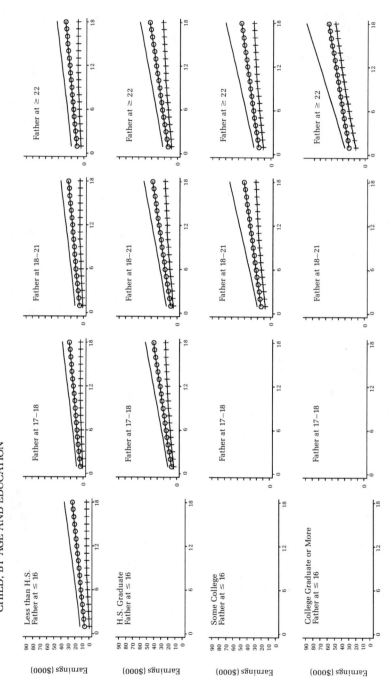

Key: + = 25th Percentile   O = 50th Percentile   — = 75th Percentile

Figure 4B.2 BLACK MEN: PREDICTED EARNINGS AT 25TH, 50TH, AND 75TH PERCENTILE FOR YEARS FOLLOWING BIRTH OF CHILD, BY AGE AND EDUCATION

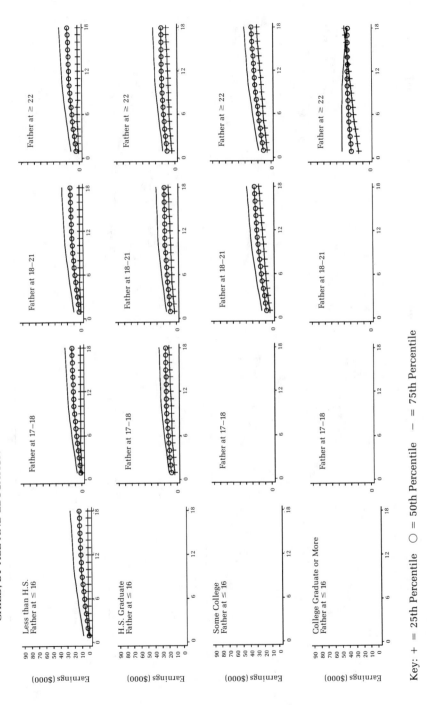

Key: + = 25th Percentile   ○ = 50th Percentile   – = 75th Percentile

Figure 4B.3 PREDICTED NUMBER OF ADDITIONAL BIRTHS TO UNMARRIED FATHERS FOR YEARS FOLLOWING BIRTH OF CHILD, BY AGE AND EDUCATION

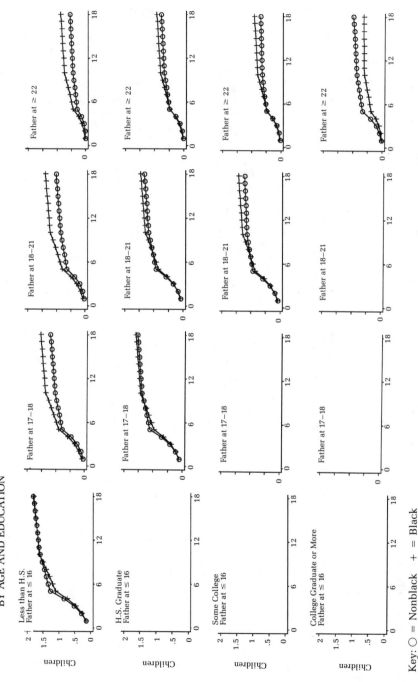

Key: ○ = Nonblack   + = Black

Figure 4B.4 PREDICTED CHILD-SUPPORT OBLIGATIONS OF UNMARRIED FATHERS FOR YEARS FOLLOWING BIRTH OF CHILD, BY AGE AND EDUCATION

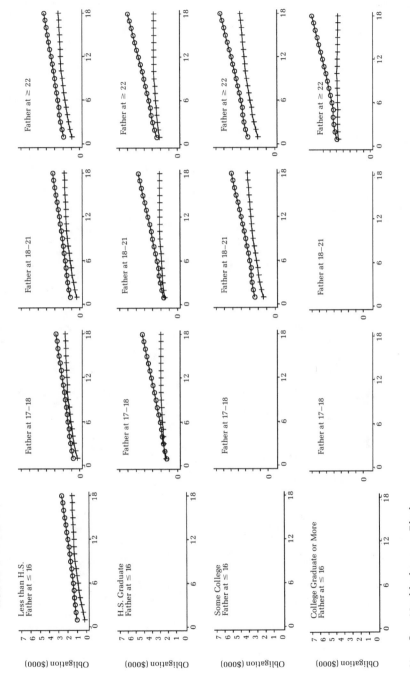

Key: ◯ = Nonblack   + = Black

Chapter Five

EFFECTS ON THE CHILDREN BORN TO ADOLESCENT MOTHERS

Kristin Anderson Moore, Donna Ruane Morrison,
and Angela Dungee Greene

The common assumption is that children's development and well-being suffer serious adverse consequences when their mothers themselves have not reached adulthood. However, whether teenage childbearing itself entails deficits for children raises a set of complex issues, and available research has not resolved all of them.

The younger the mother, for example, the more disadvantaged her background is likely to be (Moore et al. 1993)—a difference that accounts in part for differences in well-being across children born to early and later childbearers. In addition, full assessment of the effects of early childbearing for children requires consideration of a broad range of child outcomes, possible discontinuities across the years of childhood, differentials by race, and whether any effects of early motherhood hold for the first birth only or for subsequent births as well. Yet another challenge, which we do not address here, is identifying the actual mechanisms by which teen motherhood affects children. Poverty, marital disruption, single motherhood, low father contact, and inadequate parenting are all possible conduits through which being born to a young mother may affect child well-being.

The primary goal of this chapter is to examine differences between children born to women in their early teens and children whose mothers were ages 20 to 21 at their birth. We use two national data sets that have paid particular attention to children—the National Longitudinal Survey of Youth-Child Supplement (NLSY-CS) and the National Survey of Children (NSC)—to answer six questions:

- To what extent are children disadvantaged by being born to a teen mother?
- Are the consequences of teen childbearing specific to certain aspects of child well-being?
- Do the negative consequences of being born to a teen mother vary across the child's life cycle stage? That is, do risks to positive

development increase or decline as the children of teen mothers grow up?

- To what extent do mothers' background characteristics, rather than the fact of the birth itself, account for the negative effects, if any, of being born to a teen mother?
- Are race differences found in the effects of being born to a teen mother?
- Are the subsequent children born to a teen mother at a disadvantage, or just the firstborn?

FRAMING THE QUESTIONS

The strength of the evidence depends importantly on how the questions to be answered are framed. Six issues, in particular, shaped our framing of the questions.

In addressing the use of early teen versus later parenting, it is important to be specific, first of all, about which groups are being compared. Although our analysis includes several different ages of the mother at the child's birth, we focus our discussion primarily on a specific portion of the childbearing age continuum: mothers who have a child when they are less than 18 years old versus those who delay motherhood until they are 20 to 21. We highlight this particular contrast for two reasons. We think it unrealistic to assume that policy interventions would persuade young women already predisposed to becoming adolescent mothers to postpone motherhood more than a few years. In addition, we think the effects of being born to a minor (i.e., a woman under 18) may be different from the effects of being born to a mother who is still in her teens but who is old enough to be legally an adult.

In addition to being precise about the age groups of mothers being compared, it is also important to recognize the findings from previous research that the effects of early motherhood can span a wide array of outcomes. For example, despite overall declines in the incidence of low-birth-weight babies, babies of teens continue to be more likely to be underweight at birth than babies of older mothers (National Center for Health Statistics 1993), a deficit that exposes them to greater risk of illness and developmental difficulties (Strobino 1987). The children of teen mothers have also been found to score somewhat lower on measures of cognitive development and school performance than children of women who delay childbearing. They have also been found to be at greater risk of exhibiting behavior problems at home and in school (Baldwin and Cain 1980, Brooks-Gunn and Furstenberg 1985, Hayes 1987). Moreover, a longitudinal study of adolescent mothers from Baltimore documented elevated levels of grade repetition, delinquency, and other behavior problems among the children born to teen mothers (Furstenberg, Brooks-Gunn, and Morgan 1987). Here we examine the effects of being born to a teen mother for children in four major areas: the quality of the home environment provided to the child; cognitive development and educational attainment; behavior problems, delinquency, and substance abuse; and health and psychological well-being. Not only does this strategy provide a broad assessment of the implications of maternal age at first birth for children's well-being (see Zill and Coiro 1992), but it also allows us to explore how the relative importance of fertility timing may differ for different outcomes.

Tracing effects over the life cycle of the child is also important because deficits in social and emotional development may increase as the children of adolescent mothers grow older. For example, Furstenberg et al. (1987) found that, although the children born to teen mothers did not appear problematic as preschoolers, by ages 15 to 17 they had notably higher rates of misbehavior than their counterparts born to mothers who were not teens. We use two national data sets to address the issue of whether being born to a teen mother has increasing effects over the life course of the children. The NLSY-CS allows us to focus on effects for younger children and adolescents, ages 4 to 14 in 1990, while the NSC allows us to address outcomes in adolescence (among 12- to 16-year-olds in 1981) and young adulthood (youth ages 18 to 22 in 1987).

Mothers' background characteristics must also be identified and controlled for in the analysis, because teen childbearers may be "selectively recruited" as a result of their socioeconomic characteristics—factors that might also affect the quality of their children's lives and their development. Because both the NLSY-CS and the NSC contain unusually complete sets of multigenerational variables, we are able to hold constant the mother's socioeconomic background characteristics, such as whether she grew up in an intact family and the level of education of her parents, when we assess child development among the offspring of younger versus older mothers.[1]

We estimate models separately for blacks and whites for the five child outcomes where significant effects of early maternal age at the child's birth were observed for the full sample in order to assess whether the effects of being born to a teen mother vary by race.

Finally, we repeat these analyses for children classified by their mother's age at *first* birth, to examine whether risks to child development differ for later children born to mothers who had their first birth as a teen.

In order to trace a broad array of outcomes and to assess different life cycle stages of having been born to a teen mother, as noted, we use two data sets. The NLSY-CS allows us to examine effects on the offspring as young children. The NSC allows us to focus on effects on the offspring when they are adolescents and young adults.

The NLSY is a longitudinal survey of U.S. youth who were 14 to 21 when the study began in 1979. In 1986, the data collection effort added the NLSY-CS—a substantial battery of assessment information about the children of the women who had given birth. The children were reassessed in 1988, 1990, 1992, and 1994, and all newborn children were added to the sample. The present analysis draws upon assessment data for the children in 1990. Our sample is limited to children ages 4 to 14. Younger children are not old enough to have participated in the cognitive assessment tasks, and older children are few in number and rather unusual in that all were born to very young teen mothers.

Due to the nature of the NLSY-CS—children born to a cohort of women who were ages 14 to 21 in 1979—our oldest age at first birth was 27 in this sample and the children born to the oldest mothers are disproportionately younger. Although most of our outcomes (e.g., health care in the first year of life) either are not sensitive to the child's current age, except perhaps in terms of maternal recall, or are age standardized (e.g., measures of cognitive achievement), we control for the child's age in our multivariate models.

The NSC is a nationally representative household survey of children ages 7 to 11 living in the contiguous United States in 1976. A subset of the children were reinterviewed in 1981, when they were ages 12 to 16, and again in 1987, when they were ages 18 to 22. Up to two children between the ages of 7 and 11 in each household and the parent most knowledgeable about them, usually the mother, were interviewed in person.

The primary focus of the 1981 wave of interviews was to examine the consequences of marital disruption for children's development and well-being. Data were obtained from the child, a parent, and (in 80 percent of the cases) a teacher. The 1987 wave of interviews obtained data on outcomes in early adulthood. Between 1976 and 1987, there was substantial sample attrition, most notably among the most disadvantaged youth. This loss may reduce the likelihood of detecting relationships between early motherhood and child outcomes in the early adult years. Nevertheless, over 1,150 youth were interviewed via telephone in 1987, and in most cases, a parent, usually the mother, was also interviewed.

METHODS

To the extent possible, we investigate comparable outcomes across the two data sets. However, as noted, one advantage of using two separate data sets is our ability to focus on outcomes that are appropriate measures of well-being at different developmental stages. For example, for the NLSY-CS children, who range in age from 4 to 14, we examine scores on tests of cognitive ability; for the NSC, older youth and young adults, we include measures of high school graduation and substance use.[2]

In both data sets, we use available birth date information to construct the mother's age at the birth of the child. (The mother's age at the birth of the particular child is also the mother's age at *first* birth for those children in each sample who are first borns or only-borns.) We construct five groupings of mother's age at the particular child's birth—≤17, 18–19, 20–21, 22–24, and ≥25, using the 20- to 21-year-old group as the comparison group in our multivariate analyses.[3]

As with the mother's age at the birth of the child, data on the mother's age at first birth were provided by mothers in the NLSY-CS and constructed in the NSC. If the oldest child in the NSC sample is deceased, age at first birth may be underestimated. Both data sets have a broader distribution of mothers' ages at first birth, allowing us to create the following categories: ≤15, 16–17, 18–19, 20–21, 22–24, and ≥25. As before, we use the 20 to 21 age group as our comparison group in multivariate analyses.

We use measures available in each data set to account for pre-existing characteristics of young mothers and their families. The NLSY-CS gives us characteristics of the child's grandparents, including their level of education, whether the grandmother was employed outside the home, as well as the mother's number of siblings, the mother's rural or urban residence at age 14, the presence of reading materials in her home, whether the mother lived with two biological parents at age 14, and whether the child was conceived outside marriage. The NSC gives us whether the child's grandmother was ever on welfare, whether the mother ever lived apart from both of her parents while she was growing up, urban/rural residence and religion of both grandparents, and whether the focal child was conceived outside of marriage.

We present two multivariate models for each child outcome: Model 1 includes dummy variables for each category of mother's age at child's birth, providing an assessment of the bivariate relationship between mother's age at the birth of the focal child and the particular outcomes under consideration.[4] Because preexisting maternal characteristics and attributes of the child are also presumed to relate to mother's age at childbirth as well as the outcome variables, Model 2 adds child's characteristics such as age, race, and ethnicity, maternal background characteristics, the child's birth order, and whether the child was conceived outside marriage. In analyses of the NSC, we also control for whether the mother never wanted to have the child, whether the mother wanted the child later, and whether the mother was not in high school and had fewer than 12 years of education at the conception of her first child.[5]

We begin with an examination of outcomes among young children, using the NLSY-CS, followed by comparable analyses of outcomes in adolescence and young adulthood, using the NSC.[6]

RESULTS FOR YOUNG CHILDREN

We have evidence on outcomes for young children on all four of our major areas of interest—home environment, cognitive development and academic achievement, behavior problems, and health and psychological well-being. The findings are shown in tables 5.1 and 5.2. In each case Model 1 shows the differences by age of mother at child's birth without controlling for mother's background characteristics and other factors. Model 2 shows differences with these background characteristics controlled.

HOME ENVIRONMENT.

With respect to their home environments, children born to mothers age 17 or under are at a clear disadvantage. This appears in table 5.1, column 1, which shows the quality of the environment provided to the child as measured by an indicator standardized for the age of the child. It covers both cognitive and emotional support, based on both maternal report and interviewer observation. The mean of the indicator is 100, and the standard deviation is 15. Children born to a mother age 17 or under show a statistically significant and fairly substantial disadvantage of 3.5 points. In contrast, the home environment scores of children whose mothers were slightly older teens (18- to 19-year-olds) at their births are not statistically different from children whose mothers were in the 20 to 21 age category. Strikingly, when we hold mother's background characteristics constant (column 2), the deleterious effect of early teen childbearing on the quality of the home environment provided to the child increases (to −4.4), and a statistically significant deficit (−1.5) emerges for children of mothers ages 18 to 19 at the child's birth.

Cognitive Development and Academic Achievement

Children born to the youngest teen mothers are also at a statistically significant disadvantage in terms of cognitive development and academic achievement compared with peers whose mothers were 20 to 21 at their birth. This is shown in table 5.1, columns 3 to 8, with achievement tests age standardized, with a mean of 100.

Specifically, children whose mothers were 17 or younger at their births scored lower in mathematics, reading recognition, and reading comprehension than did children in the primary comparison group, even when mothers' socioeconomic backgrounds are held constant (−3.6, −3.9, and −3.1, respectively). Given a standard deviation of 15, the magnitude of these effects is notable. Again, children of 18- to 19-year-old mothers are not at a disadvantage compared with children whose mothers were 20 to 21 at the time of the child's birth.

Behavior Problems

The results for behavior problems do not follow those for home environment or cognitive achievement. Scores on the mother-rated index of problem behavior are shown in table 5.1, columns 9 and 10. As before, this index is standardized and has a mean of 100. However, in this case higher scores indicate more behavioral problems. There is no significant difference in the number of behavioral problems between children of teen mothers age 17 or younger and the primary comparison group of children born to mothers ages 20 to 21. Contrary to expectations, when the mother's background is controlled (Model

Table 5.1 HOME ENVIRONMENT, COGNITIVE DEVELOPMENT AND ACADEMIC ACHIEVEMENT, AND BEHAVIOR PROBLEMS, CHILDREN AGES 4 TO 14 IN 1990

Independent Variable	Home Environment		Math		Reading Recognition		Reading Comprehension		Behavior Problems	
	Model 1	Model 2	Model 1	Model 2	Model 1	Model 2	Model 1	Model 2	Model 1	Model 2
Mother's age at focal child's birth										
≤ 17	−3.5***	−4.4***	−3.2***	−3.6***	−4.0***	−3.9***	−5.9***	−3.1***	0.6	−2.7**
18–19	−0.6	−1.5*	0.1	−0.1	−0.1	−0.1	−1.5	−0.2	−0.2	−1.8*
20–21	—	—	—	—	—	—	—	—	—	—
22–24	2.0***	2.3***	2.1***	2.0***	2.3***	2.1***	4.7***	2.9***	−2.6***	−0.9
≥ 25	2.9***	3.9***	2.7***	2.5***	1.8*	1.2	6.3***	2.2*	−6.1***	−2.8***
Child controls										
Child's gender (male)		1.2**		0.3		2.4***		2.0***		1.3**
Child's age in months		0.1***		0.0*		0.0		−0.1***		0.1***
Child's race (black)		−7.3***		−4.1***		−1.7**		−3.0***		−1.0
Child's ethnicity (Hispanic)		−2.4***		−2.4***		−0.8		0.0		−1.9**
Mother's background characteristics										
Education of highest-educated grandparent		0.5***		0.7***		0.7***		0.6***		−0.1
Grandmother was employed when mother was 14		−0.2		−0.4		−0.1		0.5		1.6***
Index of reading materials in mother's home at 14		2.5***		1.0***		1.1***		1.0***		−1.1***
Mother's number of siblings at 14		−0.2**		−0.1		−0.2		−0.2*		0.1
Mother lived with two biological parents		0.6		0.3		0.4		0.1		−2.0***
Mother's residence was rural at 14		−0.1		1.1*		0.4		0.6		−0.5

	(1)	(2)	(3)	(4)	(5)	(6)	(7)	(8)	(9)	(10)
Circumstances at child's birth										
Child's birth order		-3.3***		-1.8***		-3.3***		-3.3***		-0.1***
Not married at conception of focal child		-3.2***		-0.1		-0.9		-0.7		0.05
Intercept	99.4***	88.2***	99.2***	91.1***	103.1***	97.0***	102.2***	107.4***	108.2***	104.5***
R^2	0.02	0.23	0.02	0.12	0.02	0.13	0.07	0.09	0.03	0.05
N	3,680		3,197		3,150		2,556		3,659	

Source: Public use files from the National Longitudinal Survey of Youth—Child Supplement, 1986–1990.

Note: These are unstandardized OLS coefficients for models predicting the outcomes of interest. Home environment is measured by the HOME-SF indicator. Math, reading recognition, and reading comprehension are measured by the Peabody Individual Achievement Tests (PIAT) tests. Behavior is measured by the Behavior Problems Index. Table values (except Ns) are based on weighted data; means imputed for missing values on independent variables.

*p ≤ .10; **p ≤ .05; ***p ≤ .01.

Table 5.2 LOW BIRTHWEIGHT, WELL-BABY CARE, CHILD'S DISABILITY, AND PSYCHOLOGICAL WELL-BEING, CHILDREN AGES 4 TO 14 IN 1990

Independent Variable	Low Birthweight		Well-Baby Care		Disability/Limitation		Psychologist/Psychiatrist	
	Model 1	Model 2	Model 1	Model 2	Model 1	Model 2	Model 1	Model 2
Mother's age at focal child's birth								
≤ 17	1.4	1.5	1.8**	1.0	0.8	0.8	0.9	0.7
18–19	1.2	1.2	1.4	1.0	1.0	1.0	0.8	0.6
20–21 (omitted category)	—	—	—	—	—	—	—	—
22–24	0.9	0.9	1.2	1.6**	0.7**	0.7**	0.7	0.9
≥ 25	0.7	0.7	0.9	1.6**	0.4**	0.4***	0.4***	0.7
Child controls								
Child's gender (male)		1.1		0.9		0.6***		0.8
Child's age in months		1.0		1.0***		1.0		1.0***
Child's race (black)		1.7**		0.9		0.7**		0.7*
Child's ethnicity (Hispanic)		0.9		1.1		1.1		1.1
Mother's background characteristics								
Education of highest-educated grandparent		1.0		1.0		1.0		1.0
Grandmother was employed when mother was 14		1.1		1.1		1.0		1.1
Index of reading materials in mother's home at 14		1.0		1.3***		1.0		1.2
Mother's number of siblings at 14		1.0		1.0*		1.0		1.1
Mother lived with two biological parents at 14		1.2		0.8		0.9		0.7**
Mother's residence was rural at 14		1.1		1.0		1.0		1.3
Circumstances at focal child's birth								
Child's birth order		1.5***		0.7***		1.1		1.0
Not married at conception of focal child		2.0		0.9		1.0		0.9
N	3,796		3,678		3,905		3,776	

Source: Public use files from the National Longitudinal Survey of Youth-Child Supplement, 1986–1990.
Note: These are odds ratios for models predicting the outcomes of interest. Psychological well-being is measured by visits to psychologist or psychiatrist. Table values (except Ns) are based on weighted data; means imputed for missing values on independent variables.
* $p \leq .10$; ** $p \leq .05$; *** $p \leq .01$.

2), children born to teen mothers (both younger and older teens) do better than those born to mothers ages 20 to 21.

HEALTH AND PSYCHOLOGICAL WELL-BEING

None of the measures of child health and psychological well-being captured on the NLSY-CS appear to show any association with adolescent childbearing (table 5.2). When controls are added (Model 2), race and birth order are the only variables that significantly predict the likelihood of being born underweight. Since Vital Statistics data indicate that children born to younger mothers are of low birth weight more often, the nonsignificance of the association may reflect the small sample of young mothers. For well-baby care, children born to the youngest mothers are nearly twice as likely (odds ratio = 1.8) to receive well-baby care in the first year of life as those whose mothers were 20 to 21 at their births. This association does not remain statistically significant, however, when we introduce child and maternal controls. The odds of having a disability or limitation are no greater for children born to teen mothers than they are for those whose mothers were in their early 20s. The same pattern is apparent for the receipt of psychological care.

DIFFERENCES BY RACE

Given that previous studies have found differences by race in the effects of early childbearing on child well-being, we reestimated, separately for blacks and nonblacks, the five models where significant associations between early maternal age at focal child's birth were observed for the full sample: home environment; mathematics, reading recognition, and reading comprehension; and behavior problems. Different patterns do indeed emerge for the two groups. For blacks, children born to the youngest mothers have worse home environment scores and more behavior problems than do children whose mothers were 20 to 21 at their births. When maternal background characteristics and other factors are controlled, however, mathematics and reading recognition scores are higher among black children of 18- to 19-year-old mothers than among those whose mothers were slightly older—a finding that does not hold for black children of the youngest teens. Among nonblacks, children of the youngest teen mothers have significantly less favorable math and reading comprehension scores than children whose mothers were 20 to 21 at their births. Nonblack children born to comparatively older mother have more behavior problems than those born to teen mothers, however.

EVIDENCE FOR ADOLESCENTS AND YOUNG ADULTS

We now turn to outcomes in adolescence and young adulthood. As noted, the longitudinal nature of the NSC allows us to assess outcomes in 1981, when youth were 12 to 16, and again in 1987, when youth were ages 18 to 22. Some measures were taken at only one of these dates, others were taken twice.

COGNITIVE DEVELOPMENT AND EDUCATIONAL ATTAINMENT

We have three measures for this outcome area: ratings as one of the best students, grade repetition, and high school graduation. The results show little evidence that being born to a young teen mother has major effects on the academic achievement of adolescents or young adults. If the odds ratios shown in table 5.3 are less than 1.0, youths born to mothers in a particular age group are *less* likely than those born to mothers ages 20 to 21 to have the characteristic in question as long as the ratio in question is statistically significant. There are no significant differences for the model that does not control for mother's background characteristics and other factors. When these factors are controlled, however, youth born to mothers age 17 or younger are 70 percent less likely (odds ratio = 0.3) to be rated one of the best students in the class by their teachers at ages 12 to 16, but also less likely to have repeated a grade by ages 18 to 22. However, teen motherhood has no effect on the *parents'* rating of school performance or grade repetition, net of other factors. For these outcomes, the age association is significant only for youth born to mothers 25 or older, who were more likely than youth born to mothers 20 to 21 to be rated one of the best students by their parents at ages 12 to 16 and less likely to have repeated a grade by ages 18 to 22.

HEALTH AND PSYCHOLOGICAL WELL-BEING

Teen motherhood has no effect on adolescent or young adult health or psychological status (table 5.4) for any of the measures examined. Rather, controls for child and other maternal characteristics are the important predictors. For instance, black adolescents are 40 percent less likely (odds ratio = 0.6) to have this favorable health status. Also, the odds of being rated in good health are significantly reduced by having a mother who never wanted the child and by having a mother who was not in high school and had less than 12 years of education at the conception of her first child.

DEPRESSION AND BEHAVIOR PROBLEMS

Offspring of young teen mothers are neither more nor less likely to be depressed than their counterparts born to mothers ages 20 to 21 (table 5.5). While youth born to mothers in the oldest group, ages 25 and over, are less likely to be depressed than those born to mothers ages 20 and 21, the association falls to nonsignificance when controls are included. Age of motherhood is not associated with behavior problems reported by the mother in either adolescence or young adulthood. When controls for mother's background and other factors are included, young teen motherhood still makes no significant difference compared to motherhood at ages 20 or 21. However, youth born to mothers age 25 and older have significantly fewer behavior problems as adolescents and young adults with and without controls than children whose mothers gave birth at ages 20 or 21.

MAJOR DELINQUENCY, ILLEGAL DRUG USE, AND RUNAWAY BEHAVIOR

Major delinquency includes behavior such as arson, assault, theft, or prostitution in the past year. The odds of having committed one or more delinquent acts during the past year are not significantly different for youth born to teen mothers than for those born to mothers in the comparison group (table 5.6). The only age effect is within the category of youth born to mothers age 25 or older, with these youth 50 percent less likely to commit one or more delinquent acts than those born to mothers ages 20 and 21. There is also no association between mother's age at the child's birth and illegal drug use reported by these young adults. Youth born to mothers ages 18 to 19 are significantly more likely to have run away from home at least once compared with youth born to 20- to 21-year-old mothers, however. But the relatively small number of youth who reported runaway behavior suggests caution in interpreting this result.

EFFECTS OF TEEN MOTHERHOOD ON SUBSEQUENT CHIILDREN

To address the question of whether teenage motherhood affects subsequent children, we categorize children according to the ages of their mothers at the time of their *first* births. For these analyses, we distinguish between children born to teen mothers who were ≤15, 16 to 17, and 18 to 19 at first childbirth.

Table 5.3 ACADEMIC ACHIEVEMENT, YOUTH AGES 12 TO 16 AND 18 TO 22

| Independent Variable | One of the Best Students, Ages 12–16 | | | | Grade Repetition | | | | High School Graduate | |
| | Teacher's Rating | | Parent's Rating | | Ages 12–16 | | Ages 18-22 | | Ages 18-22 | |
	Model 1	Model 2	Model 1	Model 2	Model 1	Model 2	Model 1	Model 2	Model 1	Model 2
Mother's age at focal child's birth										
≤ 17	0.5	0.3*	0.8	0.8	1.4	1.5	0.7	0.4*	0.7	0.7
18–19	0.6	0.5	0.8	0.9	1.1	1.2	1.6	1.5	0.9	0.9
20–21 (omitted category)	—	—	—	—	—	—	—	—	—	—
22–24	1.2	1.4	1.2	1.2	0.6	0.7	1.0	1.2	1.1	0.8
≥ 25	1.4	1.3	1.4	1.6*	0.7	0.6*	0.8	0.9	1.7	1.9
Child controls										
Child's age in months		1.0		1.0**		1.0		1.0*		1.0
Child's gender (male)		0.8*		0.7**		1.4		1.2		0.8
Child's race (black)		0.5		0.7		1.2		1.8**		1.2
Mother's background characteristics										
Mother's smoking behavior before age 15		0.9		1.0		1.3**		1.3**		0.7***
Mother's parents were Catholic		1.0		1.2		0.9		1.0		1.8
Mother's parents were Protestant Fundamentalists		0.4*		1.3		1.4		1.4		0.8
Mother's parents received welfare at some time		1.3		0.7		1.0		1.3		0.8
Mother's residence was urban during childhood		1.2		1.5*		0.9		0.8		0.8
Mother's residence was rural during childhood		0.8		1.0		1.1		1.5		0.9
Mother lived away from parents before age 14		1.5		1.0		1.6		1.5		0.5**

Mother/Child Characteristics					
Mother never wanted to have child	1.3	0.7	1.3	1.2	0.5**
Mother wanted to have child later	0.5**	0.8	1.6*	1.3	1.0
Mother was not in H.S. and had <12 yrs of education at conception of first child	0.5*	0.6*	1.7**	2.0***	0.4***
Not married at conception of child	2.2**	1.0	1.0	1.6*	0.9
Child's birth order	1.0	1.0	1.2***	1.0	0.9
N	921	1.334	1.339		1.078

Source: National Survey of Children.

Note: These are odds ratios for models predicting the outcomes of interest. Table values (except Ns) are based on weighted data; means imputed for missing values on independent variables.

*$p \leq .10$; **$p \leq .05$; ***$p \leq .01$.

Table 5.4 HEALTH AND PSYCHOLOGICAL STATUS, YOUTH AGES 12 TO 16 IN 1981 AND 18 TO 22 IN 1987

Independent Variable	Good Health/No Limitations				Receive/Need Psychological Help	
	Ages 12–16		Ages 18–22		Ages 18–22	
	Model 1	Model 2	Model 1	Model 2	Model 1	Model 2
Mother's age at focal child's birth						
≤ 17	1.4	1.7	0.9	1.1	0.9	0.8
18–19	0.8	0.8	0.7	0.7	0.7	0.6
20–21 (omitted category)	—	—	—	—	—	—
22–24	0.9	0.7	1.3	1.1	0.7	0.8
≥ 25	0.7	0.7	1.2	0.9	0.6*	0.7
Child controls						
Child's age in months		1.1		1.6***		0.6**
Child's gender (male)		1.0		1.0		1.0
Child's race (black)		0.6***		0.9		0.5**
Mother's background characteristics						
Mother's smoking behavior before age 15		0.9		0.8**		1.3***
Mother's parents were Catholic		1.6**		1.3		0.8
Mother's parents were Protestant Fundamentalists		0.6*		0.6**		1.4
Mother's parents received welfare at some time		1.0		0.9		0.7
Mother's residence was urban during childhood		0.8		1.1		0.8
Mother's residence was rural during childhood		0.9		1.0		0.8
Mother lived away from parents before age 14		0.8		0.9		2.1**

Mother/Child Characteristics			
Mother never wanted to have child	0.5***	0.9	1.0
Mother wanted to have child later	1.0	0.7	1.6
Mother was not in H.S. and had <12 yrs of education at conception of first child	0.7*	0.7	0.6
Not married at conception of child	1.0	1.0	1.3
Child's birth order	1.0	1.0	1.0
N	1,339	1,080	1,080

Source: National Survey of Children.

Note: These are odds ratios for models predicting the outcomes of interest. Table values (except Ns) are based on weighted data; means imputed for missing values on independent variables.

*p ≤ .10; **p ≤ .05; ***p ≤ .01.

Table 5.5 DEPRESSION AND BEHAVIOR PROBLEMS, YOUTH AGES 12 TO 16 IN 1981 AND 18 TO 22 IN 1987

Independent Variable	Depression		Behavior Problems			
	Ages 18–22		Ages 12–16		Ages 18–22	
	Model 1	Model 2	Model 1	Model 2	Model 1	Model 2
Mother's age at focal child's birth						
≤17	−1.0	−1.6	1.1	1.2	0.6	−0.2
18–19	−0.5	−0.5	−0.0	0.1	0.9	0.7
20–21 (omitted category)	—	—	—	—	—	—
22–24	−1.7	−1.0	−0.7	−0.4	−0.9**	−0.5
≥25	−1.9*	−1.6	−1.2*	−1.0*	−0.9**	−0.7*
Child controls						
Child's age in months		−0.0		−0.0		−0.0
Child's gender (male)		−1.2**		0.6		0.4*
Child's race (black)		0.3		−0.7		0.8*
Mother's background characteristics						
Mother's smoking behavior before age 15		0.6*		0.4*		0.2
Mother's parents were Catholic		−0.8		0.9**		0.5
Mother's parents were Protestant Fundamentalists		−0.7		1.1*		0.3
Mother's parents received welfare at some time		−0.2		0.5		0.9*
Mother's residence was urban during childhood		1.7**		−0.6		0.4
Mother's residence was rural during childhood		−0.1		−0.3		0.0
Mother lived away from parents before age 14		0.8		1.1		0.6

Mother/Child Characteristics						
Mother never wanted to have child	0.9			1.3**		0.7
Mother wanted to have child later	0.4			0.7		−0.1
Mother was not in H.S. and had <12 yrs of education at conception of first child	0.2			2.1***		0.7*
Not married at conception of child	0.5			0.1		0.6
Child's birth order	0.1			−0.0		−0.0
Intercept	10.0***	12.5***	8.5***	8.4***	3.9***	4.7***
R²	0.01	0.05	0.01	0.07	0.03	0.08
N	1,080		1,339		999	

Source: National Survey of Children.
Note: These are unstandardized OLS coefficients for models predicting outcomes of interest. Table values (except Ns) are based on weighted data; means imputed for missing values on independent variables.
$*p \leq .10; **p \leq .05; ***p \leq .01.$

Table 5.6 DELINQUENCY, ILLEGAL DRUG USE, AND RUNNING AWAY, YOUTH AGES 18 TO 22 IN 1987

Independent Variable	Delinquency		Illegal Drug Use		Running Away	
	Model 1	Model 2	Model 1	Model 2	Model 1	Model 2
Mother's age at focal child's birth						
≤17	0.5	0.5	0.9	0.8	2.3	3.2
18–19	1.1	0.9	0.7	0.6	5.7***	6.9***
20–21 (omitted category)	—	—	—	—	—	—
22–24	0.7	0.7	0.7	0.8	1.3	1.4
≥25	0.6	0.5**	0.6*	0.7	2.0	1.2
Child controls						
Child's age in months		1.0		1.0		1.0*
Child's gender (male)		3.8***		0.6**		0.7
Child's race (black)		0.6		0.5**		0.3**
Mother's background characteristics						
Mother's smoking behavior before age 15		1.1		1.3***		1.0
Mother's parents were Catholic		0.9		0.8		0.8
Mother's parents were Protestant Fundamentalists		0.7		1.4		1.0
Mother's parents received welfare at some time		0.6		0.7		0.3
Mother's residence was urban during childhood		1.1		0.8		1.2*
Mother's residence was rural during childhood		0.8		0.8		1.1
Mother lived away from parents before age 14		1.0		2.1**		1.4
Mother/Child Characteristics						
Mother never wanted to have child		1.2		1.0		1.8
Mother wanted to have child later		1.2		1.6		1.1
Mother was not in H.S. and had <12 yrs of education at conception of first child		0.8				1.5
Not married at conception of child		1.5		1.3		1.6
Child's birth order		1.0		1.0		1.3**
N	1,079		1,080		1,080	

Source: National Survey of Children.
Note: These are odds ratios for models predicting the outcomes of interest. Table values (except Ns) are based on weighted data; means imputed for missing values on independent variables.
$*p \leq .10$; $**p \leq .05$; $***p \leq .01$.

The patterns are similar whether we categorize children according to mother's age at the particular child's birth or mother's age at first birth. Measures of child health and psychological well-being are not related to the mother's age at first birth; however, the quality of the home environment is lower for children whose mothers began child-bearing when they were 17 or younger than for mothers who began childbearing at 18 or 19. The same is true for reading and math achievement test scores. Grade repetition is more common among children of teen mothers (age 19 or younger). And children whose mothers were 15 or younger when their first child was born are less likely to complete high school and more likely to have behavior problems in early adulthood.

SYNTHESIS OF THE FINDINGS

We synthesize the findings presented for 4- to 14-year-olds using the National Longitudinal Survey of Youth-Child Supplement (NLSY-CS) and adolescents and young adults using the National Survey of Children (NSC), by discussing each of the six questions we posed at the outset.

- To what extent are children disadvantaged by being born to a teen mother?

The answer to the question of whether the children of teen mothers have less positive development does indeed depend on the comparison group one uses. When children born to 20- to 21-year-olds are used as the comparison group, there are important but not pervasive disadvantages associated with being born to an adolescent mother (table 5.7). When delayed childbearers (≥ 25) are used as the contrast group, however, differences in child outcomes are larger and broader and include not only cognitive outcomes, teacher's rating of school performance, the home environment, and running away, but also behavior problems, delinquency, psychological problems, well-baby care, the presence of a disability or limitation, grade repetition, and the parent's rating of school performance.

- Are the consequences of early teen childbearing specific to certain areas of child well-being?

The effects of early teen motherhood are concentrated in two areas: the quality of the home environment provided to the child and cog-

Table 5.7 OUTCOMES OF BIRTH TO A MOTHER AGES 20 TO 21 RELATIVE TO BIRTH TO A MOTHER AGES 17 OR YOUNGER AND 18 TO 19

	NLSY-CS				NSC			
	Bivariate		Multivariate		Bivariate		Multivariate	
	≤ 17	18–19	≤ 17	18–19	≤ 17	18–19	≤ 17	18–19
Home Environment								
Home Scale	✓	0	✓	✓				
Cognitive Development and Educational Attainment								
Mathematics score	✓	0	✓	0				
Reading Recognition score	✓	0	✓	0				
Reading Comprehension score	✓	0	✓	0				
Child never repeated grade	0	0	1	1				
Child one of the best in the class	0	0	1	1				
Youth never repeated a grade as of 1981					0	0	0	0
Youth never repeated a grade as of 1987					0	0	✓	0
Teacher rated youth one of the best students					0	0	✓	0
Parent rated youth one of the best students					0	0	0	0
Youth is a high school graduate or soon will be					0	0	0	0

Health and Psychological Well-being					
Not Low Birth Weight	0	0	0	0	0
Received Well-Baby Care	✓	0	0	0	0
No Child Disabilities/Limitations	0	0	0		
Health status excellent or very good with no limitations in 1981	0	0	0	0	0
Health status excellent or very good with no limitations in 1987	0	0	0	0	0
Did not visit psychiatrist/psychologist in past year	0	0	0		
Youth never received or needed psychological help between 1981 and 1987	0	0	0	0	0
Youth's CES-Depression Score in 1987	0	0	0	0	0
Behavior Problems and Substance Abuse					
Behavior Problems Index (positive association = positive outcome)	0	0	x	x	0
Behavior Problems Index—1981	0	0	0	0	0
Behavior Problems Index—1987	0	0	0	0	0
No delinquent acts in the past year	0	0	✓	0	0
Youth has never run away from home	0	0	✓	0	✓
No illegal drug use during the past year	0	0	0	0	0

Source: Child Trends, Inc. based on public use files from the National Longitudinal Survey of Youth-Child Supplement, 1986–1990, and the National Survey of Children, 1976–1987.

Key: ✓: Indicates a relative advantage among children born to mothers ages 20 to 21.
0: no association
x: Indicates a relative advantage among children born to mothers ages 17 or younger and 18 to 19.
¹Too few cases to permit estimation of a model.

nitive development, with some negative effects also found for behavior problems.

In terms of the quality of the home environment, children of both younger (≤ 17) and older (18 to 19) teen mothers rate significantly less favorably than do those born to mothers in their early 20s. Children born to the youngest teen mothers also perform significantly more poorly on tests of mathematics achievement, reading recognition, and reading comprehension than do children born to 20- to 21-year-olds. However, these negative effects are not observed for children born to older teen mothers.

For youth and young adults, negative effects of having been a child of a teen mother appear for academic attainment and one measure of behavior problems. Compared to children born to 20- to 21-year-olds, the offspring of mothers age 17 or younger are more likely to repeat a grade and are less likely to be rated by their teachers as among the best students in the class. Children born to 18- and 19-year-olds are significantly more likely than their counterparts born to 20- and 21-year-olds to have run away from home.

- Do the negative consequences of being born to a teen mother vary by life cycle stage? That is, do risks to positive development tend to increase or decline as the children of these mothers grow up?

Negative effects of early childbearing on cognitive development show up for children and adolescents. The 4- to 14-year-olds born to the youngest teen mothers perform more poorly on tests of cognitive ability, and the offspring of teens are more likely to be retained in grade and less likely to be perceived by their teachers as performing favorably by the time they reach high school age. In addition, running away from home emerges as a problem among older children. Although having a young teen mother does not affect the number of behavior problems of younger children, by the time these children reach adolescence, they are more likely to run away from home.

- To what extent do mothers' background characteristics account for the negative effects of being born to a teen mother?

Where we find significant bivariate associations (i.e., the home environment, cognitive attainment, and running away), the relationships hold even when socioeconomic background characteristics of mothers are held constant. Differences in academic outcomes between the children of early childbearers and those of mothers ages 20 to 21 were not statistically significant in the bivariate formulation. But net of background variables, children of young teen mothers are more likely to repeat a grade and less likely to be described by their teacher as one of the best students in the class.

- Are race differences found in the effects of being born to a teen mother?

Among blacks, children born to young teen mothers have less cognitively stimulating and less nurturing home environments and more behavior problems than do children whose mothers were 20 to 21 at their births, net of controls for maternal background and other factors. Among nonblacks, the comparative disadvantage of being born to a teen mother is observed among the offspring of both younger and older teen mothers in both home environment and reading achievement. Children of the young teen mothers have significantly lower math and reading comprehension scores than do their counterparts whose mothers were 20 to 21 at their births. However, black children of older teen mothers have higher mathematics and reading recognition scores than do their counterparts whose mothers were 20 to 21 at their births. Surprisingly, nonblack children of 20- to 21-year-olds have more behavior problems than their counterparts born to young teen or older teen mothers.

- Are the subsequent children born to a teen mother at a disadvantage, or just the firstborn?

The patterns look very similar whether one classifies children according to mother's age at the particular child's birth or mother's age at first childbirth—with slightly different variables showing significant differences. When we classify children according to their mother's age at their own births, the outcomes on which children of teen mothers, particularly the young teen mothers, compare less favorably with children born to 20- to 21-year-old mothers include the quality of the home environment, mathematics achievement, reading comprehension, reading recognition, grade repetition by the end of high school, teachers' rating of school performance, and runaway behavior. When the classification is by mother's age at first childbirth, outcomes on which children of teen mothers compare less favorably with the children of 20- to 21-year-olds include the quality of the home environment, mathematics achievement, reading recognition, grade repetition by the end of high school, high school graduation, and behavior problems in young adulthood.

DISCUSSION

Our aim was to document the extent to which, on a variety of indicators of well-being, children born to young teen mothers compare less favorably with peers born to somewhat older mothers. We focused on the children of 20- to 21-year-olds as our primary contrast, based on the assumption that a year or two of delay in childbearing is more realistic than a ten-year delay from the standpoint of policy intervention. We distinguished between the children of young teens (≤17 years old) and somewhat older teens (18 to 19 years old).

When no statistical controls are included except the mother's age at the birth of the child, a few marked differences appear between the children of teen mothers and the children of 20- to 21-year-olds. Children of the youngest teen mothers are less likely to have received well-baby care in the first year of life, have less cognitively stimulating and less nurturing home environments, and obtain lower cognitive achievement scores than peers whose mothers were 20 to 21 at their births.

As with previous research, our analyses show that teenage childbearers have socioeconomic disadvantages that are apparent even before they enter motherhood. Young teen mothers disproportionately come from single-parent families, have more siblings, had less well educated parents, and were more often recipients of welfare at some point during their own childhoods. When we statistically account for their less favorable circumstances and compare the well-being of children born to young teen mothers to that of children whose mothers were 20 to 21 at their births, we generally find that the bivariate differences still hold. These children are more likely to have lower cognitive achievement scores and less cognitively stimulating and less nurturing home environments. But we found little evidence of disadvantage for the offspring of young teen mothers in physical or psychological well-being or in behavior problems, however, either as children or as adolescents or young adults.

Do these modest results mean that being born to a young teen mother does not matter much for children? Our results persuade us not to draw that conclusion, for several reasons. First, although we did not observe negative effects across a large array of areas, the effects we did observe are compelling. For example, the magnitude of the effect that being born to a mother ≤17 years old has on the quality of the child's home environment (− 4.4) is nearly one-third of a standard deviation, putting these children at a sizable disadvantage relative to their peers. The sizes of the effects for the three tests of cognitive achievement are similar—about one-quarter of a standard deviation. The long-term implications of this poorer academic performance among the younger children are not clear, but are suggested by the fact that the offspring of the youngest mothers are more likely when they reach adolescence to repeat a grade in school and to be rated unfavorably by their teachers.

Another key point is that the group one uses for comparison purposes makes an important difference to the conclusions drawn. The children of teen mothers experience considerably greater disadvantage in considerably more areas on considerably more measures when compared with children born to mothers who delayed childbirth until the mid- to late 20s or older.

Finally, we found that the negative effects of teen childbearing for the firstborn children generally extend to the subsequent children of teen mothers as well.

Notes

1. Factors such as family structure, maternal education, family size, receipt of public assistance, level of support from the young mother's parents, amount of father involvement, and parenting behaviors of the adolescent mothers themselves are prominent among the mechanisms through which researchers have found the mother's age at first birth to indirectly affect child well-being (see Hofferth 1987 for a review). However, the aim of this chapter is *not* to illuminate the processes through which an early birth affects child well-being but rather to document the extent to which there is an effect of being born to a teen mother. Therefore, we do not include these variables in our models.

2. Appendix 5A provides detailed descriptions of the dependent variables we investigate.

3. Our dummy variables denote each age-at-first-birth group as "one" and our contrast group as "zero" to detect differences between each group and the contrast group. In our multivariate analyses, we include both measures of our independent variable (age at focal birth) and control variables.

4. Appendix 5B shows how mothers' background characteristics relate to their ages at focal children's births. Regarding methods, we use ordinary least squares (OLS) regression when the dependent variable is continuous (e.g, cognitive test scores) and logit models when the dependent variable is dichotomous (e.g., being low birth weight or not).

5. We were interested in exploring whether the inclusion of the mother's performance on the Armed Forces Qualifying Test (AFQT), a cognitive achievement measure available in the NLSY-CS, changed our estimates of the effect of mother's age at the birth of the focal child on selected measures of child well-being. We found that mothers' AFQT scores were significantly associated with the child's level of behavior problems; the child's mathematics, reading recognition, and reading comprehension scores; and the quality of the child's home environment. The disadvantages associated with being born

to a teen mother remained statistically significant when the AFQT was added to our models but became smaller.

6. Both the NLSY-CS and the NSC include more than one child per household. In the NLSY-CS, 40 percent of the sample members are siblings; in the NSC, 25 percent of sample members are siblings. We account for the problem of nonindependence statistically by estimating (maximum-likelihood) standard errors based on Huber's formula (Huber 1967) for individual-level data. We use the standard errors calculated with this procedure (estimated with the statistical package called STATA) as the basis for determining the statistical significance of our parameter estimates. Both the NSC and the NLSY-CS oversampled minority subgroups. To produce percentages that accurately reflect national distributions of oversampled groups, all analyses are based on weighted data. The sample sizes presented reflect unweighted numbers.

References

Achenbach, T. M. 1981. *Child Behavior Checklist for Ages 4–16*. Burlington: University of Vermont, Department of Psychiatry.

Adams, G. C., and R. C. Williams. 1990. *Sources of Support for Adolescent Mothers*. Washington, D.C.: Congress of the United States, Congressional Budget Office.

Bacon, L. 1974. "Early Motherhood, Accelerated Role Transition, and Social Pathologies." *Social Forces* 52(3): 333–41.

Baker, P. C., and F. L. Mott. 1989. *NLSY Child Handbook*. Columbus, Ohio: Center for Human Resource Research.

Baldwin, W., and V. Cain. 1980. "The Children of Teenage Parents." *Family Planning Perspectives* 12(1): 34–43.

Brooks-Gunn, J., and F. F. Furstenberg Jr. 1985. "Antecedents and Consequences of Parenting: The Case of Adolescent Motherhood." In *The origins of Nurturance*, eds. Fogel and Melson. Hillsdale, N.J.: Lawrence Erlbaum.

Butler, A. C. 1992. "The Changing Economic Consequences of Teenage Childbearing." *Social Service Review* (March): 1–31.

Dillard, K. D., and L. G. Pol. 1982. "The Individual Economic Costs of Teenage Childbearing." *Family Relations* 31(April): 249–59.

Furstenberg, F. F., Jr., J. Brooks-Gunn, and S. P. Morgan. 1987. *Adolescent Mothers in Later Life*. Cambridge: Cambridge University Press.

Hayes, C., ed. 1987. *Risking the Future: Adolescent Sexuality, Pregnancy, and Childbearing*. Washington, D.C.: National Academy Press.

Hofferth, S. 1987. "The Children of Teen Childbearers." In *Risking the Future*, vol. 3, 174–206, eds. L. Hofferth and C. D. Hayes. Washington, D.C.: National Academy Press.

Huber, P. J. 1967. "The Behavior of Maximum Likelihood Estimates under Non-standard Conditions." *Proceedings of the Fifth Berkeley Symposium on Mathematical Statistics and Probability* 1: 221–33.

Moore, K. A. 1986. *Children of Teen Parents: Heterogeneity of Outcomes.* Final report to NICHD, under grant number HB 18427-02. Washington, D.C.: Child Trends.

———. 1992. *The Consequences of Early Childbearing in the 1980s.* Final report to NICHD, under contract number NO1-HD-9-219. Washington, D.C.: Child Trends.

———. 1994. *Facts-at-a-Glance.* Washington, D.C.: Child Trends.

Moore, K. A., D. E. Myers, D. R. Morrison, C. W. Nord, B. V. Brown, and B. Edmonston. 1993. "Age at First Childbirth and Later Poverty." *Journal of Research on Adolescence* 3(4): 393–422.

National Center for Health Statistics. 1993. "Advance Report of Final Natality Statistics, 1991." *Monthly Vital Statistics Report* 42(3), supplement.

National Center for Health Statistics. 1994. "Advance Report of Final Natality Statistics, 1992." *Monthly Vital Statistics Report* 43 (5, October), supplement.

Peterson, J. L., and N. Zill. 1986. "Marital Disruption, Parent-Child Relationships, and Behavior Problems in Children." *Journal of Marriage and the Family* 48(May): 295–307.

Strobino, D. M. 1987. "The Health and Medical Consequences of Adolescent Sexuality and Pregnancy: A Review of the Literature." In *Risking the Future,* vol. 2, 93–122, eds. S. L. Hofferth and C. D. Hayes. Washington, D.C.: National Academy Press.

United Nations. 1994. *Demographic Yearbook, 1992.* New York: United Nations.

U.S. House of Representatives, Committee on Ways and Means. 1993. *Overview of Entitlement Programs—1993 Green Book.* Background material and data on programs within the jurisdiction of the Committee on Ways and Means. Washington, D.C.: U.S. Government Printing Office.

Zaslow, M. J., and C. D. Hayes. 1986. "Sex Differences in Children's Responses to Psychosocial Stress: Toward a Cross-Context Analysis." In *Advances in Developmental Psychology,* vol. 4, 285–337, eds. M. Lamb, A. Brown, and B. Rogoff. Hillsdale, N.J.: Lawrence Erlbaum.

Zill, N., and M. Coiro. 1992. "Assessing the Condition of Children." *Children and Youth Services Review* 14: 7–27.

APPENDIX 5A: DEPENDENT VARIABLES USED IN ANALYSES OF EFFECTS OF TIMING OF CHILDBEARING ON CHILDREN

National Longitudinal Survey of Youth-Child Supplement (Children Ages 4 to 14 in 1990)

Low Birth Weight. Survey ascertains child's actual weight at birth in ounces. Low birth weight (less than 5.5 pounds): mean = .05; range = 0, 1.

Well-Baby Care during the First Year. Mothers reported whether the child was taken to a doctor/clinic/HMO/community health center for well-baby care during the first year: mean = .92; range 0, 1.

Physical, Mental, Emotional Condition. Mothers were asked to report whether their child has a wide variety of physical, mental, and emotional conditions, including learning disability, minimal brain dysfunction, hyperkinesis/hyperactivity, asthma, respiratory disorder, speech impairment, serious difficulty in seeing or blindness, serious hearing difficulty or deafness, allergic conditions, serious emotional disturbance, speech impairment, crippled or orthopedic handicap, mental retardation, chronic nervous disorder, heart trouble, or other health limitations. Any disability or limitation (all of the above): mean = .08; range = 0, 1.

Psychological Help. Mothers reported whether the child had seen a psychiatrist or psychologist in the past 12 months. Mean = .05; range = 0, 1.

Home Observation for Measurement of the Environment. The HOME instrument consists of both maternal self-reports and interviewer observations. It was developed to assess quantitative and qualitative aspects of the child-rearing environment. Items are concerned with how the mother interacts with the child and structures the home environment. Different versions of the instrument are administered depending on the age of the child. The instrument consists of separate subscales for emotional support (reliability = .49 for children ages 3–6) and cognitive stimulation (reliability = .69) (Baker and Mott 1989; Zill and Coiro 1992). Mean = 96.7; s.d. = 16.2; range = 29.5 to 130.2.

Peabody Individual Achievement Test—Mathematics. The mathematics subscale of the PIAT assesses ability in mathematics, increasing in difficulty from simple recognition of numerals to advanced concepts such as geometry and trigonometry. Mean = 97.7; s.d. = 13.0; range = 65 to 135.

Peabody Individual Achievement Test—Reading Recognition. The reading recognition subscale measures word recognition and pronunciation ability. Children read a word silently, then say it aloud. The 84 items included in the subscale range from pre-school to high school levels. Mean = 101.7; s.d. = 14.0; range = 65 to 135.

Peabody Individual Achievement Test—Reading Comprehension. The reading comprehension subscale measures ability to derive meaning from sentences that are read silently, by having the child select the one out of four pictures that best portrays the meaning. The subscale consists of 66 increasingly difficult items. Mean = 101.0; s.d. = 14.4; range = 65 to 135.

Grade Repetition. Mothers report whether their child has ever re-peated any grades for any reason as well as the reason he/she repeated any grades: academic failure or lack of ability; imma-ture, acts too young; truancy; etc. Mean = .28; range = 0, 1.

Behavior Problems Index (standardized). The Behavior Problems In-dex contained in the NLSY-Child Supplement data is a subset of items developed by Peterson and Zill (1986), primarily from Achenbach's (1981) Child Behavior Checklist. The BPI is admin-istered to children ages four or older and measures mothers' reports of the frequency and types of behavior problems. The items selected for inclusion in the NLSY test battery have a demonstrated ability to distinguish children referred for psycho-logical treatment from typical children. The total scale score (reliability = .86) has psychometric properties preferable to any of the available subscales (Baker and Mott 1989). We use same-sex standard scores in our analyses. Higher scores on the index imply a greater level of behavior problems. Mean = 106.4; s.d. = 14.5; range = 68 to 149. (See Behavior Problems Index in the NSC section for a list of items.)

National Survey of Children
(Youth Ages 12 to 16 in 1981 and 18 to 22 in 1987)

Overall Health Rating (1981). Mothers were asked to rate their child's health as excellent, very good, good, fair, or poor. They were also asked to indicate whether the child has any physical or mental limitations. Excellent or very good health with no limitations: Mean = .78; range = 0, 1.

Overall Health Rating (1987). Youth were asked to rate their own health as excellent, very good, good, fair, or poor. They were also asked to indicate whether they have any physical or mental limitations. Excellent or very good health status with no limitations: Mean = .71; range = 0, 1.

Psychological Help (1987). Youth received psychological help between 1981 (based on parent report) and 1987 (based on youth report), and/or in 1987 youth reported they felt the need for psychological help in the past 12 months. Mean = .20; range = 0, 1.

Depression Scale (1987). The NSC contains a modified version of the Center for Epidemiological Studies Depression (CES-D) scale. This scale measures depressive symptoms in the general population and consists of 12 items. The range is from 0 to 36; if five or more items are missing, the scale is coded as missing. Individual items include "During the past week . . . I felt sad; I was bothered by things that usually don't bother me; I did not feel like eating/my appetite was poor; I felt that I could not shake off the blues, even with help from my family or friends; I had trouble keeping my mind on what I was doing; I felt depressed; I felt that everything I did was an effort; I felt fearful; my sleep was restless; I talked less than usual; I felt lonely; I could not get going." Mean = 8.7; s.d. = 6.7; range = 0 to 36.

Parent Rating of School Performance (1981). Parent report of youth's class standing is measured by responses to the question "Is s/he: one of the best students in the class, above the middle of the class, in the middle of the class, below the middle of the class, or near the bottom of the class?" One of the best in the class: mean = .26; range = 0, 1.

Teacher Rating of School Performance (1981). Teachers are asked to report on youth's class standing via the question "How did this student compare with others in his/her class last year in overall performance? One of the best students in the class, above the middle of the class, in the middle of the class, below the middle of the class, or near the bottom of the class." One of the best in the class: mean = .17; range = 0, 1.

Grade Repetition (1981). Parent-reported response to "Has (he/she) repeated any grades for any reason?" Mean = .16; range = 0, 1.

Grade Repetition (1987). Youth-reported response to "Have you ever been held back or repeated a grade for any reason?" Mean = .15; range = 0, 1.

High School Graduation. Youth has completed at least 12 years of high school, or youth is 17 or 18 years old and has completed the 11th grade. Mean = .89; range = 0, 1.

Behavior Problems Index. Parents completed a brief rating scale of behavior problems, rating the number of problems that were "often true" or "somewhat true" of the youth during the past four weeks. For the NSC analyses, each positive response counted as one point on the scale. If six or more of the items were missing, the scale was coded missing. Individual items include "Tell me whether each statement has been often true, sometimes true, or not true of (YOUTH) during the past four weeks . . . feels or complains that no one loves her/him; cheats or tells lies; is too fearful or anxious; has difficulty concentrating, cannot pay attention for long; is easily confused, seems to be in a fog; bullies, or is cruel or mean to others; does not seem to feel sorry after s/he does something wrong; is impulsive, or acts without thinking; feels worthless or inferior; is not liked by others of the same age; has difficulty getting his/her mind off certain thoughts, has obsessions; is restless or overly active, cannot sit still; has a very strong temper and loses it easily; is unhappy, sad, or depressed; is withdrawn, does not get involved with others; feels others are out to get her/him; and hangs around with kids who get in trouble." The 1987 measure consisted of these 17 items. Mean = 3.4; s.d. = 3.6; range = 0 to 17. The 1981 measure included the 17 aforementioned items and eight additional items: has sudden changes in mood or feelings; is rather high strung, tense or nervous, argues too much; is disobedient at home; is disobedient at school; is stubborn, sullen, or irritable; is secretive, keeps things to (himself/herself); worries too much. Mean = 7.9; s.d. = 5.8; range = 0 to 25.

Illegal Drug Use. A Gutman-type scale was constructed to measure youth-reported drug use in 1987. Categories are: (0) no use of illegal drugs (marijuana/hashish, cocaine/crack, nonprescription drugs), alcohol, or tobacco; (1) used alcohol/tobacco but no illegal drug; (2) used marijuana but no other illegal drugs; (3) used an illegal drug other than marijuana, but used less than once a month; and (4) used an illegal drug other than marijuana at least once a month. For multivariate analyses, we combined categories two through four and referred to any illegal drug use during the past year. Mean = .22; range = 0, 1.

Delinquency Scale. A scale created from nine items. The following items are coded not at all, 1 or 2 times, 3 to 11 times, or 12 or more times: "How often did you do this in the past 12 months . . . purposely damaged or destroyed property belonging to someone else? carried a hidden weapon other than an ordinary pocket knife? stole or tried to steal a motor vehicle such as a car or motorcycle? stole or tried to steal something else worth more than $50? purposely set fire to a building, a car, or other property or tried to do so? attacked someone with the idea of seriously hurting or killing her or him? got paid for having sexual relations with someone? sold marijuana or hashish? sold hard drugs such as heroin, cocaine, or LSD?" Mean = .15; range = 0, 1.

Whether Youth Ever Ran Away. Youth reported whether, before they turned 18, they ever ran away from home. Mean = .05; range = 0, 1.

APPENDIX 5B: INDEPENDENT VARIABLES

Table 5B.1 MOTHER'S FAMILY BACKGROUND CHARACTERISTICS, BY MOTHER'S AGE AT FOCAL CHILD'S BIRTH FOR CHILDREN AGES 4 TO 14 IN 1990 (WEIGHTED MEANS AND PERCENTAGES), NATIONAL LONGITUDINAL SURVEY OF YOUTH-CHILD SUPPLEMENT 1986–1990

Mother's Characteristics	Mother's Age at Focal Child's Birth						Total (Unweighted N)
	≤ 17	18–19	20–21	22–24	25 +	Total	
Unweighted N	429	763	939	1135	639	—	(3905)
Average education of highest educated parent	10.6	10.9	11.2	11.8	12.4	11.5	(3738)
Percent mothers worked when R was 14	52.1	53.1	54.1	52.7	50.3	52.6	(3814)
Average reading materials in the home at 14 (range 1 to 3)	1.7	1.8	1.9	2.2	2.2	2.0	(3891)
Average number of siblings	4.5	4.3	4.1	4.0	3.7	4.1	(3893)
Percent lived with two biological parents at 14 (range 1 to 3)	57.5	62.6	62.9	69.8	78.5	67.4	(3896)
Percent rural residence at 14	26.0	23.5	24.9	22.6	21.2	23.3	(3886)
Percent not married at conception of focal child	83.4	56.1	38.4	27.3	19.2	38.8	(3905)

Table values (except Ns) are based on weighted data.

Table 5B.2 MOTHER'S FAMILY BACKGROUND CHARACTERISTICS BY MOTHER'S AGE AT FOCAL CHILD'S BIRTH (WEIGHTED PERCENTAGES), NATIONAL SURVEY OF CHILDREN, 1976–1987

Mother's Characteristics	Mother's Age at Focal Child's Birth						Total (Unweighted N)
	≤ 17	18–19	20–21	22–24	25 +	Total	
Unweighted N	77	135	199	283	649	—	(1343)
Mother's parents were Catholic	28.4	16.2	23.9	36.5	30.6	29.4	(1343)
Mother's parents were Protestant Fundamentalists	12.1	8.1	9.8	10.8	8.1	9.1	(1343)
Mother's parents received welfare at some time[1]	32.3	12.0	10.9	6.4	8.4	9.7	(1031)
Mother's residence was urban during childhood	79.4	70.5	76.4	66.5	72.3	71.8	(1343)
Mother's residence was rural during childhood	16.4	24.7	20.1	31.1	26.2	25.8	(1343)
Mother often smoked cigarettes before age 15[1]	13.2	13.2	7.7	5.4	3.3	5.7	(1032)
Mother lived away from both parents before age 14[1]	1.4	5.0	8.9	3.9	10.4	7.9	(1032)
Mother never wanted to have focal child	14.5	4.7	6.4	7.1	20.1	13.5	(1334)
Mother wanted to have focal child later	41.1	38.3	30.2	23.7	10.4	20.2	(1334)
Mother was not in H.S. and had <12 years of education at conception of first child	18.3	24.2	29.4	14.9	24.8	23.1	(1017)
Mother was not married at conception of focal child[1]	77.3	40.2	22.0	7.7	3.9	13.6	(993)

1. Variable based on 1987 interview (unweighted N = 1080).
Note: Table values (except Ns) are based on weighted data.

Chapter Six

TEEN CHILDREN'S HEALTH AND HEALTH CARE USE

Barbara Wolfe and Maria Perozek

Chapter 5 examined a whole variety of dimensions along which the children of teen mothers may differ from the children of older mothers, including a few limited measures of health. In this chapter we focus intensively on more comprehensive measures of health and on medical care utilization and expenditures. With respect to utilization and expenditures, we present descriptive statistics as well as comparisons that control for factors that influence use and expenditures, namely, the child's health, gender, and race.

We can readily think of reasons why the health of teen mothers' children could be better or worse than the health of the children of older mothers. Children of teen mothers, for example, may face increased risk of medical problems if their mothers have lower educational levels (leading to poorer parenting skills) and/or lower incomes (leading to worse nutrition, for example, and less preventive health care). Alternatively, the mothers' youth could be associated with fewer problems during childbirth and a greater likelihood of giving birth to a healthy infant. Any negative outcomes could outweigh positive outcomes or vice versa.

Even if children of teens are more likely to be in poor health than are the children of older mothers, they will not necessarily incur higher medical costs or have greater medical care utilization. First, persons with lower incomes and those without insurance are less likely to take their children to medical care providers (Wolfe 1994). Second, if they do take their children, they are more likely to use lower-cost providers such as subsidized clinics and primary care providers, rather than specialists (Mitchell 1991). Finally, since Medicaid generally reimburses providers at a lower level than private insurers do, reported expenditures are likely to be lower for those who are covered by Medicaid. If the cost of the medical care of teens' children is disproportionately paid by Medicaid or shifted to other payers, then other members of society are paying these costs.

We use a nationally representative data set, the 1987 National Medical Expenditure Study (NMES), to investigate the association between teen parenting and health and medical care costs of the children. This is the most recent data set to collect detailed data on medical care utilization, health status, and insurance coverage for a national sample. We use these data to construct a sample of 3,047 children who were less than 14 years old at the time of the last interview and who had mothers less than 33 years old. Maternal characteristics are merged onto the child's observation to complete our analysis file. The sample is restricted to children and mothers for whom complete information is available.

Unfortunately, the NMES data set is not ideally suited for studying the fertility decisions of the women in the sample. In fact, we know very little about their fertility histories. Instead, we infer the age at which women had their first child by subtracting the age of the mother's oldest child in the sample from the mother's age. Clearly, this approach has several problems. First, since the sampling unit is the household, we only observe the mother and the child if they are living in the same household at the time of the first interview. If the mother's oldest child moved away from home sometime prior to the initial interview, for example, we would underestimate the age at which the mother had her first child. Our restriction of the sample of mothers to those who were less than 33 years old at the time of the last interview is designed to minimize the chances that one or more of the mother's children will no longer be living in the household.

A second problem, which we cannot ameliorate, results from restricting our sample to children whose mothers live in the same household, thus omitting children who live only with their fathers or other relatives. It seems reasonable to assume that children of teenage mothers might disproportionately live with other family members. To the extent that this is true, we do not have a representative sample of children of teen mothers. (The overall means, standard deviations, minimums, and maximums of the variables used in our analysis are presented in table 6.1.)[1]

We study differences in health status, medical care utilization and expenditures, insurance coverage, and public cost of medical care. To make these comparisons, we present the results from two separate analyses. First, we present average (mean) utilization and medical expenditure figures for the following three groups of children: chil-

Table 6.1 DEFINITIONS, MEANS, AND STANDARD DEVIATIONS OF VARIABLES
USED IN TOBIT ESTIMATES ON SAMPLE OF ALL CHILDREN OF
WOMEN AGES 16–32 AS OF 1987

	Mean	Standard Deviation	Minimum	Maximum
Dependent variables				
Total number of medical				
care visits	3.76	8.22	0	196
Total medical care				
expenditures	$406.40	$2,305.00	$0.00	$101,200.00
Total dollars paid by others	$198.00	$1,258.00	$0.00	$ 38,080.00
Independent variables				
Age of child	5.52	3.46	0	14
Race of child is white	.61	.49	0	1
Sex of child is male	.52	.50	0	1
Child has excellent health	.52	.50	0	1
Child has poor health	.07	.26	0	1
Mother first gave birth when				
17 or under	.20	.40	0	1
Mother first gave birth when				
18 to 19	.24	.43	0	1
Mother first gave birth when				
20 to 21	.23	.42	0	1
Child born when mother was				
17 or under	.13	.34	0	1
Child born when mother was				
18 to 19	.14	.34	0	1
Other variables				
Mother a high school graduate	.69	.46	0	1
Mother's age in 1987	27.62	3.41	16	32
Mother's number of children				
in 1987	2.27	1.11	1	7
n = 3,463				

Source: National Medical Expenditure Survey (NMES).

dren born to mothers who first gave birth as a young (less than 18)
teen, children born to mothers who first gave birth as an older (ages
18 to 19) teen, and children born to mothers who never gave birth as
a teen (nonteen, or late-fertility, mother). We then present these means
for children grouped into the following six age groups: 0 to 1 year, 2
to 3 years, 4 to 5 years, 6 to 7 years, 8 to 10 years, and 11 to 14 years.
The first group comprises children who are the appropriate age to
receive well-baby care. The second group are at the age when vacci-
nations are usually given. The third group are nursery school age; the
6- to 7-year-olds are in their first years of elementary school; the 8- to

10-year-olds have completed most of elementary school; and the 11- to 14-year-olds are entering their early adolescent years.

The next sections present descriptive analyses showing the relationship between teen childbearing and health status, health care utilization, sources of payment for medical care, and expenditures on care, respectively. These discussions are followed by a section presenting the results of our second set of analyses using multivariate regression to control for child's race, sex, and health status, which can be expected to influence health care use.

HEALTH STATUS

We use four measures of health status. The first two are based on parents' self-assessment and are perhaps the most widely used of all health status measures.[2] The first measure is a dummy variable for whether the child is reported to be in excellent health (*excellent*), and the second measure is a dummy variable for whether the child is reported to be in poor or fair health (*poor-fair*). We also use two other indicators of health problems, one that indicates the presence of acute health conditions (*acute*) and a second that indicates the presence of chronic health conditions (*chronic*). Both variables are based on a series of questions asked of parents. The chronic conditions included differ slightly for children less than 5 years old relative to children over 5 (see Appendix 6B for more detail). The overall proportion of children in excellent health is clearly lower for children whose mothers were teens at first birth than for those whose mother never gave birth as a teenager (table 6.2). Considerably more than half of children born to nonteen mothers are reported to be in excellent health, whereas slightly less than half of children born to older teen mothers (ages 18 to 19) report excellent health, and considerably less than half (38 percent) of those born to a young teen mom (age 17 or younger) are least likely to report excellent health. Further, the reported health status of children born to teen mothers is never better than that of children born to mothers who first gave birth at a later age for any age child. There are also differences in the proportion of children with reported poor or fair health status by mother's age at her first birth, although the proportions themselves are small: 5 percent of children born to older mothers had poor or fair health reported, compared to 9 percent of children born to mothers who ever gave birth as a young or older teen. The pattern for acute and chronic illness is rather dif-

Table 6.2 CHILDREN'S HEALTH STATUS, BY MOTHER'S AGE AT BIRTH OF FIRST
CHILD

	Excellent Health	Fair or Poor Health	Health Condition		(N)
			Acute	Chronic	
Young Teen Mother					
Age of Child (years)					
0 to 1	0.36	0.08	0.68	—	(54)
2 to 3	0.43	0.13	0.52	—	(89)
4 to 5	0.40	0.06	0.59	0.63	(67)
6 to 7	0.39	0.13	0.48	0.05	(85)
8 to 10	0.37	0.06	0.45	0.01	(132)
11 to 14	0.35	0.07	0.51	0.05	(150)
All	0.38	0.09	0.52	—	(577)
Older Teen Mother					
Age of Child (years)					
0 to 1	0.48	0.07	0.74	—	(53)
2 to 3	0.48	0.11	0.63	—	(133)
4 to 5	0.45	0.16	0.64	0.63	(110)
6 to 7	0.49	0.09	0.54	0.07	(134)
8 to 10	0.50	0.06	0.50	0.10	(164)
11 to 14	0.52	0.03	0.50	0.07	(120)
All	0.49	0.09	0.50	—	(714)
Nonteen Mother					
Age of Child (years)					
0 to 1	0.60	0.04	0.70	—	(248)
2 to 3	0.62	0.08	0.67	—	(456)
4 to 5	0.64	0.05	0.60	0.61	(320)
6 to 7	0.56	0.05	0.58	0.07	(301)
8 to 10	0.58	0.03	0.59	0.06	(221)
11 to 14	0.57	0.03	0.57	0.11	(50)
All	0.60	0.05	0.63	—	(1,596)

ferent: in these cases, the proportions with acute or chronic conditions
are somewhat greater for children of older mothers. These differences
may reflect real health differences or simply differences in diagnosis
rendered at the site of care.

UTILIZATION

We use five measures of utilization: outpatient visits to medical providers, outpatient visits to hospital clinics, visits to an emergency
room, number of inpatient or hospital stays, and total number of visits.

Table 6.3 MEANS OF HEALTH CARE UTILIZATION, BY MOTHER'S AGE AT BIRTH
OF FIRST CHILD

	Medical Provider Visits	Hospital Outpatient Visits	Emergency Room Visits	Inpatient Stays	All Medical Visits	(N)
Young Teen Mother						
Age of Child (years)						
0 to 1	3.90	0.56	0.66	0.11	5.24	(61)
2 to 3	2.87	0.28	0.38	0.10	3.64	(105)
4 to 5	1.93	0.27	0.25	0.01	2.47	(110)
6 to 7	1.33	0.03	0.25	0.04	1.63	(98)
8 to 10	1.14	0.10	0.22	0.02	1.52	(152)
11 to 14	1.42	0.08	0.16	0.02	1.68	(174)
All	1.84	0.18	0.27	0.04	2.33	(700)
Older Teen Mother						
Age of Child (years)						
0 to 1	4.41	0.54	0.77	0.08	5.80	(65)
2 to 3	2.27	0.28	0.38	0.08	3.01	(155)
4 to 5	3.52	0.28	0.27	0.04	4.11	(160)
6 to 7	3.51	0.19	0.20	0.02	3.72	(144)
8 to 10	2.21	0.16	0.21	0.03	2.60	(184)
11 to 14	1.28	0.11	0.18	0.06	1.63	(136)
All	2.71	0.23	0.29	0.05	3.27	(844)
Nonteen Mother						
Age of Child (years)						
0 to 1	6.89	0.58	0.47	0.12	8.06	(282)
2 to 3	4.96	0.32	0.40	0.05	5.74	(516)
4 to 5	3.36	0.26	0.26	0.05	3.93	(462)
6 to 7	3.53	0.20	0.24	0.03	4.00	(346)
8 to 10	2.16	0.17	0.17	0.01	2.51	(259)
11 to 14	2.25	0.33	0.14	0.00	2.71	(54)
All	4.15	0.31	0.31	0.05	4.82	(1,919)

Our reasoning for using these measures of utilization is as follows.
Much of the literature suggests that emergency room visits often represent inappropriate medical care utilization. In many cases, such
visits take place when access to providers is restricted and care is
postponed until it is an "emergency." Further, some inpatient stays
are the result of postponed medical care and may represent lack of
access—rather than access as normally interpreted—to medical care.
Finally, in some areas of the country, outpatient visits to hospitals
may indicate a lack of access to private providers as well as the lack
of a regular provider.

The pattern of utilization of medical providers provides clear evidence that children born to mothers who never gave birth as a teen

have greater use in terms of visits to medical care providers (table 6.3). This is true for every age of child, although the differences are greater at younger ages. Note in particular the comparison of 6.89 medical provider visits for infants and 1-year-olds of older mothers, compared with 3.90 and 4.41 for infants and 1-year-olds born to young teen and older teen mothers, respectively. The overall differences are also large: 4.15 for children of older mothers versus 1.84 for children born to a young teen mother and 2.71 for those born to an older teen mother. In each of these tabulations, the same pattern exists: children of young teen mothers have the lowest utilization, whereas children born to nonteen mothers have the highest utilization. A similar pattern appears for hospital outpatient visits. There is greater use among children born to older mothers, although the differences are smaller and the utilization is far smaller on average. Emergency room visits suggest little difference by age of the mother at her first birth. However, in the youngest age group, the pattern shows greater use for infants of teen mothers. In this case, the mean use is .66 for children born to young teen mothers, .77 for those born to older teen mothers, and .47 for nonteen mothers. The pattern for inpatient stays is not clear because they are so infrequent in this age group. Finally, since total medical care visits are dominated by visits to a medical provider, the patterns of total visits are essentially identical to those for utilization of medical providers: significantly greater use among children born to older mothers. A comparison of children born to a young teen mother versus those born to a nonteen mother shows that children in the first group have fewer than half the number of total visits as those in the latter group.

SOURCE OF PAYMENT FOR MEDICAL CARE

We look here at the ratio of medical expenditures paid for by three sources: self-payment (payment by parents), private insurance, and other members of society. Payment by other members of society includes payments made by Medicaid, by the Civilian Health and Medical Program for the Uniformed Services (CHAMPUS), and by Medicare (for a small number of disabled children), with an adjustment for uncompensated care (see appendix 6B).

Children born to older mothers are more likely than those born to younger or older teens to have their care paid for directly by their parents (table 6.4). About 47 percent of the cost of care was paid out-

Table 6.4 MEANS OF PROPORTION OF MEDICAL EXPENSES PAID BY SOURCE,
BY MOTHER'S AGE AT BIRTH OF FIRST CHILD

	Percentage Self-Paid	Percentage Paid by Private Insurance	Percentage Paid by Others in Society	(N)
Young Teen Mother				
Age of Child (years)				
0 to 1	0.34	0.10	0.56	(50)
2 to 3	0.25	0.15	0.60	(80)
4 to 5	0.29	0.16	0.56	(72)
6 to 7	0.41	0.18	0.42	(47)
8 to 0	0.45	0.14	0.41	(82)
11 to 14	0.35	0.21	0.44	(85)
All	0.35	0.16	0.49	(416)
Older Teen Mother				
Age of Child (years)				
0 to 1	0.36	0.09	0.55	(58)
2 to 3	0.42	0.20	0.38	(116)
4 to 5	0.27	0.26	0.47	(105)
6 to 7	0.42	0.20	0.39	(80)
8 to 10	0.41	0.29	0.31	(103)
11 to 14	0.43	0.28	0.30	(73)
All	0.38	0.23	0.39	(535)
Nonteen Mother				
Age of Child (years)				
0 to 1	0.49	0.30	0.21	(268)
2 to 3	0.48	0.32	0.20	(429)
4 to 5	0.50	0.33	0.17	(368)
6 to 7	0.45	0.31	0.24	(243)
8 to 10	0.40	0.37	0.25	(172)
11 to 14	0.39	0.32	0.30	(38)
All	0.47	0.32	0.20	(1,518)

of-pocket for children born to older parents, compared with only 38
percent of the costs for children of older teen mothers and 35 percent
for children born to young teen mothers. The proportion covered by
private insurance also differs by mother's age at first birth. On average,
32 percent of medical costs were paid for by private insurance for
children born to older-fertility mothers, compared to 23 and 16 percent for children of older teen mothers and younger teen mothers,
respectively. The ratio paid by others in society is again consistent
with expectations: far more children born to teen mothers, especially
young teen mothers, had publicly provided insurance. Whereas only
20 percent of medical care costs were paid by others in society for

children born to older-fertility mothers, nearly half (49 percent) the costs for children born to young teen mothers were paid by others in society.

EXPENDITURES

As expected, given the patterns of utilization, expenditures are greater for children born to an older mother than for those born to a teen mother (table 6.5). Overall, in 1987 dollars, the average is $469 for children born to nonteen mothers versus an average of $312 for children born to a young teen mother.[3] The pattern is not consistent across all age groups. For infants (0–1), the highest average expenditures are among children born to a late-fertility (older) mother; the lowest are among those born to an older teen mother. For ages 4–5 the pattern differs: the highest expenditures are for children born to older teen mothers, and the lowest are for those born to young teen mothers.

For expenditures by other members of society, the pattern is different. Even though average expenditures are greatest for children born to older mothers, the amount paid by other members of society is greatest for children born to mothers who first gave birth as young teens. Children born to young teen mothers, for example, incurred $187 in social costs, compared to about $165 incurred by children born to older teen and nonteen mothers (table 6.6). Since acute health problems may explain differential medical expenditures, we include means by whether or not the child has a reported acute condition. On average, those with acute conditions report far greater social and total expenditures than do those with no acute conditions. For those with

Table 6.5 TOTAL ANNUAL EXPENDITURES, BY MOTHER'S AGE AT BIRTH OF FIRST CHILD (1987 DOLLARS)

Child's Age (years)	Young Teen Mother	(N)	Older Teen Mother	(N)	Nonteen Mother	(N)
0 to 1	$926.88	(61)	$783.01	(65)	$1,167.64	(282)
2 to 3	472.76	(105)	348.01	(155)	512.60	(516)
4 to 5	271.20	(110)	405.63	(160)	336.49	(462)
6 to 7	324.35	(98)	165.52	(144)	289.44	(346)
8 to 10	222.22	(152)	173.58	(184)	156.76	(259)
11 to 14	121.34	(174)	315.53	(136)	188.07	(54)
All	311.77	(700)	311.96	(844)	469.22	(1,919)

Table 6.6 TOTAL EXPENDITURES AND AMOUNT PAID BY OTHERS IN SOCIETY,
BY MOTHER'S AGE AT BIRTH OF FIRST CHILD AND CHILD'S HEALTH
(1987 DOLLARS)

	Dollars Paid by Others	Total Expenditures
Young Teen Mother		
Child's Health		
Not Sick	$ 83.64	$141.02
Sick	282.49	459.66
All	186.70	306.17
Older Teen Mother		
Child's Health		
Not Sick	85.76	149.28
Sick	224.66	474.25
All	164.79	334.19
Nonteen Mother		
Child's Health		
Not Sick	56.60	214.45
Sick	226.50	672.31
All	163.78	503.27

Note: Sick is defined as having an acute condition.

acute conditions, children born to a young teen have the highest expenditures paid by others in society ($282), compared with about $225 for the other two groups.

RESULTS WHEN HEALTH STATUS, RACE, AND BIRTH ORDER OF CHILD ARE CONTROLLED

The means above provide us with a picture of differences in health status, medical care use, and expenditures, by whether or not a child was born to a young teen mother, an older teen mother, or a nonteen mother. Since the distribution of children's ages is not constant across these groups, we use multivariate analysis to better isolate the impact that having a mother who first gave birth as a teen has on her children's medical care use. To this analysis, we also add whether a particular child was the mother's first born or not. We look at three measures of medical care use: total number of visits, total expenditures, and societal expenditures (expenditures paid by others).

Three models are estimated for each dependent variable. Model 1, the simple, or limited, model, includes only the child's age at the time he or she is observed in 1987; dummy variables indicating that the child's mother first gave birth as a young teen, older teen, or at age 20–21; and dummy variables indicating that the child's mother was a young or older teen at the time of *this* child's birth. Model 2 adds the child's race and sex to the equation. We include these variables because race and sex are associated with some illnesses and may be associated with barriers to medical care. Model 3 adds two measures of a child's health to the estimates: a dummy variable for poor-fair health and a dummy variable for excellent health. The former is expected to lead to greater use of care, the latter to less use, other things being equal. Other variables normally included in utilization estimates, such as insurance coverage and income, are not included for three reasons. Both variables are likely to be related to the mother's fertility decisions. Reported income may belong to the mother's parents as the mother may not have her own household. And there are documented problems with the income imputations at the tails of the distribution.[4]

The estimated determinants of total medical care visits are consistent with the means presented earlier (table 6.7). Older children have fewer visits. Children with mothers who first gave birth prior to age 22, for all three categories of young mother, use less care, with the magnitude of the reduction increasing as age of first birth gets younger. There is also some indication that the first child born to a

Table 6.7 DETERMINANTS OF TOTAL MEDICAL CARE VISITS: TOBIT ESTIMATES

	Model 1		Model 2		Model 3	
Mother first gave birth when 17 or under	− 3.79	(5.2)	− 2.94	(4.0)	− 3.45	(4.1)
Mother first gave birth when 18 to 19	− 1.80	(3.0)	− 1.15	(1.9)	− 1.37	(2.0)
Mother first gave birth when 20 to 21	− 1.52	(3.3)	− 1.35	(2.9)	− 1.38	(2.6)
Young teen at child's birth	.84	(1.0)	.94	(1.1)	1.05	(1.1)
Older teen at child's birth	− .81	(1.1)	− .91	(1.3)	− .83	(1.0)
Child's age	− .55	(9.8)	− .54	(9.8)	− .57	
Child's sex = male			.15	(0.4)	.16	(0.4)
Child's race = white			2.69	(7.3)	2.79	(6.6)
Child's health						
Excellent					− .96	(2.3)
Fair to poor					4.49	(5.8)
Constant	6.49	(17.8)[a]	4.38	(9.0)	4.83	(7.8)
Log likelihood	− 10,254		− 10,227		− 8,666	
n = 3,463						

Note: Mean of the dependent variable = 3.76; standard deviation = 8.22.
a. *T*-statistics are in parentheses.

young teen mother may use somewhat more care than her later children. Children's health status plays the expected role and is quite significant. In addition, white children have relatively more medical visits than nonwhite children, even after controlling for the child's health status, age, sex, and mother's age at birth.

The estimated determinants of medical care expenditures are similar to those for visits, with the following exception: even after a child's health is taken into account, first-born children of young teens have significantly greater expenditures than do subsequent children born to these mothers (table 6.8).

The estimated determinants of medical care cost borne by other members of society show that others in society bear significantly greater costs for the medical care of children born to mothers in each of the three young mother categories than for children of other mothers, although when health status is controlled the children of young teen mothers do not cost more than children in the other two young-mother categories (table 6.9). First-born children of young teen mothers have greater costs, however, than do subsequent children born to the same mothers, a finding that suggests some learning. This pattern does not hold for first borns of older teen mothers.

As argued above, the health status of the child may vary systematically with the mother's age at birth. Indeed, the descriptive statistics

Table 6.8 DETERMINANTS OF MEDICAL EXPENDITURES: TOBIT ESTIMATES

	Model 1		Model 2		Model 3	
Mother first gave birth when 17 or under	−460.3	(2.2)	−361.2	(1.7)	−704.8	(2.9)
Mother first gave birth when 18 to 19	−420.9	(2.4)	−343.2	(1.9)	−437.5	(2.2)
Mother first gave birth when 20 to 21	−110.3	(0.8)	−90.4	(0.7)	−95.6	(0.6)
Young teen at child's birth	179.8	(0.7)	190.5	(0.8)	504.3	(1.8)
Older teen at child's birth	125.9	(0.6)	11.4	(0.5)	202.3	(0.9)
Child's age	−141.7	(8.7)	−141.6	(8.7)	−150.1	(8.3)
Child's sex = male			−17.3	(0.2)	−72.6	(0.06)
Child's race = white			311.5	(2.9)	377.2	(3.1)
Child's health						
Excellent					−360.6	(3.0)
Fair to poor					899.7	(4.0)
Constant	$671.10	(6.3)[a]	$443.90	(3.1)	$647.80	(3.6)
Log likelihood	−23,692		−23,688		−19,955	
n = 3,463						

Note: Mean of the dependent variable = $406.44; standard deviation = 2,305.3.
a. T-statistics are in parentheses.

Table 6.9 DETERMINANTS OF MEDICAL EXPENDITURES PAID BY SOCIETY: TOBIT ESTIMATES

	Model 1		Model 2		Model 3	
Mother first gave birth when 17 or under	870.7	(3.8)	712.2	(3.1)	398.4	(1.7)
Mother first gave birth when 18 to 19	857.9	(4.4)	736.1	(3.7)	565.9	(2.9)
Mother first gave birth when 20 to 21	607.4	(3.8)	576.9	(3.6)	589.9	(3.8)
Young teen at child's birth	475.1	(1.9)	455.6	(1.8)	672.2	(2.6)
Older teen at child's birth	−75.5	(0.3)	−52.4	(0.2)	49.5	(0.2)
Child's age	−165.9	(9.1)	−166.7	(9.1)	−156.9	(8.9)
Child's sex = male			135.2	(1.2)	66.5	(0.6)
Child's race = white			−510.2	(4.3)	−327.1	(2.8)
Child's health						
Excellent					−486.4	(4.1)
Fair to poor					1,150.2	(5.8)
Constant	−$1,572.3	(11.9)[a]	−$1,269.0	(7.6)	−$959.1	(5.4)
Log likelihood	−10,341		−10,331		−8,477	
n = 3,463						

Data source: 1987 National Medical Expenditure Study.
Notes: Mean of the dependent variable = $198.00; standard deviation = 1,257.9.
a. T-statistics are in parentheses.

in table 6.2 suggest that children of teen mothers are less likely to be reported in excellent health than the children of nonteen mothers. However, the descriptive statistics do not allow us to control for demographic variables such as sex and race. When we control for these factors we find that teen motherhood is significantly associated with a lower likelihood of excellent health (table 6.10). This negative effect on health status is greatest for young teen mothers and decreases in magnitude as the mother's age increases. Further, the negative effect of young teen motherhood on health status does not appear to be offset by birth order. There is also a suggestion that having a mother who was a teen when she first gave birth raises the child's risk of having fair to poor health. But this finding is only statistically significant for children of older teen mothers.

ESTIMATED IMPACTS OF DELAYED CHILDBEARING ON HEALTH CARE EXPENDITURES AND USE

We can now simulate the expected impact on children's health care utilization and expenses of delaying childbearing, based on the tobit

Table 6.10 DETERMINANTS OF CHILD'S HEALTH STATUS: PROBIT ESTIMATES

	Fair-Poor	Excellent
Mother first gave birth when 17 or under	.06 (.44)	−.49* (−4.9)
Mother first gave birth when 18 to 19	.25* (2.1)	−3.4* (4.0)
Mother first gave birth when 20 to 21	−.20* (1.9)	−.13* (−1.9)
Young teen at child's birth	.11 (.66)	.05 (.47)
Older teen at child's birth	−.17 (−.13)	.08 (.83)
Child's age	−.03* (−2.5)	.004 (.53)
Child's sex = male	−.16* (−2.3)	−.05 (−.98)
Child's race = white	−.13 (−1.7)	.21* (4.2)
Constant	-1.19 (11.9)	.12 (1.8)
Log likelihood	−727.04	−1,953.8
n = 2,887		

*Statistically significant at the 5 percent level.
Note: T-values are in parentheses.

estimates presented in tables 6.7 to 6.9 and the probit estimates in table 6.10. The tobit estimates allow us to calculate the expected value of the outcome of interest for all children in the sample. Then we recalculate that value as the mother is "aged" at her first birth. Our simulations provide a range of estimates. The upper bound of the range is calculated under the assumption that all covariates in the analysis are held constant except age of the mother at first birth. However, this may not be a very good assumption. For example, as the results in table 6.10 show, the health status of the child itself is affected by a change in the mother's age at first birth. Hence, we also calculate a lower bound that incorporates the expected change in health status when the mother's age changes (simulated using the probit results).

How average total medical expenses would be expected to vary if the mother were older when she had her first child, given no health change, is shown in table 6.11. The values assuming child health changes as predicted by the estimates are shown in table 6.10. The figures in table 6.11 are upper-bound estimates; those in table 6.12 are lower-bound estimates. The discussion here is based on the 1987 values. As a baseline case, column 1 presents the average "expected" value for different groups of children in the sample using the actual values. The first row suggests that if a woman who first gave birth as a young teen postponed childbirth until she was 18 to 19 years old, until 20 or 21, or until 22 or over, then the expected medical expenses for one of her children would increase from $829 to $859, $949, or $992, respectively. These upper-bound estimates do not incorporate the potential improvement in the child's health status as the age of the mother increases. When the expected change in health status is

Table 6.11 TOTAL EXPECTED MEDICAL EXPENSES, GIVEN NO CHANGE IN CHILD'S HEALTH

	Baseline Value	If Mother Delayed until Age			(N)
		18 to 19	20 to 21	22 or over	
Age of mother at first birth was 17 or under	$829.15	$858.54	$949.27	$991.52	(577)
First born	835.26	821.61	877.89	917.95	(377)
Later child	817.45	928.15	1,083.82	1,130.22	(200)
Age of mother at first birth was 18 to 19	894.94		997.22	1,040.93	(714)
First born	858.33		916.42	957.71	(394)
Later child	940.02		1,096.80	1,143.38	(320)
Age of mother at first birth was 20 to 21	1,057.79			1,103.51	(661)
Age of mother at first birth was 22 or over	1,238.62				(935)
Total	1,030.39				(2,887)

Note: These figures denote simulated expenses on the assumption that the child's health does not change. Figures are 1987 dollars. Comparable 1994 dollars would be 1.622 times larger, based on the Consumer Price Index for medical care.

Table 6.12 TOTAL EXPECTED MEDICAL EXPENSES, GIVEN CHANGES IN CHILD'S HEALTH

Population	Baseline Value	If Mother Delayed until Age			(N)
		18 to 19	20 to 21	22 or over	
Age of mother at first birth was 17 or under	$1,344.74	$1,392.41	$1,539.55	$1,608.08	(577)
First born	1,354.81	1,332.51	1,423.79	1,488.76	(377)
Later child	1,325.76	1,505.30	1,757.77	1,833.02	(200)
Age of mother at first birth was 18 or 19	1,451.44		1,617.32	1,688.21	(714)
First born	1,392.07		1,486.28	1,553.24	(394)
Later child	1,524.55		1,778.66	1,854.37	(320)
Age of mother at first birth was 20 to 21	1,715.56			1,789.71	(661)
Age of mother at first birth was 22 or over	2,008.83				(935)
Total					(2,887)

Note: These figures denote simulated expenses on the assumption that the child's health changes as predicted by the probit estimates in table 6.10. Figures are 1987 dollars. Comparable 1994 dollars would be 1.622 times larger, based on the Consumer Price Index for medical care.

included in the simulations (table 6.12), the change in expenditures is smaller for each incremental increase in the mother's age. For example, the upper-bound calculation reported above indicates that annual medical expenses would increase by $163 if a mother who was a young teen at the time of her first birth were to postpone childbearing until she was 22 or over. The lower-bound calculation, in contrast, suggests that total medical expenses would increase by only $126 if the mother waited until age 22 or over.

Similar simulations for expected medical visits (table 6.13) show that medical visits increase when the mother is older at the time of her first birth. Once again, the expected differences in medical care utilization decrease somewhat when the change in health status is included in the simulation. If a young teen mother were to delay childbearing until she was 22 or over, the number of medical visits would increase from 3.8 to 5.3 (without expected health change) and 3.8 to 5.1 (with expected health change).

Table 6.13 TOTAL ANNUAL EXPECTED MEDICAL VISITS

Population	Baseline Value	If Mother Delayed until Age			(N)
		18 to 19	20 to 21	22 or over	
Age of mother at first	3.8	4.2	4.5	5.3	(577)
birth was 17 or under	3.8	4.2	4.3	5.1	
First born	3.7	3.8	4.2	4.9	(377)
	3.6	3.7	4.0	4.7	
Later child	4.0	5.1	5.1	5.9	(200)
	4.0	5.1	4.9	5.8	
Age of mother at first	4.6		4.8	5.6	(714)
birth was 18 to 19	4.5		4.6	5.4	
First born	4.0		4.5	5.2	(394)
	4.0		4.3	5.1	
Later child	5.3		5.3	6.1	(320)
	5.2		5.0	5.9	
Age of mother at first	5.2			6.1	(661)
birth was 20 to 21	5.2			6.1	
Age of mother at first	6.8				(935)
birth was 22 or over	6.8				
Total	5.3				(2,887)
	5.3				

Note: The top figure in the cell denotes simulated expenses on the assumption that the child's health does not change; the bottom figure denotes simulated expenses on the assumption that the child's health changes as predicted by the probit estimates in table 6.10.

The total expected expenses paid for by others in society, assuming children's health does and does not change, are shown in tables 6.14 and 6.15, respectively.

The results are striking. If a younger teen mother were to postpone childbearing until she was 22 or over, the expenses paid for by others in society on behalf of each of her children would decrease from $405 to $224 (45 percent). Since the total medical expenses for each member of this group would increase from $829 to $992, the reduction in the share of the health expenses of her children paid by others is even greater. The single greatest expected reduction is young teen moms delaying childbirth until age 22 or over: from $414 to $171 for their firstborn.

Although these simulations provide an interesting first step toward measuring the effects of teen childbearing on the health status and health expenses of children, it is important to highlight their limitations. The estimates on which the simulations are based are reduced form regressions. Because we do not have a structural model of the process in which teen childbearing plays a major part, we cannot make policy predictions based on our simulations. For example, several important factors that may be correlated with both health care utilization and teen motherhood are necessarily omitted from our

Table 6.14 TOTAL EXPENSES PAID BY OTHERS IN SOCIETY, GIVEN NO CHANGES IN CHILD'S HEALTH

| Population | Baseline Value | If Mother Delayed until Age | | | (N) |
		18 to 19	20 to 21	22 or over	
Age of mother at first					
birth was 17 or under	$405.36	$346.22	$344.85	$223.94	(577)
First born	425.96	311.76	306.11	196.77	(377)
Later child	366.52	411.19	417.88	275.15	(200)
Age of mother at first					
birth was 18 to 19	357.11		356.96	233.00	(714)
First born	312.15		306.49	197.06	(394)
Later child	412.46		419.10	277.24	(320)
Age of mother at first					
birth was 20 to 21	345.49			223.04	(661)
Age of mother at first					
birth was 22 or over	265.95				(935)
Total	334.57				(2,887)

Note: These figures denote simulated expenses on the assumption that the child's health does not change. Figures are 1987 dollars. Comparable 1994 dollars would be 1.622 times larger, based on the Consumer Price Index for medical care.

Table 6.15 TOTAL EXPENSES PAID BY OTHERS IN SOCIETY, GIVEN CHANGES IN CHILD'S HEALTH

	Baseline Value	If Mother Delayed until Age			(N)
		18 to 19	20 to 21	22 or over	
Age of mother at first birth was 17 or under	$657.43	$561.51	$559.29	$363.19	(577)
First born	690.83	505.62	496.46	319.13	(377)
Later child	594.43	666.88	677.73	446.25	(200)
Age of mother at first birth was 18 to 19	579.17		497.07	319.60	(714)
First born	668.94		679.71	449.64	(394)
Later child	668.94		679.71	449.64	(320)
Age of mother at first birth was 20 to 21	560.33			361.73	(661)
Age of mother at first birth was 22 or over	431.33				(935)
Total	542.62				(2,887)

Note: These figures denote simulated expenses on the assumption that the child's health changes as predicted by the probit estimates in table 6.10. Figures are 1987 dollars. Comparable 1994 dollars would be 1.622 times larger, based on the Consumer Price Index for medical care.

analysis. These include educational attainment, earnings opportunities, and income of mothers—all likely to be correlated with teen motherhood and health care utilization. Insurance status is another important omitted variable that is likely to be correlated with both medical utilization and teen motherhood. Hence, although our results provide a useful description of the differences in medical care use and expenses between children born to teenage mothers and other children, we are unable to predict behavioral responses to alternative policies.

CONCLUSION

The children of teenage mothers tend to be in poorer health than are the children of older mothers. In addition, although the children of teen mothers visit medical providers less frequently and have lower *total* medical expenses, more of the expenses they do incur are paid by others in society than is the case among children of nonteen mothers, both proportionately and absolutely.

Our simulations suggest that the medical expenses paid by society would be reduced dramatically if teenage mothers were to wait until they were older to have their first children. These simulations are based on the assumption that current teen mothers will "act" like older mothers, not only in terms of their fertility behavior but also in their educational attainment, earnings, and insurance. If these assumptions do not hold, our results are likely to overstate the savings to society from postponing the childbearing of current teenage mothers.

Notes

1. A discussion of outliers appears in appendix 6A.

2. The validity of this measure has been tested for older population age groups. See, for example, Maddox and Douglass (1973) and Fylkesnes and Forde (1991).

3. All dollar amounts are expressed in 1987 dollars, which can be converted to current dollars by using the consumer price index for medical care.

4. For all three dependent variables, a number of children have zero values; hence we use tobit analysis. In an alternative specification, we add a dummy variable for high income. Although this inclusion did not significantly affect the results for the total medical expense regressions or the total medical visits regressions, the results from the regressions for total dollars spent by others in society were significantly different. The general pattern of the coefficient estimates remains the same, but the magnitude of the effects is somewhat diminished. Not surprisingly, the coefficient estimate for the dummy variable for high income is large, negative, and statistically significant at the 1 percent level.

References

Fylkesnes, K., and O. Forde. 1991. "The Tromso Study: Predictors of Self-Evaluated Health: Has Society Adopted the Expanded Health Concept?" *Social Science and Medicine* 32: 141–46.

Maddox, G., and E. Douglass. 1973. "Self-Assessment of Health: A Longitudinal Study of Elderly Subjects." *Journal of Health and Social Behavior* 14:87–93.

Mitchell, J. 1991. "Physician Participation in Medicaid Revisited." *Medical Care* 29 (July): 645–53.

Wolfe, B. 1994. "Reform of Health Care for the Nonelderly Poor." In *Confronting Poverty: Prescriptions for Change*, eds. S. Danziger, G. Sandefur, and D. Weinberg. Cambridge: Harvard University Press.

APPENDIX 6A: OUTLIERS

Whenever medical care use or expenditures are studied, the mean (average) can be influenced by a few outliers. In this appendix, we report the results obtained after eliminating observations that might be considered as outliers in the sense of possibly changing the direction or magnitude of the results substantially. Our definition of "outlier" for this test of robustness is values of the dependent variable that exceed two standard deviations above the mean.

For total medical care visits, the overall mean is 3.76, and the standard deviation is 8.22. Our definition would eliminate all those with more than 20 visits (70 observations). If we do so, the mean becomes 2.95 with a standard deviation of 3.48. The pattern of coefficients is similar, though each is smaller than those reported in the text. For mothers who first gave birth before age 18, for example, the coefficient is negative and statistically significant at the 1 percent level, as is the negative and smaller coefficient on mothers who first gave birth at age 18 or 19, and the still smaller negative coefficient on mothers who first gave birth at age 20 or 21. The one change from table 6.7, where the coefficient on mothers who were 18 or 19 at first birth is negative but not statistically significant, is that in the regression omitting those with 20-plus visits, the coefficient becomes positive and significant at the 5 percent level. The other variables are consistent with the initial specification.

A similar exercise for the total medical expenditures yields comparable results. Here we eliminate observations with expenditures more than two deviations above the mean, or greater than $5,017. This omits 48 observations. The mean is reduced from $406.44 to $239.85 and the standard deviation from $2,305 to $576. In this case, the pattern of coefficients on the variables for age at which the mother first gave birth is identical to those reported in table 6.8.

Finally, excluding amounts more than two standard deviations above the mean for the average dollars paid by other members of society eliminates values greater than $1,714 (88 observations). This reduces the mean from $198 to $58 and the standard deviation from $1,258 to $181. Again, the pattern of coefficients on the dummy variables on mother's age at birth are consistent with those reported. All are positive.

These tests of the potential impact of "a few" possible outliers suggest that our results are fairly robust. Since no a priori reason exists to exclude these observations or to believe they are not representative of the general population, the results for the full sample are reported in the text.

APPENDIX 6B: GLOSSARY OF VARIABLES

Demographic Variables

Age of child (LASTAGE)	Child's age at last interview.
Mother's age (MOMAGE)	Mother's age at last interview.
Child born to teen mother	1 if mother had this child while a teen (less than 19: MOMAGE − LASTAGE ≤ 19); 0 otherwise.
Teen mother	1 if mother ever had a child when less than 19 years old (MOMAGE − LASTAGE of oldest child) ≤ 19; 0 otherwise.
Race of child	1 if child is white; 0 otherwise.

Health Variables

acute	This variable is intended to capture acute health problems. For all children, the dummy variable is equal to 1 if any of the following conditions were reported to occur within 30 days prior to the interview at which the health status questionnaire was administered (between rounds 1 and 2): stomachache for at least two days, stomach flu with vomiting or diarrhea lasting at least three days, ear infection or earache lasting at least two days, skin infection, sore throat, and high fever lasting at least two days, diarrhea lasting at least two days, poor eating habits, or trouble with school work. In addition, the acute variable is equal to 1 if the child had any of the following conditions in the 12

months prior to the interview: asthma, hay fever, two or more ear infections, stammering/stuttering, migraines, anemia, heart problems, enuresis, parasites, or digestive problems.

chronic   This variable is intended to capture chronic health problems. For children less than 5 years old, this variable equals 1 if the parent answered yes to any of the following questions:

1. During the past three months, has the child been unable to take part in the usual kind of play activities done by most children his age?

2. During the past three months, has the child been limited in the kind or amount of play activities due to a health problem or impairment?

3. Is the child limited in any way due to a health problem or impairment?

Also, this variable equals 1 if the child has difficulty seeing with glasses or hearing with a hearing aid.

For children who are between 5 and 14 years old, the chronic variable is equal to 1 if the parent answered yes to any of the following questions:

1. Does this child attend (or need to attend) a special school or special classes due to an impairment or health problem?

2. Is this child limited in school attendance or unable to attend school due to her health?

3. Is this child limited in any way because of an impairment or health problem?

Again, this variable is equal to 1 if the child has difficulty seeing with glasses or hearing with a hearing aid.

excellent   Self-reported health status (reported by primary respondent for the children) is excellent.

fair–poor   Self-reported health status (reported by primary respondent for the children) is fair or poor.

Utilization

ER visits   Total number of emergency room visits, measured over all rounds.

Hospital inpatient visits   Total number of inpatient hospital stays, measured over all rounds.

Hospital outpatient visits Total number of hospital outpatient visits, measured over all rounds.

Medical provider visits   Total number of visits to medical providers measured over all rounds.

All medical visits   Total of all reported visits to medical providers, hospital outpatient departments, emergency rooms, and inpatient hospital stays.

Expenses

The NMES has detailed data on medical expenditures. The visit data include information on payment source. Expense variables include total medical expenses corresponding to all reported visits, including facility and physician charges where applicable. In addition, the data include the fraction paid by (1) self; (2) private; and (3) public—Medicare, Medicaid, CHAMPUS,* other federal program, other state program, workers' compensation, other, or free from provider.

---

*The Civilian Health and Medical Program for the Uniformed Services is a health insurance package provided to active and retired military personnel and their families.

Chapter Seven

ABUSE AND NEGLECT OF THE CHILDREN

Robert M. Goerge and Bong Joo Lee

Whether or not children of teenage mothers are more likely than children of older mothers to be abused or neglected and subsequently to use foster care or other child welfare services is a critical issue for both public policy and program development.[1] Although the human and financial costs of abuse and neglect investigations and foster care are significant and growing, little is known about the determinants of the events that lead children and families to these child welfare services.

Families suspected of abusing or neglecting their children are typically reported to a centralized "hot line" or registry. These reports are investigated by public agency workers to determine whether or not credible evidence of abuse or neglect exists. Once abuse or neglect has been substantiated, a decision is made as to whether the child needs to be protected by removal from the family's home. The decision is usually made by a public agency worker, which must be confirmed by a judicial determination. The out-of-home care, typically called foster care, may be with a relative, with a foster family, or in an institutional setting. Children remain in foster care until the court determines they can be safely returned to their parents. A child who cannot be returned to his or her parents may be adopted, placed with a relative, or placed in long-term foster care.

This chapter focuses on the effect a mother's age at the birth of her child has on the incidence of substantiated child abuse/neglect reports[2] and on the rate of foster care placements during a child's early years. We then examine whether early childbearing leads to longer duration in foster care. Finally, we estimate the cost to the nation of child protective and child welfare service systems and on abuse/neglect investigations.

APPROACH

To estimate the independent effect of maternal age on child protective and child welfare services, we use multivariate analysis to control for the effects of a set of confounding demographic factors: the child's birth order, race/ethnicity, sex, and region. Ideally, one would include additional background factors such as poverty or education of mothers; however, because our analysis of incidence rates of indicated abuse/neglect and foster care placement employs aggregate-level birth certificate data as at-risk population estimates, we were unable to disaggregate the birth certificate data from the other factors.[3] Instead, we employed race/ethnicity and region (Chicago versus the rest of the state) as proxies for the socioeconomic status of a child. Therefore, the results of our multivariate analyses should be interpreted as adjusted population incidence rate differences between teen mothers and nonteen mothers after controlling for basic demographic factors. Given our previous experience with these demographic variables, poverty may account for additional variance but would not greatly change the effects of teenage parenthood on child protective and child welfare service experiences. Our results should not be interpreted as implying anything about causation.

To examine the costs of teenage childbearing with regard to abuse/neglect and child welfare services, we employ a two-stage process. First we model the process of first contact with the service system. Specifically, we estimate the effect of maternal age on the probability of a child's becoming a reported case of child abuse or neglect or of entering the child welfare service system in a foster care placement during the first five years of life. We estimate models at the individual-child level to examine the effect of maternal age on the probability of the child's being involved in the two service systems. We estimate models at the family level to examine the effect of maternal age at *first* birth on the family's becoming a case in the service systems. The cohorts we study are all births in Illinois from 1982 through 1988 and all new families in Illinois during the same period.

The second stage of the analytical process addresses whether children of teenage mothers use foster care for longer periods once they are placed in that system. Specifically, we use proportional hazards models to examine the effect of teenage parenthood on the duration of the foster care spell. The study population is all children placed in foster care from 1982 through 1992.

Using the models we develop in stages 1 and 2, we then estimate the amounts of child protective and child welfare services associated with teen childbearing. First we estimate the expected changes in substantiated abuse/neglect incidence rates, foster care placement rates, and the length of time children remain in foster care when mothers delay childbearing past their teenage years. Using our findings on the changes expected by delaying childbearing with the Illinois population, we then present the estimated overall foster care and abuse and neglect investigation costs associated with teen childbearing at the national level.

We use simulation results based on the Illinois population to derive these estimates because child protective and child welfare service data with detailed family information are not available at the national level. The Illinois child protective and child welfare administrative data are one of very few available data sources, even at the state level, that provide detailed family information, including mother's age and sibling information. In addition, the overall demographic characteristics of the Illinois child population are very comparable to those of the population in the nation; this makes Illinois data quite suitable for approximating national figures. For example, analysis of Current Population Survey data indicates that the Illinois and U.S. child populations have similar racial/ethnic and metropolitan residence distributions (Center for the Study of Social Policy 1993).

DATA

The data used in this study are drawn from the Integrated Database on Children and Family Services (IDB) and Illinois birth certificate data. The IDB is a unique state-level database that uses the computerized administrative data that contain demographic, family composition, case status, service status, outcomes, and cost information for the entire population of abuse/neglect cases and foster children between 1982 and 1994 (Goerge, Van Voorhis, and Lee 1994). These data provide longitudinal information on service contacts and subsequent experiences of all families and children receiving child protective and child welfare services during the study period.

One limitation of most research in the child welfare area has been lack of adequate data. Since child abuse/neglect and foster care placement are relatively rare events, a typical survey of the general population would not provide a sample size sufficient to allow generalization of results to the entire population of children who come to the attention of the child welfare service system. As a result, previous research has tended to rely on cross-sectional aggregate data from administrative sources or very-small-scale sample studies in clinical settings. Both strategies are limited in their ability to identify the independent effects of various demographic factors on events that children and their families experience (Panel of Research on Child Abuse and Neglect 1993). Because aggregate-level analyses have often failed to disentangle aggregate data into their components, the results have not been comparable across different subpopulations. In addition, most aggregate-level analyses have employed cross-sectional data. As a result, very little is known about the temporal dimension of events (such as sequence, duration, and outcome of services) or incidence rates of an entire population experiencing certain events over long periods of time. At the other end of the spectrum, small-scale sample studies have been impeded by their limited sample sizes and the ensuing problems in generalizing findings to the population of children and families that come into contact with child protective and child welfare services.

DESCRIPTIVE STATISTICS

To estimate the population incidence rates of being a substantiated child abuse/neglect case or being placed in foster care, one first needs to identify the population at risk. The base population in this study is defined in two ways: (1) at the individual level, all children born from 1982 through 1988, and (2) at the family level, all new families formed during the same period.[4] Using the first base population, we examine the effect of mother's age at birth on an individual child's probability of becoming an indicated victim of child abuse and neglect or of being placed in foster care. The base population at the family level allows us to follow entire cohorts of new families and examine the effect mother's age at *first* birth has on the family's becoming a child abuse/neglect case or having a child placed in foster care. We use Illinois birth certificate data to calculate these two base population sizes.

Since our administrative data contain information on *all* children and families who come to the attention of abuse/neglect and foster care systems in Illinois, we can estimate population incidence rates of a particular birth cohort or new family cohort by using total live births or total first live births as the denominator data. Further, classifying the birth certificate data by birth order, maternal age, race/ethnicity, sex, and region allows us to estimate the population incidence rates for each stratum of a particular birth cohort.

Between 1982 and 1988, 1,257,149 live births took place in Illinois (table 7.1). Roughly 40 percent of all children born in each year were

Table 71 SELECTED CHARACTERISTICS OF ILLINOIS LIVE BIRTHS, BIRTH COHORTS 1982–88

| Birth Year | Total Births | % First Birth | % by Mother's Age at Birth | | | | | % by Race/Ethnicity | | | | % Chicago | % Female |
			≤ 15	16–17	18–19	20–21	≥ 22	White	Black	Hispanic	Other		
All births													
1982	181,856	40.9%	1.0%	4.4%	8.6%	11.4%	74.7%	67.4%	21.2%	9.1%	2.2%	30.2%	48.7%
1983	176,875	40.5	1.0	4.2	8.4	10.8	75.5	67.7	21.2	8.9	2.1	30.2	48.8
1984	177,932	39.9	1.0	4.0	8.0	10.4	76.6	67.7	21.2	9.0	2.0	30.1	48.7
1985	180,346	39.8	1.0	3.9	7.6	10.0	77.5	67.7	21.2	9.3	1.8	30.0	48.7
1986	176,103	39.8	1.1	3.9	7.6	9.6	77.9	66.7	21.7	9.9	1.8	30.5	48.8
1987	179,843	39.5	1.1	4.1	7.3	9.4	78.2	65.2	22.2	9.9	2.6	30.6	48.8
1988	184,194	39.5	1.1	4.1	7.4	8.9	78.5	64.4	22.5	10.3	2.8	30.6	48.7
Total	1,257,149	40.0	1.0	4.1	7.8	10.1	77.0	66.7	21.6	9.5	2.2	30.3	48.8
First births													
1982	74,427		2.4	9.0	14.5	14.8	59.3	70.9	19.1	7.8	2.2	29.2	48.8
1983	71,590		2.4	8.8	14.5	13.9	60.4	70.8	19.7	7.3	2.2	29.4	48.6
1984	70,943		2.3	8.3	13.8	14.0	61.7	70.6	19.7	7.5	2.2	29.3	48.6
1985	71,816		2.4	8.1	13.1	13.3	62.9	70.5	19.8	7.7	2.0	29.3	48.6
1986	70,176		2.6	8.1	13.0	12.7	63.6	69.4	20.2	8.5	1.9	29.9	48.9
1987	71,099		2.6	8.5	12.5	12.2	64.1	67.7	20.7	8.6	3.0	29.7	48.7
1988	72,780		2.6	8.6	12.6	11.6	64.7	66.6	20.9	9.2	3.2	30.1	48.7
Total	502,831		2.5	8.5	13.4	13.2	62.4	69.5	20.0	8.1	2.4	29.5	48.7

Source: Illinois birth certificate data, 1982–88.

born to first-time mothers. These first births represent the formation of 502,831 new families during the period. About 13 percent of all births and 24 percent of first births were to mothers less than 20 years of age.

Of the children born during that period, 68,024 had an indicated abuse and neglect report by age five. Of the children who had a first-time indicated abuse and neglect report, 12 percent did not live with their mothers at the time of the report. As a result, mother's information was missing for them. Since we could not calculate mother's age at birth for these children, we dropped them from our analysis sample, leaving us with a total of 59,799 children for the subsequent analyses.

To analyze cohorts of new families becoming reported cases of child abuse or neglect, we selected all families with an indicated child abuse/neglect report in which the eldest child was born in the period 1982–88 and was the only child living in the household at the time of birth. A total of 19,786 new families formed during those years had an indicated child abuse or neglect report within the first five years after family formation (birth of the first child).

To study the incidence rates of foster care, we took similar steps to identify the relevant populations. Of the children born during the study period, 19,045 were placed in foster care in the first five years of life. Among them, the 16,702 children for whom the mother's age at birth could be calculated were selected for the analysis. Our family-level analysis shows that 4,784 of the new families formed during the years in question had a child placed in foster care by the time the first child reached age five.[5]

Children born to teen mothers (under age 20 at the time of the child's birth) are much more likely to be indicated victims of abuse and neglect than are those born to nonteenage mothers (table 7.2, top panel). Among those children born to teen mothers, the children born to young teens (≤17 years old) were more likely to be indicated victims than were those born to older teens (18 to 19 years old). By age 5, on average, children born to age 17 or younger mothers were about one and one-half times more likely to become victims of indicated child abuse and neglect than were children born to 20- to 21-year-old mothers. The mother's age at first birth also has a strong effect on the probability of the family's being an indicated case of child abuse or neglect. New families in which the mother's age was under 18 at the time of first birth were about two and one-half times more likely to become an indicated case of abuse and neglect than were those families in which the mother was age 20 or 21. The abuse/neglect incidence rates have also been increasing rapidly in recent years for all children and for

Table 7.2 INCIDENCE RATES (PER 1,000) OF CHILD ABUSE/NEGLECT AND FOSTER CARE

| | Child Birth Cohorts | | | | | New Family Cohorts | | | | |
| | Mother's Age at Birth | | | | | Mother's Age at First Birth | | | | |
Cohort Year	≤ 17	18–19	20–21	≥ 22	All Children	≤ 17	18–19	20–21	≥ 22	All New Families
Abuse/neglect										
1982	105.8	77.0	61.8	25.9	38.7	95.9	60.0	38.7	17.0	35.4
1983	118.2	87.0	69.7	28.9	42.9	106.7	62.0	43.7	16.6	37.0
1984	127.5	95.0	77.5	31.3	46.0	118.7	71.6	43.0	17.9	39.5
1985	118.2	98.4	82.1	32.8	47.0	108.6	72.4	49.7	19.3	39.8
1986	128.9	101.2	86.3	34.2	48.9	113.2	74.1	47.7	19.5	40.2
1987	124.8	109.3	94.0	38.3	53.2	115.9	77.3	52.2	20.5	42.2
1988	126.9	104.7	99.2	41.6	55.8	109.4	74.8	50.7	21.7	41.6
Total period	121.3	95.5	80.6	33.4	47.5	109.6	69.9	46.2	19.0	39.3
Foster care										
1982	29.3	18.7	14.3	6.0	9.3	25.3	13.5	8.2	3.3	8.0
1983	28.3	23.0	16.5	7.7	11.0	23.9	14.5	8.6	3.7	8.2
1984	36.5	24.0	20.0	7.2	11.3	29.8	15.0	8.7	3.3	8.5
1985	35.9	26.5	21.8	8.7	12.7	30.3	18.4	10.7	4.9	10.1
1986	34.9	29.9	24.2	9.6	13.8	27.0	18.5	11.4	4.9	9.8
1987	36.9	33.9	30.0	11.8	16.4	32.4	19.8	12.4	4.9	10.7
1988	39.4	35.6	32.4	13.6	18.3	31.1	20.0	14.3	5.6	11.3
Total period	34.4	27.1	22.3	9.3	13.3	28.5	16.9	10.4	4.4	9.5

new families. At both the child and the family level, members of the 1988 cohort were one and one-half times more likely than those in the 1982 cohort to become a case of indicated abuse/neglect.

Foster care incidence rates show that 13 children out of 1,000 born from 1982 through 1988 were placed in foster care in the first five years of their lives (table 7.2, bottom panel). Children of mothers age 17 or younger were over one and one-half times more likely to be placed in foster care than were children whose mothers were 20–21 at their births. New families in which the mother was a young teen (≤17 years old) at the time of first birth were also much more likely— over two and one-half times more likely—than were families with 20- to 21-year-old mothers to have a child placed in foster care by the time the first child reached age five.

To study whether a mother's early childbearing leads to a longer foster care duration once a child is in a foster care placement, we selected those children who entered substitute care for the first time in 1982 through 1992. During this period, 63,122 children were placed in foster care for the first time, of whom 52,690 had maternal age data available.

Of these 52,690 children, 65 percent were born to mothers whose age was less than 20 at the time of first birth (table 7.3). (For this analysis, once a woman has had a child as a teen, she will always be

Table 7.3 SELECTED CHARACTERISTICS OF ILLINOIS CHILDREN PLACED IN FOSTER CARE BETWEEN 1982 AND 1992

Characteristic	Percentage of Total	Characteristic	Percentage of Total
Mother's age at first birth		Type of indicated allegation	
15 or under	14.5%	Abuse	31.0%
16–17	26.5	Neglect	43.0
18–19	24.0	Not identified	26.0
20–21	13.5	Age at placement (in years)	
22 and over	21.4	Less than 1	20.8
Race/ethnicity		1–2	18.4
White	31.5	3–5	18.7
African American	62.2	6–8	13.6
Hispanic	4.9	9–11	10.6
Other	1.4	12–14	11.0
Region		15–17	6.9
Chicago	52.1	Birth order	
Rest of state	47.9	First birth	38.2
(n)	(52,690)	Second or higher	61.8

Note: Includes only those children for whom mother's information is available.

a teen mother.) About 62 percent placed were African American, 52 percent were living in Chicago, and 21 percent were infants at the time of placement. About 31 percent of children placed during the period had an abuse allegation.[6]

Using the population that entered foster care during the period, we examined the average duration of foster care (summarized by the median) by each of the demographic factors. Table 7.4 presents sum-

Table 7.4 DURATION OF FIRST SUBSTITUTE CARE PLACEMENT SPELL, ILLINOIS 1982–92

	Median (days)	95% Confidence Interval
Total state	505	495-516
Mother's age at first birth		
15 or under	719	686-770
16–17	607	580-628
18–19	471	449-493
20–21	418	397-441
22 and over	381	362-399
Type of indicated allegation		
Abuse	415	398-429
Neglect	727	701-751
Not identified	380	366-395
Age at placement (in years)		
Less than 1	709	682-736
1–2	589	555-616
3–5	581	551-617
6–8	603	561-632
9–11	533	502-568
12–14	290	274-303
15–17	182	168-198
Region		
Chicago	875	843-908
Rest of state	298	291-310
Race/ethnicity		
White	254	244-266
African American	782	758-807
Hispanic	373	349-412
Other	324	258-386
Sex		
Male	529	516-550
Female	479	465-496
Birth order		
First birth	371	359-383
Second or higher birth	626	609-642

Note: Median duration is estimated using Kaplan-Meier method to control for the effect of the many incomplete cases (right censoring).

mary statistics on the first foster care spell duration of the population. The median first spell of children born to mothers whose age at first birth was 16 to 17 lasts just over 600 days, whereas the median first spell in substitute care of children born to mothers ages 20 to 21 lasts about 420 days. Children with neglect-type allegations, younger children, children from the Chicago area, African American children, and second or higher birth order children also tend to stay longer in foster care than other children.

These descriptive data show a significant relationship between maternal age and the likelihood of child abuse/neglect and foster care placement. The results also show that maternal age is a significant factor in predicting how long a child will stay in foster care. However, these statistics do not necessarily reflect the independent effect of maternal age. The rate and the duration of foster care are known to vary considerably with many other observable demographic factors. In addition, as shown in table 7.4, duration of foster care varies considerably by factors other than maternal age. Clearly these other factors are not independent of each other and are highly correlated with maternal age. To study the independent effect of maternal age on child abuse/neglect and foster care, it is necessary to control for the other confounding factors, using multivariate methods. The next section describes the methods we used to study the independent effect of maternal age on child abuse/neglect and foster care. Readers more interested in results than in mathematical computations may jump ahead to the next section.

MULTIVARIATE METHODS

We use two multivariate methods in our analysis. First, we use logistic regression to examine the independent effect of maternal age on child abuse/neglect and foster care incidence rates. Second, we employ a proportional hazards model to estimate the independent effect of mother's age at first birth on foster care duration.

For the study of first contact with service systems, logistic regression is used to approximate the log-linear Poisson regression to investigate the effects of early childbearing on the probability of having a substantiated abuse/neglect report and being placed in foster care. Poisson regression represents statistical methods for the analysis of the relationship between an observed count with a Poisson distribution and a set of explanatory variables (Koch, Atkinson, and Stokes

1986). This method has been widely used in the studies of infant morbidity, mortality, and cancer incidence with aggregate-level data that are cross-classified according to demographic and other factors (Breslow and Day 1975; James and Segal 1982; Frome 1983). The general form of a log-linear Poisson regression model is given by

$$\mu(x) = [N(x)] [\exp(x'\beta)]$$

where $\mu(x)$ is the expected value of the number of events $n(x)$ from the subpopulation corresponding to known vector x of explanatory variables, $N(x)$ is the known (estimated) total exposure to risk of the subpopulation where the events occur, and β is the vector of unknown regression parameters. In the model, $N(x)$ are regarded as fixed numbers that are sufficiently large and events $n(x)$ sufficiently rare that the data are well represented by the Poisson distribution.

Having base population estimates and the number of children experiencing their first indicated abuse/neglect report or foster care placement corresponding to the demographic factors, as discussed in the previous section of this chapter, we can fit the logistic Poisson regression to estimate the unknown vector β.

To determine the effect of teenage parenthood on the duration of foster care, we employed a particular type of event-history model, a proportional hazards model (Kalbfleisch and Prentice 1980). This regression-like model allows us to determine the effects of covariates on the risk of leaving foster care. We can estimate the coefficients using censored data, which is necessary in this case because many of the children in our population were still in foster care as of June 30, 1994 (when our observation of foster care spells ended). The proportional hazards model is nonparametric in the specification of the variation of the hazard rate with time, since it uses an unspecified distributional form for the baseline hazard function. The equation of the proportional hazard function that must be estimated is

$$\lambda(t{:}z) = \lambda_o(t)\exp(z\beta)$$

where z is a vector of covariates, β is the coefficient vector, and t is the associated failure time.

INDICATED CASES OF ABUSE OR NEGLECT AND FOSTER CARE PLACEMENT

We take two approaches to the task of estimating the effects of maternal age on the probability of having a substantiated abuse/neglect report or being placed in foster care. We first estimate the impact of maternal age on the probability of a child's involvement. We then estimate the impact of the mother's age at *first* birth on her family's involvement.

Abuse/Neglect Reports

We use four models to consider the effect of maternal age on the probability of having an indicated child abuse/neglect report within the first five years of the child's life (table 7.5). The estimated effects

Table 7.5 RELATIONSHIP BETWEEN MOTHER'S AGE AT BIRTH AND AN INDICATED CHILD ABUSE/NEGLECT REPORT, BIRTH COHORTS 1982–88

Characteristic	Model 1	Model 2	Model 3	Model 4
Mother's age at birth				
15 or under	2.06	1.90	2.96	2.20
16–17	1.45	1.39	1.90	1.60
18–19	1.21	1.18	1.38	1.28
20–21	1.00	1.00	1.00	1.00
22 and over	0.39	0.40	0.34	0.39
Birth year				
1982		1.00	1.00	1.00
1983		1.13	1.13	1.13
1984		1.23	1.23	1.23
1985		1.27	1.27	1.27
1986		1.33	1.33	1.33
1987		1.46	1.46	1.43
1988		1.54	1.54	1.51
Region				
Chicago		1.43	1.35	0.91
Rest of state		1.00	1.00	1.00
Sex of child				
Male			1.00	1.00
Female			0.99[a]	0.99[a]
Birth order				
First birth			0.42	0.46
Second + birth			1.00	1.00
Race/ethnicity				
White				1.00
African American				2.68
Hispanic				0.84
Other				1.83

Note: These are relative odds of having an indicated child abuse/neglect report written five years after child's birth, estimated from logit models. Baseline levels are indicated by relative odds of 1.

a. These are the only estimates not statistically significant at the 0.05 level.

for all models are expressed as changes in the expected incidence rate of being an indicated victim of child abuse/neglect, relative to a baseline group. For example, Model 1, which includes only mother's age at the birth of the child, shows that the relative odds of having an indicated abuse/neglect report for the mother's age group ≤15 are 2.06. In other words, children born to mothers age 15 and under are two times more likely to become an indicated case of child abuse/neglect in the first five years of their lives than are children born to mothers ages 20–21 (the baseline category). Since Model 1 does not include any other demographic factors, it should be interpreted as "unadjusted" differences in the incidence rate of child abuse/neglect across the mothers' age groups considered in the study.

Model 2 adds the child's birth year and region to the model. After controlling for the birth cohort and region effects, we still find significant differences in odds ratios between teen and nonteen mothers. Also, the results of Model 2 show that incidence rates of indicated child abuse/neglect have been increasing significantly in recent years. For instance, a baby in the birth cohort of 1988 was one and one-half times more likely to become an indicated case of abuse/neglect than one in the birth cohort of 1982. In Model 2, region also seems to be a significant factor in predicting the incidence rate of child abuse and neglect, with children in Chicago being one and one-half times more likely to become an indicated case of abuse/neglect than are children in the balance of the state.

Model 3 adds two more factors: sex and birth order of the child. One interesting result is that first-born children are much less likely to become indicated cases of abuse and neglect than subsequent children are. The relative odds of becoming an indicated abuse/neglect case are 0.46. This means that first-born children are less than one-half as likely as their other siblings to become indicated cases of child abuse/neglect. After controlling for birth order of the child, we find that the effect of young motherhood on the rate of child abuse/neglect increased significantly. This might suggest a close relationship between the birth order of the child and maternal age. For example, if the risk of child abuse/neglect increases with the birth order of a child, the maternal age-specific rates, after controlling for birth order of a child, should be higher than the rates one would estimate before controlling for the birth order effect. Based on the results in Model 3, we can conclude that once we take into account the fact that most births to teens are first births, adjusted incidence rates of child abuse/neglect for teen mothers tend to be even higher than unadjusted rates (especially for young teen mothers).

Model 4 adds race/ethnicity. African American children are about two and one-half times as likely to become indicated cases of child abuse/neglect as non-Hispanic white children. We also find that the Chicago effect almost disappears once we control for race/ethnicity. This is a result of the high concentration of African American children in the group of children indicated in the Chicago area. Thus, after controlling for all the other demographic factors, we still find that children born to teen mothers are significantly more likely to have an indicated child abuse/neglect report during their early childhood than are those born to nonteen mothers. Children born to young teen mothers are also at greater risk of being indicated cases of child abuse/neglect than are those children born to older teen mothers. For example, compared with children born to mothers ages 20–21, children born to mothers age 15 or younger are over two times more likely to have an indicated child abuse/neglect report, and children born to mothers ages 16–17 are about one and one-half times more likely to become indicated victims of child abuse/neglect.

To examine the effect of mother's age at her *first* birth on her family's involvement in the child protective services system, we use three models (table 7.6). Model 1, as before, includes only mother's age at first birth. Any differences in odds ratios across the mother's age group considered here should again be interpreted as unadjusted differences. Families with mothers who had their first birth during their teen years are much more likely to become indicated cases of child abuse and neglect than are families with nonteen mothers. For instance, families with mothers who were 15 or under at the time of the birth of their first child are over three and one-half times more likely to become an indicated case of abuse and neglect than are families with 20- to 21-year-old mothers. The odds ratio for the mother's age group 18 to 19 is 1.55. In other words, these families are over one and one-half times more likely to become an indicated case of abuse and neglect than are families with 20- to 21-year-old mothers.

Model 2 adds birth year of the first child and region. The magnitude of the effect of mother's age at first birth decreases somewhat, although those effects are still significant and large. Our multivariate results on the cohort effects support our descriptive findings on recent trends in rates of substantiated child abuse and neglect. Even after controlling for any possible changes in demographic composition of the population, we still find an increasing cohort effect in recent years. This indicates an upward trend in the incidence rate of substantiated child abuse and neglect reports that is independent of other demographic changes in the population.

Table 7.6 RELATIONSHIP BETWEEN MOTHER'S AGE AT FIRST BIRTH AND AN
INDICATED CHILD ABUSE/NEGLECT REPORT, NEW FAMILIES 1982–88

Characteristic	Model 1	Model 2	Model 3
Mother's age at first birth			
15 or under	3.56	3.45	2.87
16–17	2.26	2.23	2.02
18–19	1.55	1.54	1.49
20–21	1.00	1.00	1.00
22 and over	0.40	0.40	0.41
First-birth year			
1982		1.00	1.00
1983		1.06[a]	1.05[a]
1984		1.16	1.15
1985		1.18	1.18
1986		1.20	1.19
1987		1.26	1.24
1988		1.25	1.22
Region			
Chicago		1.10	0.91
Rest of state		1.00	1.00
Race/ethnicity			
White			1.00
African American			1.72
Hispanic			0.67
Other			2.12

Note: These are relative odds of having an indicated child abuse/neglect report written
five years after first child's birth, estimated from logit models. Baseline levels are
indicated by relative odds of 1.
a. Estimates not statistically significant at the 0.05 level.

Model 3 adds race/ethnicity. The maternal age effect falls somewhat
because African American women are having children at younger
ages. These results suggest that part of the overall age-of-mother effect
(unadjusted) is a race/ethnicity effect. Even when this is taken into
account, however, families with teen mothers are still substantially
more likely to have an indicated case of child abuse/neglect than are
families with nonteen mothers, even after controlling for the other
demographic factors considered in the study. The estimated odds ratio
for mother's age at first birth—$\leq$15, 16 to 17, and 18 to 19—are 2.87,
2.02, and 1.49, respectively, compared with the 20- to 21-year-old
mothers.

Foster Care

The effects of maternal age on foster care placement parallel those for
indicated abuse/neglect reports. Here again we use four models to

explore the impacts of maternal age on the probability of a child's involvement (table 7.7) and three models to explore the impacts of mother's age at first birth on the family's probability of involvement (table 7.8).

The unadjusted estimates indicate that the relative odds of a child being placed in foster care for the maternal-age group ≤15 and the age group 16 to 17 are 1.84 and 1.22, respectively, compared to the age group 20 to 21 (table 7.7, Model 1). The findings for families are similar, with a slightly larger effect of maternal age on the family's having a

Table 7.7 RELATIONSHIP BETWEEN MOTHER'S AGE AT BIRTH AND PLACEMENT IN SUBSTITUTE CARE, ILLINOIS, BIRTH COHORTS 1982–88

Characteristic	Model 1	Model 2	Model 3	Model 4
Mother's age at birth				
15 or under	1.84	1.55	2.68	1.79
16–17	1.22	1.16	1.40	1.24
18–19	1.22	1.17	1.39	1.25
20–21	1.00	1.00	1.00	1.00
22 and over	0.41	0.44	0.37	0.48
Birth year				
1982		1.00	1.00	1.00
1983		1.20	1.20	1.20
1984		1.25	1.25	1.24
1985		1.42	1.42	1.41
1986		1.54	1.55	1.53
1987		1.85	1.84	1.80
1988		2.06	2.06	1.99
Region				
Chicago		2.21	2.07	1.12
Rest of state		1.00	1.00	1.00
Sex of child				
Male			1.00	1.00
Female			0.99[a]	0.99[a]
Birth order				
First birth			0.36	0.42
Second + birth			1.00	1.00
Race/ethnicity				
White				1.00
African American				4.49
Hispanic				0.90
Other				1.54

Note: These are relative odds of being placed in substitute care within five years after child's birth, estimated from logit models. Baseline levels are indicated by relative odds of 1.

a. Estimates not statistically significant at the 0.05 level.

Table 7.8 RELATIONSHIP BETWEEN MOTHER'S AGE AT FIRST BIRTH AND
PLACEMENT IN SUBSTITUTE CARE, ILLINOIS, NEW FAMILIES 1982–88

Characteristic	Model 1	Model 2	Model 3
Mother's age at first birth			
15 or under	3.62	3.25	2.37
16–17	1.60	1.55	1.42
18–19	1.64	1.60	1.48
20–21	1.00	1.00	1.00
22 and over	0.42	0.42	0.47
First-birth year			
1982		1.00	1.00
1983		1.04[a]	1.03[a]
1984		1.10[a]	1.08[a]
1985		1.33	1.31
1986		1.29	1.27
1987		1.41	1.36
1988		1.48	1.44
Region			
Chicago		1.45	1.01[a]
Rest of state		1.00	1.00
Race/ethnicity			
White			1.00
African American			2.61
Hispanic			0.72
Other			1.75

Note: These are relative odds of having a child placed in substitute care within five
years after first child's birth, estimated from logit models. Baseline levels are indicated
by relative odds of 1.
a. Estimates not statistically significant at the 0.05 level.

child placed in foster care (table 7.8, Model 1). Families in which the
mother was 16 or 17 at the time of her first birth, for example, are over
one and one-half times more likely than those families with 20- to 21-
year-old mothers to have a child placed in foster care by the time the
first child reaches age five.

The fully adjusted models do not change the basic picture. Children
born to mothers ages 16–17 are about one and one-half times as likely
to be placed in foster care in the first five years of their lives as are
those born to mothers ages 20 to 21 (table 7.7, Model 4). And new
families in which the mother was 16 or 17 at the time of her first birth
are about one and one-half times more likely to have a child placed
in foster care than are the families with mothers ages 20 to 21 (table
7.8, Model 3).

FOSTER CARE DURATION

Our descriptive statistics show a clear relationship between maternal age and foster care duration. However, as we discussed earlier, maternal age-specific duration measures do not necessarily reflect the independent effect of maternal age on how long a child remains in foster care. For example, we find substantial variation across a range of demographic characteristics in the length of time foster children remain in first placement spells. It would be reasonable to expect that the other demographic factors might be correlated with maternal age and duration. Here we explore the relationship between maternal age and likelihood of leaving foster care, while controlling for the effects of the other demographic factors.

The findings are presented in terms of changes in the expected odds of leaving foster care relative to a baseline group (table 7.9). In other words, the estimated ratios represent the relative risk that a child with a given attribute will leave foster care, other things being equal (a larger risk ratio implies a shorter placement spell; a smaller ratio implies a longer placement spell). Model 1 includes only mother's age at first birth. Children born to teen mothers (defined here as those mothers who had their first birth during their adolescent years) tend to stay longer in care than do children born to nonteen mothers. For example, a first foster care spell of a child whose mother had her first child between the ages of 16 and 17 would be expected to be about 20 percent longer than the first placement spell of a child of a 20- to 21-year-old mother. Because Model 1 does not include any other control variables, these findings should be interpreted as unadjusted differences in foster care spells across the maternal age groups.

Model 2 adds the type of indicated allegations, showing that children entering foster care with neglect allegations stay in care longer than those with abuse allegations. Models 3 and 4, respectively, add placement year and region, and child's age at placement. The maternal-age effect is more modest but still statistically significant for young teen mothers. The results also indicate that placement year, region, and child's age at placement all have systematic effects on duration. The duration of first spells in foster care is more than 50 percent longer for the cohort of 1992 than the cohort of 1982. The Chicago region has durations that are 40 percent longer than in the rest of the state. The duration of first spells in foster care is 53 percent longer for infants at the time of placement than for children ages 12–14.

Table 7.9 DURATION OF FIRST PLACEMENT SPELLS, ILLINOIS, 1982–92

Characteristics	Risk Ratios				
	Model 1	Model 2	Model 3	Model 4	Model 5
Mother's age at first birth					
15 or under	0.72	0.75	0.83	0.85	0.92
16–17	0.79	0.82	0.89	0.91	0.96
18–19	0.93	0.94	0.96	0.98[a]	1.00[a]
20–21	1.00	1.00	1.00	1.00	1.00
22 and over	1.03[a]	1.02[a]	1.02[a]	0.98[a]	0.97[a]
Indicated allegation type					
Abuse		1.00	1.00	1.00	1.00
Neglect		0.75	0.83	0.85	0.89
Not identified		1.06	0.94	0.91	0.93
Placement year					
1982			1.00	1.00	1.00
1983			1.00[a]	1.00[a]	1.00[a]
1984			0.94	0.92	0.92
1985			0.96[a]	0.94	0.94
1986			0.89	0.86	0.86
1987			0.74	0.74	0.74
1988			0.71	0.71	0.72
1989			0.66	0.65	0.67
1990			0.60	0.59	0.61
1991			0.51	0.51	0.53
1992			0.47	0.47	0.49
Region					
Chicago			0.59	0.61	0.68
Rest of state			1.00	1.00	1.00
Placement age (in years)					
Less than 1				1.00	1.00
1–2				1.05	1.03[a]
3–5				1.05	1.03[a]
6–8				1.03[a]	1.01[a]
9–11				1.13	1.10
12–14				1.53	1.45
15–17				2.01	1.86
Sex of child					
Male					1.00
Female					1.01[a]
Birth order					
First birth					1.09
Second + birth					1.00
Race/ethnicity					
White					1.00
African American					0.75
Hispanic					1.12
Other					1.08[a]

Note: These are relative risk ratios from proportional hazards models. Baseline levels are indicated by risk ratio of 1.

a. Estimates not statistically significant at the 0.05 level.

Model 5, the final model, adds sex of child, birth order, and race/ethnicity. The maternal-age effect on the foster care duration almost disappears. Although the maternal-age effect is still statistically significant for mothers age 15 or younger and mothers ages 16–17, the effects are very small relative to 20- to 21-year-old mothers (8 percent and 4 percent longer foster care durations, respectively).The full model also finds that first-born children tend to stay in foster care for a slightly shorter time than do other siblings, and African American children remain in foster care significantly longer than whites.

Overall, once the effects of a range of demographic factors are controlled for, for the children in foster care there are no substantially significant differences in foster care duration between children born to teen mothers and children born to nonteen mothers.

COST ESTIMATES

To focus on the costs of teenage childbearing to child protective and child welfare services, we use estimates of the effects of maternal age on abuse/neglect rates and foster care placement rates to produce five alternative cost scenarios (table 7.10).[7] Since our proportional hazards results of foster care duration show no substantial effect, we assume that the ratio of the expected foster care spell duration is constant between children of teen mothers and those of nonteen mothers.

The first three scenarios show the effects of delaying from a range of younger to older ages. Delaying the age at first birth from age 15 or younger to ages 16 to 17 has very small effects on the child abuse/neglect and foster care rates (simulation 1). Such a delay results in about a 0.6 percent decrease in indicated abuse/neglect rates and a 1.5 percent decrease in foster care rates. While delaying from age 17 and under to ages 18 to 19 has somewhat greater effects (simulation 2), we note that delaying the age at first birth from teenage years to ages 20–21 has very large effects on the child abuse/neglect and foster care rates. If all women delayed childbirth at least until ages 20 to 21 (simulation 3), the expected child abuse/neglect rate would be 26.2 per 1,000, representing a 12.3 percent decrease from the observed 29.9 per 1,000 (simulation 3). The foster care placement rate would decrease by 10.9 percent.

Simulations 4 and 5 turn from specific ages to show the effects of delaying for two and four years, respectively. Simulation 4 shows the expected changes in child abuse/neglect and foster care placement

Table 7.10 THE EFFECT OF DELAYED CHILDBEARING ON CHILD PROTECTIVE AND CHILD WELFARE SERVICE SYSTEMS

Scenario	Estimated Population Incidence Rate of Being an Indicated Child Abuse/Neglect Case Falls from 29.9 per 1,000 to:	Percentage Decrease in Overall Indicated Abuse/Neglect Rate	Estimated Population Incidence Rate of Having a Child Placed in Substitute Care Falls from 6.4 per 1,000 to:	Percentage Decrease in Overall Foster Care Placement Rate
If age of first birth changes:				
Simulation 1: from age 15 to 16 or 17	29.7	0.6	6.3	1.5
Simulation 2: from age 17 or under to 18 or 19	28.7	4.0	6.3	1.5
Simulation 3: from age 19 or under to 20 or 21	26.2	12.3	5.7	10.9
If all women delayed childbearing:				
Simulation 4: for average of 2 years	24.5	18.0	5.4	15.6
Simulation 5: for average of 4 years	21.0	29.7	4.7	26.5

Note: Estimates are based on Model 3 of table 7.6 and table 7.8 of new family's involvement with each respective service system.

rates when the age group 15 and under delays childbirth until ages 16–17, the age group 16–17 delays to 18–19, and so forth. We interpret these results as the expected changes with an "average" two-year delay. An average delay of two years in the age at first birth among teenagers results in 18.0 percent and 15.6 percent decreases, respectively, in indicated child abuse/neglect rates and foster care placement rates (simulation 4). An average four-year delay results in a 29.7 percent decrease in abuse/neglect rates and a 26.5 percent decrease in foster care placement rates (simulation 5).

The availability of information on foster care costs in Illinois and nationally allows us to estimate, using the simulation results presented in table 7.10, foster care costs at the national level (table 7.11). We estimate the annual cost of foster care in the United States in 1993 to have been $10 billion, based on information about federal reimbursement for foster care (U.S. House of Representatives 1993). About half the children in foster care in that year (236,000) were reimbursed from the federal government through Title IV-E at about a 50 percent level ($2.5 billion) (Goerge, Wulczyn, and Harden 1994). Title IV-E of the Social Security Act is the primary federal source of funding for foster care maintenance payments and administrative costs. States and local areas paid the remainder of the costs of foster care through general revenue funds and federal block grants, such as Title XX.

Table 7.11 NATIONAL COST SAVINGS IN FOSTER CARE SERVICES FROM DELAYED CHILDBEARING

	Percentage Decrease in Overall Foster Care Placement Rate	Cost Savings in Foster Care (Dollars in Millions)
If age of first birth changes:		
Simulation 1: from 15 or under to 16 or 17	1.5%	$150
Simulation 2: from 17 or under to 18 or 19	1.5	150
Simulation 3: from 19 or under to 20 or 21	10.9	1,090
If all women delayed childbearing:		
Simulation 4: for average of 2 years	15.6	1,560
Simulation 5: for average of 4 years	26.5	2,650

Note: Cost savings estimates are based on decreases in incidence rates among families with children ages birth to 5 years and estimated U.S. national foster care costs (1993) of $10 billion.

From our simulation results, table 7.11 presents the foster care costs savings assuming that one would have a program or policy that could delay teenage childbearing. Note that we are projecting from simulation results on the experiences of the Illinois cohort of new families with young children (ages birth to five) to the entire child population in the nation.

Delaying the maternal age at first birth from age 15 or younger to ages 16 to 17 (simulation 1) would reduce the cost of foster care at the national level by $150 million annually. Delaying the age at first birth from age 17 and under to at least ages 18–19 (simulation 2) would result in savings of the same magnitude. Although unrealistic, if a policy or program could delay childbearing until at least ages 20–21, the saved costs in foster care would be $1.1 billion per year nationally (simulation 3). An average delay of two years (simulation 4) and four years (simulation 5) in maternal age at first birth would result in the reduction of foster care costs by $1.6 billion and $2.7 billion per year, respectively.

The available information on the national expenditures for the investigation of abuse and neglect reports is less available and reliable than that for foster care. Nevertheless, it was clear that Illinois contains about 5 percent of all of the families reported for abuse or neglect nationally. We also estimated, with the assistance of Illinois Department of Children and Family Service administrators, that about $40 million was spent on the investigation of these cases in fiscal year 1993. Our conclusion is that roughly $800 million was spent on abuse and neglect investigations in the United States in fiscal year 1993.

From our abuse/neglect investigation simulation results, table 7.12 presents the abuse and neglect investigation costs savings, again assuming that one would have a program or policy that could delay teenage childbearing. Also again, we are using simulation results on the experience of the Illinois cohort of new families with young children (ages birth to five) to approximate the estimates for the entire child population in the nation.

Table 7.12 shows that delaying the maternal age at first birth from age 15 or younger to ages 16–17 (simulation 1) would reduce the national cost of abuse/neglect investigations at the national level by $4.8 million annually. Delaying the age at first birth from age 17 and under to at least ages 18–19 results in approximately a $32 million savings in abuse/neglect investigations. Although unrealistic, if a policy or program could delay childbearing until at least ages 20–21, the saved costs in abuse/neglect investigations would be $98 million per year nationally. The results of simulation 4 and simulation 5 show

Table 7.12 NATIONAL COST SAVINGS ON ABUSE/NEGLECT INVESTIGATIONS
FROM DELAYED CHILDBEARING

	Percentage Decrease in Overall Indicated Abuse/Neglect Rate	Cost Savings in Abuse/Neglect Investigations, Based on 1993 National Estimate (Dollars in Millions)
If age of first birth changes:		
Simulation 1: from age 15 to 16 or 17	0.6%	$4.8
Simulation 2: from 17 or under to 18 or 19	4.0	32
Simulation 3: from 19 or under to 20 or 21	12.3	98
If all women delayed childbearing:		
Simulation 4: for average of 2 years	18.0	144
Simulation 5: for average of 4 years	29.7	237

Note: Cost savings estimates are based on decreases in incidence rates among families with children ages birth–5 years and estimated U.S. national abuse/neglect investigations costs (1993) of $800 million.

that an average delay of two years and four years in maternal age at first birth would also result in the reduction of abuse/neglect investigations costs by $144 million and $237 million per year, respectively.

CONCLUSION

Our results provide evidence of a significant relationship between maternal age and the likelihood of substantiated child abuse/neglect and foster care placement. They indicate, even after we controlled for other demographic characteristics, that children born to teen mothers are significantly more likely to have an indicated child abuse/neglect report and to be placed in foster care during early childhood than are those born to nonteenage mothers. Furthermore, our analyses provide evidence that children born to young teen mothers are at greater risk of being an indicated case of abuse/neglect and being placed in foster care than are those born to older teen mothers. In terms of foster care duration, the results provide somewhat mixed evidence. The seemingly large effect of maternal age on foster care duration that we found in our univariate analyses almost disappeared when we controlled for other demographic factors.

Extrapolating from our results with Illinois data, we estimate that delaying the age at first birth from teenage years to nonteenage years would significantly reduce the cost of foster care at the national level. The estimated annual reduction realized by delaying the age at first birth ranged from $150 million to $2.5 billion, depending on the extent of simulated delay in the age at first birth.

Finally, the reader will recall that we have made two major assumptions in the cost estimates: (1) that policy interventions that can increase the mother's age at first birth are possible and (2) that adolescent childbearing is the cause of the abuse and neglect and increased use of foster care that we find. The challenges of testing these two assumptions are great, and research designs to test them must address cause. Until they are tested, the conclusions of this paper must be seen as the best social researchers can do at this time, although less than ideal.

Notes

1. In this study, we define foster care as all out-of-home placements supervised by the public child welfare agency of the state. The state has temporary custody of the children. Foster care includes foster family care, care with kin, group care, specialized foster care, and residential care.

2. With this indicator, we are measuring not who actually is abused or neglected but who is reported for abuse or neglect and subsequently indicated. We use indicated abuse/neglect as a proxy of the incidence of abuse or neglect among all children and families. See Coulton et al. (1994) for further discussion.

3. We were also unable to obtain birth certificates with identifying information that could be linked on an individual level to the abuse and neglect or foster care records.

4. A new family is defined as a family, either single-parent or two-parent, with its first child.

5. In this case, we count new families with any child (not necessarily the first child) placed during the five-year period.

6. While a child may have multiple indicated allegations of abuse or neglect, table 7.3 reports only the most serious of these allegations. Thus a child reported as physically abused and medically neglected would be coded as "abuse" in the study, since physical abuse is generally considered more harmful than medical neglect.

7. The simulations are based on the final models presented in tables 7.6 and 7.8 and use the coefficients of the mother's age at first birth.

References

Breslow, N. E., and N. E. Day. 1975. "Indirect Standardization and Multiplicative Models for Rates, with Reference to the Age Adjustment of Cancer Incidence and Relative Frequency Data." *Journal of Chronic Disease* 28:289–303.

Center for the Study of Social Policy. 1993. *Kids Count Data Book 1993.* Washington, D.C.: Center for the Study of Social Policy.

Coulton, C., J. Korbin, M. Su, and J. Chow. 1994. *Community Level Factors and Child Maltreatment Rates.* Cleveland: Center for Urban Poverty and Social Change, Case Western Reserve University.

Frome, E. L. 1983. "The Analysis of Rates Using Poisson Regression Models." *Biometrics* 39:665–74.

Goerge, R., J. Van Voorhis, and B. J. Lee. 1994. "Illinois's Longitudinal and Relational Child and Family Research Database." *Social Science Computer Review* 12(3): 351–65.

Goerge, R., F. Wulczyn, and A. Harden. 1994. *Foster Care Dynamics 1983–1992: A Report from the Multistate Foster Care Data Archive.* Chicago, Ill.: Chapin Hall Center for Children, University of Chicago.

James, I. R., and M. R. Segal. 1982. "On a Method of Mortality Analysis Incorporating Age-Year Interaction, with Application to Prostate Cancer Mortality." *Biometrics* 38:33–43.

Kalbfleisch, J., and R. Prentice. 1980. *The Statistical Analysis of Failure Time Data.* New York: John Wiley & Sons.

Koch, G. G., S. S. Atkinson, and M. E. Stokes. 1986. "Poisson Regression." In *Encyclopedia of Statistical Sciences, Vol. 7.* Eds. S. Kotz, N. L. Johnson, and C. B. Read. New York: John Wiley & Sons.

Panel of Research on Child Abuse and Neglect, National Research Council. 1993. *Understanding Child Abuse and Neglect.* Washington, D.C.: National Academy Press.

Tatara, T. 1992. "Characteristics of Children in Substitute and Adoptive Care: Based on FY 82 through FY 88 Data." Washington, D.C.: American Public Welfare Association.

U.S. House of Representatives, Committee on Ways and Means. 1993. *Overview of Entitlement Programs: Green Book 1993.* Washington, D.C.: U.S. Government Printing Office.

Chapter Eight

INCARCERATION-RELATED COSTS OF EARLY CHILDBEARING

Jeffrey Grogger

Two of the most troubling trends facing society are an increase in early fertility and the concomitant rise in reported crime. Between 1950 and 1975, the proportion of births to teenage mothers rose from 12 to 19 percent of all births (National Center for Health Statistics, various years). Since 1965, when children born in 1950 would have reached their crime-prone teenage years, the reported crime rate has risen from about 2.5 crimes per 1,000 residents to nearly 6 per 1,000 (Freeman 1991).

A natural question to ask is whether these trends are linked—that is, whether early fertility on the part of the mother actually leads to increased crime on the part of her children. Equivalently, one could ask whether the amount of crime committed by an adolescent would have been less if that adolescent's mother had delayed her childbearing. It is hard to imagine otherwise. Teen childbearing has been shown to reduce the mother's educational attainment, her employment, her earnings, and her likelihood of marriage (Geronimus and Korenman 1992; Grogger and Bronars 1993). Single parents with lower human capital and lower income may transmit to their children the kinds of economic and social disadvantage that give rise to adolescent crime. Furthermore, a young mother simply may lack the maturity required to be a good parent. As a result, her children may act out; as adolescents, they may commit crime.

In this chapter, I focus on one of the most socially costly aspects of the crime problem: imprisonment. I first ask whether a mother's early fertility leads to a greater likelihood that her son will be incarcerated at some point during his teens or 20s. I then estimate the incarceration-related costs that early childbearing imposes on the economy.

Unfortunately, the importance of these questions is nearly matched by the difficulty of obtaining valid answers. Studying the intergenerational link between early childbearing and crime imposes stringent data demands; the analyst requires data linking the fertility history of mothers to the criminal careers of their children. Indeed, valid measures of crime are themselves hard to come by. The subjective self-reports of criminals are tainted by obvious incentive problems, whereas police records and the like capture only a fraction of all crime. No ideal solution exists to this measurement problem; ultimately, criminal justice researchers must choose between objectivity and completeness.

Finally, there arises the methodological problem posed by confounding factors. The question of whether delayed fertility on the part of the mother would reduce the amount of crime committed by her children necessarily involves an unobserved counterfactual. Measuring the causal effect of early fertility requires an estimate of the extent to which the children born to a young mother would have committed less crime if that same mother had delayed her childbearing. Simply comparing the children of two mothers, one who started her family early and one who waited, is not the same. The same factors that lead different mothers to initiate their childbearing at different ages may also influence the subsequent behavior of their children. Failing to control for such influences would lead to overstating the effect of early fertility on crime, for one would also attribute the effects of the confounding factors to early childbearing.

A strategy for estimating the intergenerational effect of early fertility on crime must confront all these potential problems. For the requisite intergenerational data, I use the National Longitudinal Survey of Youth (NLSY), an annual panel study. This survey provides fertility histories for the mothers of most of its respondents. It also includes an objective if incomplete measure of respondents' criminal behavior over the period from 1979 to 1991.

Furthermore, the NLSY provides some background information on the mothers of the survey respondents, which allows me to use multivariate statistical methods to control for some of the factors that confound the relationship between maternal age and filial crime. Because the focus of the NLSY is on the youths, however, the information on their mothers is rather limited. As a result, many confounding factors are not observed. To deal with this problem, I propose a simple statistical approach designed to hold constant the effect of unobservables as well.

DATA

The NLSY began in 1979 as a survey of 12,686 youths aged 14 to 21. It is stratified, providing an oversampling of minorities and disadvantaged whites. When properly weighted, however, it yields estimates that are representative of the entire population of its age cohort. Survey respondents have been reinterviewed annually. This study makes use of data through 1991, the most recent data available when this study was begun.

One source of crime data in the NLSY is its 1980 crime module, which queried respondents about the crimes they had committed over the previous year. A major problem with these data, however, as with almost all self-reported offending (SRO) data, concerns their validity. Criminologists have noted that SRO data differ in several ways from police records. Most notably, in SRO surveys, blacks and whites appear to participate in crime in roughly the same proportion, a feature that stands in sharp contrast to estimates based on police records (Blumstein et al. 1986). While in principle a number of explanations could reconcile this discrepancy, an extensive cross-checking study of self-reports and police records concluded that it was due largely to underreporting by young black men (Hindelang, Hirschi, and Weis 1981).

Because of the questionable validity of the NLSY self-report data, I do not use them for the main component of the analysis. Rather, I use a different, albeit more limited, source of information to measure crime among the survey respondents. At each annual interview between 1979 and 1991, survey interviewers recorded the type of residence—including jails and prisons—in which the respondent was housed. By 1991, members of the sample ranged from 27 to 34 years of age. Since crime is disproportionately the pursuit of men in their late teens and early 20s, the jail interview data provide a measure that spans most of the criminal careers of most of the sample criminals.

The jail interview data also have the benefit of objectivity, although this benefit comes with a cost. First, the data limit the scope of the analysis to incarceration rather than to more general aspects of crime. Furthermore, they provide no information about the offense that led to the observed jail spell. Finally, using these data I can observe only those jail spells that are ongoing at the time of the annual interview; I may miss many short stays in jail. Although this is clearly a limitation of the data, I am able to provide some evidence below on the extent to which it affects my cost estimates.

The NLSY provides better measures of maternal childbearing. Indeed, two different measures can be constructed: the mother's age at the respondent's birth and her age at her first birth. Both of these measures require data on the mother's age. Also, the former requires the age of the respondent, and the latter requires the age of the oldest sibling in the family.

For respondents who lived with their parents in 1979, the mother's age, generally reported by the mother herself, is available from the household enumeration conducted that year. The 1987 and 1988 questionnaires included further questions about the mother's age, to which the respondent provided answers. When the 1979 data were available, I used them in the analysis.

Not all respondents were certain about their mother's age, however, as was revealed by analysis of the responses of siblings in the survey. Sibling data are available because the NLSY was initially a household survey and included all youths in the target age group in all of the households it sampled. When siblings disagreed about their mother's age, choosing any one sib's report was difficult to rationalize. The approach I took was to use the average among all siblings for whom data were available. The average of the mother's age across siblings was then assigned to each sib within the family.

Siblings likewise disagreed about the age of their oldest sib. I averaged these responses, as well, and assigned the average to each child in the family. For each respondent, the mother's age at her first birth is simply the mother's (average) age in 1979 less the (average) age of the oldest sib in 1979. The mother's age at the respondent's birth was constructed similarly.

DESCRIPTIVE STATISTICS

Incarceration rates and birth rates to teen mothers among all males in the NLSY, weighted to provide estimates representative of the entire population of males who were 14 to 21 years old in 1979, are shown in table 8.1. Throughout the study, I restrict the analysis to males, because males account for over 90 percent of the jail and prison population in the United States.

Over the 13 years from 1979 to 1991, nearly 5 percent of all men in the NLSY age cohort were interviewed in jail at least once (table 8.1, row 1). Given that my incarceration measure misses many short spells, this 5 percent *observed* incarceration rate may imply a very high rate of *actual* incarceration. Since respondents are interviewed annually, spells that last one year or more are observed with certainty. Data from various sources, however, suggest that the average incarceration spell, among the roughly 10 million spells completed annually, lasts only 46 days.[1] Since the probability of observing a 46-day spell by sampling on any randomly chosen day over a one-year period is only 12.6 percent (= $46 \div 365$), the 5 percent observed incarceration rate in the NLSY reflects what must be a substantially larger underlying rate of

Table 8.1 INCARCERATION AND YOUNG TEEN BIRTH RATES, YOUNG MALE
POPULATION

Sample	Total Number	% of Total Sample	% White	% Black	% Hispanic
Full sample					
Ever interviewed in jail	6,403	4.82	2.99	14.23	6.85
Analysis sample					
Born to young teen mother (17 or under)	5,204	12.06	9.07	27.89	15.89
Ever interviewed in jail	5,204	4.58	2.82	14.18	6.29
Born to young teen mother (17 or under)	851	10.32	6.97	17.71	6.76
Born to older mother	4,353	3.80	2.41	12.82	6.20
Differential		6.52	4.56	4.89	0.56

Note: Based on data from the NLSY, weighted to provide estimates representative of
the population of males ages 14 to 21 years in 1979.

actual incarceration. The observed incarceration rate varies substantially
by race, a pattern consistent with data from police records.

Data from the sample to be analyzed include only those respondents
for whom the mother's age at first birth could be calculated. The
overall incarceration rate in the analysis sample is 4.58 percent, only
slightly lower than the full sample. Variation by race is similar to that
from the full sample as well.

The fraction of males of this age group born to young teen mothers,
whom I define as women 17 years old or younger at the age of their
first birth, is shown in row 2 of table 8.1. Roughly one-eighth of the
children in this cohort were born to young teens. Early teen births
vary substantially by race, which is consistent with data from *Vital
Statistics of the United States* (National Center for Health Statistics)
and various fertility surveys.

Overall, incarceration rates among the children of young teen mothers were 10.32 percent, which is 6.52 percentage points, or 2.7 times,
higher than the 3.8 percent incarceration rate among the children of
older mothers. This differential varies substantially by race. Whereas
among whites the children of young teens are nearly three times more
likely to be observed in jail than their counterparts, among blacks the
differential is only 38 percent. Among Hispanics the association between maternal age and filial incarceration is negligible.

Thus the raw data show a clear intergenerational association between maternal age and the likelihood of incarceration, at least among
whites and blacks. It would be improper to attribute this correlation

entirely to the mother's early fertility, however, because of the possibility that the same factors that contributed to the mother's early childbearing also influenced her children's proneness to delinquency.

MULTIVARIATE ANALYSES

In this section, I provide estimates of the effect of early fertility that attempt to disentangle causality from simple correlation.

Estimation Technique

Multivariate statistical techniques provide a means to control for many observable factors that may confound the relationship between maternal age and filial incarceration. Given the binary (yes or no) nature of the incarceration outcome, the probit model is a natural technique to choose.

Denote the incarceration variable by I, so $I = 1$ if the respondent is ever interviewed in jail, and $I = 0$ otherwise. Denote the young teen mother dummy by Y; $Y = 1$ if the respondent's mother first gave birth at age 17 or earlier, and $Y = 0$ otherwise. Probit analysis allows one to assess the relationship between I and Y while holding constant the influence of observable, potentially confounding, variables X. The model is motivated by proposing that the probability (P) of ever being interviewed in jail, as a function of maternal age and the background variables, is given by

$$P(I = 1|Y, X) = \Phi(\alpha Y + X\beta)$$

where Φ is the standard normal distribution function. Symbolically, this states that the probability of incarceration is a function of the mother's age at her first birth, a number of background characteristics, and unknown parameters α and β. The larger α is, the stronger is the relationship between maternal age and the risk of filial incarceration.

The characteristics to be included in the variables, X, merit some discussion. Ideally I would include all characteristics of the mother that might affect both the a priori likelihood that she would become a young mother and the likelihood that her sons eventually would go to jail. Unfortunately, since the focus of the NLSY was on the respondent rather than his parents, the survey provides little a priori information about the mother.

The variables in X also should capture those characteristics of the respondent that are not under his direct control but that influence his risk of incarceration independently of the age of his mother. Among these characteristics are the respondent's birth order and his age at the beginning of the observation period. Birth order is clearly beyond the respondent's control but may affect his participation in crime. Birth order affects educational attainment, which in turn affects wages (Hanushek 1992). Wages in turn play an important role in young men's decisions to commit crime (Grogger 1996).

The respondent's age may capture differences in crime-proneness. Alternatively, it may control for the fact that different sample respondents are observed over different portions of their criminal careers. The late teens are typically the ages at which young men commit the most crimes. Therefore, the older NLSY respondents may appear to face a lower incarceration risk over the observation period simply because most of their criminal careers are already behind them.

Many other variables are deliberately excluded from the model. Some of these, such as the mother's education and ultimate family size, may themselves be affected by the mother's early fertility (Bronars and Grogger 1994; Grogger and Bronars 1993). Because I exclude these variables from the regression, the probit model provides an estimate of the total effect of early fertility, which includes both direct effects and indirect effects that operate through the mother's educational attainment and family size.

I also exclude variables that may reflect the mother's response to early signals about her child's delinquency, which could mask the effect of early fertility per se. Examples include the mother's employment and marital status during her son's childhood, that is, after he is born but before he is observed in the sample. For example, the mother of a youngster who acts out in school may decide to work part-time rather than full-time in order to keep closer tabs on her child. Or she may more readily pursue a potential husband in order to provide a male role model for her son.

Both these actions may reduce the child's likelihood of eventual incarceration. However, because they resulted from early, unobservable (to the analyst) behavior on the part of the child (behavior that itself may have stemmed from the mother's early childbearing), the results of this type of action on the part of the mother should not be netted out in measuring the effect of early childbearing per se. In other words, variables that potentially represent the response of the mother in attempting to mitigate the effects of her early childbearing are endogenous and should not be included in the model.

Estimates with Observable Factors Controlled

I present a number of specifications that include different sets of background characteristics to illustrate the effect of potentially confounding factors on the estimated effect of early fertility (table 8.2). Model 1 is the simplest; the only explanatory variable is the young teen mother dummy. The probit coefficient of 0.511 on the young teen mother variable is roughly six times the magnitude of its standard error, indicating that it is statistically quite significant. The magnitude of the coefficient itself, however, is difficult to interpret. For this reason, I provide an estimate of the "average treatment effect" associated with young teen motherhood in square brackets below the estimated coefficient. This gives the difference in the probability between the children of young teen mothers and the children of older mothers of

Table 8.2 RELATIONSHIP BETWEEN MALE OFFSPRING'S INCARCERATION RISK
AND MOTHER'S AGE AT BIRTH (PROBITS)

Variable	Model 1	Model 2	Model 3	Model 4
Young teen	0.511	0.345	0.331	0.320
mother (17 or under)	(0.079)[a]	(0.087)	(0.088)	(0.100)
	[0.065[b]]	[0.037]	[0.035]	[0.033]
Mother 18 to 19 at first birth				0.106
				(0.107)
Mother 23 or older at first birth				−0.105
				(0.098)
Birth order			0.025	0.024
			(0.016)	(0.016)
Respondent's age in 1979		−0.050	−0.049	−0.047
		(0.017)	(0.017)	(0.018)
Black		0.813	0.796	0.776
		(0.076)	(0.076)	(0.080)
Hispanic		0.258	0.242	0.230
		(0.098)	(0.099)	(0.131)
Log likelihood	−947.1	−878.3	−876.9	−874.5
n = 5,204				

Note: Estimates, derived from probit models, are based on weighted data. In addition to the variables shown, all regressions include a dummy for urban residence, for residence in the western census region, and for missing region. Also included in each regression are missing value flags associated with all included regressors. These missing flags take on the value one if data were missing for the associated regressor, and zero otherwise. Missing values of the associated regressor are set to zero.
a. Standard errors, corrected for dependent observations within families, are in parentheses.
b. Average treatment effects are in square brackets.

being observed in jail, holding constant the other variables in the equation.[2] It has the advantage of being directly comparable to the unadjusted difference in incarceration rates between the sons of teen and older mothers. Indeed, for Model 1, the average treatment effect is 6.5 percentage points, reflecting (as it should) exactly the same differential in incarceration rates as was obtained by simply cross-tabulating the raw data (table 8.1).

Several background characteristics, including race, the respondent's age in 1979, and indicator variables for the respondent's region of residence and for residence in an urban area,[3] are added to Model 2. The coefficients associated with these variables show that older survey respondents are less likely to be observed in jail than their younger counterparts and that blacks and Hispanics are more likely to be incarcerated than whites (the omitted race category). The background variables have a substantial bearing on the estimated effect of early fertility: the probit coefficient is 0.345, and the average treatment effect has fallen to 3.7 percentage points.

The respondent's birth order is added to Model 3. Its coefficient indicates that later-born offspring are more likely to be incarcerated than their older siblings, although this effect is only marginally significant. Adding birth order to the model reduces the estimated effect of early childbearing only slightly.

A more general specification of the relationship between the mother's age at her first birth and the likelihood of incarceration on the part of her male children is allowed in Model 4. Compared to the omitted base group of children whose mothers first gave birth between the ages of 20 and 22, the children of older teen mothers—18- and 19-year-olds—were only slightly and insignificantly more likely to be incarcerated as young adults. Likewise, the children of the mothers who waited the longest to start their families were only slightly and insignificantly less likely to end up in jail eventually. These estimates suggest that there is an important difference in the jail-proneness of the children of young teen mothers but not of the children born to older teenage mothers.

Two conclusions emerge. First, the qualitative relationship between maternal age and filial incarceration remains significant even after controlling for a number of important background characteristics. Second, the quantitative association falls a great deal as one controls for a broader set of background measures. In particular, the unadjusted 6.52 percentage point differential in incarceration rates grossly overstates the true effect of early childbearing.

Using the Mother's Age at Her First Birth to Control for Unobservable Confounding Factors

Due to the presence of unobservable confounding factors, even the estimates with controls for the broadest set of background character- istics may overstate the true effect of maternal age. Indeed, maternal characteristics that may affect both the age at which a woman first gives birth and the ultimate success of her children are easy to think of but difficult to measure. Emotional maturity and orientation toward the future are two examples.

For this reason, I need to devise an approach that controls for unob- served differences across mothers in estimating the effect of maternal age on filial incarceration. The approach I propose is based on a simple observation: a mother is older at the births of her later children than she is at the births of her earlier children. Put differently, there is necessarily a delay between the birth of one child and the birth of the next. In contrast, a mother's age at her first birth is a fixed trait that does not vary across her children.

These two observations give rise to a simple estimation strategy. I use the young teen mother dummy as a control variable, to account for all unobservable characteristics of the mother that led her to be- come a young teen mother. I then use the variation in the mother's age at the birth of her various children, controlling for birth order as before, to measure the effects of delaying childbearing.[4]

This approach is appealing for its simplicity, but it warrants some further scrutiny. Recall that I have defined the effect of early fertility on the likelihood of imprisonment as the difference in the likelihood of imprisonment facing a child born to a young mother and the like- lihood of imprisonment that same child would have faced if his mother had delayed her childbearing. My approach approximates this unobservable counterfactual by basing an estimate of the effect of early fertility—or equivalently, of the effect of delaying childbirth—on the difference in incarceration outcomes between, say, the first and sec- ond children of the same mother, holding constant her age at her first birth. If maternal maturation has the same effect on child outcomes, independent of whether the mother has yet had her first child, then my approach provides a valid estimate of the effect of delay as defined by the counterfactual. If not, then I may either over- or underestimate the effect of interest.

To illustrate this point further, consider an example. I would like to compare the outcome of a child born when his mother was, say, 16 to the outcome that *same* child would have experienced had his mother not had him until she was, say, 20. Instead, I compare two children born to the same mother, one at age 16 and the other at age 20. In both cases, the mother matures four years. In the counterfactual case, those four years come before her first birth; in the observable case, they come after her first birth. If maternity enhances the effect of maturation, then four years as a mother reduce the likelihood that the son eventually goes to jail by a greater amount than four prematernal years; in this case, my approach overstates the beneficial effect of maternal maturation on the likelihood of incarceration. If, instead, maternity hinders maturation, then four years of maturation as a mother are less effective in reducing the likelihood of filial incarceration, and my approach underestimates the beneficial effect of maternal maturation on incarceration rates. Unfortunately, the counterfactual nature of the comparison prevents empirical verification of either the presence or magnitude of either of these countervailing effects.

The estimates are presented in table 8.3 for mother's age at respondent's birth as a dummy variable (young teen or not, Model 1) and for mother's age as a continuous variable (Model 2). In addition to the variables shown, models include all variables included in Model 3, table 8.2.

When mother's age at the respondent's birth is either teen or non-teen, age appears to have little effect on the likelihood that her son eventually goes to jail. When mother's age at the respondent's birth is allowed to vary continuously, it has a negative and significant coefficient, indicating that delaying childbearing reduces the likelihood of

Table 8.3 RELATIONSHIP BETWEEN INCARCERATION AND MOTHER'S AGE AT BIRTH, USING THE MOTHER'S AGE AT HER FIRST BIRTH TO CONTROL FOR UNOBSERVABLES

Variable	Model 1	Model 2
Young teen mother	0.320	0.216
(17 or under at first birth)	(0.095)[a]	(0.097)
Mother under 18 at respondent's birth	0.043	
	(0.197)	
Mother's age at respondent's birth		−0.019
		(0.008)
Log likelihood	−876.8	−873.3
n = 5,204		

Note: Based on weighted data. In addition to variables shown, all regressions include the full set of regressors from Model 3 of table 8.2.
a. Standard errors, corrected for dependent observations within families, are in parentheses.

the child's eventual incarceration. The latter specification also provides a better fit to the data, as indicated by the log likelihood. The linear specification yields a higher value (i.e., a smaller negative number), indicating that it has a greater likelihood of being the model that gave rise to the observed data. As before, however, attaching an intuitive quantitative interpretation to the coefficient is difficult. Because, moreover, the mother's age at the respondent's birth appears in the model linearly, to speak of the average treatment effect associated with delayed childbearing makes no sense.

To aid in interpreting these estimates, I provide the results of some simulations based on the coefficient of the mother's age at the respondent's birth from Model 2 of table 8.3.

The simulations address the question, "By how much would the likelihood of incarceration fall among all children born to a young teen mother, if the young teen mother were to delay her childbearing?" To answer this question, one must first specify the magnitude of the delay being considered. I present three scenarios. The first asks how these mothers' children would have fared had the mothers delayed the birth of their first child until the age at which their second child actually was born, which on average was age 18.5. The second asks how the children would have fared if the young teen mothers had waited until just beyond their teens, giving birth at age 20.5. The third asks how the children's risk of incarceration would have differed had their mothers waited till the age of 22.9 to have their first child, where 22.9 is the average age at first birth among all women whose first birth occurred after age 17.[5]

These three scenarios (table 8.4) reflect the benefits that one could expect from policies designed to encourage delayed childbearing, as a function of the effectiveness of those policies. For example, the first scenario is informative about policies that succeed in encouraging young teen mothers to delay their first birth just beyond the young teen threshold. The third scenario depicts the results of a highly effective policy that succeeds to the extent that women who would have been young teen mothers actually delay their childbearing to the point where, on average, their age at first birth is the same as that of older mothers. The second case represents the effects of a policy of intermediate effectiveness.

Delaying the age at first birth from 16 to 18.5 results in an incarceration rate of 9.68 percent among the sons of young teen mothers (scenario 1, table 8.4). This amounts to a reduction of only six-tenths of 1 percentage point, or equivalently only 6 percent of the observed incarceration rate of 10.32 percent.

Table 8.4 EFFECT ON INCARCERATION RATES OF DELAYED CHILDBEARING, SIMULATION RESULTS

	Change Mean Age at First Birth among Young Teen Mothers from 16.0 to:	Incarceration Rate (percent) among Sons of Young Teen Mothers Falls from 10.32 to:	Percentage Change in Incarceration Rate among Sons of Young Teen Mothers	Overall Incarceration Rate (percent) Falls from 4.58 to:	Percentage Change in Overall Incarceration Rate
Scenario 1	18.5	9.68	−6.2	4.49	−2.0
Scenario 2	20.5	9.10	−11.8	4.42	−3.5
Scenario 3	22.9	8.56	−17.1	4.35	−5.0

Note: Simulations are based on Model 2 of table 8.3 and use the coefficient on the mother's age at the respondent's birth to estimate the effect of delayed childbearing.

Longer delays have greater effects. A delay in the age at first birth from 16 to 20.5 would result in a filial incarceration rate of 9.10 percent, a reduction of 1.22 percentage points, or 12 percent (scenario 2). If young teen mothers were to delay their childbearing by 6.9 years, so that on average their first birth occurred at age 22.9, then the incarceration rate among their sons would fall to 8.56 percent (scenario 3). This 1.76 percentage point differential amounts to 17 percent of the actual incarceration rate.

To simulate the incarceration rate among the entire cohort, I construct a weighted average of the simulated incarceration rate among the sons of young teen mothers and the predicted incarceration rate among the sons of older mothers, using weights that reflect each group's representation in the cohort.[6] Under scenario 1, the overall incarceration rate falls 0.09 percentage points, from 4.58 percent to 4.49 percent, which amounts to a 2.0 percent reduction. Under scenario 2, the overall reduction is 0.16 percentage points, or 3.5 percent of the actual incarceration rate. For the greatest delay, the overall incarceration rate falls to 4.35 percent. This reduction of 0.23 percentage points amounts to 5.0 percent of the actual incarceration rate.

These simulation results show that policies that successfully encouraged young teen mothers to delay their childbearing would reduce the likelihood of incarceration on the part of their sons. Not surprisingly, they also show that policies that encouraged longer delays would have greater effects. I next consider the cost savings associated with these various reductions in incarceration rates.

COSTS

We would like to know how the costs of corrections, as borne by state, federal, and local governments, would fall in response to delayed childbearing on the part of young teen mothers. To go from reductions in observed incarceration rates to reductions in correctional costs, however, requires some theoretical work. I first consider what information would be needed to estimate the expected lifetime cost of incarcerating a particular individual as a function of his mother's age at birth. I then discuss how such a lifetime cost measure may be expressed in terms of annual expenditures.

The expected lifetime cost of incarcerating a criminal is the product of the cost per unit of time of keeping him behind bars times the expected total amount of time he spends in jail. His total expected time in jail, in turn, is the product of the probability that he ever goes to jail and the expected number of times he is incarcerated, times the expected length of his jail spells. To express this relationship symbolically, let C denote the lifetime cost of incarcerating a particular individual, let T denote the total amount of time he spends behind bars, and let c be the cost of incarceration per unit of time. Let J denote the event that the individual is ever incarcerated, let N denote the number of times he goes to jail, and let S denote the length of a typical jail spell. Then, conditional on the mother's age at birth, denoted by A, we have

$$C = cE(T|A) \qquad (8.1)$$

where

$$E(T|A) = P(J|A)E(N|A)E(S|A) \qquad (8.2)$$

In equations (8.1 and 8.2), E denotes a mathematical expectation, and $P(\ )$ denotes the probability of an event. The costs of incarceration due to early childbearing are then given by the expression

$$c[E(T|\text{early childbearing}) - E(T|\text{later childbearing})] \qquad (8.3)$$

Expressions (8.1) through (8.3) show that, to estimate the incarceration-related costs of early childbearing directly, one would need to know the cost per unit of time in jail and be able to estimate the effect of early fertility on the probability of ever going to jail, on the expected number of jail spells, and on the expected length of a jail spell. The annual costs of incarceration are readily available in published reports. The other information, however, is harder to come by. The NLSY, given its sampling scheme, provides data on the likelihood of being observed in jail but not on the likelihood of ever going to jail. Although the two are likely to be closely related, direct cost estimation requires the more comprehensive measure.

Likewise, the sequences of interviews at which NLSY respondents were observed in jail can be used together with intervening employment histories to provide a count of observed jail spells for each sample member. Again, although observed and actual jail spells are likely to be highly correlated, direct cost estimation requires the actual number. Finally, the NLSY provides only qualitative information about the length of jail spells. If a respondent is observed in jail at two sequential interviews, then I presume that he spent at least one year (the length of time between interviews) behind bars, provided that he was not observed in the labor force in the intervening period. For a jail spell that spans a single interview, however—roughly 60 percent of all observed spells—we know much less about its duration. In some cases, the longitudinal employment records in the NLSY can be used to determine the maximum amount of time the respondent could have spent in jail. In about half these cases, however, the employment data are largely uninformative. Thus the NLSY provides only qualitative information about the length of observed jail spells. Specifically, I can classify some of the spells as long (i.e., as lasting a year or more), and I can classify some of the others as short. Although these qualitative indicators are likely to be correlated with the average length of actual spells, they fall short of the quantitative information required to estimate the average spell length as a function of maternal age.

Because there are such formidable barriers to estimating the incarceration-related costs of early childbearing directly, I take an indirect approach instead. The NLSY data have permitted me to estimate the likelihood that a respondent is observed in jail given that he was born to a young mother, relative to the likelihood of being observed in jail given that he was born to an older mother. Letting I denote the event of being interviewed in jail, as above, this can be expressed symbolically as

$$\frac{P(I \mid \text{early childbearing})}{P(I \mid \text{later childbearing})} \tag{8.4}$$

To estimate the incarceration-related costs of early childbearing indirectly, I begin by determining the conditions under which the ratio of total time spent in jail, as a function of maternal age, is equal to the relative probability of ever being interviewed in jail, as a function of maternal age. Symbolically, I provide conditions under which

$$\frac{E(T \mid \text{early childbearing})}{E(T \mid \text{later childbearing})} = \frac{P(I \mid \text{early childbearing})}{P(I \mid \text{later childbearing})} \tag{8.5}$$

Manipulating equations (8.2) through (8.5), the necessary conditions are

(A) $\dfrac{P(J \mid \text{early childbearing})}{P(J \mid \text{later childbearing})} = \dfrac{P(I \mid \text{early childbearing})}{P(I \mid \text{later childbearing})}$

(B) $E(N \mid \text{early childbearing}) = E(N \mid \text{later childbearing})$

(C) $E(S \mid \text{early childbearing}) = E(S \mid \text{later childbearing})$

Condition (A) says that the odds of actually going to jail given birth to a young mother must equal the odds of being observed in jail given birth to a young mother. Condition (B) says that on average the number of jail spells served is independent of the age of one's mother's age at birth, and condition (C) says that the average sentence length must also be independent of maternal age.

Under conditions (A) through (C), the effect of early fertility on the total time an individual spends in jail over his lifetime will equal the effect of early fertility on the probability of being observed in jail. If one also assumes prisons are characterized by constant marginal costs, then a delay in age at birth that brings about a p percent reduction in the likelihood that the son will ever be observed in jail also brings about a p percent reduction in the cost of incarcerating him. If data were available on the lifetime cost of imprisoning a typical criminal, then I could estimate the reduction in lifetime incarceration costs associated with scenarios 1 through 3 above by invoking assumptions (A) through (C), together with the constant cost assumption, and applying the proportionate reductions in observed incarceration rates from the last column of table 8.4.

Such lifetime cost data, however, do not exist. Rather, correctional authorities report the annual expenditures: expenses they incur in order to maintain the current year's set of prisoners. These annual data are nonetheless useful under a set of three assumptions, which I will refer to as steady state assumptions. If (1) the proportion of births to young teen mothers is constant over time, (2) the effect of early childbearing is likewise constant across cohorts, and (3) the overall incarceration rate does not change over time, then the proportionate reduction in lifetime incarceration costs for a fixed birth cohort that results from a given delay in childbearing can be approximated by the same proportionate reduction in the cost of incarcerating the current year's set of prisoners. I can do this because, in the steady state, the current behavior of older cohorts is the same as the future behavior of younger cohorts. In other words, in the steady state, a snapshot view of all prisoners at a point in time mirrors a prospective view of a fixed age cohort over the lifetime of its members. Thus, under conditions (A) through (C), the constant cost assumption, and the steady state assumptions (1) through (3), I can estimate the steady-state incarceration cost savings attributable to a given delay in early childbearing on the part of young teen mothers by multiplying the proportionate reduction in observed incarceration rates attributable to that delay by reported annual corrections costs.

Incarceration-Related Costs of Early Childbearing

Correctional expenditures by all levels of government amounted to $24.96 billion in 1990 (U.S. Department of Justice 1992c). In 1994 dollars, that amounts to $28.94 billion. Roughly 90 percent of the budget, or $26 billion, goes to incarcerate men.

A 2.0 percent reduction in this amount, which is the predicted result of young teen mothers delaying their childbearing by 2.5 years (last column of table 8.4), comes to $522 million. Longer delays result in greater savings. If young teen mothers first gave birth at, on average, age 20.5 rather than at age 16, incarceration costs would fall by 3.5 percent, or $920 million. If they waited till age 22.9, the mean age at first birth among older mothers, the savings would amount to $1.29 billion.

This general approach also can be used to provide a more detailed breakdown of the incarceration-related costs of early childbearing. The estimated cost savings[7] that would obtain if different groups of young teen mothers were to delay their first births by varying amounts (table 8.5) largely reinforce the earlier conclusions: small delays lead to small cost savings, whereas large delays have substantial effects.[8]

These cost figures also provide an implicit estimate of how the prison population would fall in response to delayed childbearing on the part of young teen mothers. The cost of incarcerating one criminal for one year is widely estimated to average $20,000 to $25,000 (DiIulio and Piehl 1991; General Accounting Office 1991; U.S. Department of Justice 1992b; Zedlewski 1987). Thus a delay in childbearing on the part of young teen mothers of 2.5 years, which is estimated to reduce annual correctional expenditures by $522 million, implies a reduction in the prison population of roughly 21,000 to 26,000 men.[9] At the extreme, if young teen mothers were to delay their first births till age 22.9, the prison population would fall by 52,000 to 65,000 men.

Testing the Assumptions

The population estimates and the corresponding cost estimates are both based on a number of assumptions. Because the estimates are valid only if the assumptions hold, providing at least some indirect evidence on the validity of the assumptions is desirable. I begin with evidence on conditions (A) through (C). Condition (A) requires that the odds of a young male's ever actually going to jail given a young teen mother must equal the odds of being interviewed in jail given a young teen mother. This will tend to be true if the crimes committed by the sons of young teen mothers are no more likely to result in a jail term than the crimes committed by the sons of older mothers and if, at each conviction, the length of the offender's previous criminal record does not depend on his mother's age at birth.

Table 8.5 COST SAVINGS ASSOCIATED WITH VARIOUS DELAYS IN CHILDBEARING

Ages at First birth	Cost savings ($ Millions/Year) if First Birth Had Been Delayed until:				
	Ages 16 or 17[b]	Ages 18 or 19[c]	Ages 20 or 21[d]	Ages 22 to 41[e]	Ages 20 or over[f]
15 or under[a]	162.7	293.5	421.9	727.5	638.0
16 or17	NA	240.2	498.8	1,111.3	932.3
18 or 19	NA	NA	NA	NA	NA
Total	162.7	533.7	920.7	1,838.8	1,770.3

Note: Mean ages used in calculated savings are:
a. 14.2
b. 16.7
c. 18.6
d. 20.5
e. 25.5
f. 24.0
See endnote 7 of the text for a complete discussion.
NA = not applicable

Robbery is the crime most likely to result in an incarcerative sentence, both because of its severity and because it involves face-to-face contact between the victim and the offender. If, among the youths who commit crime, the sons of young teen mothers commit, on average, a higher proportion of robberies than the sons of older mothers, then the sons of the young teen mothers would be more likely to be incarcerated, all else equal. Using the NLSY 1980 self-reported offending crime module, I can ask whether the fraction of reported offenses that involves robbery depends on maternal age. Likewise, I can determine whether the age at first arrest or age at first conviction, both of which will be correlated with the extent of the offender's arrest record, vary by maternal age.

Condition (B) requires the number of jail spells to be unaffected by maternal age, whereas condition (C) requires that the average length of a jail spell be independent of the mother's age at birth. The number of observed jail spells can be used to examine the validity of condition (B), and the qualitative data on lengths of spells provide information about condition (C).

The results of a series of regressions provide substantial support for conditions (A) through (C) (table 8.6). Each row gives the results of a different regression. In addition to the variables shown, all regres-

Table 8.6 EARLY FERTILITY AND VARIOUS CRIMINAL JUSTICE OUTCOMES

Dependent Variable	Young Teen Mother (17 or under)	Mother's Age at Respondent's Birth
1. Robbery rate	−0.002	0.004
(n = 3,798)	(0.004)[a]	(0.005)
2. Age at first arrest	−0.296	0.008
(n = 807)	(0.229)	(0.016)
3. Age at first conviction	−0.538	−0.005
(n = 463)	(0.293)	(0.021)
4. Number of observed jail spells	0.384	−0.003
(n = 378)	(0.147)	(0.011)
5. Long jail spell	0.078	0.003
(n = 626)	(0.131)	(0.010)
6. Short jail spell	0.035	−0.018
(n = 626)	(0.141)	(0.011)

Note: Each row reports the results of a separate regression. Estimates are based on weighted data. In addition to the variables shown, all regressions include the full set of regressors from Model 3, table 8.2. For regressions 5 and 6, the unit of observation is the jail spell rather than the respondent.
a. Standard errors, corrected for dependent observations within family, are in parentheses.

sions include all variables from Model 3, table 8.2.[10] I employ the same statistical procedure as above to control for unobservable confounding factors associated with both the mother's early fertility and her sons' proneness to crime, using the young teen mother dummy as a control variable and using variation in the mother's age at the births of her children to estimate the effect of delayed childbearing.

None of the coefficients on the mother's age at the respondent's birth are significant. Young teen childbearing is positively correlated with the number of observed jail spells. Given the specification, this provides evidence of confounding factors but not of a causal relationship. The apparent validity of assumptions (A) through (C) provides greater confidence in the cost estimates based on those assumptions.

For evidence on the remaining assumptions, I turn to the existing literature. California prisons exhibit roughly constant marginal costs (Block and Ulen 1979). Federal prisons, in contrast, exhibit increasing marginal costs (Schmidt and Witte 1984). The vast majority of the nation's prisoners are held in state rather than federal facilities (U.S. Department of Justice 1992a). To the extent that the California state system is more representative of state prisons generally than are those run by federal authorities, the constant marginal cost hypothesis receives some support.

The evidence is more mixed for the steady state assumptions. The proportion of births to young teen mothers has varied within a fairly narrow band over time. In 1950, the share of all births that women under 18 years old accounted for was 3.7 percent; this rose to 7.6 percent in 1975 and fell again to 4.6 percent in 1989 (National Center for Health Statistics, various years).

No evidence whatsoever exists on changes in the intergenerational effect of early childbearing on crime. The only other study on the topic also used the NLSY, albeit the 1980 SRO data (Morash and Rucker 1989). To determine whether the effect of maternal age on filial crime had changed over time would, however, require studies based on cohorts of different vintages of youths.

Finally, recent data show that the assumption of constant incarceration rates is false. According to the 1980 census, there were roughly 479,000 prisoners in the United States. By 1990, that figure had risen to 1.1 million, a 130 percent increase. The concomitant growth in population, in contrast, was only 9.8 percent. Recent "three strikes" proposals would reinforce this trend in the future.

The implication of this trend for my cost estimates is clear. As imprisonment increases, prison costs rise, and a given proportionate reduction in prison costs translates to a larger absolute cost savings. Therefore my cost estimates, which are based on the assumption of constant incarceration rates, are conservative.

CONCLUSIONS

The results of this study provide evidence that early childbearing and youth crimes are linked. Based on a model that provides controls for unobservable characteristics of the mother that may be correlated with her early age at first birth, I conclude that delayed childbearing on the part of young teen mothers—women under the age of 18 at the time of their first births—would reduce the risk of incarceration on the part of their sons. Specifically, if a young teen mother were to delay her childbearing until just beyond her 18th birthday, then her son's incarceration risk would fall by about 6 percent. If all young teen mothers so delayed their fertility, then the number of men behind bars in the United States would fall by 21,000 to 26,000, and annual corrections budgets could be reduced by roughly $522 million.

Longer delays would have larger effects. If would-be young teen mothers were to delay their first births until they were almost 23 years old—the average age at which other women begin their families— then their sons' incarceration risk would fall by 17 percent. As a result, prison populations would fall by 52,000 to 65,000, and corrections costs incurred by local, state, and federal governments would decrease by $1.29 billion per year.

Because these figures reflect only correctional costs, they almost certainly substantially understate the full crime-related costs of early childbearing. In 1990, correctional expenditures accounted for only one-third of the roughly $75 billion devoted to criminal justice activities by all levels of government (U.S. Department of Justice 1992c). In addition, direct costs to crime victims have been estimated at $17 billion (Klaus 1994). Although this latter figure includes victims' losses due to theft, which constitute social transfers rather than true social costs, it excludes the costs of private security measures and insurance. It also excludes the costs associated with peoples' fear of being victimized. Thus the total crime-related costs of young teen childbearing may exceed the incarceration-related costs by a great deal.

Nevertheless, even though the crime-related costs of early child-bearing may be substantial, early childbearing per se explains only a small fraction of the difference in incarceration rates between the children of young teen mothers and the children of older mothers. The sons of young teen mothers are 2.7 times more likely to be incarcerated at some point during their 20s than the sons of older mothers. Even if young teen mothers were to delay their first birth till age 23, however, their sons would still be 2.2 times more likely to end up in jail than the sons of their older counterparts. Thus even large changes in young teen mothers' age at first birth would have a relatively modest effect on their sons' incarceration risk.

Why is this true? The age of the mother is but one of the differences in the circumstances facing the children of young teen mothers as compared to the children of older mothers. Other factors contribute to the risk of delinquency among the children of young teen mothers. These factors in total have greater effects than early childbearing itself. Although the precise definition of these factors is unclear, what is clear is that social policy designed to reduce teen childbearing will have only relatively small effects on youth crime. In order to have large effects, social policy would have to identify and address the other risk factors, as well.

Notes

1. Source data are from U.S. Department of Justice (1991, 1992b, 1994). The author's calculations are available on request.

2. Formally, the average treatment effect is given by

$$n^{-1} \sum_{i=1}^{n} w_i [\Phi(\hat{\alpha} + X_i\hat{\beta}) - \Phi(X_i\hat{\beta})]$$

where the hat notation denotes the maximum likelihood estimates, the i subscript indexes individual observations, n is the sample size, and w_i is the sampling weight for the ith observation.

3. The coefficients of the region dummies and the urban dummy are omitted from the table to save space.

4. Formally, I estimate the probit model given by

$$P(I = 1|Y, A, X) = \Phi(\alpha Y + \gamma A + X\beta)$$

where A denotes the mother's age at the respondent's birth and γ is a parameter to be estimated.

5. The simulated incarceration rate among the sons of young teen mothers is given by

$$\hat{I}_1(\Delta) = n_1^{-1} \sum_{i=1}^{n_1} w_i \Phi[\hat{\alpha}Y_i + \hat{\gamma}(A_i + \Delta) + X_i + \hat{\beta}]$$

where the summation runs over the n_1 respondents whose mothers' first births occurred prior to age 18. The term Δ is calculated as the mean difference between the actual age at first birth among the young teen mothers and the target age for the given scenarios. Thus, for the simulations in the first row of table 8.4, $\Delta = 18.5 - 16.0 = 2.5$.

6. The simulated incarceration rate for the entire cohort is constructed as

$$\hat{I}(\Delta) = \pi (\Delta)\hat{I}(\Delta) = \pi \hat{I}_1(\Delta) + \hat{I}_0$$

where π is the fraction of youths born to young teen mothers ($= 0.1206$ from table 8.1) and $\hat{I}_0$ is the predicted incarceration rate among the sons of older mothers. It is calculated as

$$\hat{I}_0 = n_0^{-1} \sum_{i=1}^{n_0} w_i \Phi[\hat{\alpha}Y_1 + \hat{\gamma}(A_i + \Delta) + X_i\hat{\beta}]$$

where the summation runs over the n_0 sample members whose mothers were 18 or older at their first births.

7. The cost savings are based on simulated reductions in overall incarceration rates computed similarly to the manner described in footnote 6. A word on the calculation of Δ is in order, however. In each cell, Δ is equal to the difference between the mean age at first birth among sample mothers in the target age range and the mean age at first birth of the indicated group of young teen mothers. For example, the mean age at first birth among sample mothers who first gave birth at age 15 or earlier was 14.2. Among mothers who first gave birth at ages 20 or 21, the mean age at first birth was 20.5. Thus, for the cell in the first row, third column, $\Delta = 20.5 - 14.2 = 6.3$. Mean ages used in calculating Δ for each cell are given in the notes to table 8.5.

8. No cost savings are calculated for delays on the part of older teen mothers (i.e., 18- and 19-year-olds), because the estimates reported in table 8.3 showed no significant association between births to older teens and higher rates of filial incarceration.

9. Strictly speaking, this is a reduction of 21,000 to 26,000 man-years of incarceration.

10. Regressions 1 through 4 are ordinary least squares. Regressions 5 and 6 are probit.

References

Block, M. K., and T. S. Ulen. 1979. "Cost Functions for Correctional Institutions." In *The costs of Crime*, ed. C. M. Gray, pp. 187–212. Beverly Hills, Calif.: Sage Publications.

Blumstein, A., J. Cohen, J. A. Roth, and C. A. Visher. 1986. *Criminal Careers and "Career Criminals."* Washington, D.C.: National Academy Press.

Bronars, S. G., and J. Grogger. 1994. "The Economic Consequences of Unwed Motherhood: Using Twin Births as a Natural Experiment." *American Economic Review* 84(5):1141–56.

DiIulio, J. J., Jr., and A. M. Piehl. 1991. "Does Prison Pay? The Stormy National Debate over the Cost-Effectiveness of Imprisonment." *Brookings Review* 9(Fall 1991): 28–35.

Freeman, R. B. 1991. "Crime and the Employment of Disadvantaged Youths." NBER Working Paper no. 3875. Cambridge, Mass.: National Bureau of Economic Research.

General Accounting Office. 1991. *Prison Costs: Opportunities Exist to Lower the Cost of Building Federal Prisons.* Washington, D.C.: U.S. Government Printing Office.

Geronimus, A., and S. Korenman. 1992. "The Socioeconomic Consequences of Teen Childbearing Reconsidered." *Quarterly Journal of Economics* 107(4): 1187–214.

Grogger, J. 1996. "Market Wages and Youth Crime." Santa Barbara: University of California Department of Economics. Mimeograph.

———, and S. G. Bronars. 1993. "The Socioeconomic Consequences of Teenage Childbearing: Findings from a Natural Experiment." *Family Planning Perspectives* 25(4): 156–61.

Hanushek, E. A. 1992. "The Trade-off between Child Quantity and Quality." *Journal of Political Economy* 100(1): 84–117.

Hindelang, M. J., T. Hirschi, and J. G. Weis. 1981. *Measuring Delinquency.* Beverly Hills, Calif.: Sage Publications.

Klaus, P. A. 1994. *The Costs of Crimes to Victims.* Washington, D.C.: U.S. Department of Justice, Bureau of Justice Statistics.

Morash, M., and L. Rucker. 1989. "An Exploratory Study of the Connection of Mother's Age at Childbearing to Her Children's Delinquency in Four Data Sets." *Crime and Delinquency* 35(1): 45–93.

National Center for Health Statistics. Various years. *Vital Statistics of the United States, Vol. I, Natality.* Washington, D.C.: U.S. Government Printing Office.

Schmidt, P., and A. D. Witte. 1984. *An Economic Analysis of Crime and Justice.* Orlando, Fla.: Academic Press.

U.S. Department of Commerce, Bureau of the Census. 1989. *Statistical Abstract of the United States: 1989.* Washington, D.C.: U.S. Government Printing Office.

U.S. Department of Justice, Bureau of Justice Statistics. 1991. *Census of Local Jails, 1988: Volume I.* Washington, D.C.: U.S. Government Printing Office.

———. 1992a. *Census of State and Federal Correctional Facilities, 1990.* Washington, D.C.: U.S. Government Printing Office.

———. 1992b. *Correctional Populations in the United States, 1990.* Washington, D.C.: U.S. Government Printing Office.

———. 1992c. *Justice Expenditures and Employment, 1990.* Washington, D.C.: U.S. Government Printing Office.

———. 1994. *National Corrections Reporting Program, 1991.* Washington, D.C.: U.S. Government Printing Office.

Zedlewski, E. W. 1987. *Making Confinement Decisions.* Washington, D.C.: National Institute of Justice.

Chapter Nine

CHILDREN OF EARLY CHILDBEARERS AS YOUNG ADULTS

Robert Haveman, Barbara Wolfe, and Elaine Peterson

Few social issues have attracted as much attention in the popular press as the high level of and rapid increase in the number of births to teenagers—especially those who are not married. The reason for this is easy to discern. Children born to teen mothers often do not have an even start in life. They are more likely to grow up in a poor and mother-only family, to live in a poor or underclass neighborhood, and to experience high risks to both their health status and potential school achievement. For people in society who value equal opportunity as a social goal, the high rate of births to teens is viewed with great apprehension.

Teen mothers, too, often appear to be harmed by the experience. The probability that these mothers will be receiving welfare benefits within a short period after giving birth is high. Moreover, a smaller percentage of teen mothers finish high school than do their peers who do not give birth as teens. Teen mothers clearly prejudice economic and, in many cases, marriage opportunities that they might otherwise have had, and they experience a sudden end to their own childhood. (See chapter 3 in this volume.)

The high level of and recent growth in the number of teen births also have implications for public policy. Twenty-seven percent of teenage mothers receive welfare within a year of giving birth. Among recipients of Aid to Families with Dependent Children (AFDC) benefits who are less than 30 years old, three-quarters first gave birth as a teenager, in most cases out of wedlock. About $25 billion is paid annually through AFDC, food stamps, and Medicaid to women who are or were teenage mothers. Each family that begins with a birth to a teenager is expected to cost the public an average of about $17,000 in some form of support over the next 20 years (see Center for Population Options 1990).

Although the implications of the unmarried teen birth rate noted above seem consistent with both casual observation and common sense, the birth of a child to a teenager is not necessarily responsible for the observed patterns of poverty, failure to complete high school, and welfare recipiency. The girls who give birth as teens may have these poor outcomes even if they had not had the birth; they might have family backgrounds or personal characteristics that foster low attainments. The experience of a birth to a teenager may be just another manifestation of this poor outlook for future success.

This position has been suggested by a number of researchers (Luker 1991; Nathanson 1991). Moreover, a recent study comparing sisters (hence, controlling for family background) who become mothers at different ages found only negligible differences between teen and non-teen mothers in a wide variety of outcomes (see Geronimus and Korenman 1992). For several reasons the results from this study do not appear robust. A recent critique (and reanalysis of its model) concludes that "the socio-economic effects of teen motherhood do not disappear, nor, indeed, are they small" (Hoffman, Foster, and Furstenberg 1993).

The presence, direction, and magnitude of impacts on the mother of the teen birth itself, as opposed to non-birth-related factors, are still being debated. Chapter 3 of this volume, for example, using the natural quasi-experiment of miscarriage (an almost random event) to control for non-birth-related factors, finds reduced long-term welfare receipt and no long-term earnings deficit attributable to timing of the birth.

Whether or not early childbearing per se has negative impacts on the mother's long-term earnings and welfare receipt, however, adverse impacts on factors affecting her family life and the rearing of her children are certainly plausible. And those impacts may well have negative effects on her children. This is the issue we examine here. We study two questions: Do the children of teen mothers experience adverse effects from the teen birth—and the accompanying shift in the life path of their mothers? Can these effects be measured some two decades after the mothers' early fertility?

THREE DIFFERENT VIEWS OF THE TEEN MOTHER–CHILD OUTCOME RELATIONSHIP

To answer questions about adverse effects, we consider three models that reflect three different views of the effect on children of having an "early fertility" mother (one who first gave birth when she was very young [15 or less], a young teen [16–17], or an older teen [18–19]).

Model 1 presumes that initially, prior to giving birth, teen mothers are not very different from other girls. Then, when they become mothers at an early age, motherhood interferes with their human capital formation (in terms of schooling and work experience), marriageability, and general living situation. Their life path then diverges from the trajectory it would have taken if they had delayed childbearing until later in life, especially until their postadolescent years. If this is the case, we would not expect to observe significant *prebirth* differences between girls who are early-fertility mothers and those who are not. Nevertheless, the *postbirth* life paths of the early-fertility mothers will differ from those of later-fertility mothers, and these life path differences are at least in part attributable to early fertility. These differences may then also affect the early mothers' children's lives, and these intergenerational effects would be due to early fertility. Hence, to measure the total effect that having an early-fertility mother has on a particular outcome for children, we estimate a simple equation relating a measure of the outcome for the child to dummy variables (those taking on a value of either zero or one) indicating whether the child was born to an early (or very early)-fertility mother.

Model 2 reflects the view that, even in prebirth years, differences exist between early- and later-fertility mothers that are likely to influence the development and attainments of their children. To the extent that such *prebirth* differences are reasonably represented by descriptive characteristics of these mothers, the *total* effect that being born to a teen, or early-fertility, mother has on children's outcomes can be measured by an equation relating some child's outcome measure to a dummy variable indicating whether the child was born to an early-fertility mother, but also including variables to control for prebirth differences in the mother's choices and background. The coefficient on the early-fertility mother dummy variables would then reflect this effect, apart from the other prebirth differences between teen and later-fertility women.

Model 3 suggests not only that the early- and later-fertility mothers might differ in some important *prebirth* ways but that the environments in which the children grow up and reach adolescence also differ in ways potentially related to the policy regimes in effect. Hence, in addition to controlling for differences in the observed prebirth characteristics between teen and later-fertility mothers, we control for selected differences in the policy regimes confronting their children. The coefficients on the early-fertility dummy variables should not change (will be robust) if these policy regimes are truly exogenous (i.e., predetermined outside of the model). However, if children of adolescent mothers are at a disadvantage, the coefficients on these variables may give some insight into whether poor outcomes can be mitigated by public policy.[1]

DATA

Our estimation is based on a sample of 1,705 persons who were 0 to 6 years old in 1968 and were then surveyed for each of 21 years (through 1988). The data come from the Panel Study of Income Dynamics (PSID) and include background information such as age of the mother when she had her first child. Some retrospective information on when the mother was growing up is available in the PSID; we added data on state welfare generosity and state spending on family planning services, based on where the child lived while growing up.[2]

Individuals who did not respond for two consecutive years were excluded from the sample. Observations with missing data were generally assigned values based on an interpolation of their data for the prior and subsequent year. In a few cases, additional dummy variables indicating missing data were also created. Our sample does not include anyone who was incarcerated or died between 1968 and 1988.[3]

We focus on four outcomes: (1) the probability that the teen mother's child will graduate from high school, (2) the probability that her female children will give birth as a teenager, (3) the probability that her female children will give birth out of wedlock as a teenager, and (4) the probability that her child will be economically inactive at age 24. Youths are defined as inactive if they fall into none of the following categories: (1) a mother of an infant or of two or more children, one of whom is less than six years old; (2) working 1,000 or more hours per year; (3) a full-time student; (4) a part-time student and working at least 500 hours per year; or (5) a part-time student and a mother with one child less than six years old.[4]

We use a set of dummy variables to capture alternative definitions of early fertility. Thus, in each model, four dummy variables describing ages of childbearing of 21 years or less are included in the specification:

- Childbearing at age ≤15
- Childbearing at ages 16 or 17

- Childbearing at ages 18 or 19
- Childbearing at ages 20 or 21

The omitted category is childbearing at age 22 or older. Delineation of these early childbearing categories allows us to explore impacts of early fertility and to simulate the effect that fertility delays of various magnitudes will have on children's outcomes.

Since Model 1 presumes that early- and later-fertility mothers are similar in their family background and the policy environments that influence their childbearing decisions, only dummy variables for the gender of the child and whether or not the child is firstborn are added to the variables describing the mother's early childbearing experience. Model 2 tests the hypothesis that early- and later-fertility mothers have different observed preadolescent characteristics that might influence their children's attainments and be correlated with (or causal to) their choice of when to first give birth. Because we wish to estimate the total, direct, and indirect effects of adolescent motherhood on the children's eventual outcomes, we omit any variables for the period while the child was growing up that might have been affected by the mother's life path. We add to the variables in Model 1 the following:

- Whether the mother lived with both her parents when she was growing up
- Whether the mother's father ("grandfather") had a high school education or more
- Whether the mother's mother ("grandmother") had a high school education or more
- The mother's score on a sentence completion test (and a dummy variable indicating whether the mother's score is missing)
- Whether the mother is an African American
- Whether the mother is a Catholic
- The number of times the mother attended religious services each month (based on earliest response available between 1968 and 1972)
- Whether the mother grew up in a poor family

Since Model 3 tests the hypothesis that early and later-fertility mothers have different observed preadolescent characteristics and that the two groups may have faced a different policy environment, we add the following variables:

- Average adult unemployment rate in the neighborhood in which the child lived during ages 6 to 15

- Average real maximum state welfare benefits in state where daughter lived during ages 15 to 18[5]
- Average real public per capita family planning expenditures in state where daughter lived during ages 13 to 19.[5]

High School Graduation

Early childbearing reduces the chances that the child will graduate from high school (table 9.1). Our estimates for the simplest model (Model 1) are in the first column. The coefficients on all of three childbearing variables representing early motherhood are negative and statistically significant at the 1 percent level.[6]

As the additional, prebirth characteristics of the mother and the policy environment when the child was growing up are added in Models 2 and 3, the magnitude of the negative impacts of early-fertility variables shrinks, as does the significance level. However, in all cases, the coefficients on the variables for childbearing prior to age 20 are statistically significant at conventional levels. And in both Model 2 and Model 3, the set of early childbearing variables passes the log likelihood ratio test, again rejecting the null hypothesis that age of motherhood does not matter.

Being a female child and being firstborn each increase the probability of graduating from high school, and these variables are statistically significant in all models. The firstborn variable also indicates that this is the child born to the teen mother (if the mother gave birth as a teen). The positive coefficient suggests that being born to an early-fertility mother while she was a teen has no additional negative impacts beyond those experienced by all of her children.

The control variables indicating the mother's prebirth characteristics are generally as expected and are often significant. If the mother lived with both of her parents, had a mother (the child's grandmother) who graduated from high school, is African American, or is Catholic, the probability that the child is expected to graduate high school increases and is statistically significant in each case. Although the education of the mother's father (grandfather), the economic status of her family while she was growing up, and the frequency of her attendance at religious services have the expected sign, none of these variables is uniformly statistically significant. The higher the mother's sentence completion score, the higher the probability that the child will graduate high school, and this effect is significant. The policy variable—the unemployment rate in the neighborhood in which the

Table 9.1 PROBABILITY THAT CHILD GRADUATED FROM HIGH SCHOOL

	Model 1 Coefficient (S.E.)	Model 2 Coefficient (S.E.)	Model 3 Coefficient (S.E.)
Mother became a mother at age ≤15	−0.526 (0.154)***	−0.392 (0.166)**	−0.391 (0.166)**
Mother became a mother at age 16–17	−0.384 (0.113)***	−0.244 (0.121)**	−0.225 (0.122)*
Mother became a mother at age 18–19	−0.273 (0.101)***	−0.206 (0.107)*	−0.219 (0.107)**
Mother became a mother at age 20–21	−0.060 (0.109)	0.002 (0.116)	−0.006 (0.116)
Female child	0.133 (0.075)*	0.135 (0.077)*	0.135 (0.078)*
Firstborn child	0.364 (0.099)***	0.294 (0.103)***	0.296 (0.104)***
Mother lived with both her parents		0.277 (0.083)***	0.260 (0.083)***
Maternal grandfather had a high school education or more		0.144 (0.123)	0.104 (0.123)
Maternal grandmother had a high school education or more		0.411 (0.108)***	0.401 (0.108)***
Mom's sentence completion score		0.104 (0.029)***	0.105 (0.029)***
Missing mom's sentence completion score		0.462 (0.086)***	0.431 (0.087)***
Mother is African American		0.337 (0.094)***	0.437 (0.099)***
Mother is Catholic		0.302 (0.116)***	0.287 (0.117)***
Number of times mother attends religious services each month		0.033 (0.030)	0.033 (0.030)
Mother grew up poor		−0.109 (0.082)	−0.140 (0.083)*
Average adult neighborhood unemployment rate at child's ages 6–15			−0.034 (0.010)***
Constant	1.057 (0.083)***	−0.687 (0.300)**	−0.425 (0.310)
Log likelihood	−720.65	−670.35	−664.56
Chi-square	41.952	142.56	154.13
Percentage of zeros correctly predicted	0.0	3.7	4.1
Percentage of ones correctly predicted	100	99.4	99.4
N = 1,705			

Source: Michigan Panel Study of Income Dynamics.
S.E. = Standard error.
* Denotes significance at the .10 level; ** denotes significance at the .05 level; *** denotes significance at the .01 level.

child lives—has a distinctly negative effect on the probability that the child will graduate high school, and it too is statistically significant.[7]

Giving Birth as a Teenager

The probability that a child will give birth as a teenager is clearly greater for women whose mothers were also teens at their first birth (table 9.2).

In the simple case (Model 1), all the early-fertility variables indicating a birth prior to age 19 are statistically significant. The positive signs indicate that early childbearing by the mother increases the probability that her daughter will give birth as a teen. The test statistic for a log likelihood ratio test of the significance of the full set of the early childbearing variables exceeds the critical value at the .01 level, leading to rejection of the null hypothesis that early fertility of the mother has no effect on the outcome of the child.[8]

As additional, prebirth characteristics of the mother and the policy environment when the child was growing up are added in Model 2 and Model 3, the magnitudes of the coefficients on the early-fertility variables again fall, as does the significance level. However, in all cases, the coefficients on the variables for childbearing prior to age 20 are statistically significant at conventional levels.[9]

As before, the impact of being born to an early-fertility mother is essentially the same for the first child and for the additional children. The impacts of the mother's prebirth characteristics are again as expected, though fewer of them are statistically significant than in the case of high school graduation. The mother's test score and the grandfather's education are both negatively related to the probability that the daughter will give birth as a teenager, and in each case the coefficient is statistically significant. The education of the grandmother and whether or not the mother's family was poor do not have a statistically significant effect, however, although in both cases the signs are as expected. In this case, unlike the results for teen out-of-wedlock childbearing discussed below, none of the policy variables has a statistically significant effect on the probability that the daughter will give birth as a teenager.[10]

Giving Birth Out of Wedlock as a Teenager

The relationship between mother's age at first birth and whether her daughter will give birth out of wedlock as a teenager is less clear than for teen childbirth itself (table 9.3). In the simple model in column 1,

Table 9.2 PROBABILITY THAT CHILD HAD A BIRTH AT AGE <19:
FEMALE SAMPLE

	Model 1 Coefficient (S.E.)	Model 2 Coefficient (S.E.)	Model 3 Coefficient (S.E.)
Mother became a mother at age ≤15	0.707 (0.209)***	0.437 (0.222)**	0.421 (0.224)*
Mother became a mother at age 16–17	0.594 (0.150)***	0.373 (0.159)**	0.341 (0.161)**
Mother became a mother at age 18–19	0.415 (0.139)***	0.291 (0.146)**	0.270 (0.147)*
Mother became a mother at age 20–21	0.223 (0.143)	0.140 (0.150)	0.140 (0.150)
Firstborn child	−0.083 (0.126)	0.032 (0.131)	0.033 (0.131)
Mother lived with both her parents		−0.127 (0.112)	−0.104 (0.114)
Maternal grandfather had a high school education or more		−0.325 (0.165)**	−0.305 (0.169)*
Maternal grandmother had a high school education or more		−0.051 (0.133)	−0.036 (0.134)
Mom's sentence completion score		−0.080 (0.039)**	−0.079 (0.039)**
Missing mom's sentence completion score		−0.340 (0.114)***	−0.329 (0.115)***
Mother is African American		0.181 (0.121)	0.147 (0.134)
Mother is Catholic		−0.327 (0.166)**	−0.279 (0.171)
Number of times mother attends religious services each month		−0.062 (0.041)	−0.064 (0.041)
Mother grew up poor		0.091 (0.107)	0.106 (0.109)
Average public family planning expenditures per capita in states child lived at ages 13–19			−0.195 (0.153)
Average adult neighborhood unemployment rate at child's ages 6–15			0.023 (0.014)
Real average maximum state welfare benefits at child's ages 15–18			−0.001 (0.001)
Constant	−1.167 (0.101)***	−0.009 (0.400)	0.259 (0.518)
Log likelihood	−412.67	−387.24	−384.43
Chi-square	23.974	74.852	80.471
Percentage of zeros correctly predicted	100	98.6	98.6
Percentage of ones correctly predicted	0.0	4.2	6.0
n = 873			

Source: Michigan Panel Study of Income Dynamics.
S.E. = Standard error.
* Denotes significance at the .10 level; ** denotes significance at the .05 level; *** denotes significance at the .01 level.

Table 9.3 PROBABILITY THAT CHILD HAD AN OUT-OF-WEDLOCK BIRTH AT
AGE <19: FEMALE SAMPLE

	Model 1 Coefficient (S.E.)	Model 2 Coefficient (S.E.)	Model 3 Coefficient (S.E.)
Mother became a mother at age ≤ 15	0.716	0.391	0.381
	(0.221)***	(0.237)*	(0.239)
Mother became a mother at age 16–17	0.568	0.308	0.252
	(0.163)***	(0.176)*	(0.180)
Mother became a mother at age 18–19	0.437	0.273	0.232
	(0.151)***	(0.162)*	(0.165)
Mother became a mother at age 20–21	0.263	0.179	0.177
	(0.156)*	(0.168)	(0.169)
Firstborn child	−0.284	−0.186	−0.182
	(0.145)*	(0.154)	(0.154)
Mother lived with both her parents		−0.161	−0.120
		(0.122)	(0.124)
Maternal grandfather had a high school education or more		−0.174	−0.152
		(0.180)	(0.185)
Maternal grandmother had a high school education or more		0.034	0.062
		(0.146)	(0.148)
Mom's sentence completion score		−0.128	−0.129
		(0.042)***	(0.043)***
Missing mom's sentence completion score		−0.257	−0.239
		(0.124)**	(0.127)*
Mother is African American		0.501	0.475
		(0.136)***	(0.153)***
Mother is Catholic		−0.242	−0.170
		(0.191)	(0.197)
Number of times mother attends religious services each month		−0.103	−0.109
		(0.046)**	(0.047)**
Mother grew up poor		0.001	0.018
		(0.119)	(0.121)
Average public family planning expenditures per capita in states child lived at ages 13–19			−0.394
			(0.174)**
Average adult neighborhood unemployment rate at child's ages 6–15			0.031
			(0.015)**
Real average maximum state welfare benefits at child's ages 15–18			−0.001
			(0.001)
Constant	−1.338	0.086	0.695
	(0.112)***	(0.430)	(0.575)
Log likelihood	−346.54	−313.87	−307.4
Chi-square	24.002	89.343	102.28
Percentage of zeros correctly predicted	100	99.3	98.8
Percentage of ones correctly predicted	0.0	4.8	8.8
n = 873			

Source: Michigan Panel Study of Income Dynamics.
S.E. = Standard error.
* Denotes significance at the .10 level; ** denotes significance at the .05 level; *** denotes significance at the .01 level.

all the early-fertility variables indicating the mother gave birth prior to age 19 are statistically significant. The positive sign on these variables indicates that early childbearing by the mother increases the probability that her daughter will give birth out of wedlock as a teen.[11] As before, adding the additional prebirth characteristics of the mother and her environment as she grew up reduces the magnitude of the impacts. They are still statistically significant at the .1 level for Model 2, but not for Model 3.[12]

Being a firstborn child decreases the probability that the daughter will give birth out of wedlock as a teenager, but this variable has a statistically significant coefficient only in the simplest model (column 1). This again suggests that the impact of being born to an early-fertility mother is essentially the same for the first child and for the additional children. The control variables indicating the mother's prebirth characteristics are again signed as expected, and several are statistically significant. If the mother is African American, the probability that her daughter will give birth out of wedlock as a teenager increases, and the coefficient is statistically significant in each of the specifications. The mother's test score and the regularity of her attendance at religious services are both negatively related to the probability that the daughter will give birth out of wedlock as a teenager, and in each case the coefficient is statistically significant. Here, as opposed to the results for high school completion, the education of the mother's parents and whether or not her family was poor do not have a statistically signficant effect on the outcome, although in both cases the signs are as expected.

With respect to the policy variables, an increase in the unemployment rate tends to increase the probability of a teen nonmarital birth, increases in state family planning expenditures tend to reduce the probability, and generosity of state welfare spending has no statistically significant effect.

Being Economically Inactive at Age 24

The relationship between early fertility and being inactive as a young adult is weak (table 9.4). Only for the simple model are all of the early-fertility variables indicating a birth prior to age 19 statistically significant, indicating that early childbearing increases the probability that a mother's child will be economically inactive as a young adult.[13] Being firstborn decreases the probability that the child will be economically inactive as a young adult, but this variable is only statistically significant in the simplest model. Again, adding the additional

Table 9.4 PROBABILITY OF CHILD BEING ECONOMICALLY INACTIVE AT AGE 24

	Model 1 Coefficient (S.E.)	Model 2 Coefficient (S.E.)	Model 3 Coefficient (S.E.)
Mother became a mother at ≤15	0.581	0.362	0.360
	(0.213)***	(0.226)	(0.226)
Mother became a mother at age 16–17	0.327	0.190	0.187
	(0.158)**	(0.166)	(0.166)
Mother became a mother at age 18–19	0.376	0.276	0.275
	(0.134)***	(0.140)**	(0.140)**
Mother became a mother at age 20–21	0.038	0.016	0.016
	(0.144)	(0.148)	(0.148)
Female child	0.308	0.302	0.302
	(0.102)***	(0.104)***	(0.104)***
Firstborn child	−0.259	−0.209	−0.199
	(0.133)*	(0.136)	(0.137)
Mother lived with both her parents		−0.118	−0.106
		(0.114)	(0.115)
Maternal grandfather had a high school education or more		0.101	0.109
		(0.155)	(0.155)
Maternal grandmother had a high school education or more		−0.234	−0.229
		(0.138)*	(0.138)*
Mom's sentence completion score		−0.089	−0.088
		(0.041)**	(0.041)**
Missing mom's sentence completion score		−0.061	−0.052
		(0.115)	(0.116)
Mother is African American		0.198	0.165
		(0.127)	(0.133)
Mother is Catholic		−0.252	−0.250
		(0.152)*	(0.152)
Number of times mother attends religious services each month		0.053	0.052
		(0.042)	(0.042)
Mother grew up poor		−0.057	−0.043
		(0.108)	(0.110)
Average adult neighborhood unemployment rate at child's ages 6–15			0.013
			(0.015)
Constant	−1.015	−0.160	−0.264
	(0.114)***	(0.407)	(0.426)
Log likelihood	−409.36	−397.49	−397.15
Chi-square	29.917	53.663	54.34
Percentage of zeros correctly predicted	100	98.6	98.4
Percent of ones correctly predicted	0.0	4.8	7.0
n = 765			

Source: Michigan Panel Study of Income Dynamics.
S.E. = Standard error.
* Denotes significance at the .10 level; ** denotes significance at the .05 level; *** denotes significance at the .01 level.

prebirth characteristics of the mother and her environment as she grows up reduces the magnitude of the relationship between early motherhood and being economically inactive as a young adult, with only one of the age category variables statistically significant.[14] Most of the control variables indicating the mother's prebirth characteristics are again signed in the direction expected, though only three are statistically significant. The mother's test score and grandmother's education are both negatively related to the probability that the child will be economically inactive as a young adult, and in each case the coefficient is statistically significant.

THE EFFECTS OF DELAYED CHILDBEARING

The predicted effects of delays in childbearing are shown in tables 9.5 through 9.8. For these simulations, we group the children based on when their mothers first gave birth. We hold constant all the observed characteristics of the mothers who gave birth in each of the age categories, except for the variables indicating when the mother first gave birth. We then use the previously estimated coefficients to obtain the predicted probability of each outcome (e.g., high school graduation) for each child under alternative sets of childbearing variables and take the weighted average of the newly predicted probabilities for each group. Model 3 is the basis for the simulations.[15]

There is a clear benefit from delayed childbearing with respect to high school graduation (table 9.5). The probability of graduating high school for a child born to a mother who gave birth at age ≤15 is about 71 percent. If her mother had delayed childbearing until age 16 to 17, the probability would rise to 76 percent, an increase of 5 percentage points. If her mother had delayed childbearing until age 18 to 19, the

Table 9.5 SIMULATIONS OF IMPACT DELAYING CHILDBEARING HAS ON HIGH SCHOOL GRADUATION OF THE CHILDREN: FULL SAMPLE

For Children of Mothers First Giving Birth While:	Number of Observations in Group	Estimated Probability for the Child if the Mother Delayed Her First Birth until Age:				
		Original	16–17	18–19	20–21	≥22
Age ≤15	98	.710	.760	.762	.819	.820
Ages 16–17	262	.785		.786	.839	.840
Ages 18–19	427	.832			.877	.878
Ages 20–21	380	.885				.886

probability that the child would graduate high school would rise to 76.2 percent. Delay until age 20 to 21 or after age 22 would increase the probability to 82 percent.[16]

For the daughters' probability of adolescent childbearing, the results are equally clear (table 9.6). If the mothers with the earliest fertility delayed their childbearing until age 22 or older, for example, the probability of their daughters having an adolescent birth would drop by over 11 percentage points. The patterns are similar for those who give birth under age 18 and under age 20. For the daughters' probability of adolescent out-of-wedlock childbearing, the effects are similar but somewhat smaller (table 9.7). If mothers with the earliest fertility delayed their childbearing until they were age ≥22, for example, the probability of their daughters having an adolescent out-of-wedlock birth would drop by 7.9 percentage points.

Delays in childbearing also reduce the probability of the child being economically inactive at age 24 (table 9.8). If the mothers with the earliest fertility delayed childbearing until age ≥22, the probability of their children being economically inactive would drop by about 12.3 percentage points. In this table, uncertainty as to the relative magnitude of the effects of early fertility at ages 16 to 17 leads to a strange result. A one- to two-year delay in childbearing by mothers who had their first child while ages 16 to 17 appears to increase the probability of their children being economically inactive. This suggests that the most reliable estimates in this table are those based on the statistically significant estimated coefficient for the children of mothers who first became mothers at ages 18 to 19. For this group, delayed childbearing by the mothers is estimated to decrease the probability of the child being economically inactive by about 7.5 percentage points.[17]

THE BENEFITS OF DELAYING BIRTHS

These simulation results indicate that in a variety of dimensions— schooling attainments, early fertility, early nonmarital fertility, and economic activity—children's attainments would have been greater if their mothers had delayed giving birth until reaching, say, ages 20–21 or older. Viewed alternatively, when a mother gives birth before that age, our evidence suggests that the child—and hence society—bears a cost that could be avoided if the mother's childbearing had been delayed.

Table 9.6 SIMULATIONS OF IMPACT DELAYING CHILDBEARING HAS ON ADOLESCENT CHILDBEARING: FEMALE SAMPLE

Age of Daughter at Childbearing	Age at which Mother First Gave Birth	Number of Observations in Group	Estimated Probability for the Child if the Mother Delayed Her First Birth until Age:				
			Original	16–17	18–19	20–21	≥22
<18	≤15	50	.185	.169	.143	.142	.129
	16–17	137	.158		.133	.132	.119
	18–19	203	.089			.089	.079
	20–21	203	.090				.080
<19	≤15	50	.279	.255	.234	.200	.166
	16–17	137	.248		.227	.193	.159
	18–19	203	.168			.139	.112
	20–21	203	.141				.113
<20	≤15	50	.358	.291	.305	.255	.222
	16–17	137	.286		.300	.250	.217
	18–19	203	.229			.185	.157
	20–21	203	.189				.161

Table 9.7 SIMULATIONS OF IMPACT DELAYING CHILDBEARING HAS ON ADOLESCENT OUT-OF-WEDLOCK CHILDBEARING: FEMALE SAMPLE

Age of Daughter at Out-of-Wedlock Childbearing	Age at which Mother First Gave Birth	Number of Observations in Group	Estimated Probability for the Child if the Mother Delayed Her First Birth until Age:				
			Original	16–17	18–19	20–21	≥22
<18	≤15	50	.142	.116	.116	.128	.102
	16–17	137	.098		.098	.110	.085
	18–19	203	.060			.068	.051
	20–21	203	.070				.053
<19	≤15	50	.205	.175	.171	.160	.126
	16–17	137	.164		.159	.148	.116
	18–19	203	.104			.095	.071
	20–21	203	.095				.071
<20	≤15	50	.234	.200	.205	.189	.164
	16–17	137	.193		.197	.181	.156
	18–19	203	.130			.117	.098
	20–21	203	.116				.097

Table 9.8 SIMULATIONS OF IMPACT DELAYING CHILDBEARING HAS ON ECONOMIC INACTIVITY AT AGE 24 OR OLDER

For Children of Mothers First Giving Birth While:	Number of Observations in Group	Estimated Probability for the Child if the Mother Delayed Her First Birth until Age:				
		Original	16–17	18–19	20–21	≥22
Age ≤15	45	.376	.314	.345	.258	.253
Ages 16–17	108	.262		.290	.212	.207
Ages 18–19	187	.242			.171	.167
Ages 20–21	173	.171				.167

So far, our estimates of these "costs" of mothers' early childbearing (or, conversely, the benefits of delayed childbearing) have been stated in terms of the child's schooling, early childbearing and early non-marital childbearing among daughters, and changes in economic activity when a young adult. For policy purposes, it is helpful to express the burden implied by these negative effects of early childbearing (or benefits of delays in childbearing), on either the children or society, in dollar terms. Policymakers can compare the reductions in costs (increases in benefits) in these dimensions with the costs of policies that might be able to reduce the incidence of early childbearing.

Unfortunately, placing dollar values on these intergenerational attainment effects is very difficult. Stipulating the dollar value of the benefits to society of reducing the prevalence of economic inactivity or early childbearing in the next generation must of necessity be based on numerous assumptions, few of which are verifiable. This problem is no less difficult than that faced by researchers who are asked to tell policymakers the cost of, say, an anticipated increase in the probability of a disaster, such as long-run global warming or a nuclear melt-down in some Chicago-area facility in the year 2010.

Moreover, serious ethical considerations are involved in making such estimates. Because many of the benefits that might be obtained from finding a way to reduce the incidence of early childbearing accrue to people who have not yet been born, the researcher has the impossible task of imputing to them values that those children might not have. One of the difficulties is translating into today's values benefits or costs that occur far into the future. Because subsequent generations might value the passage of time quite differently than do people living today, one is left with a difficult and ultimately unre-solvable dilemma.

Yet some discussion of these benefits and costs in dollar terms is required if we are to get any realistic sense of the magnitude of the issues with which we are concerned. Hence, we present tentative estimates of the benefits (in dollars), to both society and taxpayers, of a particular policy scenario: the delay until ages 20 to 21 of all births in a year to women who are less than 20 to 21 years old when they give birth. These benefit estimates can equally well be thought of as the costs to society and taxpayers of the present and observed annual incidence of childbearing that occurs before the mother is age 20 to 21.

It would be helpful to have dollar estimates of benefits and costs for all the outcomes we have estimated—schooling attainment, early childbearing, early nonmarital childbearing, and economic inactivity. However, we judge that responsible estimates are feasible only for the education outcome.[18] We therefore present estimates of the dollar benefits society and taxpayers would accrue from the increased productivity if the births of children who are born to early-fertility mothers were delayed until the mother was at least 20 to 21 years of age. The gain in economic productivity is measured as the increase in earnings of these children, attributable to the increase in their schooling levels that we predict would occur from the delay in mothers' childbearing until ages 20 to 21.

Methods

To obtain these benefits (or, alternatively, the cost estimates associated with early childbearing), we first fit a tobit model similar to Model 3 described earlier in this chapter. Although the estimates above focused on the likelihood of high school graduation, here we use years of education as the dependent variable.[19]

Using this estimated equation and holding the other variables constant, we simulate the number of years of schooling each of the children born to an early-fertility mother might have completed should the mother have delayed giving birth until age 20 to 21. We then multiply these predicted increases in schooling levels by the number of children born each year to mothers who would belong to each of the early-fertility age groups.[20] Summing across the birth-age groups, we obtain an estimate of the total increase in the years of education that would be experienced for children born to early-fertility mothers should their birth have been delayed.

The next step is to transform the resulting estimate of the increase in years of schooling for each of the children into an estimate of the increased lifetime productivity or earnings of each child attributable to the simulated delay in their mothers' childbearing until ages 20 to

Table 9.9 ESTIMATES OF THE PRESENT VALUE OF BENEFITS OF DELAYING
EARLY CHILDBEARING UNTIL MOTHERS' AGES 20–21,
IN BILLIONS OF 1994 DOLLARS

	Using a Real Discount Rate of:	
	5 percent	3 percent
Value of increased earnings stream discounted to children's age 0	$2.26	$4.86
Value of increased taxes to government discounted to children's age 0	.52	1.12

21. To accomplish this, we multiply the estimated change in years of
education for each child by a projection of the increase in the present
value of the child's lifetime earnings attributable to an incremental
year of education.[21] The resulting dollar estimates are then converted
to 1994 values.

Results

These dollar estimates are shown in the first row of table 9.9, for
discount rates of 3 and 5 percent. Because the change in childbearing
behavior that we are analyzing is the delay of birth by the mother, the
increment in earnings streams is discounted to that point in time. We
designate this point as children's age 0. Using a discount rate of 3
percent, we calculate the benefits of delaying childbearing to the
mother's age 20 to 21 for all children born to younger mothers to be
just under $5 billion; a similar calculation using a 5 percent discount
rate yields an estimate of slightly over $2 billion.[22]

An alternative calculation would estimate the benefits to taxpayers
from the increased tax revenue attributable to the increased earnings
from the delayed birth. Following the procedures for this calculation
used by other authors in this project, we estimate the present value
of the additional taxes likely to be paid to the government as 23 percent
of the estimated increase in the present value of earnings. The resulting estimates of the benefits of delayed childbearing are shown in the
second row of table 9.9.

CONCLUSION

Having a mother who first gave birth as a teen has negative consequences for her children. This is so even after taking into account the
differences we observe in the backgrounds of these mothers compared
to later-fertility mothers. On a statistical basis, the impact is more
significant for the child's education level than for the daughter's fertility behavior or the child's economic inactivity at age 24. If teenagers
could be convinced to postpone childbearing, their children (and
hence society) would have improved life chances and outcomes.

If teenagers who gave birth before age 15 could be induced to postpone their first births to ages 16 to 17, for example, the probability that
their children would graduate high school would increase by about 7
percent, from .71 to .76. Similarly, the probability that their daughters
would give birth by age 19 would be decreased by about 9 percent.
We estimate an even larger decrease, about 16 percent, the biggest
estimated impact, in the probability that the daughters would give
birth out of wedlock by age 19. We also expect that the probability of
children being economically inactive as young adults would decrease
by about 16 percent.

If teenagers who are currently having their first birth between the
ages of 16 and 17 could be induced to postpone that birth until they
are 18 to 19, the expected increase in the probability of their children
graduating high school is quite small. However, postponement until
age 20 or later leads to sizable expected increases of about 7 percent,
from .785 to .839. In the case of subsequent early fertility for the
daughters born to these teenage mothers, a one- to two-year postponement of the age when the mother first gave birth (from 16 to 17
to 18 to 19) is not expected to have a sizable impact on her daughter's
probability of giving birth as a teen; however, a shift to age 20 or older
again has a much larger expected impact.

The characteristics of early-teen mothers differ from women who
first give birth at later ages. Nevertheless, a policy to postpone their
initial age at first birth would be expected to have sizable impacts on
the future attainments of their children. Beyond this, if young teens
do not give birth at these young ages, they may change their life course
in other ways as well (e.g., increase their own levels of schooling and
job opportunities). Such changes could have additional positive impacts on the well-being of their children.

Notes

1. We also considered a model in which important unobserved premotherhood differences between adolescent and older mothers would make the outcomes of the children differ. Because of the difficulty of determining why some mothers become early-fertility mothers and others do not, however, our estimations were not satisfying. Hence, we cannot rule out the possibility that unobserved characteristics are the true cause of both the mother's early fertility and the children's subsequent disadvantages. Further details, including the estimates of our two-stage estimation procedure, are available from the authors upon request.

2. Data on state welfare generosity were obtained from Robert Moffitt. Data on state spending for family planning services come from *Family Planning Perspectives*. State population and price index data come from the *Statistical Abstract of the United States*.

3. Appendix table 9A.1 presents the means and standard deviations for the variables we use.

4. Because each of the outcomes is a limited dependent variable taking on the values of zero and one, we fit the models using maximum likelihood probit estimation.

5. Variable included only in specifications for the teen childbearing and teen out-of-wedlock childbearing outcomes.

6. As a set, these early childbearing variables are statistically significant at the .01 level, when a log likelihood ratio test of the null hypothesis of no significant effect of early childbearing is tested. The critical value for the log likelihood ratio test at the .01 level is 13.28; the test statistic equals 21.8.

7. For the Model 2 and Model 3 results, tests of structural differences in the parameters for these equations and estimates based on subsamples of African Americans and non-African Americans could not reject the null hypothesis of no structural difference. The chi-square test statistics for these equations are 15 and 13, and the .1 critical values are 25 and 26.

8. The critical value for the log likelihood test at the .01 level is 13.28; the test statistic equals 22.99.

9. In Model 2, the set of early childbearing variables passes the log likelihood ratio test, again rejecting the null hypothesis that age of motherhood does not matter. The log likelihood ratio test statistic for whether the four estimated coefficients on the early-fertility dummy variables are statistically different from zero for Model 2 is 8, and the .1 critical value is 7.78. The test statistic for Model 3 is 6.7, statistically significant only at the .15 level.

10. However, for the results in Model 3 of table 9.2, a test of structural difference in the parameters for this equation and estimates based on subsamples of African Americans and non-African Americans rejected the null hypothesis of no structural difference. The chi-square test statistic for the third model is 31.98 (versus only 19.38 for the second model, which doesn't include the policy variables) and so rejects the null hypothesis at the .05 level, for which the critical value is 25. In the estimates based on non-African Americans, an increase in the unemployment rate tends to increase the probability of a teen birth; in the estimates based on African Americans, increases in state family planning expenditures tend to reduce the probability. The generosity of state welfare spending appears to have no statistically significant effect on this outcome in any of the estimations.

11. The test statistic for a log likelihood ratio test of the significance of the full set of the early childbearing variables exceeds the critical value at the .01 level, leading to rejection of the null hypothesis that early fertility of the mother has no effect on the

outcome of the child. The critical value for the log likelihood test at the .01 level is 13.28; the test statistics equals 18.95.

12. As a set, the log likelihood ratio test indicates rejection of the null hypothesis at the .05 level. We also estimated several variants of these models. We considered variants using out-of-wedlock childbearing by the daughters when they were ≤19 and ≤17 as the dependent variables and variants using one dummy variable for early maternal fertility based on whether the mother had her first child while ≤19, ≤18, and ≤17. In addition, we considered each of these variants for the full sample and for separate subsamples of non-African Americans and African Americans. Tests for structural differences in the parameters for these equations and estimates based on subsamples of African Americans and non-African Americans rejected the null hypothesis of no structural differences. The chi-square test statistics for the second and third models are 26.5 and 37.25 and so reject the null hypotheses at, respectively, the .05 and .01 levels. The .05 critical value for Model 2 is 25, and the .01 critical value for Model 3 is 35. From these we learned that the relationship between the mother's early fertility and adolescent out-of-wedlock childbearing for the daughters is strongest for non-African Americans. For that sample, we found the early-fertility dummies jointly statistically significant from zero for all three models when looking at out-of-wedlock childbearing at age ≤18 (with significance levels of .05, .05, and .04) and at age ≤17 (with significance levels of .012, .015, and .013). When one dummy variable for having an early-fertility mother is used in these equations, the estimated coefficient is also statistically significant.

Estimates for out-of-wedlock childbearing at ≤19 are jointly significantly different from zero only for the full sample using the first model, although for non-African Americans several estimated coefficients on the dummy variables are individually statistically significant in each of the three models. For the subsample of African Americans, the estimated coefficients on the dummy variables for early maternal fertility are not statistically significant in any of these estimations.

13. The test statistic for a log likelihood ratio test of the significance of the full set of the early childbearing variables exceeds the critical value at the .01 level, leading to rejection of the null hypothesis that early fertility of the mother has no effect on the outcome of the child. The critical value for the log likelihood test at the .01 level is 13.28; the test statistic equals 15.07.

14. As a set, the log likelihood ratio test does not indicate rejection of the null hypothesis for Model 2 or Model 3. The log likelihood ratio test statistics for Models 2 and 3 are both 5.9 and so would only be significant at the .2 level.

15. The weights on the PSID are intended to represent proportions of the U.S. population. Even though some of the coefficients are not statistically significant, they are our best predictor of the likely impact on children of the mother postponing her first birth. Nevertheless, the lack of significance reduces the confidence one should place on some of these results. One further caveat also applies: although we include a broad set of background factors of the mother, unobserved factors may still play a role. To the extent this is the case, our simulations may over- or underestimate the expected change caused by delay in childbearing.

16. Mothers who first gave birth while less than 15 years old tended to have other characteristics that put their children at a disadvantage. Hence, although delaying childbearing increases the probability of the children graduating, it does not mean the children will have as great a chance of graduating as the children of mothers in the other groups. For example, although delaying childbearing until 20 or 21 raises the probability of their children graduating from high school by 10.9 percentage points, this is less than the 17.5 percentage points difference in the probabilities of graduation for children in the different groups.

17. The simulated results for both African Americans and non-African Americans were also estimated based on equation estimations on these subsamples but are not shown here. Most of the coefficients relevant for simulating these results are not statistically significant for African Americans, which may be attributable to small sample sizes in many of the age-at-first-birth categories.

18. In chapter 3 of this volume (and Hotz et al. 1995), Joseph Hotz, Susan McElroy, and Seth Sanders find that mothers who give birth prior to adulthood draw more on governmental resources for welfare assistance than they contribute in taxes over their lifetime. From this calculation they conclude that "teen mothers, on average, are a net cost to government" (Hotz et al., 43). Using a discount rate of 5 percent and an assumed tax rate of 23 percent, they calculate the discounted present value of the net fiscal burden of a teen mother to be about $34,000 in 1993 dollars. This estimate rests on their projections of the lifetime earnings of teen mothers and the costs of their participation in welfare programs. Based on these same assumptions, the present discounted value of the demands on welfare benefits is estimated to be $72,624, and tax contributions are estimated at about $39,000.

The authors then compare these tax contributions and welfare costs with analogous estimates of contributions and welfare costs for women with similar characteristics who delayed their childbearing until adulthood. The $73,000 of welfare costs for the teen mothers falls to about $65,375 for women who delay their childbearing until adulthood. However, the authors find that mothers who delay their childbearing until adulthood earn *less* over their lifetime than do the teen mothers and hence contribute less in the way of taxes; for these adult mothers, the discounted present value of tax contributions is about $31,000, or about $8,000 less than the contributions of the teen mothers. These adult mothers are also found to be "a net cost to government—indeed, a net cost of $35,000, or about $1,000 *more costly* than the teen mothers."

From the government's point of view then, both teen mothers and mothers who delay childbearing are costly, with the costs of adult mothers exceeding the costs of teen mothers.

If one accepts these estimates and assumes that the welfare system now in place will be in place when the children of both teen and adult mothers become eligible for benefits, the discounted present value of the increased welfare costs attributable to the increased early childbearing of the children of teen mothers can be calculated. This calculation would involve discounting from the average age of a teen birth, or for about 17.98 years, the $7,249 of net increased welfare costs of teen mothers relative to adult mothers ($73,000–$66,000). Using a 5 percent discount rate, this value equals about $3,015. Multiplying this value by the number of daughters born to teen mothers each year weighted by the increased probability of the daughters becoming teen mothers themselves gives a value of the additional welfare costs to government of the early childbearing of the children of teen mothers: $48.7 to 105.3 million in 1994 dollars depending on the method used to estimate the number of daughters born to early-fertility mothers each year.

To calculate the additional tax contributions of the children of teen mothers deriving from their increased productivity and earnings using an equivalent procedure would be double counting; our estimates of increased governmental revenues from the increased earnings of the children of teen mothers operating through the increases in their educational attainment already capture this value. Note that our estimates of the increased productivity and earnings attributable to the increased education of children from delaying childbearing are different in both sign and magnitude from those estimated by Hotz, McElroy, and Sanders.

19. In this tobit analysis, the dependent variable (years of education completed) was limited to range from 0 to 14 because at the youngest age of children in our sample (age 21) they could still be in school and hence not have completed their education. At this

age, they have at most completed 15–16 years of education if they persistently attended school. The choice of 14 years as the upper truncation is consistent with an interruption of a year or two. In this estimation (as in the high school graduation specification presented in table 9.5), the coefficients on the early-fertility dummy variables were negative and statistically significant at the .05 level. These estimated equations are available from the authors upon request.

20. The number of children born to each age group of early-fertility mothers is based on the number of first births to women in each age group plus the number of higher order births to women in each of the age groups that suggest the mother is in an early-fertility birth group. This calculation is based on data taken from Table 1-53 in U.S. Department of HHS (1994). An alternative method would approximately double the number of children.

21. For the earnings increases attributable to increased years of schooling, we used estimates developed by the Children's Defense Fund to measure the benefits attributable to reducing children's poverty. Their estimates are based on measures taken from Bureau of the Census earnings profiles for men and women. By multiplying the simulated increases in education by estimates of the present value of the increased future earnings stream related to increased schooling (allowing for 1 percent annual growth in overall productivity, the probability of surviving to various ages, and the probability of being employed at various ages), we obtain an estimate of the benefits of the additional productivity benefits of the increased schooling attributable to delayed childbearing. For additional details on the calculation, see Children's Defense Fund (1995, 141–43). This calculation assumes that the increased earnings attributable to additional education come from increases in the wage rate of more highly schooled workers and not an increase in their work hours. The calculation also ignores the costs to society of providing the additional schooling.

22. There is a question as to what is the most appropriate base year (age of future child) for purposes of discounting the changed earnings stream. One could argue that both the earnings of the child whom we observe and those of the unobserved hypothetical child (the child whose birth is delayed) should be discounted back to the year at which the mother delayed birth. Our calculations assume that the benefits of the delayed birth reflect the present value of the earnings of the counterfactual child at the time of his or her birth less the present value of the factual child at the time of his or her birth. A calculation reflecting the difference in present values at the time of the decision to delay the birth would result in slightly smaller values for both discount rates.

References

Center for Population Options. 1990. *Teenage Pregnancy and Too-Early Childbearing: Public Costs, Personal Consequences.* Washington, D.C.: Center for Population Options.

Children's Defense Fund. 1995. *Wasting America's Future.* Washington, D.C.: Children's Defense Fund.

Geronimus, A., and S. Korenman. 1992. "The Socioeconomic Consequences of Teen Childbearing Reconsidered." *Quarterly Journal of Economics* 107(November): 1187–214.

Gold, R. B., and S. Guardado. 1988. "Public Funding of Family Planning, Sterilization and Abortion Services, 1987." *Family Planning Perspectives* 20(5, September–October): 228–33.

Gold, R. B., and J. Macias. 1986. "Public Funding of Contraceptive, Sterilization and Abortion Services, 1985." *Family Planning Perspectives* 18(6, November–December): 259–64.

Gold, R. B., and B. Nestor. 1985. "Public Funding of Contraceptive, Sterilization and Abortion Services, 1983." *Family Planning Perspectives* 17(1, January–February): 25–30.

Hoffman, S., M. Foster, and F. Furstenberg. 1993. "Reevaluating the Costs of Teenage Childbearing." *Demography* 30(February): 1–13.

Hotz, V. J., S. W. McElroy, and S. G. Sanders. 1995. "The Costs and Consequences of Teenage Childbearing for Mothers." Chicago: University of Chicago, Harris Graduate School of Public Policy Studies. Mimeograph.

Luker, K. 1991. "Dubious Conceptions: The Controversy over Teen Pregnancy." *American Prospect* 5(Spring): 73–83.

Nathanson, C. A. 1991. *Dangerous Passage: The Social Control of Women's Adolescence.* Philadelphia: Temple University Press.

Nestor, B. 1982. "Public Funding of Contraceptive Services, 1980–1982." *Family Planning Perspectives* 14(4, July–August): 198–203.

Orr, M. T., and L. Brenner. 1981. "Medicaid Funding of Family Planning Clinic Services." *Family Planning Perspectives* 13(6, November–December): 280–87.

Torres, A., and J. D. Forrest. 1983. "Family Planning Clinic Services in the United States, 1981." *Family Planning Perspectives* 15(6, November–December): 272–78.

Torres, A., J. D. Forrest, and S. Eisman. 1981. "Family Planning Services in the United States, 1978–1979." *Family Planning Perspectives* 13(3, May–June): 132–41.

U.S. Bureau of the Census. 1994. *Statistical Abstract of the United States 1994.* 114th ed. Washington, D.C.: U.S. Government Printing Office.

————. 1993. *Statistical Abstract of the United States 1993.* 113th ed. Washington, D.C.: U.S. Government Printing Office.

————. 1987. *Statistical Abstract of the United States 1987.* 107th ed. Washington, D.C.: U.S. Government Printing Office.

U.S. Department of Health and Human Services (HHS). Public Health Service. Centers for Disease Control and Prevention. National Center for Health Statistics. 1994. "Live Births by Single Year of Age of Mother and Live Birth Order." In *Vital Statistics of the United States, 1990.* Vol. 1, *Natality.* Washington, D.C.: U.S. Government Printing Office.

————. 1993. "Advance Report of Final Natality Statistics, 1990," by S. J. Ventura and J. A. Martin. *Monthly Vital Statistics Report* 41(9), supplement.

Table 9A.1 MEANS AND STANDARD DEVIATIONS OF VARIABLES
         USED IN ESTIMATION
A. Full-Sample Statistics (N = 1,705)

Variable	Mean	Standard Deviation
Mother became a mother at age ≤15	0.06	0.23
Mother became a mother at age 16–17	0.15	0.36
Mother became a mother at age 18–19	0.25	0.43
Mother became a mother at age 20–21	0.22	0.42
Mother lived with both her parents	0.70	0.46
Maternal grandfather had a high school education or more	0.20	0.40
Maternal grandmother had a high school education or more	0.29	0.46
Mom's sentence completion score	8.56	1.20
Missing mom's sentence completion score	0.70	0.46
Mother is African American	0.43	0.49
Mother is Catholic	0.19	0.39
Number of times mother attends religious services each month	1.95	1.29
Mother grew up poor	0.46	0.50
Average public family planning expenditures per capita in states child lived at ages 13–19	1.06	0.36
Firstborn child	0.23	0.42
Female child	0.51	0.50
Child graduated from high school	0.84	0.36
Average adult unemployment rate in neighborhood at child's ages 6–15	7.08	4.08
Real average maximum state welfare benefits at child's ages 15–18	$353.95	$78.45

Table 9A.1 MEANS AND STANDARD DEVIATIONS OF VARIABLES
          USED IN ESTIMATION (continued)
B. Female Sample Statistics (N = 873)

Variable	Mean	Standard Deviation
Mother became a mother at age ≤15	0.06	0.23
Mother became a mother at age 16–17	0.16	0.36
Mother became a mother at age 18–19	0.23	0.42
Mother became a mother at age 20–21	0.23	0.42
Mother lived with both her parents	0.70	0.46
Maternal grandfather had a high school education or more	0.19	0.40
Maternal grandmother had a high school education or more	0.29	0.45
Mom's sentence completion score	8.52	1.20
Missing mom's sentence completion score	0.71	0.46
Mother is African American	0.45	0.50
Mother is Catholic	0.18	0.39
Number of times mother attends religious services each month	1.97	1.27
Mother grew up poor	0.48	0.50
Average public family planning expenditures per capita in states child lived at ages 13--19	1.07	0.36
Firstborn child	0.21	0.41
Female child	1.00	0.00
Child graduated from high school	0.86	0.35
Average adult unemployment rate in neighborhood at child's ages 6–15	7.14	4.10
Real average maximum state welfare benefits at child's ages 15–18	$354.07	$77.15
Child had a birth at age <20	0.24	0.43
Child had a birth at age <19	0.19	0.39
Child had a birth at age <18	0.13	0.33
Child had out-of-wedlock birth at age <20	0.18	0.38
Child had out-of-wedlock birth at age <19	0.14	0.35
Child had out-of-wedlock birth at age <18	0.10	0.30

Table 9A.1 (*Continued*)
C. Sample Age ≥24 in 1988 Statistics (*N* = 765)

Variable	Mean	Standard Deviation
Mother became a mother at age ≤15	0.06	0.24
Mother became a mother at age 16–17	0.14	0.35
Mother became a mother at age 18–19	0.24	0.43
Mother became a mother at age 20–21	0.23	0.42
Mother lived with both her parents	0.71	0.45
Maternal grandfather had a high school education or more	0.19	0.39
Maternal grandmother had a high school education or more	0.28	0.45
Mom's sentence completion score	8.54	1.22
Missing mom's sentence completion score	0.67	0.47
Mother is African American	0.43	0.49
Mother is Catholic	0.19	0.40
Number of times mother attends religious services each month	1.94	1.23
Mother grew up poor	0.47	0.50
Average public family planning expenditures per capita in states child lived at ages 13–19	1.14	0.39
Firstborn child	0.21	0.40
Female child	0.54	0.50
Child graduated from high school	0.86	0.35
Average adult unemployment rate in neighborhood at child's ages 6–15	6.64	3.72
Real average maximum state welfare benefits at child's ages 15–18	$371.59	$83.11
Child economically inactive at age 24	0.24	0.43

Source: Michigan Panel Study of Income Dynamics.

THE COSTS OF ADOLESCENT CHILDBEARING

Rebecca A. Maynard

Previous chapters have focused on specific facets of the complex web of behavior, social circumstances, and economic transactions associated with young teen childbearing. My task in this chapter is to build upon the findings of earlier chapters to produce some idea of the overall consequences of teen pregnancy and its concomitants, and to provide some assessment of the measurable costs attributable to young teen pregnancy that could be prevented by policy interventions that (1) delayed the age of childbearing and produced no other changes and (2) delayed the age of childbearing and were successful in preventing at least some of the other risk factors associated with young teen childbearing. Although I build on the estimates of the other authors, this analysis does not represent a consensus view of cost implications of the findings from these other studies.[1] Rather, it reflects my own analysis and interpretation of those findings.

Why include a cost chapter in a volume like this? The findings of the contributing authors speak for themselves. Some readers may find it unnecessary and even unhelpful to provide any overall assessment. But for many would-be users, the value of the *Kids Having Kids* research depends on being able to extract messages that can be readily translated into policy terms. In particular, policymakers (and increasingly the public) want to know how much adolescent parenthood is costing. When confronted with proposals for new programming to prevent adolescent parenting or to mitigate its consequences, they want some idea of the range of savings that could be achieved through such expenditures. Even practitioners are asking for summative cost data. How much, if anything, is the decision to have a baby as a young teen costing these young women? Are they making large financial sacrifices when they chose to have babies or do they actually make out financially? How much can we potentially save taxpayers if our programs are successful? For completeness, the cost analyst also wants to encourage readers to focus on the question of the aggregate costs of young teen childbearing from the broader social welfare perspective. How much is young teen parenthood costing the nation as a whole—the parents and the rest of society combined?

Is there a best answer to each of these questions? There is no "best" answer to these questions. However, any attempt to answer them must consider a broader set of consequences than has guided previous cost estimates, which have tended to focus narrowly on public welfare costs.[2] Moreover, generally these studies make only crude attempts to distinguish between that portion of costs attributable to early childbearing and that portion due to other related factors, such as poverty.[3]

Deriving a more comprehensive set of costs of young teen childbearing is an extremely complex enterprise. I draw on six of the preceding chapters of research (chapters 3, 4, and 6 through 9) in this effort, using an analytic framework that necessarily embodies a number of important assumptions, including assumptions about the time period over which costs will be measured, the assumed rate of time preference or discounting, and the costs (or *shadow prices*) associated with various measured consequences of young teen parenting.

As is evident from the preceding chapters, estimating each of the myriad consequences of young teen childbearing is complex, constrained by available data, and sensitive to assumptions about the alternative life courses for would-be adolescent parents, if they were to delay childbearing. How long would they delay? Under what circumstances would the delays occur? Would they delay childbearing but otherwise experience no changes in life circumstances or would the delay in childbearing be accompanied by improvements, for example, in perceived educational and career options or in the available social and economic support?

How sensitive are the results to the assumptions used in the cost estimates? The qualitative conclusions tend not to be sensitive to the underlying assumptions. However, the dollar estimates vary. My first step in this chapter is to generate a *baseline* set of cost estimates using the outcome estimates generated in the preceding chapters and a reasonable set of assumptions regarding the time frame for the analysis, discount rates, and shadow prices. I then explore the sensitivity of the cost estimates to changes in the underlying assumptions.

In the baseline cost estimates, I make only those manipulations of the outcome estimates reported in the preceding chapters that are necessary to fit them into the cost accounting framework (see further below). I have not, for example, omitted any of the estimates because the measured consequences failed standard tests for statistical significance. Nor have I adjusted estimates upward or downward because of possible biases due to limitations of the data or study methodologies. With few exceptions, I have not included indirect costs associated with specific outcomes measured in the *Kids Having Kids* studies; and, again with few exceptions, I have not truncated the time horizon from that underlying the original analysis.

Each of the studies has certain limitations, most of which are discussed by the authors themselves. For this reason, other analysts or end users of the results might prefer to make certain adjustments when estimating overall costs. Rather than impose my own view as to which adjustments are most appropriate, I instead show the results of a series of sensitivity analyses illustrating the change in the bottom-line cost estimates that occurs when I alter certain of the assumptions underlying the analysis. In this way, I offer readers the option of mixing and matching assumptions to generate a bottom-line estimate that most closely conforms to their views regarding what, if any, adjustments in the estimated consequences reported in the previous chapters or assumptions in my analytic framework seem warranted.

How do I deal with those outcomes that cannot easily be translated into a dollar value? In my discussion of these bottom-line costs, I also reflect on the many adverse consequences of young teen childbearing identified in the *Kids Having Kids* research that are not easily denominated in costs—for example, the lower rates of high school graduation and higher rates of single parenthood for the young mothers, as well as the myriad developmental, educational, and social consequences for the children.

What do the baseline cost estimates say? Adolescent childbearing alone has relatively modest impacts on the average level and sources of financial support mothers have available to them. When a would-be young teen parent bears her first child, whether before age 18 or later, she can look forward to a net income stream over her first 13 years of parenthood that averages only $14,000 to $15,000 annually (discounted to the year she becomes a parent). At one extreme, the baseline estimate of the impacts of the early parenting itself (the lower bound estimate because it assumes nothing is changed in the wider environment) suggests that the young mothers average $852 more income annually than would be the case if they postponed their childbearing until age 20 or 21. At the other extreme, if we had the perfect intervention that simultaneously induced them to delay childbearing until age 20 to 21 *and* addressed the maximum feasible set of policy-influenceable factors that precipitate and/or compound the consequences of early childbearing—such as motivation, educational opportunities, peer group influences, and various social and economic support needs that contribute to the poor observed outcomes for adolescent mothers—the baseline estimates indicate that would-be young teen mothers potentially would gain an estimated $10,000 in average annual income. The modest success of teen pregnancy prevention initiatives to date indicate that the very best interventions that currently exist would eliminate or mitigate only a portion of the consequences of these other factors (Moore, Sugland et al. 1995; Maynard, Kelsey, and McGrath 1996; Kirby forthcoming).

In a steady state with the number of births annually mirroring the current level of nearly 185,000 first births to teens under the age of 18, the lower-bound baseline estimate implies that the fact of young teen childbearing alone costs U.S. taxpayers nearly $7 billion annually for social services and forgone tax revenues.[4] These are primarily costs related to lower productivity levels of the fathers and the taxpayer costs of addressing the poor outcomes for children. Our upper-bound estimate of the *potential* savings to taxpayers from eliminating adolescent childbearing through means that also address the maximum feasible set of precipitating and compounding factors is $15 billion annually.

The costs to society are roughly twice as large as those borne by taxpayers. An estimated $15 billion would be saved if young teen childbearing were delayed and nothing else changed. Twice that amount would be saved if we assume a policy that is able to simultaneously prevent adolescent childbearing and address the myriad other factors that potentially could be addressed through effective interventions.

THE ANALYTIC APPROACH

My approach to the cost analysis rests on four key sets of assumptions and design decisions. The first two define the structure of the accounting framework for the analysis. One is the particular outcomes or consequences of young teen childbearing that will be included in the analysis. These are bounded by the scope of the core studies reported in previous chapters. The other concerns the question: From whose perspective are we measuring costs and benefits: that of adolescent mothers, that of taxpayers, or that of society as a whole?

The third and fourth sets of assumptions relate to the particular subset of young teen parents that is the focus of the estimates and the counterfactual conditions against which we are comparing outcomes of these young teen parents. For example, if a would-be young teen mother delays childbearing beyond age 18, what do we assume about her future? Does it look like that of the average nonadolescent mother, or that of a typical young woman who gives birth at a particular older age, such as 20 or 21? Do we assume that childbearing is delayed but that nothing else changes, or that the same policy changes that would delay childbearing also would address other sources of poor outcomes typically observed for young teen parents? If we assume the latter, which background and environmental circumstances of the would-be young teen mothers do we assume could not be affected through any program or policy intervention? Rather than focus the analysis on any one set of assumptions, I opt for a range of assumptions that illustrate how different answers to these questions affect the measured cost (and benefit) estimates.

The Measured Economic Consequences[5]

The measured economic consequences of young teen childbearing fall into three broad categories. The first relates to *earned income* for the young mothers, the fathers of their children, and their spouses (who often are not the father of their first child). The studies measure directly the effects of young teen parenthood on income due to employment efforts and productivity levels of the mothers, the fathers of their babies, and their spouses (my analysis; Hotz, McElroy, and Sanders, chapter 3; Brien and Willis, chapter 4). The measured earnings effects then provide the basis for estimating the changes in consumption and other taxes attributable to young teen parenting.[6]

The second category of economic consequences is *public assistance* to the mother. The studies measure directly the level of cash and in-kind transfer payments through the Aid to Families with Dependent Children (AFDC) and food stamp programs (my analysis; Hotz, McElroy, and Sanders, chapter 3). They also measured the change in incidence of public housing residence and rent subsidies, which I then translated into an approximate dollar value using published data on average subsidy levels.[7]

Public health care subsidies are also included in this category. Health care subsidies for children are measured directly (Wolfe and Perozek, chapter 6). Since the *Kids Having Kids* research does not measure directly the consequences of young teen childbearing on health care subsidies for the parents themselves, I adopted another strategy. I used published data on the level of Medicaid dollars spent for health care of adult AFDC recipients in conjunction with chapter 3's findings on the AFDC payments to young teen and later child-bearers to estimate the dollar value of the health care subsidies for both groups and the differences.[8]

I also use national data on the size of program administrative costs relative to direct program benefits as the basis for estimating the administrative costs associated with changes in AFDC benefits, food stamp receipt, and health care subsidies. Published data suggest that, for every dollar of AFDC benefits, 12.1 cents are spent administering the program; for every dollar spent on food stamp benefits, 13.9 cents are spent on administration; and for every dollar of medical assistance through Medicaid, which is the largest source of public funds for health care for young poor families, 3.7 cents are spent on administration.[9]

The third category of outcomes includes various *other consequences* for the parents and their children that impact on the parents themselves, taxpayers, and society in a variety of ways: out-of-pocket costs of children's health care, foster care placement, incarceration costs, and the costs of lower productivity of the children.

Out-of-pocket costs borne by parents for children's health care result from a combination of the fertility effects of early childbearing and the health consequences for children of being born to adolescent mothers. The per-child consequences of early childbearing for out-of-pocket health care costs for children are measured directly as part of the *Kids Having Kids* research (Wolfe and Perozek, chapter 6). I simply adjust these costs for the estimated effects of early childbearing on the number of children women have. I use direct estimates of the consequence of early childbearing on the likelihood of a foster care placement (Goerge and Lee, chapter 7) in combination with estimates of changes in family size and published data on the average annual cost of supporting foster children to calculate an estimate for the total foster care costs associated with early childbearing.[10] I use the incarceration rate results (Grogger, chapter 8), together with data on the average prison costs per inmate year, to estimate the average annual costs associated with the higher rates of incarceration attributed to young teen childbearing and, in some cases, closely linked factors.[11] Finally, I use estimates of the consequences of early childbearing on the years of schooling completed by children to calculate an estimate of lost worker productivity due to the lower levels of educational attainment by children born to a young teen as compared with older mothers (Haveman, Wolfe, and Peterson, chapter 9).[12]

The Accounting Perspectives

These various outcome measures have been arrayed in a framework that make it possible to easily aggregate the costs and compare them across the three perspectives (table 10.1). The framework indicates whether a positive measured outcome from delaying childbearing reflects a gain, a loss, or no consequence from the particular perspective—that of young teen parents themselves, that of taxpayers, or that

Table 10.1 ANALYTIC FRAMEWORK FOR THE COST ANALYSIS

	Impact of Positive Values of the Measured Consequence From the Perspective of:		
Benefit (Cost) Component	Adolescent Childbearers	Taxpayers	Society
Earnings-Related Outcomes			
Mother's earnings	Gain	Neutral	Gain
Spouse's earnings	Gain	Neutral	Neutral
Father's earnings	Neutral	Neutral	Gain
Child support	Gain	Neutral	Neutral
Mother's income and consumption taxes	Loss	Gain	Neutral
Spouse's income and consumption taxes	Loss	Neutral[a]	Neutral
Father's income and consumption taxes	Neutral	Gain	Neutral
Public Assistance			
AFDC benefits	Gain	Loss	Neutral
Food stamp benefits	Gain	Loss	Neutral
Rent subsidies	Gain	Loss	Neutral
Medical assistance for parents	Gain	Loss	Neutral
Medical assistance for children	Neutral	Loss	Loss
Administrative costs of public assistance programs	Neutral	Loss	Loss
Other Consequences			
Out-of-pocket cost of children's health care	Loss	Neutral	Loss
Foster care	Neutral	Loss	Loss
Incarceration of young men	Neutral	Loss	Loss
Productivity of young adult children	Neutral	Neutral	Loss
Income and consumption taxes of young adult children	Neutral	Loss	Neutral

a. We have assumed that changes in spouses earnings, as distinct from those of fathers of the children born to adolescent childbearers, represent shifts in the allocation among families rather than net changes in the productivity and tax revenues. That portion of the spouse's earnings difference that is linked to productivity effects associated with adolescent childbearing is assumed to be picked up in the estimated changes in the *father's* earnings and taxes.

of society at large. What this particular framework does not allow is to overlay the implications of various consequences of adolescent childbearing that are less easily measured in dollars—things like the developmental, educational, and social outcomes for the children of young teen parents (Moore, Morrison and Greene, chapter 5) or various markers of hardship for the parents (Hotz, McElroy, and Sanders, chapter 3). It also does not look at overall economic consequences from the perspectives of the fathers of the children born to young mothers, the spouses of these young mothers (whether the fathers of her children or not), or the children themselves.

Component Costs to Adolescent Mothers

From the perspective of the mothers, the consequences fall into four categories. The first relates to changes in *income from the mother's own employment.* This includes changes in her earnings and the partially offsetting changes in income and consumption taxes. A second category pertains to *income from her husband(s) and the father(s) of* her children. Young teen childbearing affects the amount of income a mother can expect to receive from a husband—an outcome that depends on the consequences of early childbearing for both the proportion of time that she lives with a spouse and his earnings. Young teen childbearing also influences the level of child support, both by affecting the probability of bearing a child out-of-wedlock and by altering somewhat the earnings patterns of nonresident fathers.[13]

The third category of consequences from the perspective of the young mothers is *public assistance.* This includes changes in access to and reliance on Aid to Families with Dependent Children (AFDC), food stamps, public housing and rent subsidies, and health care subsidies for parents.[14] The final category pertains to the changes in direct *out-of-pocket costs of health care for children* that arise from differences in the health care needs of children born to young teen versus older mothers and from the different fertility rates of the two groups of mothers.

This framework does not include direct estimates of the economic implications of *all* the consequences of early childbearing. For example, it ignores the effects of young teen childbearing on access to a number of educational and training resources, such as student financial aid and publicly funded job training. It also ignores adverse social consequences of young teen childbearing, including those associated with lower school completion rates, higher proportions of time spent in single parenthood, and larger family sizes (Hotz, McElroy, and Sanders, chapter 3). Then, too, it ignores the social and psychological costs associated with the poorer qualities of home environments and the poorer developmental outcomes children experience (Moore, Morrison, and Greene, chapter 5; Wolfe and Perozek, chapter 6; Goerge and Lee, chapter 7; Grogger, chapter 8; and Haveman, Wolfe and Peterson, chapter 9). It also could be argued that this framework ignores social-psychological *benefits* of early parenthood to the mothers. For example, to the extent that having a baby brings joy and love to an otherwise unhappy, lonely young woman there may be important personal pleasures that have not been valued.[15]

MEASURING THE COSTS TO TAXPAYERS

The costs of young teen childbearing to taxpayers fall into five categories. The first is *tax revenues* resulting from changes in productivity of the mothers and the fathers of their children (whether husbands or not).[16] The second is *public assistance* expenditures (AFDC, food stamps, public and subsidized housing, and health care subsidies for both parents and children) as well as the costs of administering these programs. The final category reflects the public costs of addressing the adverse consequences of young teen childbearing for children— *foster care* costs, *criminal justice* (prison) costs for young adult male children of young teen parents, and *lost tax revenues* arising from the lower work productivity of those born to young teen parents. In each of these cases, the measured adverse consequences of young teen childbearing for individual children are compounded by the fact that young teen parents have more children on average than do later childbearers.

The framework ignores certain potentially relevant costs to taxpayers that either were not measured in the *Kids Having Kids* research or do not lend themselves to conversion to dollar values. For example, changes in the demand for secondary education and publicly funded higher education are not considered. So, too, early childbearing is associated with higher levels of learning disabilities and social problems among children, which have implications for educational and social service costs not captured in this framework (Moore, Morrison, and Greene, chapter 5). Also missing are the financial and social costs to taxpayers related to socially deviant behavior, beyond the direct costs of foster care placement and incarceration rates for children of adolescent parents. Such costs include the social costs of the presumed higher levels of crime that accompany the higher incarceration rates, the child welfare investigative and support services that presumably precede and accompany the higher rates of foster care placement, and the higher levels of social dissonance associated with lower education levels.

The costs of young teen childbearing to society pertain only to those consequences that reflect real changes in the resources available for consumption by the population at large. These include changes in the productivity of the mothers themselves and in the productivity of the fathers of their children, changes in the level of resources devoted to administering public assistance (but not public assistance payments themselves), and changes in the level of medical care provided to children (that are due to poorer health). They also include those child welfare and criminal justice costs associated with higher foster care and incarceration rates for children born to young teen mothers, and the lower productivity among those adult workers who were born to and reared by mothers who began parenting as young teens.

The framework ignores a number of potentially important social cost factors. Most notably, it does not include the costs of child welfare services other than foster care, or the costs of property damage and personal injuries likely to accompany the higher incarceration rates among children of young teen mothers.

The Comparison Scenarios for the Analysis

The comparison scenarios (counterfactuals) for the analysis are defined along two dimensions: (1) the focal group of teens for whom outcomes will be estimated; and (2) the assumed circumstances under which they delay childbearing.

THE FOCAL GROUP OF TEEN PARENTS AND THEIR LATER CHILDBEARING COUNTERPARTS

In contrast to most previous research on teen parenting, which has focused on comparing outcomes for all teen parents (those giving birth before age 20) with nonteen mothers (those giving birth at age 20 or later), the *Kids Having Kids* research, and quite specifically this cost analysis, focuses on those mothers who give birth before age 18— the group we refer to as young teen, or early, or adolescent childbearers. Moreover, we compare outcomes for this group of very young mothers (mean average age at first birth of about 16.5) to those giving birth at age 20 or 21, which is, on average, about four years older than their adolescent childbearing counterparts, but still a group of relatively young mothers. By definition, then, the simulated delays in childbearing for the comparison group are shortest for the 17 year-old childbearers and longest for those who are 14 and under when they have their first baby.

This particular focus reflects the strong public concern about the high rate of childbearing among teens under age 18, who normally would not have completed their secondary education and for whom future life prospects are especially bleak (Maynard 1996; Jacobson and Maynard 1995; Hotz, McElroy, and Sanders, chapter 3). In 1996, there will be roughly 185,000 first births among this group, the vast majority of which will result, as noted in chapter 1, from unintended pregnancies, and 80 percent of which will occur out of wedlock. The *Kids Having Kids* research focuses primarily on the question of the consequences of young teen childbearing relative to delaying childbearing until age 20 or 21, feeling that this comparison has greater policy relevance than, for example, looking at the consequences relative to delaying childbearing to the national average age at first birth (age 23), which is a much longer delay than could reasonably be expected to be achieved through even extremely aggressive policy interventions.

There is one exception to maintaining this focus on the consequences of delaying childbearing from under age 18 until age 20 to 21. In their study of the consequences of adolescent childbearing *itself* on outcomes for mothers, specifically on their earnings, welfare receipt (AFDC and food stamps), and housing assistance, Hotz, McElroy, and Sanders (chapter 3) compare outcomes for a cohort of teens who became pregnant before age 18 and gave birth, with outcomes for their counterparts who got pregnant before age 18 but miscarried (or had a stillbirth). Insofar as miscarriage is a random or near random event among pregnant women, this was an extremely strong methodology for disentangling the effects of young teen parenting from the effects of various other factors that are correlated with both young parenting and subsequent outcomes.[17] One trade-off, however, is that their methodology limits them to addressing a somewhat different question from that posed by the other *Kids Having Kids* studies. It asks: For those teens who get pregnant before age 18 and carry their babies to term, what would be the effect of their delaying childbearing by the average childbearing delay caused by a miscarriage?[18] Another limitation of this approach is the very small sample size for the comparison group (fewer than 70 observations), which precluded any attempt to estimate effects by varying durations of induced delays in childbearing.

On average, three-fourths of the teens who get pregnant at age 17 deliver their babies after they turn 18, resulting in these estimated outcomes pertaining to a sample that averages about half a year older than those who actually give birth before age 18. This study design also means that the results reflect the mean impacts for the average delay in childbirth induced by a miscarriage, which rarely conforms to the duration of delay that was assumed for the comparison groups in the other *Kids Having Kids* studies. While the average duration of delay is roughly the same in the two studies if we assume those who did not have a baby before the end of the observation period had one at age 30, the distributions are quite different (see note 17). Thus, the combined effect on the outcome estimates of the older population and the high rate of inclusion of adolescent childbearers in the comparison group may mean that, while generating robust and unbiased estimates of the consequences of delays in parenthood caused by a miscarriage, the estimates may well underestimate the consequences of specifically delaying childbearing from under age 18 until age 20 or 21.[19] Nonetheless, in recognition of the advantages the statistical design afforded by the miscarriage sample for disentangling the effects of early childbearing itself from the consequences of other factors closely related to early childbearing, I use these estimates for the consequences of early childbearing itself in the baseline lower-bound cost estimates.

EARLY CHILDBEARING COMPARED WITH WHAT?

We present the estimated costs of having a baby before age 18 versus delaying childbearing until age 20 to 21 under three quite different counterfactual scenarios. One of these drives public perception, but is not relevant for policy development purposes, and two offer bounds on the size of impacts that would result from policies that were successful in preventing young teen pregnancy.

The estimates that shape public opinion. Public opinion about young teen parenthood are shaped in large part by the observed outcomes for those women who begin their families early versus those who delay childbearing. The public generally does not focus on the fact that outcomes for the mothers and their children will differ for a variety of reasons, only one of which is the fact that one group begins parenthood at a younger age. Although, as noted in chapter 1, it is pure fantasy to imagine a policy that could both induce the would-be young teen childbearers to delay childbearing and fully compensate for the myriad other differences between these two groups, I present the *combined costs of young teen childbearing and all other disadvantages* for descriptive and contextual purposes. In this calculation, I use the observed outcomes for young teen childbearers (defined as mothers who have their first child before age 18) and those who delayed childbearing until early adulthood (age 20 or 21), not adjusting for any of the differences between these two groups of mothers that will condition their future life prospects. This set of estimates is the least policy relevant, but is the most comparable to the informal calculations the public makes when formulating their beliefs about young teen childbearing.

Upper-bound estimates of the costs that could be averted through a maximally effective program. A second set of estimates answers the question: What are the *measured costs (or benefits) of having a baby before age 18 and of addressing the maximum feasible set of factors* that precipitate and/or compound the effects of adolescent childbearing? For these estimates, I use the measures of the differences in outcomes between young teen and later childbearers after controlling statistically for a "minimal" set of background factors—factors such as the mothers' race/ethnicity and the demographic characteristics of the mothers' parents—*not* expected to be affected by policy actions that would alter fertility timing.[20] In some sense, these estimates could be viewed as the maximum difference in outcomes that conceivably could be achieved from any type of policy intervention.

Lower-bound estimates of the costs that could be averted through preventing adolescent parenting. The final set of cost estimates answers the question: What are the *costs of adolescent childbearing relative to a world in which all would-be young childbearers delayed childbearing until age 20 or 21, but nothing else changed* in the lives of these young women? For these estimates, I use the results from those models that do the best job of isolating the impacts of adolescent childbearing itself from other factors that may account for the observed impacts. These can be viewed as the best estimates of the measured economic consequences of a policy that could eliminate adolescent childbearing through a combination of effective promotion of abstinence among young teens and effective contraceptive behavior among sexually active teens. They assume that such policies would not affect other aspects of the teens' lives either leading up to or concurrent with the delayed parenthood.

Other Basic Assumptions of the Cost Analysis

Two other sets of assumptions went into my development of the cost estimates. The first pertains to the time frame for the analysis and the cohort size. The second concerns the discount rate and the use of longitudinal estimates as the basis for generating current year estimates for various cohorts of adolescent mothers.

THE COHORT SIZE AND TIME HORIZON

The analysis projects forward from the present assuming that, in the absence of significant policy shifts, future cohorts of adolescent parents will be the same size as that projected for 1996, or 184,986 new mothers annually.[21] This assumption of constant cohort sizes understates future costs in so far as we have seen only modest reductions in the adolescent birth rates in recent years and we see relatively large increases in the numbers of teens through the end of the century (chapter 1). However, it overstates somewhat the actual costs today in so far as the number of current and former adolescent parents raising children is smaller today than will be the case in the future if we maintain our current teen birth rates.[22]

In measuring the costs from the perspective of the young teen mothers, I limit the analysis to the first 13 years of parenthood. This decision was largely driven by the fact that a number of the key studies (especially those measuring outcomes for the mothers and the health care costs for children) have limited or no data beyond this time frame. It happens also to be a time period which is highly relevant to the developmental prospects for the children of these very young mothers, and is a period consistent with many of the measured child outcomes reported in chapters 5 through 7.[23]

When measuring costs from the perspective of taxpayers and society, in contrast, I focused the analysis on the *aggregate* costs in a given calendar year, 1996, associated with outcomes for the young teen mothers, their spouses, and the fathers of their children over the first 13 years of parenthood. That is, I add up the current year costs for the first-time adolescent mothers, the second year costs for a cohort of adolescent mothers who gave birth for the first time a year ago, and so forth for 13 cohorts. To these costs (or benefits) I add those associated with the additional current year costs of incarcerating adolescent and young adult males born to women who had their first child before age 18, as well as the costs associated with the lower work productivity of adult children born to mothers who began childbearing before age 18.[24] These costs begin to emerge when the male children reach their midteens. Indeed, the estimates by Grogger (chapter 8) pertain specifically to males age 15 through 27.

DISCOUNT RATES

Throughout this analysis, we assume that the young mothers discount future income at a rate of 5 percent annually. The studies themselves often present estimates based on somewhat lower discount rates as well. However, the literature on adolescent development would lead one to expect that, if anything, the 5 percent rate of discount is low for teens. Thus, I do not conduct sensitivity tests with the discount rate.

In contrast to traditional benefit-cost analyses (and my analysis of the costs to the young mothers), I have not used a discounted present value concept in measuring taxpayer and social costs. Rather, I estimate the steady-state annual costs in current dollars associated with young teen childbearing as contrasted with each of the three counterfactual situations. In most cases, I do this by using the average cumulative longitudinal estimate of the various consequences of early childbearing denominated in current dollars as current-year estimates of the aggregate costs associated with 13 adolescent mothers, each in a different year of parenthood. For example, I use the average cumulative 13-year estimate of the rent and public housing subsidies to reflect the current year costs of these subsidies for one new young teen parent, plus the current year cost of these subsidies for one young teen parent who is in her second year of parenting, and so forth, through a teen in her thirteenth year of parenting. The aggregate costs per young teen mother of foster care are used to represent the current year costs for 18 adolescent mothers, each in a different year of parenthood, and those for the productivity of adult children are used to represent current year costs for children of 43 young teen mothers, again, each in a different year of parenthood.[25]

ESTIMATES OF THE COMPONENT COSTS AND BENEFITS

By almost any measure, the life prospects for those teen women who begin parenthood before age 18 are poor. The average such woman can look forward to earnings that have an average discounted value of $5,874 annually over their first 13 years of parenthood (table 10.2, column 2). To this they can add roughly $9,000 in expected income from their spouses, and an average of $563 annually in child support.[26] Their earned income will then be supplemented by an average of $2,565 annually in AFDC, food stamps, and rent subsidies combined. They receive $1,951 in health care subsidies, but still pay an estimated $3,432 in taxes. Moreover, in spite of their relatively low incomes, they bear substantial out-of-pocket costs for medical care for their children (an average of $1,573 annually). The net result is that the mothers' annual income after taxes and child health care costs

Table 10.2 ECONOMIC OUTCOMES FOR ADOLESCENT AND 20- TO 21-YEAR-OLD CHILDBEARERS AND ESTIMATED CONSEQUENCES OF DELAYING CHILDBEARING (MARCH 1996 DOLLARS, DISCOUNTED AT 5 PERCENT ANNUALLY)

(1)	Observed Outcomes (No Statistical Controls)			Change Associated with Delaying Childbearing from Under Age 18 to Age 20 to 21 and Addressing:	
	(2)	(3)	(4)	(5)	(6)
Outcome Estimates	Adolescent Childbearers	20- to 21-Year-Old Childbearers	Difference Between Older and Adolescent Childbearers	The maximum feasible set of related factors[a]	Nothing except early childbearing itself
Earnings-Related Outcomes (Average per Year)					
Mother's earnings	$5,874	$10,340	$4,466	$3,258	($288)
Spouse's earnings	$9,048	$23,985	$14,937	$12,222	($961)
Father's Earnings	$11,307	$14,698	$3,391	$2,830	$2,270
Child support	$563	$323	($240)	($136)	($20)
Mother's income and consumption taxes	$1,351	$2,378	$1,027	$749	($66)
Spouse's income and consumption taxes	$2,081	$5,517	$3,436	$2,811	($221)
Father's income and consumption taxes	$2,601	$3,381	$780	$651	$522
Public Assistance (Average per Year)					
AFDC benefits	$1,152	$487	($665)	($566)	$58
Food stamp benefits	$640	$265	($375)	($291)	$80
Rent Subsidies	$773	$556	($217)	($68)	($108)
Medical assistance for parents	$449	$190	($259)	($221)	($22)

Medical assistance for children	$1,502	$784	($718)	($720)	($637)
Administrative costs of public assistance programs	$294	$129	($165)	($141)	($7)
Other Consequences (Average per Year)					
Out-of-pocket costs of children's health care	$1,573	$1,618	$45	($200)	($77)

Source: The sources for the various estimates are detailed in Appendix 10A.

Note: Negative consequences of delaying childbearing are denoted by parentheses. Undiscounted values are presented in Appendix table 10A.1. The data on undiscounted values include estimates of the costs associated with in foster care, incarceration of adolescent and young adult males born to adolescent childbearers, and lower work productivity of working-age individuals born to adolescent childbearers.

a. Examples of other factors that might be addressed simultaneously with preventing adolescent parenthood include educational opportunities, social and economic support needs, motivation, and peer influences.

average about $15,000 (not shown). About 30 percent of this is from public assistance, which also costs taxpayers an average of $294 annually per parent to administer.

Their children spend an average of 3.3 percent of their childhood in foster care, contributing roughly $1,000 per adolescent parent to the annual child welfare costs, and an average of 10.3 percent of the male children will end up in prison, contributing an average of $3,385 to the nation's criminal justice costs for their incarceration alone (See appendix table 10A.1).[27]

The Role of Adolescent Parenting and Other Factors in Generating These Poor Outcomes

These outcomes for adolescent parents are considerably worse than those for their older childbearing counterparts in almost all dimensions (table 10.2, columns 3 and 4). However, as has been observed in a number of previous studies, much of the differences in outcomes is due to factors other than young teen childbearing itself.[28] In fact, the *Kids Having Kids* research indicates that only a minority (and, in some cases, none) of the differences in outcomes is due to young teen childbearing itself (table 10.2, column 6). A much greater portion (though still far from all) of the differences in economic outcomes for young teen and older childbearers is attributable to the combined effects of the young teen childbearing and other factors that potentially could be addressed through public policies (table 10.2, column 5).

EARNINGS OF MOTHERS AND SPOUSES

Young teen mothers and their spouses have extremely low earnings compared with their older childbearing counterparts and their spouses (table 10.2, columns 2 and 3). Young teen childbearers earn 57 percent as much as their counterparts who delay childbearing until age 20 or 21 ($5,874 a year versus $10,340) and their spouses earn 38 percent as much as the spouses of their older childbearing counterparts ($9,048 versus $23,985).[29] However, these results indicate that virtually all of this difference is accounted for by factors other than early childbearing itself. Indeed, teens who get pregnant before age 18 and give birth earn an estimated 5 percent more over the first 13 years of parenthood than do their counterparts who miscarry, and their spouses earn an estimated 12 percent more over this period (table 10.2, column 6).[30] At least in the case of the young mothers, this higher income is the result of greater work effort during their children's early school years but not before (Hotz, McElroy, and Sanders, chapter 3).

A somewhat different pattern of results is observed among the fathers of the children born to adolescent mothers, the majority of whom do not marry the mothers of their children.[31] The fathers of children born to adolescent parents are estimated to earn an average of $11,307 over the 18 years following the birth of their first child, while the fathers of babies born to mothers who are 20 or 21 when they have their first child earn an average of $14,698 annually (table 10.2, columns 2 and 3; Brien and Willis, chapter 4).[32] A sizable portion of this difference ($2,270 annually) is estimated to be attributable to early childbearing itself (or to very closely linked factors) (table 10.2, column 6).[33]

Part of the explanation for this sizable difference may relate to the marriage effect on the employment behavior of young men, in so far as the estimates of fathers' earnings are roughly 35 percent higher for those married at the birth of their first child, regardless of the age of the mother.[34] However, some also may relate to still unmeasured differences between fathers whose partners are under age 18 when they have their first child relative to those who delay childbearing.[35] One of the sensitivity analysis examines the consequence of correcting for such possible upward bias in the estimates.

Under current patterns of child support payments by nonresident fathers of children born to young mothers, the fathers of children born to adolescent mothers are estimated to pay an average of $563 annually over the first 13 years of parenthood, which is $240 per year more than paid by fathers who delayed parenthood until their partner turned 20 or 21—a difference arising from the much higher rate of out-of-wedlock childbearing among young teen mothers that more than overshadows the higher earnings of nonresident fathers of children born to older mothers. However, in large part because of the fact that most of the observed difference in fertility and out-of-wedlock childbearing behavior of adolescent women compared with their older childbearing counterparts is attributable to factors other than early childbearing (Hotz, McElroy, and Sanders, chapter 3), only about 10 percent of the higher child support payments is estimated to be due to early childbearing itself ($20 per year).[36]

PUBLIC ASSISTANCE

The $4,516 average annual public assistance (AFDC, food stamps, health care subsidies, and housing assistance) received by young teen parents over their first 13 years of parenthood is 50 percent higher than that received by their counterparts who delay childbearing until age 20 or 21 (table 10.2, column 2 and 3). Roughly 16 percent of the difference in outcomes is attributable to differences in the backgrounds of the young teen and later childbearers that potentially could be addressed through policy changes (column 5). Of the remaining 84 percent, just over one-third (about $650 annually, all from medical assistance and housing subsidies) directly attributable to early childbearing as opposed to other factors that are closely linked to early childbearing (column 6).

The administrative costs associated with adolescent childbearing parallel the outcomes for benefit levels. While the nation spends an average of $294 annually administering public assistance services for current and former young teen parents, it spends only $165 annually on administration of benefits for their 20- to 21-year-old counterparts. However, as little as $7 of this difference can be directly linked to early childbearing itself.

OTHER CONSEQUENCES

These include out-of-pocket costs for the children's health care, foster care placement, incarceration costs, and the productivity of children.

There is relatively little difference in the *out-of-pocket costs for health care for children* between the young teen and later childbearers ($1,573 versus $1,618 annually) (table 10.2, columns 2 and 3).[37] However, this difference masks the fact that the adolescent childbearers pay less *per child* out-of-pocket than do their older childbearing counterparts ($605 versus $770).[38] Indeed, there is a much larger difference in outcomes once key background characteristics are controlled for. Controlling for both background factors and health status changes that occur with delayed childbearing, as well as that portion of the fertility difference that is attributable to early childbearing itself, adolescent childbearing results in parent's paying an average of $77 more per year out-of-pocket for health care for their children than do their older childbearing counterparts (table 10.2, column 6).

Among the most significant consequences of adolescent childbearing are those that fall on the children of these young mothers. The *foster care placement* rate is 2.7 times larger among families headed by current or former young teen mothers compared with their older childbearing counterparts (28.5 versus 10.4 per 1,000) (Goerge and Lee, chapter 7). Only a small portion of this difference is accounted for by background factors. However, the *Kids Having Kids* research on abuse and neglect includes a more limited set of background control variables than is the case for other outcome areas (see table 10.2 and Goerge and Lee, chapter 8).[39] Translating these measured differences in placement rates into dollars implies that the average annual gross difference in current costs of foster care for children born to young teen childbearers relative to their older childbearing counterparts is $517 annually over the first 18 years of parenthood. Of this, $486 per young teen parent is attributable to the combination of young teen childbearing and closely linked factors; $424 is due, as closely as I can estimate, to early childbearing itself (appendix table 10A.1, column 6).[40]

Male children of adolescent childbearers have 2.7 times *higher incarceration rates* than their counterparts born to mothers age 20 or 21 (10.3 versus 3.8 percent incarcerated at some point over a 13-year observation period) (Grogger, chapter 8). Half of this difference is attributable to differences in the backgrounds of the male children born to mothers of different ages that will not be affected through short-run policies. Twenty-eight percent of the difference is attributed to factors that are closely linked to early childbearing, but not directly measurable. The remaining 18.5 percent is directly attributable to early childbearing itself.[41] While the proportion of the total observed difference in incarceration rates that is attributed directly to early childbearing is small (1.3 percentage points), this has a large aggregate impact on the criminal justice expenses, costing an average of $396 per current and former young teen parent annually (see appendix table 10A.1, column 6). The incarceration-related costs of early childbearing and all closely linked factors that potentially could be addressed through effective program interventions average an estimated $991 per adolescent parent annually (appendix table 10A.1, column 5), or 46 percent of the gross difference in prison costs for children of young teen and older childbearers.[42]

The final measured outcome relates to the *productivity of adult children* born to young teens. These estimates are based on direct measures of the consequences of young teen childbearing for the educational attainment of children and the measured productivity gains associated with each additional year of schooling (Haveman, Wolfe, and Peterson, chapter 9). Over the entire 43-year working life of these children, they are estimated to earn an average of $700 more annually as a result of their higher levels of education (appendix table 10A.1, column 2).[43] Imposing additional controls for the fertility impacts of early childbearing results in estimated differences in earnings of $646 annually (appendix table 10A.1, column 6). These higher earnings also raise tax revenues by an amount assumed to equal 23 percent of the productivity increase, or between $161 and $149 annually.[44]

COSTS AND BENEFITS FOR THE ADOLESCENT MOTHERS

Young teen mothers do not suffer earnings-related financial losses as a result of their adolescent childbearing decisions, according to the research reported in this volume. In fact, those estimates that most closely approximate the consequences of adolescent childbearing *itself* indicate that the adolescent mothers actually are slightly better off financially than if they had delayed childbearing a few years (table 10.3, column 6). Adolescent mothers have incomes averaging 6 percent ($852) more annually than if they had delayed childbearing until age 20 or 21 and there had been no other policy change. The reason is that they work and earn slightly more themselves and they receive more support from spouses. They have slightly lower public assistance support ($58), and pay slightly more out-of-pocket for their children's health care ($77).

We estimate that, on average, the net present value of measured income to young teen parents from all of the sources in the accounting framework is only about half that of their later childbearing counterparts ($13,494 versus $26,633) (table 10.3, column 2 versus the sum of columns 2 and 3). About a quarter of this difference in income is accounted for by background factors that are fixed in the short run (table 10.3, columns 3 versus 4). The remainder is due to unmeasured differences between the two groups that are correlated with, but that do not directly cause early childbearing (table 10.3, columns 4 versus 5).

The bottom line for the young teen mothers is that there is considerable room to improve their economic prospects whether or not they bear children early. In either case, would-be adolescent mothers are estimated to have average annual incomes 20 percent below the poverty level. Those who have their children before age 18 are estimated to have slightly higher average incomes than would be the case if they simply delayed childbearing. However, they get this higher income in part through their own greater work effort, perhaps prompted by the fact that they have spouses present somewhat less of the time (Hotz, McElroy, and Sanders, chapter 3). And, quite importantly, the outcomes for their children are extremely poor (Moore, Morrison, and

Table 10.3 ESTIMATED ANNUAL COSTS PER ADOLESCENT CHILDBEARERS OF NOT DELAYING CHILDBEARING UNTIL AGE 20 OR 21 (BENEFITS DENOTED BY PARENTHESES)

(1) Outcome Measure	(2) Observed Outcomes for Adolescent Childbearers[a]	(3) Gross Difference Between Older and Adolescent Childbearers	Costs (or Benefits) Measured Against a Counterfactual of Delaying Childbearing and Addressing:	
			(4) The maximum feasible set of related factors	(5) Nothing except early childbearing itself
Earnings-Related Outcomes	**$12,053**	**$14,700**	**$11,784**	**($982)**
Mother's earnings	$5,874	$4,466	$3,258	($288)
Spouse's earnings	$9,048	$14,937	$12,222	($961)
Child support	$563	($240)	($136)	($20)
Mother's income and consumption taxes	($1,351)	($1,027)	($749)	$66
Spouse's income and consumption taxes	($2,081)	($3,436)	($2,811)	$221
Public Assistance	**$3,014**	**($1,516)**	**($1,146)**	**$53**
AFDC benefits	$1,152	($665)	($566)	$58
Food stamp benefits	$640	($375)	($291)	$80
Rent Subsidies	$773	($217)	($68)	$80
Medical assistance for parents	$449	($259)	($221)	$23
Other consequences	**($1,573)**	**($45)**	**$200**	**$77**
Out-of-pocket costs of children's health care	($1,573)	($45)	$200	$77
Total Per Teen Parent	**$13,494**	**$13,139**	**$10,838**	**($852)**

Source: Component cost estimates are reported in Table 10.2. The sources and methods used to calculate them are detailed in Appendix table 10A.1.

Note: Costs are March 1996 dollars. Numbers in parentheses represent a net benefit to the adolescent parents.

a. Deductions from income to the adolescent parents are denoted by parentheses.

Greene, chapter 5). All available evidence shows that such consequences are viewed negatively by the mothers, even though the consequences often are not observed for several years following the initial
decision to have a child (Polit 1993; Quint, Ladner, and Musick 1994).

COSTS TO TAXPAYERS

Public expenditures for services to current and former young teen
parents are large (table 10.4 and appendix table 10A.1). Although many
of these expenditures would be incurred whether the would-be young
teen childbearers delayed their childbearing or not, taxpayers still pay
a sizable price for young teen childbearing. In a steady-state world
with 184,986 new adolescent parents each year, the aggregate measured costs to taxpayers of young teen childbearing *itself* totals $6.8
billion a year (table 10.4, column 4). Put another way, based on the
most highly controlled measures of the consequences of adolescent
childbearing, *each* adolescent mother in this country costs U.S. taxpayers an average of $2,831 a year that could be saved if her child-
bearing had been delayed until age 20 or 21. Of this total, 22 percent
results from earnings-related reductions in income and consumption
tax revenues attributed to adolescent childbearing; 27 percent results
from higher levels of public assistance; and the remainder (51 percent)
of the costs relates to the poor outcomes for the children of adolescent
mothers—the higher rates of abuse and neglect leading to placements
in foster care, the higher rates of delinquency and incarceration among
the male children of young teen parents, and the lower work productivity of children born to young teen mothers.

Virtually all of the tax revenue effects are due to lower earnings of
the fathers of children born to young teen mothers, the vast majority
of whom are nonresident fathers. This, presumably, is due to a combination of the lower educational attainment levels, at least among
those fathers who themselves were adolescents when they had their
first child, and the lower marriage rates caused by adolescent parenthood, which leads to a loss of some of the marriage premium (Brien
and Willis, chapter 4). However, it also seems likely that some of the
measured effect is because available data make it impossible to fully
control for background factors other than early parenthood that poten-
tialy affect fathers' earnings.[45] Because of the resulting uncertainty in
the impact estimates, we examine this issue further in our sensitivity
testing.

Table 10.4 ESTIMATED ANNUAL COSTS (OR BENEFITS) TO TAXPAYERS OF ADOLESCENT CHILDBEARING ($ BILLIONS)

(1) Outcome Measure	(2) Gross Difference Between Older and Adolescent Childbearers	Costs (or Benefits) Measured Against a Counterfactual of Delaying Childbearing and Addressing:	
		(3) The maximum feasible set of related factors	(4) Nothing except early childbearing itself
Earnings-Related Outcomes	**$5.7**	**$4.4**	**$1.5**
Mother's income and consumption taxes	$3.2	$2.3	($0.2)
Father's income and consumption taxes	$2.6	$2.1	$1.7
Public Assistance	**$6.7**	**$5.8**	**$1.8**
AFDC benefits	$2.1	$1.8	($0.2)
Food stamp benefits	$1.2	$1.2	($0.2)
Rent Subsidies	$0.8	$0.3	$0.5
Medical assistance for parents	$0.8	$0.7	($0.1)
Medical assistance for children	$1.3	$1.3	$1.7
Administrative costs of public assistance programs	$0.5	$0.5	$0.1
Other consequences	**$8.2**	**$5.2**	**$3.5**
Foster care	$1.7	$1.6	$1.4
Incarceration of young men	$5.2	$2.4	$1.0
Income and consumption taxes of young adult children	$1.3	$1.2	$1.2
Total per Year (Billions)	**$20.6**	**$15.4**	**$6.8**
Average per Teen Parent per Year	$8,569	$6,383	$2,831

Source: The undiscounted average costs and benefits per adolescent parent per year are reported in Appendix table 10A.1. The sources and methods used for generating these component cost estimates are described in Appendix 10A.

Note: Costs are expressed in March 1996 dollars. Earnings-related outcomes, health care costs, and costs of incarcerating young men reflect current-year aggregated costs over 13 cohorts; foster care costs reflect aggregate costs over 18 cohorts; and costs related to employment of young adult children are aggregated over 43 cohorts of children.

The increased taxpayer costs for public assistance benefits are the result of the higher rates of medical assistance for the children and higher rent subsidies. A portion of the higher health care costs is due to the larger family sizes, a portion is due to the higher fraction of care that is subsidized, and still another portion is due to the worse health conditions of children of young teen parents. Young teen childbearing itself, in fact, is estimated to *reduce* AFDC and food stamp benefits slightly (Hotz, McElroy, and Sanders, chapter 3). This is because, over their first 13 years of parenthood, young teen mothers and their spouses are estimated to have slightly higher average earnings than they would if the mothers delayed childbearing as a result of a miscarriage.

Roughly half of the taxpayer costs are associated with the worse outcomes for children born to young teen parents. In a steady state, taxpayers spend $1.4 billion more annually for foster care services than would be needed if childbearing had been delayed until age 20 or 21 (table 10.4, column 4). Similarly, in a steady state, taxpayers spend $1 billion more on prison costs due to the higher incarceration rates of men born to young teen parents, and they forgo $1.2 billion in tax revenues as a result of the lower productivity of children born to young teen mothers.[46]

Using intermediate levels of controls for differences in the backgrounds of young teen and 20- to 21-year-old mothers, I estimate that adolescent parenting costs taxpayers in excess of $15 billion annually (table 10.4, column 3). That is, if we could not only delay childbearing but also address the maximum feasible set of social and environmental forces that contribute to the poor outcomes of adolescent mothers, the steady-state payoff to the taxpayers could reach this higher level. The increase would occur primarily through higher earnings and lower public assistance needs.

This range of estimated cost savings from preventing adolescent childbearing ($6.8 to $15.4 billion annually), while substantial, is well below the $20 billion gross difference in taxpayer costs (table 10.4, column 2).

COSTS TO SOCIETY

The costs of adolescent childbearing to society include resources that are diverted to mitigate problems associated with young parenthood—in our estimates, the costs of administering welfare programs, providing foster care, building and maintaining prisons. They also include worker productivity changes among the young teen moms, the fathers of their babies, and their children when they reach adulthood.

The social costs of young teen childbearing *itself* total $15.2 billion annually (table 10.5, column 4). This is the estimated amount by which the social welfare of the nation would increase annually in current dollars if, projecting forward in time, all would-be young teen childbearers were convinced to delay childbearing until age 20 or 21 and the full steady-state benefits of delayed childbearing had taken hold. The estimate assumes that none of the many other factors that cause or compound the effects of adolescent childbearing are changed.

The major contributions to this social cost estimate are the productivity losses of the fathers of children born to young teen moms and the poorer outcomes for the children themselves.[47] Earnings losses of the fathers are estimated to total $7.4 billion annually over 13 cohorts of fathers, while the lower productivity of children born to young teen moms totals $5.1 billion annually over 43 cohorts ($646 per adolescent mom per year). Other major costs are those associated with the increased incarceration rates of the male children and the higher foster care costs, which together total an estimated $2.4 billion annually. Another component of the aggregate costs relates to the higher total consumption of medical care for children, which results from the combined effect of the somewhat higher number of children and the poorer health of children born to young teen childbearers as compared with children born to 20- or 21-year-old mothers (Wolfe and Perozek, chapter 6). And, as noted above, young teen childbearers earn slightly more, through greater work effort.[48]

A hypothetical policy that not only delayed childbearing but also addressed the maximum possible set of other factors that contribute to poor outcomes for adolescent mothers would save an estimated $30 billion annually (table 10.5, column 3). Such a policy would undoubtedly be much more costly to implement than one that simply addressed the teen pregnancy and birth issues.

In a fantasy world where we could fully compensate for or eliminate all differences between adolescent and later childbearers, the net gain to society in higher productivity and lower public assistance and social service costs would exceed $37 billion annually (table 10.5, column 2).

SENSITIVITY ANALYSIS

Because no two analysts would have chosen the same set of assumptions in generating cost estimates like this, it is useful to examine the

Table 10.5 ESTIMATED ANNUAL COSTS (OR BENEFITS) TO SOCIETY OF ADOLESCENT CHILDBEARING ($ BILLIONS)

| (1) | (2) | Costs (or Benefits) Measured Against a Counterfactual of Delaying Childbearing and Addressing: | |
| | | (3) | (4) |
Outcome Measure	Gross Difference Between Older and Adolescent Childbearers	The maximum feasible set of related factors	Nothing except early childbearing itself
Earnings-Related Outcomes	**$24.8**	**$19.1**	**$6.4**
Mother's earnings	$13.7	$9.8	($1.0)
Father's Earnings	$11.1	$9.3	$7.4
Public Assistance	**$1.8**	**$1.8**	**$1.9**
Medical assistance for children	$1.3	$1.3	$1.7
Administrative costs of public assistance	$0.5	$0.4	$0.1
Other consequences	**$11.0**	**$8.8**	**$7.1**
Out-of-pocket costs of children's health care	($1.4)	($0.5)	($0.5)
Foster care	$1.7	$1.6	$1.4
Incarceration of young men	$5.2	$2.4	$1.0
Productivity of young adult children	$5.6	$5.4	$5.1
Total per Year (Billion)	**$37.7**	**$29.6**	**$15.2**
Average per Teen Parent per Year	$15,670	$12,328	$6,315

Source: The undiscounted average costs and benefits per adolescent parent per year are reported in Appendix table 10A.1. The sources and methods used for generating these component cost estimates are described in Appendix 10A.

Note: Costs are expressed in March 1996 dollars. Earnings, health care costs, and costs of incarcerating young men reflect current-year aggregated costs over 13 cohorts; foster care costs reflect aggregate costs over 18 cohorts; and earnings effects for adult children are aggregated over 43 cohorts.

sensitivity of the bottom-line estimates of the consequences of adolescent childbearing *itself* (the most highly controlled of our estimates) to various alternative assumptions.[49] Specifically, I look at the following six alternative scenarios:

(1) I assume the estimated consequences of adolescent parenting itself on the mothers' earnings and public assistance receipt (AFDC, food stamps, and rent subsidies) and for the earnings of their spouses are 10 percent of those estimated by comparing outcomes for adolescent childbearers with those first giving birth at age 20 or 21 and controlling for as many background factors as possible. As noted previously, the baseline cost analysis uses estimates of these outcomes generated from a sample of teens who got pregnant before age 18, some of whom gave birth and some of whom miscarried. While technically this sample supports an exceptionally strong methodology for isolating the unique contribution of early childbearing to outcomes, operationally it has limitations. One is that it measures outcomes for a slightly older population of teen parents. Another is that it is measuring a different pattern of delays in childbearing than that assumed in the other *Kids Having Kids* studies. Indeed, over one-fourth of those teens who get pregnant before age 18 and miscarry still have their first child before age 18, and 20 percent delay until after age 21.[50] The alternative estimates for these outcomes, while arbitrary, represent a much smaller portion of both the gross and adjusted differences in outcomes between adolescent and older childbearers than have been estimated in several other studies using relatively rigorous methods to isolate the unique effect of adolescent parenting albeit different from that used by Hotz, McElroy, and Sanders (chapter 3).[51]

(2) I assume that early childbearing itself has no effect on the income available to mothers from resident spouses. The estimated higher income levels of resident spouses of adolescent childbearers accounted for virtually all of the mothers' financial gains from having a baby at a young age. There is no strong theoretical reason to expect early childbearing would lead women to marry men who earn significantly higher incomes during their first 13 years of parenthood, and the research indicates quite clearly that young teen mothers are not more likely to have a spouse. Moreover, the research did not produce robust estimates of the consequences of adolescent parenthood on spouses' earnings (Hotz, McElroy, and Sanders, chapter 3).

(3) I discount by 50 percent the measured earnings effects for the fathers of children born to adolescent childbearers as compared

with a scenario in which these fathers waited until the mothers turned age 20 or 21. The argument for arbitrarily discounting these estimates is that there is less certainty than with some of the other outcome estimates that those for the fathers are solely due to the effects of adolescent parenting rather than to other factors correlated with early parenting.

(4) I add in an estimate of the increase in criminal justice costs other than those associated with incarceration of male children of adolescent parents. In this alternative scenario, I assume that adolescent parenthood leads to a similar proportional increase in the incarceration rates of females as for males, thus increasing the prison-related costs by 10 percent. It also factors in a proportional increase in other criminal justice related costs, which are estimated to be twice the direct costs of incarceration.

(5) I add in an estimate of child welfare costs other than those for foster care. Under this alternative, I assume these other costs are 1.5 times the foster care costs.

(6) I include only the first 13 years of estimated earnings gains for workers who were born to adolescent parents. The argument here is that a steady state focusing on the employment gains of the children of 43 cohorts of adolescent parents may well be beyond a relevant time frame for all but the most patient policy makers.

The magnitudes of the costs exhibit substantial sensitivity to these assumptions although the qualitative conclusions are not greatly affected (table 10.6). Under all the alternative assumptions, we find that adolescent parents are suffering at most modest economic losses because of their decisions to bear children at a young age. The estimated economic consequences for the mothers range from a *loss* of $1,243 per year and a *gain* of $852 a year over the first 13 years of parenthood.

The estimated costs borne by taxpayers range from $6 billion to $9 billion annually—i.e., from 12 percent below to 32 percent above the $6.8 billion estimate reported in table 10.4. The larger figure includes estimates for some of the unmeasured costs, such as criminal justice costs other than prison costs and child welfare costs other than for foster care. The lower estimate adjusts the estimated productivity gains for fathers and children associated with delaying childbearing. The adjustment for possible underestimates of the consequences of adolescent childbearing for the earnings of the mothers and their spouses, as well as for their public assistance through AFDC, food stamps, and housing subsidies has an intermediate effect on the cost estimate, increasing it from $6.8 to $7.7 billion.

The estimates of social costs are the most sensitive to changes in the underlying assumptions, with the alternative estimates ranging from 24 percent below to 15 percent above the $15.2 billion baseline estimate (table 10.6). The estimates under the various assumptions range between $11.5 and $17.4 billion annual losses to society in a steady-state world. The largest estimates are those that make an "ad hoc" adjustment for the likely underestimation of productivity changes for mothers and their spouses, as well as changes in public assistance through AFDC, food stamps, and housing subsidies, and those that add in a crude estimate of the unmeasured costs of criminal justice costs other than prison costs and child welfare costs other than foster care. The lowest estimates, like the estimates of taxpayer costs, are those that discount the estimated productivity gains for fathers of children born to adolescent mothers and for the children themselves.

CONCLUSION

Each year, nearly one million teenage girls in the U.S. becomes pregnant. More than 180,000 of these pregnant teens are under the age 18 and begin adolescent parenthood. There are myriad consequences for these young mothers and their children, most of which are not easily measured in dollars and cents. The economic costs for the mothers, for example, are small to nonexistent. Rather, the consequences for them are largely nonmonetary and often not observable for several to many years following their first birth. They spend more of their early years of parenthood single and have their children over a somewhat shorter period of time than would be the case if they were to delay childbearing until their early twenties. Moreover, during their children's elementary and middle school years, adolescent mothers spend slightly more time out of the home and in the labor force than would be the case if they delayed childbearing. On the other hand, eventually, they succeed in finding mates who earn substantially more than would be the case if they delayed childbearing.

What is unambiguously clear from both the cost analysis given the taxpayer and social perspective and from the companion studies is that, by almost any measure, adolescent childbearing is having significant adverse consequences for the children and that these consequences are costing taxpayers and society dearly. The most conservative estimate yielded by my calculations suggests that, in a steady state, the current rate of adolescent childbearing has in excess of a $6

Table 10.6 SENSITIVITY OF THE ESTIMATED COSTS OF ADOLESCENT CHILDBEARING ITSELF TO ALTERNATIVE ASSUMPTIONS (BENEFITS ARE DENOTED BY PARENTHESES)

	Adolescent Parents (Per Adolescent Parent)	Perspective	
		Taxpayers ($ Billion Annually)	Society ($ Billion Annually)
Estimate under Baseline Assumptions[a]	**($852)**	**$6.8**	**$15.2**
Change in Costs if We Assume:			
1 Alternative estimates of the consequences on adolescent childbearing itself for mothers' and spouses' earnings and for AFDC, food stamps and housing subsidies	$2,095	$0.9	$2.1
2 There are no consequences for the earnings for spouses	$696	$0.2	$0.0
3 Consequences for fathers, earnings are only half the level estimated by Brien and Willis (Chapter 4)	$10	($0.8)	($3.7)
4 There are incarceration effects for female children and other criminal justice-related costs are double prison costs	$0	$2.2	$2.2
5 Total child welfare costs are 2.5 times those for foster care alone	$0	$2.1	$2.1
6 Policy makers care about the productivity gains of children of would-be adolescent parents over only the first 13 years of their working lives	$0	($0.8)	($3.7)

Cost Estimates Assuming:

1 Alternative estimates of the consequences on adolescent childbearing itself for mothers' and spouses' earnings and for AFDC, food stamps and housing subsidies	$1,243	$7.7	$17.3
2 There are no consequences for the earnings for spouses	($156)	$7.0	$15.2
3 Consequences for fathers' earnings are only half the level estimated by Brien and Willis (Chapter 4)	($842)	$6.0	$11.5
4 There are incarceration effects for female children and other criminal justice-related costs are double prison costs	($852)	$9.0	$17.4
5 Total child welfare costs are 2.5 times those for foster care alone	($852)	$8.9	$17.3
6 Policy makers care about the productivity gains of children of would-be adolescent parents over only the first 13 years of their working lives	($852)	$6.0	$11.5

a. The estimated costs under the baseline assumptions are those reported in the right-hand columns of table 10.3 through table 10.5.

billion impact on federal and state budgets annually. If reasonable estimates of *any* of the costs of a number of outcomes that were not measured directly by the studies are factored in, the costs are estimated to rise to as much as $9 billion.

As policymakers devise their plans for the new federalism, it would seem prudent to focus on the merits of up-front investments in policies aimed at breaking the cycle of adolescent parenthood. We already have a wealth of information detailing the enormity of the challenge. The solutions are not as simple as increasing spending on family planning services or supporting abstinence programs.[52] Successful strategies will have to be multi-pronged, including addressing clear messages of national values through rigorous enforcement of child support, human sexuality and values education, and more paternalistic welfare policies; ensuring access to family planning services that include aggressive follow-up with cases at risk of contraceptive failure; and creation of real opportunities for all through our education system and labor markets. In a world where we are spending $6 billion to $9 billion of taxpayers' money annually and forgoing upwards of $15 billion in our aggregate social welfare, substantial investments in teen pregnancy prevention, and its attendant ills, is worth serious consideration in our efforts to position the nation for a brighter future.

Notes

1. I am enormously grateful for the tremendous effort and contribution of Seth Sanders, who worked closely with me in framing a number of aspects of the overall analysis strategy, as well as in the actual estimation of many of the outcomes pertaining to the young mothers. I am also grateful to Meredith Kelsey, Dan McGrath, and Louise Alexander for research assistance and production support. Then, too, the analysis could not have been completed without the terrific research reported in the preceding chapters. The authors of these chapters offered generous support as I adapted the products of their efforts to the rather rigid format of the cost analysis. Michael Brien, Robert Haveman, V. Joseph Hotz, Seth Sanders, Robert Willis, and Barbara Wolfe also provided valuable comments on previous drafts of the chapter.

2. The most widely cited estimates of the cost of adolescent childbearing are those published periodically by the Center for Population Options/Advocates for Youth. These estimates as well as the few other studies of costs focus primarily on taxpayer costs associated with Aid to Families with Dependent Children (AFDC), food stamps, and Medicaid benefits (Burt 1992; Burt and Haffner 1986; Advocates for Youth 1994). In a limited number of cases, income and consumption taxes also are considered (for example, Hotz, McElroy, and Sanders, chapter 3).

3. The one exception here is the study by Hotz, McElroy, and Sanders (chapter 3), which does estimate the costs associated with adolescent childbearing itself.

4. These estimates differ from those reported by Advocates for Youth (1994) and those reported in chapter 3 in that they include only costs for all teenage parents, who have their first child before age 18 rather than all who begin parenthood before age 19 or 20, and they include costs associated with a much broader set of outcomes than the AFDC, food stamp, and Medicaid benefits included in these other studies (see footnote 2).

5. Appendix 10A provides additional detail on the measurement of the various outcomes included in the framework.

6. For consistency, I use the same income and consumption tax rate used by Hotz, McElroy, and Sanders (chapter 3), or 23 percent of earned income. This is based on the assumption that federal taxes average 15 percent of income and state taxes average 8 percent. This rate likely somewhat overstates average income and consumption taxes for two reasons. One is that average estimated federal tax rates are only 6 percent for families in the lowest income quintile and 19 percent for those in the second quintile (U.S. House of Representatives, 1993, Appendix K, table 3B, p. 1543). A second is that the Earned Income Tax Credit has been expanding (Blank, 1994; Scholz, 1994)

7. In 1993, the average housing subsidy level among recipients was $4,240 (U.S. House of Representatives, 1993, Appendix P, table 30, p. 1676), which is equivalent to $4,571 in 1996 dollars. This latter figure is used to translate the estimated effect of adolescent parenthood on the average number of years parents received housing subsidies into a dollar value.

8. In 1993, a total of $8.77 billion was spent on Medicaid benefits for adult AFDC recipients (U.S. House of Representatives, 1993, Appendix P, Table 18, p. 1655). This represents 39 cents in medical assistance benefits for adult recipients for every dollar in family AFDC benefits. This figure likely represents a lower-bound estimate of Medicaid costs attributable to adolescent mothers because, while all AFDC recipients are Medicaid eligible, many non-AFDC recipients also are eligible for Medicaid. Moreover, AFDC recipients who leave for employment are entitled to extend their Medicaid eligibility for at least a year beyond the point where they lose their AFDC benefits. Thus, using AFDC payments as the basis for estimating will tend to understate actual Medicaid benefits. Recent expansions in Medicaid eligibility also will tend to increase Medicaid benefits to both groups (Currie, 1995).

9. In 1992, the nation spent $22.22 billion on AFDC benefits and $2.70 billion on program administration (U.S. House of Representatives, 1993, section 7, table 1, p. 616). In this same year, it spent $21.88 billion on food stamp benefits and $3.03 billion administering the program (U.S. House of Representatives, 1993, Appendix P, Table 4, p. 1609). The corresponding figures for Medicaid benefits are $115.9 billion for direct services and $4.3 billion for state and federal administrative costs (Health Care Financing Administration 1993, table 11, p. 41).

10. Goerge and Lee (chapter 8) estimate that in 1993 the total costs of foster care in this country totaled more than $10 billion to serve 472,000 children, for an average annual cost per child of $21,186 in 1993 dollars ($22,259 per child in 1996 dollars). These costs constitute only about 40 percent of all child welfare costs, however (U.S. House of Representatives 1993, Section 11, Table 33, p. 958). Other costs include preventative and supportive services adoption services and staff training, and development.

11. Incarceration costs averaged $20,000 to $25,000 annually in 1990 (Grogger, chapter 8; U.S. Department of Justice 1993), which corresponds to an average of $24,000 to $30,000 in 1996 dollars.

12. The productivity loss estimates are based on estimates of the aggregate number of years of schooling "lost" as a result of adolescent parenting and estimates by the Children's Defense Fund (1995) on the average productivity gain associated with an additional year of school. See Haveman, Wolfe and Peterson (chapter 9) for details of how these estimates are generated.

13. This analysis does not specifically address differences in child support due to any impacts of young teen childbearing on divorce rates.

14. In the absence of empirical evidence to the contrary, I assume that health care subsidies for children are primarily compensating for poorer health status of the children and so are not a net benefit to the mother. Others could reasonably choose to use a different assumption.

15. For example, numerous studies of adolescent mothers document the joy parenthood brings to young women (Quint, Ladner, and Musick 1994; Polit 1993; Musick 1993; Luker 1996). However, some of these studies also highlight many negative social-psychological aspects of early motherhood, such as those that come with the responsibility of parenthood, family tensions around childrearing practices, and painful relationships with the fathers of the babies.

16. We have assumed that 23 cents of every dollar earned is spent on income or consumption taxes (see footnote 6 above).

17. Miscarriages have been linked to a number of high risk behaviors, including cigarette smoking and alcohol consumption, as well as to other factors associated with poor social and economic outcomes, including poor health and nutrition (Armstrong, Alison, McDonald, and Sloan 1992; Klein, Stein, and Susser 1989; Wilcox, Weingerg, and Baird 1990). However, causality has not been firmly established. It also is possible that there was systematic underreporting of miscarriages by some subgroups of teens who got pregnant before age 18. Fewer than 6 percent of those who got pregnant for the first time before age 18 reported that their first pregnancy ended in miscarriage, compared with 9 percent of those whose first pregnancy was at age 18 to 19 and 14 percent of those whose first pregnancy was at age 20 or 21. The later rate is more consistent with national estimates of the miscarriage rate. However, there is evidence that the rate of miscarriage increases with age (Armstrong, McDonald, and Sloan 1992).

18. More than one-fourth of those who got pregnant before age 18 and miscarried still had their first child before age 18; about a third of them had their first child at age 18 or 19, still younger than the age at first childbearing in the comparison groups used in the other *Kids Having Kids* studies; and more than 12 percent had not had a baby during the observation period, which extended to age 27 or later for all sample members (author's tabulations of the National Longitudinal Survey of Youth data).

19. An opposite hypothesis is that one consequence of the longer delays could be further disadvantage for the mothers by postponing yet further their entry into the workforce.

20. The control variables used in the various analyses are reported in table 1.2.

21. This figure is based on the actual number of first births in 1993, which was 175,259 (Moore 1996), inflated by the average growth in the size of the cohort of 14- to 17-year-olds, which is projected to be 1.8 percent annually through the end of the decade (U.S. Department of Health and Human Services 1996, table PF 1.1).

22. It would be a relatively straightforward, if tedious, exercise for the interested analyst to recalculate the cost estimates using an alternative set of assumptions regarding current and future cohort sizes.

23. Another strategey would be to focus the analysis on a period of late adolescence and young adulthood for the mothers. This has the advantage of treating the mothers similarly by chronological age, but differently at critical stages of their life cycle. For example, during late adolescence, some mothers would be parents and others not; and during their late twenties, the adolescent childbearers would tend not to have preschool age children, while a majority of the later childbearers would still have young children.

24. One of the sensitivity analyses reports the results on including productivity losses for children over only their first 13 years of employment.

25. I use the 18 cohorts so as to encompass all foster care costs associated with adolescent parenthood during the "risk" period of the oldest child.

26. The remainder of the $11,307 income of the fathers of their children is either captured under spouses' income or is assumed not to be shared with the young teen mothers.

27. These estimates are not included in table 10.2, since the data in table 10.2 are discounted and these are not. Only current costs are estimated for these outcomes. Moreover, since these outcomes are relevant only for the taxpayer and social perspectives, discounted values have not been calculated.

28. See, for example, Geronimus (1994), Geronimus and Korenman (1993), Grogger and Bronars (1993), Bronars and Grogger (1994), Hoffman and Furstenberg (1993), and Moore, Morrison, and Greene (1993).

29. The estimated outcomes for earnings of mothers and their spouses were generated through the application of two different methodologies to the National Longitudinal Survey of Youth data. The author and Seth Sanders generated those for adolescent mothers and their older childbearing counterparts under the first two counterfactual scenarios—that, when childbearing is delayed and policies address all or some of the disadvantages faced by adolescent parents that contribute to and/or exacerbate the consequences of teen childbearing. One set of estimates is predicted values of earnings at each age from the age at first birth through age 27 to 34 depending on age at first birth, for those who first gave birth before age 18 and for those who first gave birth at age 20 or 21, with no statistical controls. The second set of predicted values for these two groups controls for those background factors not expected to be amenable to policy intervention in the short run (for example, parents' education, family size, family income, and community characteristics). A third set of estimates was generated by Hotz, McElroy, and Sanders (chapter 3) using instrumental variables techniques and the sample of teens who got pregnant before age 18 and either miscarried or carried their baby to term. They then computed 13-year estimated average outcomes for the adolescent mothers and their counterfactual group of older mothers. The control variables used in both the second and third sets of estimates for the later childbearers are listed in chapter 1, table 1.2. See also appendix table 10A.1 for further description of the sources and methodologies used in generating the various outcome estimates.

30. The estimates of the consequences of adolescent parenthood itself on spouses' earnings are neither stable nor statistically significant in most time periods (Hotz, McElroy, and Sanders, chapter 2; Hotz, September 23, 1996). Therefore, one of my sensitivity analyses (below) explores the change in the overall cost estimates if we assume young teen parenthood has no effect on the earnings of spouses.

31. Only 19 percent of the teens giving birth before age 18 were married before or shortly after having their first child compared with 42 percent of those giving birth for the first time in their young twenties (Alan Guttmacher Institute 1994, p. 56).

32. The difference between the observed outcomes for fathers of children born to adolescent mothers and this estimate of the outcome for fathers of children born to older mothers likely understates the differences in actual outcomes for fathers whose first child is born to a young teen mother, compared with those whose first child is born to a 20- or 21-year-old. This is because the methodology used to generate the estimates relied on statistical matching of mothers and fathers and further controlled directly for some differences between the two groups of fathers. See Brien and Willis (chapter 4) for a discussion of the methodology used to generate the estimates used as the basis for the data reported in table 10.3. See appendix table 10A.1 for a description of our adaptation of the Brien and Willis results for the cost analysis and chapter 1, table 1.2 for the control variables used in their analysis.

33. The estimates of the fathers' earnings are based on the estimated median present values of father's earnings over the first 18 years of parenthood, broken down by age of

the mother, and by marital status, and race of the father. We reweighted these data using national estimates of the race and age distribution of mothers of first born children. Then we calculated annual discounted incomes for the fathers under three different assumptions about what happens to the marriage rate as childbearing is delayed: (1) it will mirror current national rates for the adolescent and older childbearers (19 and 58 percent married, respectively): (2) the out-of-wedlock birth rate will decrease among those who delay childbearing to 55 percent or by two-thirds of the observed difference in the current population; and (3) that the out-of-wedlock marriage rate will decrease to 67 percent of the current gap or by one-third. The first set of estimates is used as the best estimate of the actual outcomes for those who father children by younger versus those who father children by older mothers. The second set of assumptions was used to estimated the effects of delaying childbearing and addressing some but not all of the precipitating and related factors; and the third set of assumptions was used to estimate as close as we could get to the effects of adolescent childbearing itself.

34. The same core study reported that early fatherhood before age 18 resulted in earnings 10 percent lower than they would have been had the fathers delayed parenthood until they themselves were age 20 or 21 (Brien and Willis, chapter 4). However, this difference was not statistically significant.

35. In their statistical matching procedures, Brien and Willis (1996) are able to control for a relatively large number of the characteristics of the fathers. But, given the nature of the technique, they are only able to control for a very limited set of maternal characteristics (age, marital status, and race).

36. Child support payments are estimated based on the Wisconsin formula for award amounts and estimates from national data regarding the proportion of nonresident fathers who have awards and the fraction of the award amounts that are paid. The analysis assumes that, on average, nonresident fathers pay between 6 and 7 percent of their gross income for child support. Appendix 10A provides more detail on the specific assumptions and method of calculating the child support amounts.

37. These estimates are based on data largely for the period prior to the Medicaid expansions of the late 1980s and early 1990s. These expansions in coverage will tend to decrease out-of-pocket costs for low-income families (Currie 1995).

38. These per child cost estimates differ from those reported by Wolfe and Perozek (chapter 6), because they have been adjusted to reflect the flow of costs by the ages of children, the timing of subsequent births, and discounting at an annual rate of 5 percent annually.

39. These data are not included in table 10.2 because only current dollar cost estimates were generated.

40. These estimates are undisounted, since they are used only in the analysis of steady-state costs to taxpayers and society. Appendix 10A provides additional detail on the sources and methodologies used to generate the cost estimates.

41. These estimates are based on a methodology that used the natural variation in the mother's age at the birth of her various children to estimate the effects of early fertility, while using age at the birth of her first child to control for unobservable differences between early and later childbearers (Grogger, chapter 8, and appendix 10A).

42. The *Kids Having Kids* research did not look at incarceration rates for women. If there were a similar pattern of higher rates of incarceration among female children of adolescent mothers, these cost estimates will understate actual costs by roughly 10 percent since females account for 10 percent of incarcerations (Grogger, chapter 8). So also, the project did not attempt to measure other criminal justice costs that are related to the higher incarceration rates. These have been estimated at twice prison costs (U.S. Department of Justice 1992).

43. These figures are current dollars, assuming a 1 percent real wage growth annually. This estimate controls for background factors that differ between children born to

adolescent and later childbearers. The controls include measures of race/ethnicity, birth order, parents' education, family income, religion, and community context. Thus, it likely is a substantial underestimate of the *gross* difference in outcomes between children born to adolescent and older mothers.

44. This is the same tax rate used by Hotz, McElroy, and Sanders (chapter 3).

45. The *Kids Having Kids* research on outcomes for teen fathers (the first half of Brien and Willis, chapter 4) casts some doubt on whether these seemingly large earnings effects for fathers used in the cost analysis reflect the costs of fathering a child by an adolescent mother itself. Specifically, in their analysis of the consequences of adolescent fatherhood, where they were able to control for a rich array of background factors, the estimated differences in educational and earnings outcomes related to adolescent fatherhood were neither large (on the order of 5 to 10 percent) nor statistically significant. Their estimates of the consequences of fathering a child by an adolescent mother relative to postponing fatherhood until the mothers reached age 20 or 21 necessarily relied on a less rich set of control variables. Thus, one must consider the possibility that the larger estimated residual differences may reflect some degree of unobserved differences between their two groups of fathers.

46. Prison costs were estimated as steady state costs over all male children of adolescent parents. Costs of the productivity losses, on the other hand, were estimated as the net present value of work productivity losses to a cohort of adolescent parents. I convert the latter figures to an estimate of the average steady-state current-year costs associated with productivity losses for all workers born to adolescent mothers (see appendix 10A).

47. As noted above, it is possible that the true earnings losses for fathers would be smaller than this figure estimated by Brien and Willis (chapter 4), given their limited ability to control for other factors that could affect fathers' earnings.

48. It could be argued that we should deduct from the greater out-of-home productivity of the mothers the value of the work-related child care services they use, particularly since the higher earnings of the adolescent mothers result at least in part from their greater work effort.

49. The detailed worksheets underlying both the baseline analysis and these sensitivity estimates are available from the author. These worksheets also include the estimates of the costs of adolescent childbearing as compared against a counterfactual where I simultaneously address some but not all of the background and environmental circumstances that may precipitate and/or confound the consequences of young teen childbearing and a counterfactual where I fully address or compensate for all of the differences between young teen and later childbearers.

50. My tabulations of the National Longitudinal Survey of Youth.

51. For example, see Hoffman, Foster, and Furstenberg (1993); Bronars and Grogger (1994); Geronimus, Korenman, and Hillemeier (1994).

52. See, for example, the recent reviews of the state of knowledge regarding effective programming to prevent teenage pregnancy and parenthood and to mitigate the consequences of early parenting when it occurs (Moore et al. 1995; Kirby forthcoming; Maynard, Kelsey and McGrath 1996; U.S. Department of Health and Human Services, June 1996a).

References

Advocates for Youth. 1994. *Teenage Pregnancy and Too-Early Childbearing: Public Costs and Personal Consequences*, 5th Edition. Washington, DC: Advocates for Youth.

Alan Guttmacher Institute. 1994. *Sex and America's Teens.* New York, NY: Alan Guttmacher Institute.

Armstrong, B., A. McDonald, and M. Sloan. 1992. "Cigarette, Alcohol, and Coffee Consumption and Spontaneous Abortion." *American Journal of Public Health* 82(1): 85–87.

Blank, Rebecca M. 1994. "Outlook for the U.S. Labor Market and Prospects for Low-Wage Entry Jobs." *The Work Alternative: Welfare Reform and the Realities of the Job Market.* Nightingale, D.S. and R. H. Haveman (eds). Washington, DC: The Urban Institute Press.

Brown, S., and L. Eisenberg. 1995. *The Best Intentions.* Washington, DC: National Academy of Sciences.

Bronars, Stephen G. and Jeff Grogger. 1994. "The Economic Consquences of Unwed Motherhood: Using Twin Births as a Natual Experiment," *American Economic Review* (84): 1141–1156.

Burt, M. 1992. "Estimates of Public Costs of Teenage Childbearing: A Review of Recent Studies and Estimates of 1985 Public Costs." Washington, DC: Center for Population Options.

Burt, M., and D. Haffner. 1986. "Teenage Childbearing: How Much Does It Cost?" Washington, DC: Center for Population Options.

Children's Defense Fund. 1995. *Wasting America's Future.* Washington, DC: Children's Defense Fund.

Currie, J. 1995. *Welfare and the Well-Being of Children.* Chur, Switzerland. Harwood Academic Publishers.

Geronimus, A. and S. Korenman. 1993. "The Socio-Economic Consequences of Teen Childbearing Reconsidered." *Quarterly Journal of Economics,* 107(4): 1187–1214.

Geronimus, A., S. Korenman, and S. Hillemeier. 1994. "Does Young Maternal Age Adversely Affect Child Development? Evidence from Cousin Comparisons in the United States." *Development Review* (20): 585–609.

Grogger, J. and S. Bronars. 1993. "The Socioeconomic Consequences of Teenage Childbearing: Using Twin Births as a Natural Experiment." *Family Planning Perspectives* (25): 156–161.

Harlap, S. and P. Shiono. 1980. "Alcohol, Smoking, and Incidence of Spontaneous Abortions in the First and Second Trimester." *Lancet* 2: 173–176.

Health Care Financing Administration. 1993. *Medicaid Statistics: Program and Financial Statistics, Fiscal Year 1992.* Washington, DC: U.S. Department of Health and Human Services, HCFA.

Hoffman, S., M. Foster, and F. Furstenberg, Jr. 1993. "Reevaluating the Costs of Teenage Childbearing." *Demography* 30(1): 1–13.

Hotz, V. J., S. McElroy, and S. Sanders. 1996. Special tabulations of data underlying the results reported in Chapter 3 of this volume prepared for the author.

Hotz, V. J. 1996a. Personal communication with the author, July 30.

———. 1996. Personal (verbal) communication September 23.

Jacobson, J. and R. Maynard. 1995. "Unwed Mothers and Long-term Welfare Dependency." *Addressing Illegitimacy: Welfare Reform Options for Congress*. Washington, DC: American Enterprise Institute, September.

Kirby, D. Forthcoming. "Programs to Reduce Teenage Pregnancy: The Implications of Findings from Research." Washington, D.C.: National Campaign to Prevent Teen Pregnancy.

Kline, J., P. Shrout, Z. Stein, M. Susser, and D. Warburton. 1980. "Drinking During Pregnancy and Spontaneous Abortion." *Lancet* 2: 176–180.

Klaus, P. 1994. *The Costs of Crimes to Victims*. Washington, DC: U.S. Department of Justice, Bureau of Justice Statistics.

Kost, K., and J. Forrest. 1995. "Intention Status of U.S. Births in 1988: Differences by Mothers' Socioeconomic and Demographic Characteristics." *Family Planning Perspectives* 27(1): 23–27.

Luker, K. 1996. *Dubious Conceptions: The Politics of Teenage Pregnancy*. Harvard, MA: Harvard Press.

Maynard, R. (editor). 1996. *Kids Having Kids*. New York, NY: The Robin Hood Foundation.

Maynard, R., M. Kelsey, and D. McGrath. 1996. "The New Face of Teenage Childbearing: Implications for Welfare Policy." Philadelphia, PA: University of Pennsylvania. (Paper prepared for the Henry J. Kaiser Family Foundation.)

Moore, K. "Facts at a Glance." 1996. Washington, DC: Child Trends, January.

Moore, K., D. Myers, D. Morrison, C. Nord, B. Brown, and B. Edmonston. 1996. "Age at First Childbirth and Later Poverty." *Journal of Research on Adolescence* 3(4): 393–492.

Moore, K., B. Sugland, C. Blumenthal, D. Glei, and N. Snyder. 1995. "Adolescent Pregnancy Prevention Programs: Interventions and Evaluations." Washington, DC: Child Trends.

Musick, Judith S. 1993. "Young, Poor, and Pregnant: The Psychology of Teenage Motherhood." Yale University Press.

Nichols-Dasebolt, A. and I. Garfinkel. 1991. "Trends in Paternity Adjudications and Child Support Awards." *Social Science Quarterly*. 72: 83–97.

Polit, Denise. 1992. "Barriers to Self-Sufficiency and Avenues to Success Among Teenage Mothers." Princeton, NJ: Mathematica Policy Research, Inc., June.

Quint, J., J. Musick, and J. Ladner. 1994. *Lives of Promise, Lives of Pain: Young Mothers After New Chance*. Manpower Research Demonstration Project.

Scholz, John Karl. 1994. "The Earned Income Tax Credit: Participation, Compliance, and Antipoverty Effectivenss." *National Tax Journal* 47: 59–81.

U.S. Department of Health and Human Services. 1996a. *Effective Programs for Preventing Teenage Pregnancy*. Washington, DC: Assistant Secretary for Planning and Evaluation, U.S. Department of Health and Human Services, June.

————. 1996b. *Trends in the Well-being of America's Children and Youth.* Washington, DC: U.S. Government Printing Office.

U.S. Department of Justice. 1990. *Justice Expenditure and Employment, 1990.* Washington, DC: U.S. Government Printing Office.

————. 1992. *Correctional Populations in the United States, 1990.* Washington, DC: U.S. Government Printing Office.

U.S. Department of Labor. 1996a. *CPI Detailed Report, Data for December 1995*, Washington, DC: Bureau of Labor Statistics, Table 24, p. 66.

————. 1996b. *Consumer Price Index-All Urban Consumers,* http:// stats.bls.gov/cgi- bin/surveymost, April 26.

U.S. House of Representatives. 1993. *The Green Book.* Washington, DC: U.S. Government Printing Office.

Wilcox, A., R. Weinbert, and D. Baird. 1990. "Risk factors for early pregnancy loss." *Epidemiology* 1: 382–385.

APPENDIX 10A: SOURCES OF THE ESTIMATES OF THE OUTCOMES FOR ADOLESCENT PARENTS AND OF THE CONSEQUENCES OF DELAYING CHILDBEARING

Earnings-Related Outcomes

EARNINGS OF MOTHERS AND SPOUSES

Authors' calculations; Hotz, McElroy, and Sanders (Chapter 3); and Special tabulations of data supporting results reported in Chapter 3 prepared by Hotz, McElroy, and Sanders (1996) and Hotz (1996).

Data Source: National Longitudinal Survey of Youth

Method: Aggregate predicted earnings for adolescent and older childbearers over each of the first 13 years of parenthood and compute the average. The costs of early childbearing (consequences of delaying) are calculated by taking the difference between adolescent and older childbearers under each of the counterfactual assumptions.

Outcomes for adolescent childbearers: Authors' calculations of the weighted mean values of outcomes for those who had their first child before age 18.

Observed outcomes for 20- to 21-year-old childbearers (with no statistical controls): Authors' calculations of the weighted mean values of outcomes for those who had their first child at age 20 or 21.

*Outcomes if childbearing is delayed and we simultaneously address
the maximum feasible set of factors related to adolescent childbearing:* Authors' calculations of predicted values for 20- to 21-year-old
childbearers, based on a regression model that controls for measurable
background factors (see Chapter 1, Table 1.2).

*Outcomes for delaying childbearing and addressing nothing
else:* Differences in predicted outcomes for those who get pregnant
before age 18 and give birth versus those who miscarry based on
instrumental variables estimates generated by Hotz, McElroy, and
Sanders (Chapter 3) and tabulated over ages 17 through 28 for the
earlier childbearers and over ages 21 through 32 for those who miscarry. The control variables used in the estimation models are listed
in Chapter 1, Table 1.2.

Earnings of Fathers of Children

Data reported in Brien and Willis (Chapter 4, Table 4.5)

Data sources: National Longitudinal Survey of Youth; Vital Statistics

Method: Compute average annual discounted earnings estimates for
fathers of children born to adolescent mothers and for fathers of children born to would-be adolescent mothers who delay childbearing
under the three assumptions regarding the counterfactual situation.

We inflate the discounted values by a factor of 1.36, which is the
equivalent to the average annual discount rate over a 13 year period
of discounting at 5 percent annually. (We used the 13 year period
because we include only 13 years of parental outcomes in the cost
analysis.)

Outcomes for fathers of children born to adolescent parents: These
are the weighted averages of the predicted median earnings for those
who father children by a mother under age 18 reported by Brien and
Willis (Chapter 4, Table 4.5).

*Observed outcomes for fathers of children born to 20- to 21-year-old
childbearers (with no statistical controls):* These are weighted calculations of the predicted median earnings of fathers who first father
children by mothers who are age 20 or 21 reported in Brien and Willis,
Chapter 4, assuming that they will have the same 42 percent rate of
out-of-wedlock fatherhood as do those mothers who first bear children
at age 20 or 21 nationally (Alan Guttmacher Institute 1994). These
estimates control for the background factors listed in Chapter 1, Table
1.2.

Outcomes if childbearing is delayed and we simultaneously address the maximum feasible set of factors related to adolescent childbearing: These are weighted calculations of the predicted median earnings of fathers who first father children by mothers who are age 20 or 21 reported in Brien and Willis, Chapter 4, assuming that they will have an out-of-wedlock fatherhood rate of 55 percent or two-thirds of the way between the national rate for adolescent mothers and later childbearers. These estimates too control for the background factors listed in Chapter 1, Table 1.2.

Outcomes if childbearing is delayed but we address no other factors: These are weighted calculations of the predicted median earnings of fathers who first father children by mothers who are age 20 or 21 reported in Brien and Willis, Chapter 4, assuming that they will have an out-of-wedlock fatherhood rate of 67 percent or one-third of the way between the national rate for adolescent mothers and later childbearers. These estimates too control for the background factors listed in Chapter 1, Table 1.2.

CHILD SUPPORT

Brien and Willis (Chapter 4); Authors' calculations

Data: Estimated earnings outcomes for fathers of children born out-of-wedlock to adolescent and later childbearers are based on results from Brien and Willis (Chapter 4) and a methodology similar to that described above for estimating earnings outcomes for fathers of adolescent and later childbearers regardless of marital status (see above); National estimates of the proportion of teen and later childbearers who collect child support from nonresident fathers (Congressional Budget Office 1990); and the Wisconsin formula for determining award amounts as applied by Brien and Willis (Chapter 4).

Method: We assumed that child support awards equal to 17 percent of income will be levied on the nonmarried fathers for first children (see discussion above of the method for estimating fathers' incomes for the out-of-wedlock fatherhood assumptions); that awards averaging 8 percent of gross income will be levied for second children and awards averaging 4 percent of gross income will be levied for third children. We further assume that only half of a mother's second and higher order children will be fathered out-of-wedlock, and that only 30 percent of the awards will be paid. For adolescent parents, the compound rate of child support is 6.7 percent of the father's income; for later childbearers' assuming we address some or all differences in background characteristics, this rate is 6.4 percent; assuming child-bearing is delayed, but we address nothing else, the rate is 6.5 percent.

INCOME AND CONSUMPTION TAXES

Authors' calculations

Method: These are estimated to be .23 times earned income and are consistent with the assumed tax rates used by Hotz, McElroy, and Sanders (Chapter 3) and Brien and Willis (Chapter 4). As noted in the text the rate may be high, given the low average income levels of adolescent parents and their later childbearing counterparts. Whereas Hotz, McElroy, and Sanders assumed an average federal tax rate of 15 percent of earnings, estimated rates in 1993 for the bottom quintile of the income distribution was only 5.2 percent for families with children and that for the second quintile was only 17 percent (U.S. House of Representatives, Appendix K, Table 38, p. 1543). Moreover, recent expansions of the Earned Income Tax Credit would have the effect of substantially lowering tax rates for low-income workers with children.

Public Assistance

AFDC BENEFITS, FOOD STAMPS, HOUSING SUBSIDIES

Same sources, data, and methods as for earnings of mothers and spouses (see above).

RENT SUBSIDIES

Authors' tabulations; Hotz, McElroy, and Sanders (Chapter 3); and special tabulations of data supporting results reported in Chapter 3 prepared by Hotz, McElroy, and Sanders (1996) and Hotz (1996a).

Sources: National Longitudinal Survey of Youth

Method: Estimates of the proportion of years adolescent and later childbearers received some form of housing assistance using methodologies similar to those used to estimate earnings of mothers and spouses under the various scenarios (see above). We then computed an estimate of the average years of subsidies used by adolescent mothers and the later childbearers under each of the three counterfactual scenarios. Each year of housing subsidy was valued at $4,571, which is the average housing subsidy level in 1993 adjusted to equivalent 1996 dollars using the Consumer Price Index-Urban (U.S. Department of Labor 1995, 1996).

MEDICAL ASSISTANCE FOR PARENTS

Authors' calculations

Data: AFDC benefits (see above); U.S. House of Representatives 1993, Section 7, Table 1, p. 616, and Appendix P, Table 18, p. 1655.

Method: We multiplied the ratio of Medicaid benefits for adult AFDC recipients to AFDC payments (.39) times the measured outcomes for AFDC payments to adolescent and would-be adolescent childbearers to estimate Medicaid benefits paid for care of adolescent parents and their later childbearing counterparts.

MEDICAL ASSISTANCE FOR CHILDREN

Wolfe and Perozek (Chapter 6) (medical care expenditure information); Authors' calculations (number of children)

Data: National Medical Care Expenditure Survey; National Longitudinal Survey of Youth

Method: The undiscounted estimates are simply the average annual medical care costs reported for adolescent and later childbearers under the various assumptions regarding the counterfactual circumstances (Wolfe and Perozek, Chapter 6, Table 6.12), weighted by the authors' estimates of the average number of children in the family and prorated by the ratio of the 13-year cumulative expenditures to the 15-year cumulative expenditures to create an average annual cost estimate over the first 13 years of parenthood.

To compute discounted values, we used the average annual medical care costs paid by others in society (through social insurance or CHAMPUS) for children born to mothers who were under age 18 and those who were 20 to 21 when they had their first child (Wolfe and Perozek, Chapter 6, Table 6.12) to create a series of average annual expenditures over the first 15 years of childhood that conformed to these overall averages, but reflected age-specific expenditures per child that were proportional to the age-specific average number of medical care visits (Wolfe and Perozek, Chapter 6, Table 6.1).

We then created a 13-year series of per-child medical care expenditures for each child in the household, using the authors' estimates of the number of children born to mothers during their first 13 years of parenthood under the alternative counterfactual assumptions. Second children were assumed to be born in year three of parenthood and third children were assumed to be born in year five of parenthood. We discounted these costs at 5 percent annually beginning with the second year of parenthood and used the resulting average annual expenditure per family over the first 13 years of parenthood as the discounted value in the cost analysis.

Outcomes for adolescent childbearers: These estimates are based on the weighted mean outcomes per child, adjusted for the age of the child as noted above, and for the fact that these mothers have an average of 2.6 children during their first 13 years of parenthood.

Observed outcomes for 20- to 21-year-old childbearers (with no statistical controls): These estimates are based on the weighted mean outcomes per child born to a mother who has her first child at age 20 or 21, adjusted for age of the child as noted above, and for the fact that these mothers have an average of 2.1 children during their first 13 years of parenthood.

Outcomes if childbearing is delayed and we simultaneously address the maximum feasible set of factors related to adolescent childbearing: These estimates based on the methodology described above, but using predicted values of the medical care costs for 20- to 21-year-old-childbearers assuming they share some of the same background characteristics as the later childbearers, but that the health status of their children will not be affected by the delay. See Chapter 1, Table 1.2 for the control variables included in the estimation model. These estimates also assume that by delaying childbearing, would-be adolescent mothers would still have 2.1 children.

Outcomes if childbearing is delayed but we address nothing else: These estimates are based on the methodology described above, but using predicted values of medical care costs for later childbearers controlling for background factors and changes in the health status of children. The control variables are listed in Chapter 1, Table 1.2. These estimates assume that, by delaying childbearing alone, the number of children born during the first 13 years of parenthood will fall only to 2.4.

ADMINISTRATIVE COSTS OF PUBLIC ASSISTANCE PROGRAMS

Authors' calculations

Data Sources: AFDC, food stamps, and Medicaid benefits (see above); U.S. House of Representatives (1993, Section 7, Table 1, p. 616, and Appendix P, Table 30, p. 1676); Health Care Financing Administration (1993, Table 11, p. 41).

Method: From the above sources we calculated that for every dollar spent on AFDC payments, we spend 12.1 cents on administration; for every dollar spent on food stamp benefits, we spend 13.9 cents on administration; and for every dollar in Medicaid benefits, we spend 3.7 cents on administration. To estimate the administrative costs associated with these outcomes, we simply multiplied our estimated benefit levels for AFDC, food stamps, and medical assistance for adults and children (the vast majority of which is expected to be through Medicaid) by .121, .139, and .037 respectively,

Other Consequences

OUT-OF-POCKET MEDICAL CARE FOR CHILDREN

Wolfe and Perozek (Chapter 6) (medical care expenditures); Authors' calculations (number of children)

Data: National Medical Care Expenditure Survey; National Longitudinal Survey of Youth

Method: The method for calculating these costs is similar to that described for medical care assistance for children reported above. In this case, we applied the above methodology to the total expenditure estimates reported in Wolfe and Perozek (Chapter 6, Table 6.10) and subtracted the medical assistance estimates calculated as described above from the total expenditures.

FOSTER CARE

Goerge and Lee (Chapter 7); Authors' calculations (number of children)

Data: Illinois Integrated Database on Children and Family Services (IDB); National Longitudinal Survey of Youth

Methodology: Used estimates of the average rates of foster care placements among families headed by adolescent and later childbearers under various counterfactual scenarios (see below) to estimate the probability that each child in a family will be in foster care in each of the 18 years following the birth of the first child. We assumed that one-fifth of the children who would be placed in care before age 18 ended up in care in each of the first five years following their birth. Moreover, we assume that only half of the children in a family will be placed in care (or that all the children in a family will be placed in care, but for only half of their childhood years).

Having determined what fraction of first, second, and third children in the average family will be in foster care in each of the first 18 years of parenthood, we summed these proportions over the 18 years and across children to generate an estimate of the average child-years in foster care per family during each of the first 18 years of parenthood. We then multiply the child years in care by an estimate of the annual cost of a foster care placement ($22,259 in 1996 dollars). See Goerge and Lee (Chapter 7) for a discussion of the costs of foster care.

Placement rates for adolescent parents: These estimates are based on weighted tabulations of the IDS data for mothers who have their first child before age 18. We generated child-placement rates per family by using the authors' estimates of average number of children born to adolescent mothers (2.6 children).

Observed outcomes for 20- to 21-year-old childbearers (with no statistical controls): These estimates are based on weighted tabulations of the IDS data for mothers who have their first child at age 20 or 21. We generated child-placement rates per family by applying the authors' estimates of the number of children born to mothers who begin childbearing at age 20 or 21 (2.1).

Outcomes if childbearing is delayed and we simultaneously address the maximum feasible set of factors related to adolescent childbearing: These estimates are based on regression-adjusted outcomes for those having their first child at age 20 or 21, assuming they have similar background characteristics as adolescent childbearers. The control variables included in the model are listed in Chapter 1, Table 1.2. We generated child-placement rates per family using the authors' estimate of the average number of children who would be born to would-be adolescent childbearers if they delayed childbearing and we addressed some but not all of the differences between them and those who have babies at a young age (2.1 children).

Estimated placement rates if childbearing is delayed and we address nothing else. These estimates are based on the regression adjusted estimates of placement rates for those having their first child at age 20 or 21, assuming they have similar background characteristics to the adolescent childbearers. The control variables included in the model are listed in Chapter 1, Table 1.2. We generated child-placement rates per family using the authors' estimate of the average number of children who would be born to would-be adolescent childbearers if they delayed childbearing and we addressed none of the other differences between them and those who have babies at a young age (2.4 children).

INCARCERATION OF YOUNG MEN

Grogger (Chapter 8, Tables 8.1 and 8.4)

Data Sources: National Longitudinal Survey of Youth; U.S. Department of Justice (1993)

Method: We used the aggregate estimate of the incarceration costs attributable to adolescent parenthood itself reported in Grogger (Chapter 8), together with estimated incarceration rates of adolescent and would-be adolescent parents under different counterfactual scenarios to generate an estimate of the aggregate costs associated with adolescent childbearing and all related factors that distinguish adolescent from 20- to 21-year-old childbearers; adolescent childbearing and some of the differences between adolescent and later childbearers; and adolescent childbearing alone (rates of 10.3, 3.8, 7.3, and 9.1 respectively). We then computed the difference in aggregate prison costs between adolescent parents and later childbearers under the counterfactual scenarios and divided by the number of adolescent parents in the cohort to generate an average cost per adolescent parent per year.

PRODUCTIVITY OF YOUNG ADULT CHILDREN

Haveman, Wolfe, and Peterson (Chapter 9, Tables 9.2 and 9.10) (educational attainment); Authors' estimates (number of children); Children's Defense Fund (1995) (productivity returns to additional education)

Data: Panel Study of Income Dynamics; National Longitudinal Survey of Youth

Method of Analysis: Haveman, Wolfe, and Peterson (Chapter 9) estimated an aggregate net present value of the productivity loss associated with adolescent childbearing assuming that would-be adolescent childbearers who delay childbearing share as many other characteristics with the adolescent childbearers as the authors could control for. We used the net present value of the productivity loss per child associated with adolescent childbearing, together with the assumed cohort size to generate an estimate of the assumed net present value of the loss per child. We then assumed that the earnings losses were evenly distributed over time and created the equivalent undiscounted measure of a life-time learning loss per child of having been born to an adolescent parent. (The earnings gains estimates were assumed to have a 1 percent real rate of growth and to be discounted at 5 percent per year.)

We then used this per-child, undiscounted productivity loss estimate in conjunction with our estimate of the consequences of adolescent childbearing for fertility patterns, under various counterfactual scenarios, to generate estimates of the cost of adolescent childbearing per year, per adolescent parent, under these alternative scenarios.

Note: The worksheets used in each of these sets of calculations is available from the author upon request.

Table 10A.1 UNDISCOUNTED ESTIMATES OF THE ECONOMIC CONSEQUENCES OF DELAYING CHILDBEARING AMONG WOULD-BE ADOLESCENT MOTHERS (MARCH 1996 DOLLARS)

(1)	Observed Outcomes (No Statistical Controls)			Change Associated with Delaying Childbearing from Under Age 18 to Age 20 to 21 and Addressing:	
	(2)	(3)	(4)	(5)	(6)
Outcome Estimates	Adolescent Childbearers	20- to 21-Year-Old Childbearers	Difference Between Older and Younger Childbearers	The maximum feasible set of related factors[a]	Nothing except early childbearing itself
Earnings-Related Outcomes (Average per Year)					
Mother's earnings	$8,744	$14,445	$5,701	$4,070	($432)
Spouse's earnings	$13,326	$34,753	$21,427	$17,854	($1,817)
Father's Earnings	$15,406	$20,027	$4,620	$3,856	$3,093
Child support	$767	$440	($327)	($185)	($27)
Mother's income and consumption taxes	$2,011	$3,322	$1,311	$936	($99)
Spouse's income and consumption taxes	$3,065	$7,993	$4,928	$4,106	($418)
Father's income and consumption taxes	$3,543	$4,606	$1,063	$887	$711
Public Assistance (Average per Year)					
AFDC benefits	$729	($133)	($862)	($729)	$67
Food stamp benefits	$870	$356	($514)	($497)	$101
Rent Subsidies	$1,074	$740	($334)	($136)	($215)
Medical assistance for parents	$590	$254	($336)	($284)	($28)
Medical assistance for children	$1,694	$1,142	($552)	($554)	($718)
Administrative costs of public assistance programs	$379	$172	($207)	($184)	($27)

Other Consequences (Average per Year)

Out-of-pocket costs of children's health care	$1,774	$2,358	$584	$227	$190
Foster care	$1,016	$499	($517)	($486)	($424)
Incarceration of young men	$3,385	$1,240	($2,145)	($991)	($396)
Productivity of young adult children	—	($700)	($700)	($673)	($646)
Income and consumption taxes of young adult children	—	($161)	($161)	($155)	($149)

Source: The sources for the various estimates are detailed in Appendix 10A.

Note: Positive consequences of *delaying* childbearing are denoted by parentheses

a. Examples of other factors that might be addressed simultaneously with preventing adolescent parenthood include educational opportunities, social and economic support needs, motivation, and peer influences.

ABOUT THE EDITOR

Rebecca A. Maynard is Trustee Professor of education, social policy, and communication at the University of Pennsylvania. Previously, she served Mathematica Policy Research, Inc., as senior vice president, where she directed their Princeton research office, and is currently a member of the National Campaign to Prevent Teen Pregnancy advisory panel. She has published widely on welfare policy, educational innovation, employment and training, teenage pregnancy and parenthood, and evaluation design. Her research has appeared in a wide range of journals, and has been published by a wide range of presses including the Brookings Institution, Urban Institute Press, the National Academy of Sciences, Russell Sage, University of Michigan Press, and University of Wisconsin Press. She has testified before Congress on welfare policy, teenage pregnancy prevention, and child-care policy, and advised states and foreign governments on various aspects of social welfare policy.

ABOUT THE CONTRIBUTORS

Michael J. Brien is an assistant professor of economics at the University of Virginia. Prior to his appointment at Virginia, he was a National Institute on Aging Post-Doctoral Fellow at RAND in Santa Monica, California. His research interests include the consequences of early family formation and the implications for child support, economic models of marriage and divorce, racial differences in marriage patterns, and the economics of aging.

Robert M. Goerge is associate director and research fellow at the Chapin Hall Center for Children at the University of Chicago and co-directs the National Foster Care Data Archive funded by the U.S. Department of Health and Human Services Children's Bureau. Dr. Goerge also has served as a consultant to 15 states on the development of improved information systems and the use of administrative data for analysis purposes. He has published widely on service receipt of children and families, foster care, and the creation of research databases.

Angela Dungee Greene is a senior research analyst at Child Trends, Inc. Ms. Greene works with the Family and Child Wellbeing Research Network, which was established by the National Institutes of Child Health and Human Development. She has collaborated on several publications and professional presentations pertaining to various social, economic, and health-related issues of African American families.

Jeffrey Grogger is an associate professor of economics at the University of California, Santa Barbara. He studies issues related to poverty, including early childbearing, youth crime, welfare incentives, and the effects of school quality on wages. His publications include "The Economic Consequences of Unwed Motherhood: Using Twin Births as a Natural Experiment," *American Economic Review*, December 1994 (with Stephen G. Bronars). He is a research fellow of the National Bureau of Economic Research, and serves as co-editor of the *Journal of Human Resources*.

Robert H. Haveman is John Bascom Professor of economics and public affairs at the University of Wisconsin-Madison, where he is also a faculty member in the Institute for Research on Poverty and the La Follette Institute of Public Affairs. His research is in the area of the economics of poverty and social policy, where he has published widely. His most recent book is *Succeeding Generations: On the Effects of Investments in Children* (with Barbara Wolfe), and is published by the Russell Sage Foundation.

V. Joseph Hotz is a professor at the Irving B. Harris Graduate School of Public Policy Studies at the University of Chicago. His areas of specialization are labor economics, economic demography, evaluation of the impact of social programs, and applied econometrics. He is co-editor of the *Journal of Labor Economics* and his numerous published articles include "A Simulation Estimator for Dynamic Models of Discrete Choice," *Review of Economic Studies*, April 1994 (co-author).

Bong Joo Lee is a research fellow at the Chapin Hall Center for Children at the University of Chicago. He was previously an assistant professor at the Boston University School of Social Work. His research interests are the statistical modelling of the patterns of human service use, issues of childhood poverty, and demography of children and families.

Susan Williams McElroy is an assistant professor of economics and education policy at the H. John Heinz III School of Public Policy and Management at Carnegie Mellon University. Previously, she was a visiting scholar in the department of economics at the University of California, San Diego. Her research interests include the consequences of teenage childbearing, women in the labor market, and poverty.

Kristin Anderson Moore is executive director, and director of research, of Child Trends, Inc. A social psychologist, Dr. Moore has been with Child Trends, Inc. since 1982, studying the determinants of early sexual activity and parenthood, the consequences of adolescent parenthood, trends in child and family well-being, and the effects of family structure and social change on children. She is also a member of the Board of the National Campaign to Prevent Teenage Pregnancy, where she chairs the Task Force on Effective Programs and Research.

Donna Ruane Morrison joined the faculty at Georgetown University in fall 1995 with a joint appointment in the Graduate Program in Public Policy and the Department of Demography. Prior to Georgetown University, she was a senior research associate at Child Trends, Inc. Dr. Morrison has published articles examining the short- and long-term effects of marital conflict and divorce on child well-being.

Maria Perozek is completing her doctorate in economics at the University of Wisconsin-Madison. Her primary research concerns intergenerational transfers and wealth accumulation over the life cycle.

Elaine Peterson is an assistant professor at California State University, Stanislaus. She has been a research assistant in the Financial Structure Section of the Federal Reserve Board and the Institute for Research on Poverty. Her research includes work on neighborhood quality and children's success, and on policy-related determinants of teen nonmarital childbearing.

Seth G. Sanders is an assistant professor of economics and public policy at the H. John Heinz III School of Public Policy and Management at Carnegie Mellon University. His areas of research interest include poverty issues, applied econometrics, and labor economics. His recent articles include "The Decision to Work by Married Immigrant Women: Evidence from Asian Women," *Industrial and Labor Relations Review*, July 1993 (co-author).

Robert J. Willis is professor of economics at the University of Michigan, where he also is a research scientist at the Institute for Social Research and research associate of the Population Studies Center. Willis is currently the principal investigator on two large longitudinal surveys, the Health and Retirement Survey and the Assets and Health of the Oldest Old Survey, which are collecting data on Americans over age 50. He is an authority on the economics of the family, marriage, and fertility, labor economics, human capital and population, and economic development.

Barbara Wolfe is professor of economics and preventive medicine and director of the Institute for Research on Poverty at the University of Wisconsin-Madison. She is also a research associate of the National Bureau of Economic Research. Her research interests are poverty, health economics, and disabilities. She is coauthor, with Robert Haveman, of *Succeeding Generations: On the Effects of Investments in Children* (Russell Sage Foundation, 1994) and has published widely in professional journals and edited monographs.

LIST OF TABLES AND FIGURES

Tables

Figures